THE
POLITICAL LIFE AND LETTERS
OF CAVOUR

CAVOUR

THE
POLITICAL LIFE AND
LETTERS OF CAVOUR

1848–1861

BY

A. J. WHYTE

M.A., LITT.D.

GREENWOOD PRESS, PUBLISHERS
WESTPORT, CONNECTICUT

Library of Congress Cataloging in Publication Data

Whyte, Arthur James Beresford.
   The political life and letters of Cavour, 1848-1861.

   Sequel to The early life and letters of Cavour,
1810-1848.
   Reprint of the 1930 ed. published by Oxford
University Press, London.
   Bibliography: p.
   Includes index.
    1. Cavour, Camillo Benso, conte di, 1810-1861.
I. Title.
DG552.8.C3W52 1975   945'.08'0924 [B]   74-30983
ISBN 0-8371-7939-4

Originally published in 1930 by Oxford University Press,
London

This reprint has been authorized by the Clarendon Press Oxford

Reprinted in 1975 by Greenwood Press,
a division of Williamhouse-Regency Inc.

Library of Congress Catalog Card Number 74-30983

ISBN 0-8371-7939-4

Printed in the United States of America

TO
MY WIFE

PREFACE

THE aim of this volume is to give an account of Cavour's parliamentary career and a connected view of his diplomacy. In this task I have been fortunate in being able to use recently published material of great value. Cavour left behind him an enormous mass of papers, letters, and memoranda. Various hands have quarried in this mine. Some of it was used by Bianchi when writing his *Storia della Diplomazia Europea*, Chiala extracted material from it, and later it became the source for Bolléa's '*Silloge*' of Risorgimento Letters.

Now, however, for the first time it has been examined, arranged, and systematically edited in the volumes published by the Royal Commission appointed for that purpose. The four first volumes (there are others to follow) covering the years 1858–61 have been used in this volume. Much of what is to come, though no doubt of real value and interest, will probably be rather of the nature of *éclaircissements* than new material of genuine importance. The *Carteggio Minghetti-Pasolini* has proved disappointing. Both men were too absorbed in their own tasks. Minghetti was at Bologna the week before Garibaldi sailed, but he says nothing of the historic meeting of Cavour and the King upon which there have been so many conjectures. It was a pity he had not more of Greville in his composition.

Through the courtesy of the Earl of Clarendon I have been enabled to include a number of private letters from Sir James Hudson to Lord Clarendon, then Foreign Secretary, and other letters have been found at the Record Office. I have made little attempt at criticism. Cavour's consummate ability as a statesman is unquestioned. Nevertheless, the political moralist can always find materials for a case against him. But any one who studies Cavour's work from the inside cannot but feel that the tortuous policy he at times pursued is, in truth, alien from the character of the man, and was forced upon him, on the one hand, by the meagreness of his country's resources, and, on the other, by that spirit of distrust, jealousy, nervousness, and dread of revolution which characterized the policy of the Great Powers after the events of 1848.

A. J. W.

TADMARTON RECTORY,
BANBURY, 1930.

CONTENTS

INTRODUCTION

THE following volume is a sequel to my *Early Life and Letters of Cavour*, which told the story of Cavour's preparation for political life. It is based mainly upon Cavour's correspondence and speeches and is designed to give an uninterrupted view of his diplomacy. This has entailed a certain sacrifice of dramatic interest, for the war of 1859 and the Garibaldian Epic of 1860 are dealt with only as viewed from the windows of the Foreign Office at Turin.

In the statesmanship of Cavour three distinct phases may be observed. The first, which extended from his appointment as Minister of Commerce in 1850 to the close of the Congress of Paris in 1856, was characterized by an attempt to solve the Italian problem by diplomacy. The restoration of economic prosperity at home and the recovery of the national prestige abroad were the first objectives aimed at. Cavour worked to shift the moral support of Europe from Austria to Italy, and by his alliance with France and England in the Crimea and his influence with Napoleon at the Congress of Paris, so far succeeded that Austria emerged from the Congress almost isolated in Europe, while the cause of Italy became a European problem. All hopes, however, of a solution by peaceful methods proved vain. Nothing could be done without revising the Treaty of Vienna, and the nerves of Europe, badly frayed by the events of 1848, would stand no tampering with the settlement upon which the whole political structure of Europe rested.

Cavour had always believed war to be inevitable, and after the failure of the Congress of Paris to do anything for Italy, his diplomacy entered its second phase, which was to fight intervention with intervention and to make war on Austria in alliance with France. The result was the war of 1859, ending with the Peace of Villafranca and Cavour's resignation.

The third phase commenced with Cavour's return to power in January 1860. Lombardy having been won and Austrian predominance removed, a change of policy was required, because Napoleon, while anxious for Italian independence, was opposed to Italian unity. Cavour now reversed his policy and announced the principle not of intervention but of non-intervention. In this it was England who supported him, jealous of Napoleon and fearing the cession of further territory to France. Four times during 1860 Lord John Russell neutralized the policy of the Emperor and enabled Cavour to take another step forward. The first time was when in January he persuaded Napoleon to accept the principle of non-intervention, the second was the dispatch of February 28th, condemning Napoleon's solution of the problem of Central Italy as 'subversive of Italian independence', which enabled Cavour to annex Tuscany without undue fear of French resentment. The third was his refusal to join France in patrolling the Straits and thus prevent Garibaldi crossing to the mainland, and the last was his historic dispatch of October 27th, 1860, which recognized Italian unity in the face of a scandalized Europe.

The materials for a study of Cavour's diplomacy, already very extensive, have recently been enlarged by the publication of the four volumes of the *Carteggio Cavour-Nigra*, covering the years 1858–61, and revealing Cavour's private correspondence with his confidential agent in Paris, Count Costantino Nigra. We have now an almost day-to-day record of Cavour's diplomatic activity during the most critical years of his work. Perhaps the most interesting contribution made by these volumes to our knowledge of the *Risorgimento* is the light they throw upon Cavour's relations with Napoleon III and Garibaldi.

There has been a tendency among French and Italian writers to exalt Cavour at the expense of Napoleon;

to suggest that the Emperor was the dupe of Cavour; that he was forced into the war of 1859 either by Cavour's cleverness or his threats of publishing incriminating documents or by working on his fear of assassination. Such a line of argument offers perhaps an excuse to a French writer who disapproves strongly of the Emperor's 'Italian adventure', as it may compensate a patriotic Italian anxious to minimize the Emperor's share in the making of Italy; but it is unjust to the Emperor and a libel on Cavour. Any one who will read the letters of Alessandro Bixio to Cavour in these volumes, or the diary of Lord Malmesbury, must realize that the origin of such notions was contemporary gossip for which there is no evidence. They were the more or less natural conjectures of those who could not know the real truth.

Cavour's intimacy with Napoleon dates from the Congress of Paris, the most fruitful result of which was that it focussed Napoleon's thoughts on war with Austria. It took Napoleon two years to make up his mind and then he sent for Cavour to meet him at Plombières. From the resolution then taken the Emperor never went back. It was his proposal and he saw it through. It is true that more than once, owing to the strongly expressed disapproval of Europe, Napoleon thought the date of commencement would have to be postponed, and that Cavour believed that this meant surrender to the peace party; but it was not so. In the end, the war began at the prearranged time, because Napoleon's refusal to coerce Cavour, in his determination not to disarm, lasted just long enough to overlap the moment when Austria's patience became exhausted, and she dispatched her famous ultimatum, thus justifying the intervention of France and putting herself in the wrong in the eyes of Europe. Throughout the negotiations that preceded the declaration of war Cavour did not show much concern for the difficulties of the Emperor. His main object was to drive Austria to desperation; 'let them negotiate,' he wrote on

March 6th, 'and while they do so it will be our task to make the situation insupportable.' Napoleon's assistance was conditional upon an adequate *casus belli*, and the policy of exasperation employed by Cavour towards Austria finally provided exactly what he wanted. After Villafranca the situation was changed. Napoleon wanted Italian independence but not unity, and it was England rather than France who was Cavour's best friend in 1860.

On the vexed question as to Cavour's attitude towards Garibaldi and the Thousand the new volumes of Cavour's correspondence throw considerable light. Cavour desired to complete Italian unity by diplomacy, in conformity with law and order and constitutional methods. He wished to work from North to South, dealing with the Papal States before Naples. Negotiations for the evacuation of the French troops from Rome were already begun before Garibaldi's expedition developed. He wished to avoid revolutionary methods, if possible, and thus keep European opinion on his side.

The expedition of Garibaldi traversed all his plans. It introduced the undesired element, began at the wrong end, and threatened a conflict between the constituted authority and the methods of revolution. But Cavour could not stop it. Garibaldi had the strong support of the King and was backed by an enthusiastic public opinion. At the moment, Cavour's main preoccupation was to pass the treaty, giving Nice and Savoy to France, through Parliament. When the expedition of La Masa planned by La Farina and the National Society coalesced with Garibaldi's expedition organized by Bertani, Cavour's opposition became impossible, for it would antagonize the moderate liberal party upon whose support Cavour relied to pass the treaty with France. So he adopted an attitude of non-intervention, removed all fear of official interference, and left the responsibility upon Garibaldi. The amazing completeness and rapidity of Garibaldi's success produced a new danger, and in the later stages of the expedition Cavour was fighting for the prestige of the

Crown and the authority of Parliament. Happily, the
unique character of Garibaldi, the absence of all personal ambition, the devoted loyalty to Victor Emmanuel,
saved the situation, and the audacity and firmness of
Cavour, while it gathered the fruits of Garibaldi's
genius, saved the country from interference by instantly
covering the methods of revolution with the aegis of
constituted authority.

I. CAVOUR AND THE REVOLUTION OF 1848

THE Congress of Vienna in 1815 had settled the affairs of Italy on the basis of legitimacy. The former Kings and Princelings were restored to their thrones, and to ensure the stability of this arrangement, Austria, already bound by ties of relationship to the reigning Houses, assumed a general overlordship of the Peninsula. Austria herself, having acquired Lombardy and Venetia, the two richest provinces of Italy, was thus enabled with a minimum of trouble to send her troops wherever they might be needed. This system, which kept Italy outwardly quiet for thirty years, produced a twofold result, an increasing dependence on Austria on the part of the Italian rulers, and a growing hatred of all things Austrian on the part of the people.

The chance of peace and quietness for Italy under this new arrangement was ruined by two factors. The first was the character and ideas of government exhibited by the new rulers, and the second was the ever-present hand of Austria. In Naples, the States of the Church and Modena, chronic misgovernment and brutal repression drove the population into rebellions, assassinations, secret societies, and every form of legitimate and illegitimate protest. Lombardy and Venetia groaned under the iron rule of foreign soldiers. Tuscany was more fortunate, and in Piedmont, if the Government was absolute, it was at least national. But over all alike hung the spectre of Austria. It was the bayonets of Croats and Hungarians that alone kept these satellites of Austria upon their thrones. The Austrian Ambassador at each court was the real ruler of the country, and his advice savoured strongly of command. In Piedmont alone was there some independence, for Charles Albert, who came to the throne in 1831, had good reason to hate Austria and her system. Poor, ignorant, and misgoverned, with the veterans of Austria always within call, national regeneration in Italy might well have seemed past all recovery.

And yet there was hope. Beneath the surface there was a leaven working, passed hand to hand in leaflets, sometimes printed, sometimes in manuscript; brought by secret delegates to yet more secret meetings; for in 1830 Mazzini had founded 'Young Italy', and what there was of life and hope in Italy throughout the 'thirties and early 'forties was due to the faith, the vision, and the fiery energy of Giuseppe Mazzini. Unity and independence under a republican form of government was his creed, to obtain which he dreamed of a vast national uprising in the name of justice, divine and human, that no tyrant power could withstand. Alas, it petered out in futile conspiracies and useless self-sacrifice, amid general reprobation. But nevertheless, despite the uselessness of his efforts as a practical means of freeing Italy, Mazzini kept alive the spirit of revolt and the ideal of independence, and others reaped where he had sown.

Of the eight states into which the Congress divided Italy, there was only one that showed some spirit of independence, this was the Kingdom of Sardinia, embracing Piedmont, Savoy, and the island from which it took its name. For eight centuries the House of Savoy had ruled in this corner of Italy, which had thus a tradition and a history that marked it out from all the other states of the Peninsula. The Piedmontese had a character of his own. He had not the hot blood of the Romagnuol, the indolence of the Neapolitan, or the easy going nature of the Tuscan. For a southern race he was cold and phlegmatic, sturdy, hard-working, and poor; he came of a race of soldiers, devoted alike to the Throne and the Church, with a feudal loyalty to the nobility that was as yet unbroken. Between 1815 and 1840 little change was to be noted in the condition of the country. All traces of French influence were rapidly swept away. The Church was once more restored to full favour and richly compensated for the deprivations suffered under Napoleon. Education was again in the hands of the Jesuits; an elaborate system of espionage checked all revolutionary propaganda, and a strict censorship and a narrow system of protection kept the country poor and unenlightened. But the Government was economical, the taxation was not unduly heavy, and if the salaries were low there was always a balance at the Treasury.

After 1840 Piedmont began to feel the breath of the new movements in Europe. In 1842 permission was obtained from the Government to found the Agrarian Society, which, with a central body at Turin and branches throughout the country, soon commenced to exert an economic, and incidentally, a political, influence. The Bank of Genoa was opened in 1843, the railway from Turin to Genoa was commenced, and a series of Scientific Congresses held in different places, opened the national mind to modern thought and progress. In spite of every effort of the Government, the political agitation steadily increased. Self-government, freedom of the Press, the formation of a national guard and the expulsion of the Jesuits, were the principal reforms demanded. This movement was the work of the middle classes, backed by the enlightened section of the aristocracy. The working classes were inarticulate and the Church and the bulk of the nobility were definitely hostile. At length, after long hesitation, the King yielded, and in the autumn of 1847 Charles Albert granted the long-awaited reforms. The most important of these was the freedom of the Press, a concession which at once increased the difficulties of the Government, and rendered still more advanced reforms inevitable. Such was the situation when the year 1848 dawned.

The series of revolutions which were to convulse Europe throughout this year commenced with a rising in Sicily. Three weeks later the Kingdom of Naples, the most backward and ill-governed state in Europe, received a constitution. This event, followed as it was a few weeks later, by the abdication of Louis-Philippe and the formation of the second Republic in France, was the deciding factor in the struggle for a constitution which had been raging in Piedmont since the reforms granted by Charles Albert in the autumn of 1847. On the 4th of March the Constitution was officially announced. Framed on the French model, it provided for a Cabinet, a Senate nominated by the King, and a Chamber of Deputies elected on a limited franchise. The elections were fixed for April and the Chambers were to meet for the first time on May 8th.

Rapid as was Piedmont's transformation from a system of absolutism to Constitutional Monarchy, the events in Europe moved faster still. By March the revolutionary fever had reached Austria, and on the 13th, Prince Metternich, the mind and symbol of the old order, resigned and fled to England. With Vienna in the hands of the mob, and Hungary demanding autonomy at the point of the sword, the Empire of the Hapsburg's seemed breaking in pieces. Austria's difficulty was Italy's opportunity. On March 18th, Milan, the capital of Lombardy, rose, and in the famous 'Five Days' of street fighting drove Marshal Radetzky and his 13,000 men from the city. At the same moment Venice, under the leadership of Daniele Manin, threw off the Austrian yoke, and on March 22nd proclaimed the reconstitution of her ancient Republic.

Although Venice and Milan had thus for the moment freed themselves from Austrian control, Radetzky's army was still intact within the confines of the Quadrilateral, and the future of Italy depended on her ability to compel his surrender, or withdrawal into Austria,

before assistance was forthcoming from Vienna. The
eyes of Italy were fixed on Piedmont, which alone of
all her northern states had a regular army. The appeal
of Milan to Charles Albert was not made in vain, and
after painful hesitation, and just too late to force an
action before the Austrians reached the shelter of the
Quadrilateral, Charles Albert led forth his army for the
liberation of Italy.

The prospect of freedom from Austrian domination
thus suddenly opened, raised the national expectations
to dizzy heights. Strong contingents in support of the
Piedmontese army were confidently awaited from all the
Constitutional States, which had now been joined by
Tuscany and the Papal States, and though the conception of complete Italian unity was as yet only an ideal,
the formation of a kingdom of Upper Italy, comprising
Piedmont, Lombardy, Venetia, and the Duchies, was
regarded as an assured outcome of the war; a belief
shared equally by the army, the Parliament, and the
civil population. The events of the first few weeks of
fighting still further strengthened the general optimism,
and the nation expected almost daily the news of the
crowning victory.

In the midst of these events the first Piedmontese
Chamber of Deputies met in the Carignano Palace at
Turin on May 8th. The Chamber quickly divided
itself into three parties. On the Right sat a compact
body of Conservatives; on the Left a somewhat
stronger body of Democrats, together with a minority
of extreme Republicans; whilst between them were
grouped a body of Moderates, whose votes were usually
given to the stronger, or sometimes, to the more voci-
ferous, of the two extreme parties. The bench of
Ministers reflected the composition of the Chamber,
for the King, with that fatal weakness for qualifying
a decision that was characteristic of so many of his
actions, had associated with Count Balbo, the President,[1]

---

[1] On Count Balbo see Predari, *I primi vagiti della libertà Italiana in Piemonte.*

a moderate conservative of liberal tendencies, the Marquis Lorenzo Pareto, an extreme republican from Genoa.

The Chamber, regardless of the uncertainty of the military situation, at once plunged into the question of the Constitution of the future Kingdom of Upper Italy. The inevitable conflict between Monarchists and Republicans ended in a compromise. It was decided to leave the decision to a constituent assembly to be convoked when the war ended. A Bill was then brought in to define the powers of this future Assembly, but in the debate that ensued the Government was defeated, and the Cabinet resigned. As successor to Count Balbo the King nominated Count Gabrio Casati, President of the Provisional Government at Milan. With a fine but futile gesture he selected a cabinet that represented the future Kingdom of Upper Italy, containing Venetian and Lombard members as well as Piedmontese. But the Government was still born: for no sooner had it been formed than news came that the Austrians had routed Charles Albert at Custoza, and the Kingdom of Upper Italy vanished into thin air.

Ill news runs apace, and it was not long before both inside and outside Parliament rumours of a great disaster were common property. For some weeks the deputies had been uneasy. The ominous silence of ministers regarding information from the seat of war and their evasive replies when questioned, had indicated that all was not well, but few had imagined the magnitude of the disaster that was now revealed. Turin was horror-struck. Ugly crowds collected outside the Palazzo Carignano and tried to force their way into the Chamber, but the gates were closed and the National Guard dispersed the people. Angry cries of treachery against the King and the generals; accusation of betrayal against the ministers and deputies, mingled with wild rumours of the approach of the hated Austrians, threw the city into a dangerous state of uproar. It was evident that the country was in no mood to be governed by Count

Casati and his mixed Cabinet. Count Casati resigned, and to meet the crisis dictatorial powers were conferred on the King and Parliament was indefinitely prorogued.[1] A week later the Armistice of Salasco was signed, and the first phase of the struggle for liberty came to an inglorious end.[2]

It was during the debates that preceded the fall of the Balbo Cabinet that there entered the Chamber, as member for the first College of Turin, Count Camillo Benso di Cavour. At the first elections he had failed in three separate constituencies but was successful in the by-elections held in June. Count Cavour was at this time one of the best-known and most unpopular men in Piedmont. He was the editor of his own paper, *Il Risorgimento*, and a Director, both of the railway from Turin to Genoa and of the newly formed Bank of Turin, and had interests in many other commercial undertakings, as well as being one of the largest and most successful agriculturists in the country. In politics he was a Liberal, believing in monarchy and constitutional government, and in that political and individual freedom which he had studied and admired in England. He was a firm supporter of nationality, democracy, and industrial organization, as the three great principles of a nation's progress, and to obtain these for his country, not merely for Piedmont but for Italy, his whole life was henceforth consecrated. To the study of economics, industry, and foreign politics, his life had been given up, and there was no man in Piedmont so well equipped to occupy almost any office in the Government as this young man of thirty-eight.

The fact that with all this knowledge and ability he was ignominiously passed over, requires a word of explanation. Count Cavour was an aristocrat, and his father, the Marquis Cavour, had for many years been Vicario of Turin and head of the secret police. The

[1] Brofferio, *Storia del Parlamento Subalpino*, vol. i. ch. v.
[2] The terms of the armistice are in Mistrale, *Da Novara a Roma*, vol. v, Documenti No. 10.

hatred bestowed on the father was inherited by the son,
and the name Cavour was sufficient to alienate the
sympathies of the democratic party and their followers.
On the other hand, the fact that he was a business man
and a Liberal, turned his own class against him. At
a moment when political passions ran high, when
opinions were extreme and held with fervid tenacity,
the attitude of a firm and convinced moderate was condemned equally by both sides. Regarded as a traitor to
his class on the one side, and as an extreme reactionary
on the other, his political position was one of isolation. To this Cavour himself contributed by the policy
of his paper, which condemned equally the reactionary
programme of the Right and the revolutionary tendencies of the Left. Thus in spite of his consummate
ability, it took two years of unceasing parliamentary
work before Cavour could obtain official recognition.

In the few weeks that elapsed between his entry as
a deputy and the Armistice of Salasco, Cavour, though
he spoke several times, exerted no influence on the
Chamber. He was listened to with respect on financial
questions, and his suggestion of raising money by a loan
from the Bank of Genoa, instead of one secured on the
assets of the Order of SS. Maurice and Lazarus, was
adopted; but on the burning question of the hour, the
union with Lombardy, his words carried no weight.[1]
With the fall of the Casati Cabinet the country relapsed
for some months into government by the King and
Cabinet. At no time throughout the Risorgimento was
the condition of Piedmont so confused and so dangerous,
as during the months following the Armistice of Salasco.
This was due in part to the dissatisfaction with the terms
of the Armistice, which were characterized as 'dishonourable' by the extreme democratic element, but
still more to the conflicting political views held by the
leaders of the various parties.

The opening of the struggle had brought back to
Italy a crowd of exiles. Many of these men were

[1] Brofferio, *Storia del Parlamento Subalpino*, vol. i. c. iii. pp. 145 ff.

extremists, very few of them were now believers in monarchy, and still fewer put their trust in Charles Albert. Not only in Piedmont, but in Tuscany and other parts of Italy, they formed a rallying-point for republicanism and cognate views based on Government by the people, that proved a source of incessant difficulty to those who in Rome, Florence, and Turin, were endeavouring to make constitutional government a successful reality.

Early in April came Mazzini. Debarred from entrance into Piedmont, he made his way direct to Milan, where, in spite of his first resolution to suppress political propaganda while Charles Albert and his army were fighting in Austria, he gave warm encouragement to his partisans, and raised the hopes of those who looked, as he did, to an Italian Republic as the outcome of the struggle. From Milan he made his way to Florence, and from there to Rome, leaving on his trail a blaze of Republican ardour.[1] A fortnight after Mazzini came a far more imposing and popular personality, that of Vincenzo Gioberti. Fifteen years before, Gioberti, already known as a rising theologian, had been exiled for alleged complicity in the Liberal movements of 1833. After a sojourn in Paris, he accepted a teaching post in Brussels, and from there he had issued his great work on the Civil Primacy of the Italians. It is not easy to realize with what ardour and enthusiasm this ponderous work was welcomed throughout Italy. Its somewhat flamboyant title, if unjustified by history, was admirably calculated to arouse the national pride, and its theme of Italian independence re-echoed the dreams and aspirations of the whole nation. The political solution that he offered was a federation of Italian States under the Presidency of the Pope; and to render this ideal acceptable, as well as to insure his work against the severity of the censorship, he spared no pains to flatter the Italian Royalties, finding some words of praise even for Ferdinand of Naples; and to

[1] Bolton King, *Mazzini*. Tivaroni, *L'Italia durante il dominio Austriaco.*

make certain of Papal support, he bestowed a meed of recognition on the work of the Jesuits.

The ruse was successful, and the work became the text-book of Italian liberalism. But no sooner was Gioberti assured of the success of his plan, than he threw off the mask, and in response to the criticisms of his attitude towards those in power, he published his *Prolegomeni al Primato*, in which his real opinions were put forward in no uncertain voice. When this denunciation of both Kings and Jesuits aroused the inevitable opposition, by a *tour de force* he wrote in six months the five stout volumes of *Il Gesuita Moderno*, in which, with exhaustive learning and great dialectical skill, he exposed the dangers to Italy of the continued predominance of the Society of Jesus. The publication of these works, of which the dream of Italian Independence was the perpetual motif, read as they were throughout the country, put Vincenzo Gioberti on a pinnacle of popularity above all competitors, and his return to his native land became the occasion for an outburst of enthusiasm hitherto unparalleled in the story of the Risorgimento.

Arriving in Turin towards the end of April 1848, Gioberti was received with an almost royal welcome, every class in the community from highest to lowest combining to do him honour. After a few days in the capital, Gioberti visited Charles Albert at the army head-quarters at Sommacampagna. He was not very warmly received, for the King was prejudiced against politically minded priests, but Charles Albert encouraged his suggestion of making a tour of Italy to counteract the influence of Mazzini and advocate his own plan for a federative union of Italian States. He visited Milan, Genoa, Florence, and other places, finally reaching Rome. Three interviews with the Pope followed, but Gioberti failed to enlist the sympathies of Pio IX, or perhaps it would be more correct to say, that he failed to counteract the influences that surrounded him. At Rome, as elsewhere, he was acclaimed

with enthusiasm, but his tour had little political influence. Enemies of Piedmont called him 'Charles
Albert's commercial traveller,' and Mazzinian and
Jesuit influence combined to counteract his propaganda.
On his return to Turin he occupied for the first time
the position of President of the Chamber of Deputies,
to which he had been unanimously elected.

The position of Gioberti in Italy at this moment was
unique. 'He had become,' says a contemporary writer,
'by free consent, the leader, the moral dictator, of the
nation. Giuseppe Mazzini still retained around him the
most trusted of his supporters, but his voice fell cold
even on the most fervid of his followers. For whilst the
Primato, the *Prolegomeni*, and the *Gesuita Moderno* shook
and kindled princes and people, priests and laity, the
Mazzinian writings passed unobserved and unread.'
Then came the *débâcle*, and the fall of the Casati
Ministry, and all eyes were turned on Gioberti as the
saviour of the State. Gioberti himself felt it. Though
in private life a man of simple habits and unassuming
manners, his great literary success and the reception
accorded him throughout Italy, convinced him that the
political leadership of Piedmont was his right and
destiny. 'To me,' he said, 'that have commenced the
Risorgimento, it belongs to guide it and lead it to
its end.' [1]

The choice, however, of the Premier lay solely with
the King, and Charles Albert, with his army crumbling
around him and the evil breath of calumny and suspicion in his nostrils, turned first to a man whose
loyalty to his person and his House was beyond suspicion, and charged Count Ottavio di Revel with the
formation of the Ministry. Then, repeating his previous
mistake, which had led him to associate the republican
Marquis Pareto with the Conservative Count Balbo,
he requested Revel to invite Gioberti to join him.

But this time it failed. Count Revel could come to
no arrangement with Gioberti, and formed his Cabinet

[1] D. Berti, *Vincenzo Gioberti.*

without him. Gioberti had not identified himself hitherto with any party, but now, disappointed of obtaining power, and unable any longer to stand alone, he threw himself into the arms of the Democratic party with the fixed intention of overturning the Government at the earliest opportunity.

The new Cabinet known as the Revel-Pinelli Ministry was soon formed. Revel took the Finances, whilst the Presidency was accepted by the Marquis Alfieri di Sostegno, who brought a great name but small political ability to the office. The backbone of the Ministry was Dionigi Pinelli, Minister for Internal Affairs, a lawyer from Casale, a man of great courage and energy, but with no gifts of statesmanship. The Government's first task was to come to terms with Austria, and with this object in view they obtained the mediation of France and England, and negotiations for peace commenced. Their next task was the reorganization of the army and the appointment of a new commander-in-chief. The leadership of Charles Albert had been deplorable, and a deputation was sent to Paris to endeavour to obtain a French Marshal.[1] In this they failed and the appointment was ultimately given to a Polish general, Chrzanowski. The unpleasant task of informing the King fell upon the President, who, under cover of the sound principle that it was unsuitable for a Constitutional King to lead his troops in battle, broke to Charles Albert the news of his deposition, and then resigned. His place was taken by General Perrone, the Minister for Foreign Affairs.

The state of the country during these months was deplorable. Genoa was in a chronic condition of unrest, and if the remainder of the country was outwardly quiet, it was steadily becoming more and more dissatisfied. The Democratic orators, with Gioberti at their head,

---

[1] 'If Cavaignac sends us Bugeaud,' wrote Cavour at this time, 'we are saved: for far from fomenting anarchic passions he will be their bitterest enemy. But if the army continues under its present commanders and the negotiations drag, we are threatened with grave troubles in the country.' Bert, *Nouvelles Lettres inédites de Cavour.*

were busily engaged stirring up the people, decrying
the efforts of England and France for peace, lauding the
renewed spirit and discipline of the army, and preparing
the country to demand a renewal of hostilities. The
King, to whom the war with Austria had assumed the
complexion almost of a personal duel, was bent on
reopening the struggle, and whilst apparently supporting his Cabinet, was giving covert encouragement to
the war party. On the other hand, the Government,
armed with inside information, knew only too well that
the army was in no condition to fight, though for
patriotic reasons it was obliged to say the opposite.

It was not long before the Government experienced
the effect of its inability to come to a working agreement
with Gioberti. Two months were to pass before
Parliament was once more assembled, and in the meantime the members were busy trying to win over the
country to their several points of view. Before the
bitter reality of the national disaster, political animosities had been for a brief time cast aside. Differences
were forgotten, and men of all parties came together to
save the country. Deprived of parliamentary activity,
the deputies found an outlet for their energies in the
only existing political organization, the Circolo Politico
Nazionale. Though hitherto the organization of the
Democratic party, men of all shades of opinion now
became members. In the central Circolo at Turin,
under the Presidency of Angelo Brofferio, were to be
found enrolled Gioberti, Paleocapa,[1] Cavour, Alfieri,
and many other well-known names. On August 23rd,
Gioberti came down to the Circolo Politico and opened
his campaign against the Government with a bitter
polemic, stigmatizing them as 'the Government with
two programmes' and accusing them of duplicity, of
gulling the public, by talking of renewing the war when
their real intention was peace at any price. He demanded the retirement of the Ministry and a general
election, at which he doubtless hoped to be carried to

[1] Afterwards Minister of Public Works under Cavour.

power on a wave of public applause. The speech was printed and signatures of adhesion were sought for by zealous Democratic agents.[1]

Gioberti made a fatal mistake in thus identifying himself with the Circolo Nazionale, for although it provided him with a party and a pulpit, it determined the personnel of his future Cabinet and committed him to a policy that was not his own. Had he been possessed of patience and political foresight, and been content to stand apart and study the terrain during the months of the Revel-Pinelli Government, it might have been possible for him, with his immense prestige throughout Italy, to have formed a Cabinet that would have commanded respect outside Piedmont and achieved some measure of success. As it was, he flared into brilliance amid the shouts of the populace, but it was as the crackling of thorns under a pot.

We must now return to Cavour. Without any position or influence on the course of events, Cavour watched the military and political collapse of his country with a feeling akin to despair. 'Our military and political disasters,' he writes, 'have stupified me. What mistakes, grand Dieu! It is impossible to conceive a more lamentable combination of incapacity of every kind, whether in the army or the Government. All have made mistakes, but the greatest are those of Genoa. They have done immense harm to the Italian cause. The least culpable are the Piedmontese, their leaders, and the commander-in-chief above all, excepted.'[2] A week later he writes again: 'What frightens me is the moral anarchy into which we have fallen. There is no point of union anywhere, every one expresses his personal opinion and one can see nobody capable of rallying a strong party. The King is the greatest obstacle to the solution of the crisis. If he does not abdicate the country is lost beyond hope. The

[1] Cavour and others with him resigned their membership after this speech. See his letter to Émile de la Rue in Bert, No. 156, and Chiala, *Lettere di Cavour*, vol. i. Nos. 115–16.

[2] Bert, *Cavour, Nouvelles Lettres*, Nos. 151, 154.

Cabinet, which appeared completed, is again in the melting-pot. The position is most critical.' When the names of the Revel-Pinelli Cabinet were known Cavour took heart again. Most of them were his personal friends, and if he doubted their ability, he was certain of their honesty and good intentions. But the opposition of Gioberti grieved him sorely. What chance was there for the Government if Gioberti threw his weight against them? It was deplorable.

As the weeks passed the condition of things got worse rather than better. Mediation hung fire, for as Austria got a firmer grip on the situation, she became less and less disposed to make concessions. Parliament was to meet in October, and the position of the Government was precarious. The Democrats were now openly demanding a renewal of the struggle, which meant the retirement of the Government and their own accession to power. Cavour summed up the position in these words: 'The Ministry and the masses want peace. The King and the restless section of the middle classes want to try yet again resort to force.' But nevertheless he hoped that 'France and England will hold us by the coat-tails and make us keep the peace.' Early in October the events taking place in Austria gave renewed encouragement to the war party. On the 3rd, the Emperor declared Hungary in a state of siege and dissolved the Diet, and when a few days later a portion of the garrison at Vienna was ordered to Hungary, its departure was forcibly prevented and the Minister of War was hanged. On the 7th the Emperor fled to Olmütz. 'Here we are every day more warlike,' Cavour wrote when these events became known, 'I believe the Government will be forced to denounce the Armistice in spite of all that diplomacy can do.'

Such was the state of the country when, the day after these lines were written, the Chamber of Deputies met after an interval of three months. The sitting had hardly commenced when the Deputy Ravina rose and asked the President of the Council to name a day for a full

debate on the Armistice, mediation, and the condition
of the army. This was arranged for three days later,
and on the 17th of October the debate began. The Left
came down to the House that day determined if possible
to force the issue and compel the Government to make
an immediate declaration of war. They had men like
Ravina and Brofferio,[1] whose fiery eloquence they hoped
would force the Chamber into a renewal of hostilities.
The Government, on the other hand, were out to play
for time. Though they knew war was almost inevitable,
they wanted to keep in their own hands the power to
choose the moment for its declaration. They wanted
if possible to avoid revelations as to the true state of
the army, and trusted that the good sense of the
Chamber would accept the fact that the Cabinet was
the best judge of the situation. But the Government was weak and vacillating, devoid of persuasive
eloquence, and in consequence at a disadvantage in
debate.

The sitting opened with a long 'account rendered'
by the principal ministers, at the close of which
Domenico Buffa, a member of the Left, opened the
debate. The report of the Cabinet, he said, had only
emphasized the need for a clear answer to the question
which all the nation was asking. Was it to be peace or
war? The present situation was impossible. They had
130,000 men under arms at an enormous expense,
which the country could not bear much longer. As to
mediation, it was useless; England had only been
dragged in to prevent the isolated action of France.
Conversations had been going on for weeks and they
were farther from a conclusion than ever. As to intervention, no help would come to Piedmont until she
drew the sword; then France, that generous nation,
would fly to her aid, and together they would drive the
hated whitecoats from Italy. 'As we stand at present,'

---

[1] Angelo Brofferio was a leading criminal advocate, journalist, and dialect
poet. He was the democratic orator of the day and a persistent opponent of
Cavour. His *Storia del Parlamento Subalpino*, if partisan and highly coloured,
gives a graphic picture of Piedmontese parliamentary life.

he concluded, 'mediation is useless, intervention impossible, and war necessary and opportune.'

In response to Buffa, the Deputy Tola spoke from the Government side of the Chamber. His long and ineffective speech did not do much good, but he ended by expressing his disbelief in any help coming either from Italy or from abroad, and that Piedmont must be prepared to face Austria alone. Such odds were too great, he said, and it was best that they should wait until in the opinion of the Cabinet the moment was ripe to draw the sword.

Other speakers followed, and as the sitting was now drawing to a close, and the Left were determined to have the last word, Brofferio, as his phrase is, 'launched himself on the rostrum.'[1] With fervid eloquence he sought to counteract the fear of isolation. 'No,' he thundered, 'Piedmont will not be alone. The citizens of Vienna call to us to unsheath the sword. The Hungarian people call to us, the Prussians call to us: Venice is with us, Lombardy is with us, Tuscany is with us, and if the Roman Government is against us, the Romans themselves are on our side!' Then to focus the issue on one clear point he moved the following resolution:

> That the Chamber does not approve the policy of awaiting the outcome of the negotiations for mediation, before deciding upon peace or war: instead, it offers its assistance to the Government, if it will declare immediate war.

The following day Lorenzo Valerio,[2] next to Brofferio the most influential member of the Left, reopened the debate. From a slightly different angle he went over the same ground and came to the same conclusions, the uselessness of mediation and the opportuneness of immediate war. When Valerio had spoken the main attack on the Government had been delivered, and in

[1] The practice of the Deputies speaking from their seats was not adopted until later under Cavour.

[2] Valerio, for many years one of Cavour's bitterest opponents, learned to appreciate him later, and became first, Governor of Como, and then Royal Commissioner for the Marches in 1860.

reply to him they put forward Cavour. Cavour's speech was obviously designed to influence that central group whose silent vote would ultimately decide the issue. It was reasonable, unprovocative, and carefully calculated to impress the waverers with the wisdom of waiting a little longer. Cavour had always a firm trust in the common sense of his fellow-countrymen, and believed that, if clear reasons were put before them, they would know how to discount the rhetorical periods of Brofferio and the rush tactics of men like Ravina.

He began his speech by admitting that war was practically inevitable, and that the question with which they had to deal was in consequence simply one of opportuneness. He then passed on to the question of mediation, and Buffa's charge of the insincerity of England. There was no need to deal with France, whose jealousy of Austria was always a sure guarantee of her support of Piedmont. He believed, he said, in the sincerity of England's desire for peace, firstly, because war upset her trade, and this was always a vital matter with Englishmen, and secondly, because of her distrust of Germany and German policy. Then in a passage that to-day sounds curiously prophetic, he added:

> Germanism is scarcely born and already it threatens to upset the equilibrium of Europe; already it shows desire for dominion and usurpation. The Diet of Frankfort does not conceal its design of spreading its dominion to the shores of the North Sea, and of invading Holland with treaties and with force, in order to become a maritime power and contest with England the Empire of the Sea.

As to intervention, he warned the Chamber not to rely on France, illustrating his contention with an effective reference to the failure of that country to help Poland.

He then turned to consider what assistance was to be expected from Italy herself. Quietly discounting Brofferio's glowing rhetoric, by translating his rosy expectations into terms of regiments and battalions, he had no difficulty in showing that, beyond a certain probability of undisciplined enthusiasm, no practical help could be forthcoming. Finally, he dealt with the Hungarian rising in Austria, the one strong argument for immediate war. The line he took was, that, if the present state of things in Austria made a declaration of hostilities by Piedmont opportune and desirable, in the course of the next few weeks their position would be still further improved. The Piedmontese army, though it had recovered, was still not perfect, and the wise plan would be to put the finishing touches to their military preparations, while watching for the first clear signs of disintegration in the army of Radetzky, and then to strike.

This speech of Cavour's undoubtedly achieved the end he had in view. It convinced the waverers that it was wisest to wait a little longer. Its effect was strengthened by the Minister of War, who spoke soon after. His speech was cautious and somewhat non-committal, but ended on a disturbing note. Answering an interpellation as to the discipline of the army, he concluded his speech with these words:

> It is clear and evident that the Piedmontese army, composed as it is of married men and fathers of families, not of men hardened by many years of military life, cannot certainly have the discipline of the Austrian army.

The debate was wound up by Brofferio, who strove to counteract the effect of Cavour's speech and that of the Minister for War. The flamboyant oratory of Brofferio was always irresistible to the gallery, and the following example of his style is typical of the most appreciated democratic oratory:

> Too many injuries have we to avenge, too many accounts to settle, too many insults to wipe out, and too much cause for boasting has our last retreat given to Austria, for us not to seek with all our power to prove to the foreigner, who watches us and laughs, that the bells of the Sicilian Vespers and the trumpet of the Lombard League and the devouring flames of Pietro Micca, are not the symbols of an ancient

pride but the glories of the present! (prolonged applause). Pursue this policy of useless delay and what will you find in Lombardy? Leave the Bohemians to sack it, the Bavarians to burn it, and the bloodthirsty Croat to dye its soil with Italian blood, and when the hour of victory sounds, you will reconquer cities destroyed, a devastated country-side, and a people wasted with misery—you will build it again, but you will build upon ruin and ashes! When O'Connell, the great apostle of Irish liberty, rose against the oppression of Britain, 'three things I urge upon you,' he said, 'sons of Ireland: agitate, agitate, agitate!' And I, O Italians, urge three things upon you: audacity, audacity, audacity! (Clamorous and prolonged applause from all the Chamber and the galleries.)

The tremendous ovation which greeted Brofferio's speech brought Cavour to his feet to demand that the galleries should be made to respect the dignity of the Chamber. He was shouted down, and the already excited deputies took sides and for a time there was pandemonium. When order was restored (it was now 2 a.m.) the Chamber voted on Brofferio's motion. It was rejected by 77 against 58.[1]

Though the Government had staved off defeat its position was not an enviable one. It could neither make peace nor declare war. The country could not for long remain in its present position, but the Cabinet seemed to have no idea as to how to get out of it.

The next step it took, however, provided the solution. Relying on its victory, it invited the Chamber to appoint a committee of seven of its members to report on the conduct of the Government. The result was practically a vote of censure. Compelled to play its last card, the Cabinet demanded a secret session and exposed the condition of the army by reading a series of reports sent in by the commanders. From these it was evident that neither in discipline, morale, nor equipment, was the army fit for a second campaign.[2]

[1] Brofferio, *Stor. Parl. Subalp.*, vol. i. c. vii. For Cavour's speech, *Discorsi Parlamentari del Conte di Cavour*, vol. i. p. 47.

[2] According to the Minister for War, the army had neither rifles, boots, or bayonets, nor even buttons of regulation pattern. Brofferio, vol. ii. p. 6.

After this the fate of the Government was sealed. There
was some suggestion of a coalition, but this was rejected,
and in the middle of December, after defeat on a minor
issue, the Cabinet resigned.[1]

'From one aspect,' Cavour wrote upon hearing the
news, 'it is a misfortune, for it would be difficult to
find a body of men so honest and so courageous, but
on the other hand one must admit that, on the score
of ability it was not fit to cope with circumstances. It
had not a single statesman in it.' The alternative to the
recent Cabinet was of course Gioberti and the democratic Left. 'We shall have a Left Cabinet pure and
simple,' wrote Cavour, 'with Gioberti at its head. Such
a Ministry will make all kinds of foolish mistakes but
it will not probably last long. It is unfortunate, but
it will have the happy result of having these men, who
have acquired a disastrous influence over the country,
appreciated at their proper value.' As Cavour expected,
Gioberti became President. Having formed his Cabinet,
he at once committed a tactical error by dissolving the
Chamber which had brought him to power, and
announcing a general election for the middle of January
1849.

It was characteristic of Cavour that he seldom formed
an opinion without a very wide survey of all the prevailing conditions likely to affect the issue. In his letters
to his agent at Genoa, for instance, regarding the sale
or purchase of corn, his decision would always be
based, not only on the condition of the European
markets at the moment, but often on the probable
influence of political events. His political judgements
were formed on the same wide basis, and, in consequence,
we find that in his estimate of the probable effect of
Gioberti's ascent to power, he is more impressed with
what was taking place in France than in Italy, for at
this same moment Louis Napoleon was elected to the
Presidency of the new Republic. 'What has struck me,'
he writes, 'is not the immense majority given to Louis

[1] Bert, Nos. 174–82.

Napoleon, but the insignificant support given to Ledru-Rollin and the representatives of the red republicans. To me it is evident that social order is saved in France, and therefore in Europe, for revolutions which have not their *point d'appui* in Paris are abortive.'[1]

While the country under a flood of democratic oratory was thus swinging violently from right to left, Cavour was one of a small group of men busily engaged in trying to save the country from bankruptcy. In the early summer, they were occupied negotiating the loan with the Bank of Genoa. It was a delicate task, for the Finance Minister, Count Ricci, had raised the application from 12 to 20 millions, which was more than the Bank could find unassisted. Soon after this was accomplished, Count Ricci was replaced by the conservative Count Revel. The position with which he had to deal was even more difficult, and he adopted the heroic course of a forced loan. The Government, taking 4 per cent. as the average return from invested money, imposed a tax on capital, rising from ½ per cent. on small incomes to 2 per cent. on those over 100,000 lire. This was accepted and passed in the early autumn as a necessary war measure. But, although this implied the surrender of half the year's income from the wealthier classes, it did not satisfy the Left, who still believed there were untold millions in the coffers of the upper classes. Accordingly, they introduced a supplementary Bill which raised the rate by stages to 6 per cent. on the higher incomes, limiting this however to the landowning classes. The Bill was supported on the ground that in times of revolution, revolutionary measures were justified.

In the debate that followed, Cavour opposed the measure with all his power. After condemning it as unjust, and contrary to the Statuto, because it applied only to one section of the community, he pointed out that, if measures of this kind sometimes produced very large sums, they inevitably had the effect of diminishing

[1] Bert, No. 186

the returns from the usual sources of revenue. Their only justification was, if they produced a sum large enough to compensate for the loss of trade that must follow. In the present case, he said, the extra taxation could at most bring in some 2 millions of lire, which was nothing to what they would suffer through disturbance of trade. Then in a remarkable passage he continued:

> Gentlemen, if ever fatal necessity or fallacious economics should induce the Government or the Chamber to adopt this system of revolutionary means, I, after having fought them with all the energy of which I am capable, when I saw that they were inevitable, would then say to the Chamber: 'since you adopt revolutionary means, adopt them with all possible energy; act so that the loftiness of your purpose and the greatness of their result, will offer some recompense for the odiousness of the methods you employ; and, above all, avoid falling into that most deplorable of all conditions in which a Government can find itself, to be at the same time both odious and ridiculous.'

He then turned to the practical results of the Bill, if passed. It would not only disturb trade and cause loss of business, but it would seriously injure the national credit. Nor would it achieve the ends designed by the promoters of the Bill, for it was the small trades-men and the worker that would suffer, not the big capitalist, who would simply invest his money in other countries. Thus the effects of the measure would be to drive capital abroad and create unemployment at home. Cavour was frequently interrupted throughout his speech by the Left or their supporters in the galleries, who, ignorant of the truth of what he was saying, regarded him simply as a capitalist defending his pocket. The voting on the Bill was so close that a recount was necessary, when the Bill was rejected by a small majority. But though Cavour more than any one else procured the rejection of this Bill, he could not save the Government, which soon after resigned.[1]

As Cavour had foreseen, when the elections took

[1] *Discorsi*, vol. i. p. 96.

place early in January 1849, the extremists swept the country. He accepted the result philosophically. 'I beg you to believe,' he wrote to his friend Castelli, 'that the deplorable result of the last elections has neither surprised nor discouraged me. The state of bewilderment in which public opinion finds itself is one of the inevitable phases of the great transformation which is taking place in the country.'[1] Cavour himself was among the defeated candidates.[2] Though he did not recognize it as such, it was a blessing in disguise. Fate was more than once kind to Cavour in what he regarded at the time as ill-treatment. For, just as Charles Albert's refusal to employ him in his earlier years, on the ground of his liberalism, had kept him untainted from the spirit of absolutism; so now, his rejection during the democratic spell of power brought him back later to the Chamber free from the malodour of Novara, from which men like Rattazzi and Lanza afterwards found it so difficult to cleanse themselves. For it is more than likely that, if Cavour had been elected, when war became inevitable, he would have put country before party and from purely patriotic reasons have thrown himself on the side of the Government, an action which later would have cost him dear.

But in the short time that had elapsed since the fall of the Conservative Ministry a further change had taken place. While the Chamber had become more radical than before, Gioberti had developed a strong tendency to conservatism. In his opening speech to the Chamber, his opinions, wrote Cavour, were 'identical with those of Pinelli, the only difference being Gioberti's use of high-sounding phrases which mean nothing'. Gioberti, however, had a policy of his own, which proved to be neither that of his Cabinet nor of his majority, and when he raised himself to power on the shoulders of the Circolo Nazionale, he had no intention

[1] *Carteggio Politico di M. A. Castelli.*

[2] On his own defeat he wrote: 'Though little flattering to my *amour-propre*, this result is far from disgusting me with politics: I consider it as an inevitable episode to be borne without anger or weakness. Castelli, No. 23.

of having his policy dictated by Brofferio and his associates, which was precisely the aim of the democratic leaders. In his inaugural address to the Chamber of Deputies, Gioberti announced a line of policy which bitterly offended the Circolo, and which, to be understood, necessitates our glancing at the political events beyond the confines of Piedmont.

It has been mentioned that the central idea of Gioberti's political scheme was a federation of Italian States. It was a conception that sounded reasonable enough in the abstract, but one which bristled with difficulties as soon as it was treated as a practical problem, a fact which, however, did not trouble the theorists who supported it. The preliminary steps towards the application of this idea had been taken during the brief Ministry of Count Gabrio Casati (of which Gioberti had been a member without a portfolio) by the dispatch of the philosopher Antonio Rosmini to Rome, where he initiated a conference, in which, Monsignor Corboli-Bussi representing the Papacy, Bargagli, Tuscany, and Lorenzo Pareto Piedmont, endeavoured to find a common ground. A guarantee for the territory of each state, and an offensive and defensive league between the members, were to be the bases. Further progress was completely wrecked by the refusal of the Papacy to join any offensive league or declare war on any Christian nation. But the federal idea was nevertheless discussed all over Italy both by the governments and in the democratic organizations. In October, Gioberti summoned a Congresso Federativo Italiano to meet at Turin, which was attended by delegates from Rome, Naples, Tuscany, Milan, and Venetia. It devised a federal constitution consisting of two assemblies, one elected by the States and the other by the people, with an executive, to sit permanently in Rome. A practical problem, however, arose in the awkward question of the status of the hoped-for Kingdom of Upper Italy: if Lombardy and Venice wanted to be members of the Federal Union, how could the kingdom be formed? As a compromise, Gioberti suggested the formation of a Federal Union and a Kingdom of Upper Italy outside it.[1]

While these discussions were occupying the thoughts of the *federalisti*, events in Rome and Tuscany were moving to a crisis. In Rome, the fall of the Constitutional Minister, Fabbre, led to the elevation of Pellegrino Rossi. Born in Italy, Rossi had migrated to France, become a naturalized French subject, an academician, and then a peer of France, and now came to Rome as President of the Ministry, taking over also finance and internal affairs. He had scarcely been two months in office when on his way to open Parliament he was assassinated (Nov. 15th). After Rossi's death the democrats got the upper hand; the Pope fled to Gaeta; a Constituent Assembly was called together, and in February 1849 the Roman Republic was declared. In Tuscany a similar course of events took place. Under the Constitutional Government of Capponi a series of violent democratic outbreaks took place at Livorno. Unable to deal successfully with the disorder, Capponi fell. Guerrazzi and Montanelli, the democratic leaders, assumed power and proclaimed a Constituent Assembly. A few days later the Grand Duke fled and joined the Pope at Gaeta.

Gioberti assumed the Premiership while these events were maturing, when the Constituent Assembly had been summoned in Rome and Tuscany was on its way to a similar move. The first motion brought forward when Parliament met was a petition from the Circolo Politico that Piedmont should send delegates to the new Roman assembly. To the dismay of the democrats, Gioberti rose and declared that Piedmont should never participate in the Constituent Assembly in Rome. That night a deputation was sent to Gioberti from the Circolo to exhort him, as they put it, 'not to separate Piedmont from Italy'. Gioberti was unmoved, and the Government and the Circolo parted company. Gioberti

[1] Tivaroni, *L'Italia durante il dominio Austriaco*, part i, c. viii.

had asserted his independence, but he had shattered his majority.

When these facts were known the excitement in Turin became intense, and the day Gioberti came down to explain the programme of the Government to the newly elected Chamber, which, as Cavour had foreseen was even more extreme than its predecessor, the crowd not only packed every available space within the Chamber, but overflowed on to the staircase and entrance and out into the Piazza.

Gioberti's speech was, on the one hand, a denunciation of the republicans and all their works, and on the other an exposition of his own scheme of federalism. After remarking that the Italian risorgimento contained four principal stages, Reforms, Statuto, Independence, and Confederation, and that the movement might be described as an arch in the construction of which when the keystone is passed you commence to descend, he turned on those who wished to go farther than the point now reached, which he maintained would be disastrous:

> In the opinion of these people [he went on] the task will not be completed until the entire Peninsula is comprised in the absolute unity of a single state, and the monarchical system replaced by the republic: nor do they regard this work as the task of our grandsons: they wish us to carry it out. We have not yet expelled the Austrians, and they wish to overturn our Princes. We have not yet acquired full control over constitutional liberty, and they wish to give us republics. Who does not see that to unify Italy completely would mean the violation of all the rights of all our Princes, the destruction of all the present governments and defiance of the whole of Europe, to whom an Italian republic would give many reasons for jealousy and distrust? . . .

He then passed on to explain his own solution 'a fraternal confederation of all the Italian States with an Italian diet that represents it.' After mentioning the part Piedmont had taken in the preliminary federative efforts in Rome and Florence, and the Congress held in Turin, he explained the reason for his refusal to support the present Constituent Assemblies in Tuscany and the Papal States in these terms:

> We have been unable to assent to the new Constituent Assemblies in Central Italy, because we could not do so without abandoning our own programme and embracing another, not only altogether different, but contrary to it. The Assembly proposed by us is strictly federative: those of Rome and Tuscany are, or at least may become, political. The one leaves intact the autonomy of the various states and their internal affairs, the others are authorized to change them and even to overthrow them. Our Constituent is therefore incompatible with those of Rome and Florence.

Then before closing his speech, he made the assurance of republican hostility doubly sure, by announcing that the Government had proffered its good offices both to the Grand Duke and the Holy Father.[1]

When Gioberti sat down Brofferio rose amid tense excitement and proceeded to impeach the Government. Instead of uniting Italy, as it professed the desire to do, the policy of Gioberti, he declared, had split Italy into fragments. To the Premier's tenderness for the Pope he attributed the disorder in Rome; to his refusal to assist Tuscany, the difficulties of Guerrazzi. He had impugned the sovereignty of the people, encouraged a useless mediation, and lost the great opportunity of binding together Tuscany, Rome, and Piedmont. Gioberti replied, but when the sitting closed it was plain that, if he was enabled to carry out his scheme, it must be by means of more support than he could receive from his colleagues of the Left.

The exigencies of the situation had compelled Gioberti to choose his Cabinet from the members of the Left, the only exception being the Minister for War, di Sonnaz, whose politics were those of his regiment. Of the remainder, Urbano Rattazzi alone had genuine ability, the rest, Tecchio, Buffa, Ricci, and Cadorna, being men of very ordinary gifts. Gioberti himself was

---

[1] Brofferio, *Stor. Parl. Subalp.*, vol. ii. Berti, *Vincenzo Gioberti*.

peculiarly unfitted for a constitutional Prime Minister, for he could not work with others. His lonely and self-centred life precluded him from that group-thinking which is essential in Cabinet Government. Consciousness of his own outstanding intellectual ability, and personal conviction as to the practicability of his federal scheme, had driven him to seek the Premiership, and he had used his immense popularity and the democratic organization for this purpose, 'more', as he would have said, 'for Italy's sake' than from perfect identity of thought with the aims and methods of his party. His tour in Italy had shown him how far the country was from supporting unity as a practical proposition; the condition of Piedmont revealed to him with equal clearness that law and order rather than desperate military ventures was the first duty of the Government. So it was not surprising that, as soon as his ambition was realized, his views became much more moderate than was at first anticipated.

In regard to foreign policy, it was impossible to be blind to the fact that, the excesses of the democrats and republicans in Tuscany and Central Italy must soon necessitate intervention from outside, and it was only the internal difficulties in Austria and France that had hitherto saved those regions from the presence of foreign troops. Why should not Piedmont, thought Gioberti, save Italy from foreign intervention by restoring order with her own troops? The idea of restoring the Pope to Rome appealed to him both on political and religious grounds. It gratified him as a loyal Catholic; as a statesman, to put the Papacy under so real an obligation to Piedmont, might easily provide the solution of the religious question. The idea had the support not only of men like D'Azeglio and Cavour, but of the French and English ministers, neither of whom were averse to seeing the policing of Italy in the hands of Piedmont, instead of Austria. Gioberti resolved to act. He assembled a division under Alfonso La Marmora at Sarzana on the Tuscan border, and definitely offered assistance to the Grand Duke and the Pope. The former tentatively accepted, and then, under Austrian pressure, refused. At Rome his offer met with a blank refusal and angered alike the Assembly and the Pope. Gioberti nevertheless resolved to intervene, at least in Tuscany, but he made the mistake of not consulting or persuading his Cabinet, conducting the negotiations in person, in his capacity of Minister of Foreign Affairs. The matter, however, could not be kept quiet, rumour was soon busy, and his colleagues had to be informed. What transpired at the Cabinet meeting is not very clear, but it seems that Rattazzi was not present when the matter was first brought up, and in his absence some kind of consent appears to have been given. At a later meeting, however, which Rattazzi attended, consent was refused, and Gioberti, disappointed and disillusioned, somewhat unnecessarily, resigned. With the fall of Gioberti the idea of federalism as a practical issue disappeared. The last barrier to an immediate renewal of the struggle with Austria was removed and war became inevitable.

The value of Gioberti's contemplated intervention will remain a matter of opinion. If tactfully carried out it would undoubtedly have heightened the prestige of Piedmont abroad, and at the same time have been a deft back-handed blow at Austrian influence in Italy. But, on the other hand, for Piedmont to play the Austrian, to run the risk of shedding Italian blood in the name of Italian freedom, to alienate the sympathy of other states by her interference under the guise of promoting unity, were dangers real enough to justify those who regarded the fall of Gioberti as a blessing in disguise.

To Cavour the fall of Gioberti was a genuine misfortune for the country. The King, he said, had treated him scandalously, sacrificing him without pity to the extremists of the party and his own desire to renew the struggle with Austria. Gioberti's scheme of intervention might, he thought, have led to a favourable solution of the Italian question, for it would have enlisted the sympathy of France and England, which would now be lost.[1]

After the fall of Gioberti the Cabinet was hastily remodelled, Urbano Rattazzi became President, and the programme was summed up in one word—war.

Events now moved with startling rapidity. On March the 14th the Armistice was declared at an end. On the 20th hostilities commenced, and three days later the Piedmontese army was hopelessly crushed by Radetzky at Novara. That evening, after seeking death in vain all day on the battlefield, Charles Albert summoned his generals and announced his abdication, naming his eldest son, Victor Emmanuel, Duke of Savoy, as his successor. Then, without even returning to Turin to say good-bye to his wife and family, with only his valet as escort, under the title of the Comte de Barge, he made his way through the Austrian lines *en route* for Oporto, to exile and death.

On receiving the news of the disaster of Novara the Democratic Ministry at once resigned, and the young king, Victor Emmanuel, after arranging an armistice with Radetzky, chose General Delaunay, the officer in command of the National Guard, to form a Cabinet. It was only a stop-gap appointment, but he formed a Ministry. Pinelli became Minister of the Interior, Giovanni Nigra Minister of Finance, Galvagno of Public Works, with General Dabormida as War Minister.

A few weeks later General Delaunay resigned, and a new era in Piedmont's constitutional life opened, when, on the urgent request of the young king, the Marquis Massimo D'Azeglio became President of the Council and Minister of Foreign Affairs.

The revolution in Piedmont had lasted exactly a year. On March 23rd, 1848, Radetzky had evacuated Milan and Charles Albert had declared war on Austria. On March 23rd, 1849, Charles Albert was crushed at Novara and abdicated the throne of Piedmont.

[1] Bert, *Lettres*, No. 194.

In 1830, when a young man of twenty, Cavour had written to his father these words: 'Eighteen years from now the great crisis which has already begun will reach its climax, and Europe will then decide for good upon one of the great principles which now stand before it.' The prophecy had been fulfilled and the old order had triumphed. The bold attempt of Piedmont to fulfil Charles Albert's proud boast, 'L'Italia farà da sè', had ended in debt and disaster. This is not the place to examine the causes of the failure, but rather to note that, amid the misery and confusion of those days, there was one clear mind upon which the bitter lessons of the nation's disaster had been indelibly impressed. It is idle to speculate as to what might have happened had the destinies of the country during these months been in the hands of Cavour. His own opinion he made sufficiently clear: 'An excessive opinion of my abilities may deceive me,' he wrote to a friend, 'but I have the intimate conviction that if my advice had been listened to, if I had had control of the situation, without any effort of genius I could have saved the country; and at this minute, the Italian flag would be floating over the Styrian Alps. But my friends have united with my enemies to keep me from power, and I have passed my time deploring the mistakes that it would have been easy to avoid.[1] Looking back over his subsequent policy we can see how well Cavour had digested the teaching of 1848. He abandoned at once the idea that Italy could win her own redemption unaided, for as long as the existing system lasted, Italy meant Piedmont, and Piedmont alone could not defeat Austria. He reverted, therefore, to his country's historic policy of counterbalancing the influence of Austria by a French alliance.

He saw also that the question of unity, and the great problem of the Papacy that lay across the path, must be subordinated to that of independence. The Austrians once driven out of Italy, her satellites would follow her of their own accord, and then the problem

[1] *Chiala*, vol. i. p. 411.

of unity would arise. Until that moment came, Cavour left the question in abeyance and concentrated on the expulsion of Austria. Again, it showed him the need for decision and unity of command in a crisis, and the folly of submitting vital decisions to the interminable loquacity of a public assembly. 'We are no longer in 1848,' he wrote to the newly appointed Governor of Milan in 1859, 'we admit no discussion. Take no notice of the qualms of those who surround you. The least act of weakness will ruin the Government.' Lastly, it revealed quite clearly that Piedmont was the fulcrum upon which the whole possibility of effective leverage rested. If Piedmont collapsed, Italy would collapse with her. With great insight Cavour perceived that the economic prosperity of Piedmont must be the corner-stone of all future action, and henceforth he bent all his energies upon peace, reorganization, and reform.

Nothing is more remarkable about Cavour than the consistency of his principles. As a young man of one-and-twenty, under the influence of the July Revolution in France, he had adopted a political creed that he termed 'an honest *juste milieu*,' and to this he remained consistently loyal throughout his life. In the ensuing years we shall watch him guiding his country along the path of reform on moderate liberal principles. Fighting, on the one hand, the persistent attempts of Austria to bring Piedmont towards reaction and absolutism, and on the other hand, opposing an inflexible will to the revolutionary propaganda of Mazzini. We shall see him despairing at last of changing the views of the two extreme wings in Parliament, forming a centre party, which gradually drew to itself, not only all the best minds in Piedmont, but all the reasonable and progressive elements throughout the Peninsula, thus rendering possible the unity of Italy.

II. CAVOUR AS A DEPUTY

Massimo d'Azeglio and Cavour—The Treaty with Austria—The New
Chamber and the Treaty—Dissolution of the Chamber—The Pro-
clamation of Moncalieri—Triumph of D'Azeglio—The Treaty passed—
Cavour and Brofferio—Growing Influence of Cavour—The Bill on the
Foro—Cavour's Great Speech—His desire for Office—Threatens
Opposition to Government—Death of Minister for Commerce—
Cavour appointed as his Successor.

THE man to whom the young King now entrusted the
helm of State was not only his personal friend but also
one of the best-known men in Italy. Of old aristocratic
stock, brought up somewhat sternly by an affectionate
but austere father, Massimo d'Azeglio had early shown
artistic leanings and had trained as a painter in Rome
and Florence. In the years preceding the Statuto he
had suddenly turned author, and his novels, *Ettore
Fieramosca* and *Niccolò de' Lapi*, were known throughout Italy, their thinly disguised patriotic sentiment
bringing them a large and eager public. A little later,
in the interests of independence and Charles Albert,
he had toured Central Italy seeking to win the trust
of the people for the Piedmontese King. On his return
he wrote the brochure *Gli ultimi Casi di Romagna*,
which re-echoed through Europe and brought him
fame and recognition. He fought with the army in 1848,
and was badly wounded in the thigh at Vicenza, and
was scarcely convalescent when he accepted the post
of President of the Council. Tall and good-looking, with
a fine carriage and attractive manners, he was eminently
fitted to occupy his high post.[1]

Though he had no political training and no liking
or ambition for public life, and had only accepted office
from a sense of duty, no happier choice than Massimo
d'Azeglio could have been made. He brought to the
conduct of affairs certain priceless qualities, which at
that moment were of infinitely greater value to his

[1] On D'Azeglio see his own interesting *I Miei Ricordi*; N. Vaccalluzzo,
Massimo D'Azeglio; Bianchi, *La Politica di M. D'Azeglio*.

country than political genius. He was a man of the very highest character, whose name was familiar outside his own country, and one who was trusted and respected by all Italians. If, as was said, the name of Cavour when he came into office was in itself a programme, the name of D'Azeglio was a guarantee. And it was a guarantee that was wanted.

D'Azeglio and Cavour together were a very strong combination. For Cavour was strong where his colleague was weak. D'Azeglio disliked the rough and tumble of debate, especially in the Chamber of Deputies. He had no knowledge of finance or industry, and had had no experience in administration, and his wound prevented him from taking as active a part as he should have done in the parliamentary debates. These weak points in D'Azeglio were the strong points of Cavour, and their joint influence at home and abroad was the cause of Piedmont's rapid recovery from the disaster of 1849. Cavour welcomed D'Azeglio's acceptance of office: 'He is a man of infinite spirit, of sound common sense, and of a remarkable courage,' he wrote, 'those who assume power in the present circumstances make an act of devotion to their country.' Nevertheless, Cavour was very hurt that D'Azeglio had found no place for him in his Cabinet, but he soon got over his disappointment.

The first task of the Government was to arrange terms of peace with Austria. For this purpose General Dabormida and Carlo Boncompagni were sent as plenipotentiaries. Cavour was asked to go also, but he put too high a value on his services. 'I do not wish to go,' he wrote, 'unless I have power to conduct the negotiations in my own way.' The terms were signed at the end of July, and included an indemnity of 75 millions of lire to be paid to Austria in instalments. A little later Cavour was offered the London Embassy. This post, though it attracted him, he also declined, believing that he would be more useful in Parliament than in London.[1]

[1] 'If I was only to consult my personal feelings, I would very gladly go

Whilst the Government was negotiating for peace the country was involved in a general election.

When the results were known, it was plain that the hopes of the Government that the country would return a majority of moderates were grievously disappointed. Whilst in the towns a number of those who had lost their seats in the wave of democratic enthusiasm were once more successful, the country districts returned a solid body of democrats more or less pledged to make no treaty with Austria. The bitterness of defeat and the hatred of Austria were still the predominant forces, and the country had not yet the courage to acknowledge the facts and face the consequences. Cavour himself was successful in two constituencies and elected to sit as before for Turin.[1] The Chamber soon gave a fore-taste of its quality by electing as its President the Marquis Lorenzo Pareto, the former Minister, who had recently taken a leading part in a revolt at Genoa which General La Marmora had had to put down by military force.[2] But the two parties were not all the same quite so homogeneous as they appeared to be. The former ministers of the Democratic party, Rattazzi, Cadorna, and Buffa, were already separating themselves from the extremists, and were soon to develop into the Left Centre party, whilst the moderate Right was beginning to group itself round Cavour, thus forming the nucleus of the Right Centre. These *nuances* of opinion were not yet observable when it came to voting, but nevertheless these two parties, whose ultimate fusion was to give Cavour his working majority for ten years, existed in embryo after the July elections of 1849.[3]

---

to England, a country I delight in and where I have many distinguished friends. But to leave Piedmont in these difficult times seems to me an act of egotism that is repugnant to me. My decision will in any case depend on political events and the advice of my friends.' Visconti, *Cavour Agricoltore.*

[1] At Finalborgo, the only name put forward in opposition to Cavour was, of all people, King Charles Albert, dying of a broken heart in Oporto.

[2] See La Marmora, *Un episodio del Risorgimento Italiano.* For a short time the revolt at Genoa was serious.

[3] Chiala, *Une page d'histoire du Gouvernement Représentatif en Piémont.*

The first task before Parliament was the acceptance of the Treaty of Peace with Austria. Until this vital matter was out of the way all progressive legislation was impossible. The situation was a delicate one, for by the letter of the Statuto, the Government had infringed the constitution by having the treaty signed by the King and ratified, before its presentation to Parliament. But as every one knew, the reason for this was the clause which stipulated that the evacuation of the Austrians from Alessandria, should begin eight days from the signing of the treaty, and the removal of the enemy from Piedmontese soil was a first consideration. The democratic majority added to the difficulties of the Government. The fact was, that, so much electioneering capital had been made by the democrats over never making peace with Austria, until Italy was free and independent, that they feared the ordeal of meeting their constituents if they accepted the treaty. On the other hand, the Cabinet was thankful for postponement, fully realizing the seriousness of the constitutional crisis which would be brought about by the rejection of the terms of peace. The treaty was presented to the Chamber early in August,[1] but the members proved disinclined to deal with it and did no more than refer it to a Committee for report. The question came up again in September, when the Committee reported advising its acceptance, whereupon Count Balbo, the former Prime Minister, moved that it be accepted by a vote of silence and without discussion. But the negotiators, Boncompagni and Dabormida, were anxious to justify their handiwork, and Lorenzo Valerio wanted explanations of the financial clauses, so once more the treaty was postponed while the payment of the indemnity was discussed and ultimately approved. But postponement could not be indefinitely prolonged, and finally in November the critical debate was opened. Count Balbo once more

[1] Text of the Treaty in Zini, *Storia d'Italia*, vol. iii. Doc. 2.

moved its acceptance by a vote of silence, but this was negatived. Then Domenico Buffa, representing the more moderate democrats, moved that 'the treaty be regarded as an accomplished fact,' carefully avoiding the word 'acceptance.' This motion, at first accepted by the Ministry but afterwards opposed, was supported by Cavour, who saw in it a practical compromise. In the course of his speech, Cavour pointed out that if the Government had broken the letter of the Statuto by having the treaty signed before presenting it to the Chamber, its action was justified by the extreme gravity of the circumstances, and that it now came to ask for a bill of indemnity for what it had done. It need not be feared, he went on, that the action of the Ministry would form, as some members thought, a dangerous precedent; for no country could stand the strain of passing twice through such an ordeal as had been their lot. Buffa's motion was, however, rejected. For four days the debate continued without any decision being arrived at, during which every political and military action during the past six months was criticized, condemned, and defended in turn. Finally, the Deputy Cadorna moved that before accepting the treaty a bill safeguarding the interests of the Lombard and Venetian refugees should be brought in and passed. The question of the refugees had been brought up the day before, and on that occasion Cavour had declared that he was 'almost disposed to move a vote of censure on the Government for not having taken the initiative on this question and brought in before this a bill to safeguard the interests of the refugees.' Cavour had, moreover, in an endeavour to find a line of compromise between the two parties, moved an amendment in the following terms, 'that the House, declaring that the present treaty does not take from the inhabitants of the provinces united to Piedmont the rights from which they are excluded by their own Government, passes to the voting of the law.' But Cavour's amendment was lost. The motion of Cadorna was, however, so plainly the equivalent of a further indefinite suspension, that it was strongly opposed by the Ministry and by no one more strongly than Cavour. Very clearly he indicated to the Chamber the dangerous results that would follow from further delay.

> In regard to the internal conditions of our country [he said] I am persuaded that our parliamentary work cannot proceed with that rapidity and regularity which we all desire, until this vital question is settled. As to our relations abroad, I believe that the further suspension of the Treaty will have the very gravest inconveniences, and that, taking Europe as it is and not as we would like it to be, one cannot fail to perceive that this continual postponement of acceptance must have fatal results both for our diplomacy and for our international relations.

He begged the Chamber to accept the word of the Government that a bill regarding the refugees would be brought in. If the word of the Cabinet was not good enough, he said, there was a very simple way of enforcing their will. In a few weeks the Government would be asking for power to collect revenue, and the Chamber could then withhold their permission until the Government fulfilled its pledge regarding the refugees.

> This is not a question [he went on] between us and the Ministry: the Treaty is a question between us and Fate. And even if this Government was no longer in power and there was another chosen from some other part of the Chamber, they would be equally obliged to recognize this fatal treaty and accept it.

Cavour's warning was unheeded. The motion of Cadorna was put to the vote and was carried by a majority of seven. As this meant not only a Government defeat but a further indefinite postponement, D'Azeglio decided to dissolve the Chamber.

Though Cavour had on the whole supported the Government, his denunciation of their remissness regarding the refugees, and his support of Buffa's motion was resented by D'Azeglio, who, to show his displeasure, omitted him from the list of Government supporters that he called into consultation before deciding on dissolution. Cavour was offended and went off to his farm at Leri and from there wrote to his friend de la Rue:

> I departed in such haste that I had no time to write you a word. You will have approved the decree of dissolution. I believe that with a little cleverness and firmness it might have been avoided, but at the point which things had reached it was impossible to yield further. The Ministry wants to try one last electoral battle. If it loses, it will be the end of regular constitutional government. We shall be bandied about between *coups d'état* and republican reactions.

D'Azeglio fought his 'last electoral battle' with vigour and success. At the July elections, scarcely more than one-third of the electorate had voted, and a sure instinct told D'Azeglio that no better method could be devised of rousing the nation to a sense of its duty than a personal appeal from the throne.[1] The age-long loyalty to the House of Savoy and ingrained habits of obedience to Royal decrees was a far deeper sentiment in the nation than devotion to the new constitutional régime. The Proclamation of Moncalieri, which was published together with the decree of dissolution, more than fulfilled D'Azeglio's hopes, and the elections resulted in a two-thirds majority for the Government. Though unconstitutional, and as such bitterly denounced by the Democratic party, the Proclamation of Moncalieri saved the country. The excitement between the date of its publication and the elections on December 10th was tremendous, and a time of great anxiety both for the King and the Government. It was during these days when all kinds of prognostications were in the air that the following story is told of Cavour. It was snowing heavily in Turin, and Cavour and a distinguished French friend were watching the snowflakes falling in the streets from the windows of his Palazzo:

---

[1] See Appendix A.

'This is red snow, M. le Comte!' said his guest: 'Red as you like,' replied Cavour, smiling and rubbing his hands, 'but it will melt: the good sense of my fellow-countrymen can be trusted to do its work.' Cavour's trust in Gianduja [1] was not misplaced.

The elections of December 10th, 1849, were a triumph for D'Azeglio and his Government. The democrats were crushed, and a solid two-thirds majority supported the Ministry. At last the country was able to turn its attention from the struggle with Austria to its own affairs, and make a beginning with that programme of administrative and economic reform, which was to sweep away the husk of absolute government and bring Piedmont into line with the progressive nations of the West. In truth the position was anomalous. A constitutional system had been suddenly superimposed upon a people, whose whole political, economic, and ecclesiastical outlook was little less than medieval. The strain of two wars, waged concurrently with the infancy of the Constitution, had rendered it impossible to adapt the old to the new. The judicature and the magistracy were applying an obsolete code of law in the spirit of absolutism. The civil service, brought up in the atmosphere of a narrow bureaucracy, was administering the new laws without sympathy or understanding. The old protectionist system was still strangling industry and preventing the spread of modern ideas and methods. The ecclesiastical system was an *imperium in imperio*, with its own judges, codes, and punishments, which took no heed of the civil law of the land where its own functions were concerned. There was, in fact, a whole judicial, financial, and ecclesiastical system to be swept away, before the country could call its soul its own and go forward to prosperity.

The policy of D'Azeglio was one of safety first. Looking at the situation through the windows of the Foreign Office, his first care was to reassure Europe as to the non-revolutionary character of the Government,

[1] The typical figure of Piedmont, equivalent to our 'John Bull.'

to raise Piedmont's prestige abroad, and recover the trust of Europe, sadly shaken by the events of 1848. He had also to countermine the propaganda of Austria, which sought to brand Piedmont as a nest of conspirators and the centre of revolutionary activity in Europe. To do this he proposed a programme of useful internal reforms, while seeking to postpone any attempt to solve those fundamental, but highly controversial questions, which would have to be faced sooner or later. Cavour, on the other hand, believed that the revolutionary outbreak had exhausted itself and that Europe was settling down into a period of quiet. He held that this was the time for just these fundamental reforms that the Cabinet wished to postpone. From this time onward Cavour constituted himself as the leader of the progressive party in the Chamber, urging the Government forward on the path of reform, while opposing equally firmly the democratic excesses of the Left.

The first task of the Government was to accept the treaty with Austria. This was successfully accomplished after a brief discussion, though a group of extremists opposed it bitterly to the end. On the administrative side the Government was strong, but in the Chamber it was at a disadvantage. D'Azeglio preferred the more dignified atmosphere of the Senate,[1] and none of his colleagues showed any conspicuous capacity as leader of the Chamber or as a debater. Fortunately they found in Cavour the very man they required. He was already the leader of an unofficial group of members of the right centre, and the elections had strengthened his following. Recognized as one of the few financial authorities in the Chamber, he had become in the last eighteen months one of its best speakers, and he had the quick brain of the born debater. He was now quite at home in debate, and with his natural gift of leadership and fighting spirit, he rendered inestimable services to the Ministry, though as yet in an unofficial capacity.

[1] The Ministers could speak in both Houses.

He was not popular. He had the reputation of being difficult to work with, and he was still distrusted politically. His masterful personality and ironic tongue inspired both fear and dislike. But whether they liked him or not, in a few months he had become absolutely indispensable to the existence of the Government.

As soon as the treaty had been accepted the Chamber turned to its normal work. Amongst the first bills introduced was an Appropriation Bill for four millions moved by Giovanni Nigra, the Minister of Finance. Cavour was named reporter for the Committee appointed to examine it, and in this capacity announced the finding of the Committee to the Chamber, which was favourable. But the course of Nigra's four millions did not run smooth, and for this, perhaps, Cavour himself was responsible. It may be remembered that in the critical debate at the close of the previous Parliament, Cavour, in urging the Chamber to accept the word of the Government that a bill on the Lombard refugees should be brought in, taking a hint from English history, had suggested that to enforce their will they could withhold supplies until the Government made good their promise. This was the policy now adopted by Brofferio, though unfortunately for its success, it was a method that could only be effective when backed by a majority of the Chamber. Nothing daunted, however, Brofferio moved that

> The Chamber, declaring the discussion upon this law suspended, until the Ministry has at least in part fulfilled its promises, passes to the order of the day.

Brofferio was always at his best on a subject of this kind where he could deal in generalities, and no exact thinking was required. In the course of his speech he criticized almost every sphere of Government activity, beginning with the freedom of the Press and the working of the Statuto, and then dealing in turn with the judicial system, civil, criminal, and ecclesiastical, education, army reform, and the National Guard. A great deal of what he said was both true and obvious, but inevitable. The political condition of the country since the granting of the Statuto had rendered it impossible for any Government to pass progressive legislation; and the obstructive attitude of his own party in regard to the treaty with Austria had paralysed all Government action in matters of real reform. The debate that followed revealed the weakness of the Government, for the Left had the best of the argument and there appeared some chance that Brofferio's motion would be carried.

The next day as reporter of the Bill, Cavour answered Brofferio in detail. With a majority at his back he had no need to be over-anxious, but the speech which he delivered is a very good example of his style, and illustrates his happy knack of putting the Chamber in a good temper, equally with his power of irritating his opponents with the whip-lash of his irony. He began by chaffing Brofferio over the recent failure of his paper, the *Messaggiere Torinese*, 'the first child of his fertile imagination.' He then went on to point out that the delay in legislation, though partly due to the cumbersome procedure of the Chamber, was due far more to the slackness of members themselves in failing to examine and pass the measures initiated by the Government.

After dealing with questions relating to the National Guard and army reform, Cavour replied to Brofferio's stricture against the censorship of the Press. That office, he said, while giving free admittance to political books and papers as well as general literature, vetoed only such publications as were of an immoral tendency, as was both necessary and desirable, and by way of postscript, added, 'The advocate Brofferio has sought to render Parliament responsible for the misfortune of certain journals and the failure of others. On this point I am silent, feeling as I do that I must respect the natural sorrow that he feels for the decease of his own cherished offspring' (laughter).

But Cavour's bantering tone changed when he came to reply to the bitter words his opponent used against the clergy, and Cavour's attitude should be noted, for it was consistent on this question.

'As regards myself,' he said, 'I must honestly confess, I am utterly unable to appreciate the distinction which the honourable member drew, between the spirit of the clerical party and the Church. If he had uttered his severe words against the Jesuits and their adherents, I should have agreed with him. But his accusations were levelled against the monasteries and the churches alike. But, if the clerical party consists of all the clergy, both within monasteries and in the churches, where shall we find that elect few that represent the spirit of Christianity of which the orator spoke so eloquently? I truly do not know where to look for them, unless he wished to indicate that handful of priests, who, deserting their churches and works of piety, believe the political circles and meetings on the Piazza a more suitable arena for the exercise of their new apostolate (murmurs from the Left), or that he wished to indicate as new models of the evangelical spirit and of Christian charity, those few who join their force to his to maintain a constant centre of agitation in the streets of Turin' (angry murmurs from the Left).

Cavour had by now so irritated the Left and its supporters in the galleries by his sarcasm, that the Chamber began to get out of hand, and when at the close of his speech he added, 'I do not flatter myself that these explanations will satisfy the honourable Brofferio and persuade him and those who sit beside him—I do not know whether I ought to call them his friends'—a noisy outburst broke out from the galleries. Cavour continued, undisturbed: 'Personally —catcalls from the galleries do not disturb me in the least. I ignore them and shall continue as before—' and he brought his speech to an end; whereupon such a clamour broke out that the President put on his hat and closed the sitting, while the National

Guard cleared the public galleries and the bench of journalists.

It is difficult from the report of Cavour's speeches to realize the effect he had power to produce, missing as we must the tone and emphasis of his words, but the result was unmistakable. Brofferio adds the following expressive paragraph.

> Despite the firmness of the President, the tumult in the chamber re-echoed on to the Piazza, and the crowd collected outside the Chamber broke into loud cries against the bitter provocations of Count Cavour, the author of the disorders that followed. If any one in those days had said that Count Cavour would before long be the idol of the people, and be enshrined amongst the saviours of his country, he would have been thought demented.[1]

On this occasion Cavour rendered a real service to the Government. The previous days discussion had revealed only too clearly the debating weakness of the Ministry, and the honours had indubitably rested with the opposition. But Cavour's speech had restored the Government's prestige and left honours easy. It established his reputation as the best speaker on the ministerial side of the Chamber and the one real fighter they possessed. The Government had found a defender, but one who would soon demand a price for his support.

For the next two months Cavour was immersed in legislative reforms concerning roads, railways, banks, and commerce. The most important of these was his work as reporter of the scheme for Postal Reform. On this subject he made no less than sixteen speeches in the course of the Bill's progress through the Chamber. The Bill changed the existing system of a rate varying from 10 c. to 70 c. according to distance, to a uniform rate of 20 c. reduced to 10 c. for distances less than 20 kilometres. Cavour's speeches must be read to realize his grasp of the subject and his thorough knowledge of the reforms instituted, and the difficulties

---

[1] Brofferio, *Stor. Parl. Subalp.*, vol. iii. pp. 471 ff.

encountered, in all countries where the new system had been adopted.

Up to this time the Government, though they had introduced a series of useful reforms, had not shown any disposition to face those more controversial problems for a solution of which the country was waiting. Foremost amongst these was the relation of Church and State. If the provisions of the Statuto were to become in reality the law of the land, either fresh concordats would have to be made with Rome or legislation must be introduced to regularize their relationships, in conformity with the new principles of Constitutional Government. The most pressing question was that of the Ecclesiastical Courts for civil and criminal offences, those in Austria, for example, having been done away with in the reign of Joseph II. The same difficulties occurred in Piedmont as had arisen elsewhere, and before very long the injustice and inconvenience of this double code of law and punishment produced complaints and recriminations. To remedy this state of things Piedmont had sent a series of special envoys to endeavour to make a satisfactory arrangement with Rome. No success, however, had attended the efforts of the Piedmontese diplomacy and the question was still in abeyance when the D'Azeglio Cabinet came into office. Fresh negotiations were then opened through Count Cesare Balbo, who fared, however, no better than his predecessors. Finally Count Siccardi was sent to Rome, with the same lack of success. On his return the Cabinet reluctantly decided on legislation, and Count Siccardi, appointed Minister of Justice, was instructed to draw up a Bill for the abolition of the Foro Ecclesiastico. Two months later the Bill was laid upon the table of the Chamber of Deputies, with two smaller ones appended, one to limit the power of the Church in acquiring real property, and the other to restrict the excessive number of feast days. Though the Government had recognized the necessity of these measures, it had not wished to bring

them forward so quickly. The country had not yet
recovered from the turmoil occasioned by Novara, and
to open the struggle with the Church, though it was
bound to come, meant dividing the country once again
into two parties, for the Church would fight the measure
with all her strength. But Cavour had insisted that the
time was ripe for those wider measures of reform which
the country legitimately expected as the fruits of Constitutional Government. The importance of the Bill is
not to be judged entirely by the extent of the reform
it effected, for its real significance was that it broke
with the Albertian tradition of submission to Rome,
and initiated a new policy in which the supremacy of
the State on all questions, except those of spiritual
jurisdiction, was the cardinal principle. On March 6th,
1850, the debate began.

In introducing the Bill Count Siccardi, the Minister
of Justice, laid great stress upon the anomalous position
of a double system of law with different methods of
procedure and different forms of punishment. He
sketched the attempts made to reach an agreement with
Rome, and the non-possumus attitude of all the
authorities there, and closed with the words:

> Finally, gentlemen, the Government believes that this law
> satisfies the most long-standing wish of the nation. Long
> before political reforms were spoken of, long before we talked
> of liberty, there was already a universal desire for the aboli-
> tion of this anomaly. The Ministry then, believing it has
> done its duty, confidently commends this law to your de-
> cision.

Canon Pernigotti followed Count Siccardi. Taking
up a dignified attitude of injured innocence, he declared
that since the rights of the Church had been injured
and Rome had refused her consent, he would neither
vote nor take part in the discussion.

After the Church had put in her protest, Count Revel,
the leader of the Right, spoke. He opposed the Bill on
the ground of expediency, though he agreed with it in
principle. The moment was not opportune: it would

create much bitterness and probably disturbance, and he advocated its postponement until it could be brought forward with the consent of all parties. As a criminal lawyer of wide experience, Brofferio, who followed Count Revel, had no difficulty in showing the pernicious effects of the dual system of law existing hitherto in Piedmont. Nor had he much more difficulty in demonstrating that in the past the Popes had been no respectors of treaties when they conflicted with their temporal interests. But his best point was made, in showing that it was an acknowledged principle of International Law, that a nation had always the right to abrogate a contract harmful to its vital interests—a principle safeguarded by the inserted clause *rebus sic stantibus*—and therefore Piedmont was within her rights in demanding a fresh concordat. The sitting was brought to a close by Count Balbo. His speech, which was written and read to the Chamber by another member, for Count Balbo's sight was failing, was a long and moving plea for the postponement of the Bill. Though he did not deny the need for this reform he held the consent of Rome to be an essential. The possibilities of negotiation had not yet been exhausted. There was already some evidence that if persisted in they would ultimately prove successful, and in any case the delay that would result from further efforts was as nothing compared to the difficulties that must arise from the resistance and opposition of the Church. He therefore moved that the Bill be suspended until the Budget for 1849–50 had been disposed of. The esteem in which Count Balbo was held added great weight to his plea, and when the House rose the fate of the Bill still hung in the balance.

At the next sitting Cavour was the first speaker. His speech was anxiously awaited. Hitherto he had had no opportunity of addressing the Chamber on a big political issue, where the verdict was not already prejudged, or of stating the principles upon which his political creed was based. And his attitude on ecclesiastical questions was completely unknown. But whatever they expected, none could have anticipated the masterpiece of lucid reasoning and statesmanlike prevision, with which Cavour now delighted the Chamber. The tone of his speech was little less remarkable than the substance. Courteous and considerate to all sides of the House, discarding any suggestion of provocation or party bias, and treating the question as a national problem in which all were equally interested, he lifted the whole tone of the debate on to the highest level.

Cavour began by admitting his incompetence to deal with the legal or ecclesiastical aspects of the question, and turned at once to the one weak point, the question of opportuneness. Referring to the speeches made in the previous day's debate, he pointed out that, while some had urged that the times were still too unquiet for a measure such as this, others had held that it was wrong to disturb the present peace with so controversial a bill. 'Well, gentlemen,' he added, 'it is in quiet times that wise statesmen try to put in operation important reforms. I am not an alarmist, but all the same I can foresee, if not the probability, at least the possibility, of stormy times ahead of us. Now, do you know, gentlemen, the best way to prepare for such times? It is to make reforms when things are peaceful, to remove abuses before it is forced on you by the extreme parties. If you wish to render powerless, or at least greatly weaken, the power of these extremists, there is no better way than to rob them of their principal weapon, the demand for the reform of abuses whose existence cannot be denied.' He then passed on to the question of the prospect of success from further negotiations with Rome, which he personally considered hopeless, and drew a roar of laughter from the Chamber by his description of the present temper of the College of Cardinals. 'Various very well-informed persons that have returned from Gaeta,' he remarked, 'have told me that, to give some idea of the spirit that dominates the Sacred College, the member who is most favourable to

our proposals, who is, so to speak, on the extreme Left
—is Cardinal Lambruschini.'[1]

But it was when he came to the political aspect that
he was at his best. After pointing out that at the time
of the Statuto there were two parties, one who wanted
to keep things as they were, and the other who ardently
desired Liberty, and having described how the new
constitution had brought them together in a common
effort for the country, he drew their attention to the
fact that, the very cause that had united them had also
prevented the passing of those real reforms which all
had hoped would follow from Constitutional Government. The Bill before the Chamber was the first big
measure yet produced. Now what will happen, he
asked, if this is indefinitely postponed? And then he
proceeded to give a most luminous sketch of the
probable development of political thought under such
conditions. The lovers of Constitutional Government,
sickened by hope deferred, would gradually lose faith
in free Government; while those who had never wanted
it, if not strong enough to overthrow the Constitution,
would by a process of systematic obstruction render the
growth of real reform impossible. Then, if one of those
revolutionary outbreaks, to which Europe was always
liable, occurred, Piedmont would split into factions,
one wing seceding to the reactionaries, the other joining
hands with the revolutionists, leaving the Constitutional party 'reduced to a few men of knowledge, robbed
of all influence, and stigmatized by the title of doc-
trinaires.' Then coming to his last point, he dealt with
the dangers to be expected if the Bill was passed,
dangers, that is, from clerical opposition. Refusing to
believe that more than a small minority of the clergy
was against them, since no question of faith or doctrine
was involved, he declared that the only effect would be

[1] Cardinal Lambruschini had for years been regarded as the incarnation
of reaction. He had been Papal Nuncio at the Court of Charles X and was
said to have inspired the famous ordinances that led to the fall of the
Bourbons. He succeeded Bernetti at Secretary of State in 1836, and for
ten years was the genius of the reaction under Pope Gregory XVI.

to force their secret enemies into the open, 'and for my part,' he added, 'open enemies are infinitely less dangerous than secret ones.' Drawing to the conclusion he begged the Chamber to realize what country in Europe had escaped the horrors of the revolution that had devastated Europe—not France or Germany or Austria, but England alone. And why? because she had anticipated the struggle by reform. Quoting Catholic Emancipation, the Reform Bill, and the Corn Laws, he urged them to realize how reforms made in time did not weaken but strengthen authority.

> I say then to the Government [he added] imitate frankly the example of Wellington, Grey, and Sir Robert Peel, whom history will proclaim the greatest statesmen of our time; go forward boldly with reforms and do not fear they will be inopportune: do not fear that in so doing you will weaken our Constitutional Throne entrusted to your hands, for instead you will strengthen it; by such a course, this Throne will drive its roots so deep into our soil, that even should the revolutionary tempest rise against it, it will not only resist it, but drawing to itself all the living forces of Italy, will lead our nation to those high destinies to which it is called.[1]

The storm of applause and congratulation from all sides of the Chamber which greeted the close of Cavour's speech was sufficient proof of its greatness. But he had done more than win applause, he had decided the fate of the Bill, which when put to the vote was carried by an overwhelming majority.[2]

The success which Cavour achieved on this occasion gave a considerable impetus to his chances of political advancement. Not only did it consolidate his position in the Chamber, rallying a good many undecided members to his standard, but it brought him a noticeable

[1] Brofferio, *Stor. Parl. Subalp.*, vol. iii. p. 549; Discorsi, vol. i. p. 395.

[2] The excitement in the country over this reform was very great. 'Never,' wrote Constanza D'Azeglio, 'even at the opening of the second campaign, nor where invasion was at the gates, has the country been so moved. The result does not appear doubtful, but if by any chance it did not pass, I do not know what would happen in Turin and in the provinces, so great is the excitement, and one cannot even rely on the National Guard to stop disorders.' *Souvenirs Historiques.*

increase of popularity outside Parliament. It began to be recognized that it was due to the pressure exercised by Cavour's party, that the Cabinet introduced the Bill so quickly, and his own share in its success was also fully appreciated. No less decided was the change which it brought about in Cavour's personal attitude towards the Government. He now made up his mind to make a determined bid for office.

If one may interpret Cavour's line of thought from his subsequent action, he gave the Cabinet three months in which to offer him a post, after which he proposed to bring direct pressure to bear by means of an ultimatum. Cavour had two means of bringing pressure on the Government, his weight in the Chamber, and the columns of the *Risorgimento*, and he used them both. In a series of articles on the needs of the country he sketched the necessary measures the Government should introduce, implying more and more clearly that failure to do so would lead to the withdrawal of the support of himself and his friends.

At the end of June, no hint of a portfolio having been dropped by D'Azeglio, Cavour prepared his ultimatum. The occasion chosen was the new loan for six millions, which Nigra asked permission to contract before the session ended.

The general lines of his speech he laid down as follows:

> As a member of the majority, which shares in some degree the ministerial responsibility, I believe it my duty to examine the charges brought against the Government by the members of the Left, in order to see if they are exaggerated or unjust, and also, to see if amongst them there may not be some we can consider favourably.

After dealing with the points of criticism as to what the Government had already done, he gave his personal opinion, 'I believe therefore that it is my duty to declare that, taken in their complex, I think we should give our approval to what has been done. Certainly these measures were capable of improvements: but in the present condition of the country I should not have hesitated to give my approval if I had been able to take part in their discussion.'[1] He then passed on to the Government's sins of omission. After lamenting that certain important subjects had not been dealt with, he added, 'I recognize however that there are very weighty reasons that militate in favour of the Government, which may be considered as attenuating circumstances, and therefore, because of these and others that may be causes of delay, I am disposed, as far as the past is concerned, to accord the Ministry a bill of indemnity.'

The almost patronizing note which Cavour adopted, as of one in whose hands lay the fate of the Government, but who was nevertheless graciously disposed to sanction their efforts and overlook their failures, is a very noticeable feature of this speech throughout, and must have proved very irritating to the Government Bench. He then proceeded to deal with a number of suggestions for economies and new forms of taxation which had been put forward by various speakers. The first of these was income-tax. 'I honestly confess,' he went on, 'without reticence or hesitation, that I consider the income-tax, in theory, the best of all taxes: and I hasten to add that I do not believe that in practice it need always meet insurmountable difficulties. To those who know my weakness for the teaching of the English school there will be no difficulty in accepting my assertion. But, in the same way that I have made this open declaration, I must add, that I recognize that its introduction into countries where it has never been applied, is surrounded by great practical difficulties; difficulties so great that one ought not to face them, until the question has been profoundly studied and the means of overcoming them devised.' Then, after remarking that as far as he was aware the Left had so far produced nothing of any practical value on this question of income-tax, he added, 'I will not then make this subject a matter of censure on

[1] The illness and death of his father had kept him out of politics during the time these measures were before the Chamber.

the Government, but I will take a solemn pledge towards those who sit on the Left that, if in the coming
year they present to Parliament a practical plan or at
least one that does not offer insuperable difficulty, I
will support them as far as possible, in order that
this experiment of income-tax may be tried in this
country.'

After strongly supporting the principle of Government decentralization or local Government on the
English plan, as against the centralized French system
in vogue, and scouting the idea put forward by another
speaker of saving money by doing away with the
Regular Army and replacing it by a Swiss militia
scheme, he came to the real point of his speech, the
future policy of the Government. Up to this he had, so
to speak, let them off with a caution, but he now became
quite clear and definite, delivering his ultimatum with
a carefully graduated impressiveness.

Here I will speak plainly and say to the Ministry, as much
in my own name as in that of my many political friends,
that there is a condition which we attach to the support that
we are about to give.

For certainly, if in the coming session the Ministry does not
at the commencement present the Estimates for 1851; if
these estimates are compiled on the same bases as those of
1850; if they do not put into effect all the principles already
sanctioned by this Chamber; if there should still appear the
gratuities, emoluments, and pensions, retiring pensions
excepted, this would be for us an inducement to separate
ourselves from the Ministry. Further, if at the beginning of
the new session the Ministry does not present its entire
financial plan, if it does not tell us the precise manner in
which it proposes to re-establish equilibrium in the State
finances—if not at once, at least in a short space of time: if
it does not indicate the means of attaining this end, this would
be a motive for us to separate from it. And to enter still
further into this matter, that these declarations, made as
much in the name of my many political friends as in my own,
may not be regarded as those meaningless assertions made on
all occasions when money is wanted from Parliament, I will

give some particulars as to the matters upon which I insist.
If, before the end of the year, the Ministry does not present
to Parliament a scheme of Customs reform founded on the
wide bases of liberal principles, this will be sufficient for
me to vote with those that move a vote of censure against
the Government. . . .[1]

Cavour had never intended to oppose by this speech
the vote before the Chamber. Nigra's millions were the
occasion, not the subject of it, and he and his party
voted with the Government. The result was a striking
majority for D'Azeglio. Heartened by this success,
which he interpreted as a vote of confidence in the
Government, D'Azeglio discarded any thoughts he
might have had of replacing Nigra by Cavour. Writing
to Sir Ralph Abercromby, the English Minister, on the
day after the loan was passed, he said, '119 votes against
28 is a very fine majority in a vote of confidence of this
nature. The Ministry feels itself bound in honour to
respond to it, and follow the political line that has
won it such a proof of confidence. That is to say, that
I feel myself bound, not to let the strings of the purse
which has brought us so many millions, pass into other
hands.'

But although D'Azeglio in his easy-going way
imagined that his big majority put Cavour and his
threats comfortably into the background, Cavour had
in reality created a very awkward situation for the
Government. It was practically certain that what he
demanded would not be done, and this left them no
alternative, except either to bring Cavour into the
Cabinet or face the prospect of a vote of censure moved
by Cavour and backed by his 'many friends.' The first
of these seemed the easiest solution of the difficulty.
Cavour's ability was unquestioned. Until this last
speech his support had been invaluable and consistent,
why not make him a member of the Cabinet? The factors in the problem were both personal and political.
He was neither liked nor wanted by the members of

---

[1] Discorsi, vol. i. pp. 479 ff.

the Cabinet. He had only one friend in it, Alfonso La Marmora, the War Minister. To D'Azeglio he was certainly not *simpatico*. In tastes, character, and political views they differed widely, their only bond was a common patriotism. The rest of the Cabinet disliked and feared Cavour. They feared his masterful personality and his volcanic energy, and perhaps also his ability and knowledge, so that D'Azeglio was sure of the support of his colleagues if he refused him admittance. But it would be unfair to D'Azeglio to suggest that personal antipathy was the sole cause for his distaste for having Cavour in the Cabinet. A deeper reason with him was political. From the outset of his premiership D'Azeglio had laid down as a first principle the restoration of authority. It was essential to restore the prestige of Piedmont in the eyes of Europe by a régime of tranquillity and political steadiness, in order to counteract the insistent declarations of Austria that Piedmont was a hotbed of revolutionary intrigue. Rightly or wrongly, Cavour's views were held to be too advanced for safety, and D'Azeglio felt that to introduce Cavour into the Cabinet would be to prejudice foreign opinion against the Government. Nor was it possible to mistake the political implications of Cavour's speeches on the Foro and on Nigra's loan. In the one he had deliberately emphasized the incompatibility between the views of the extreme Right and those of the Government; in the other he had made it plain, that in certain circumstances, he would vote with the Left. Already Rattazzi and the Left Centre were angling warily for fusion with Cavour, though there had been no response as yet. Cavour's tendency to advance by the Left was in fact plain to observant eyes, and the whole Cabinet policy might be rendered suspect if Cavour was brought into it. With the reactionary spirit triumphant in Europe, any movement to the Left was bound to be viewed with suspicion, and for this reason D'Azeglio was anxious to avoid the necessity of introducing Cavour's 'activité diabolique' into the Cabinet.

A week after this debate the Chamber was prorogued until the autumn.

Fate now took a hand in the political game, for the first week in August, Count Pietro di Santarosa, the Minister of Commerce and Agriculture, died, thus creating a vacancy in the Cabinet.[1] The name of the successor to Santarosa became the question of the hour. Public opinion was unanimous in its support of Cavour, but no word came from D'Azeglio. 'There is no question of my entering the Ministry,' Cavour writes a little bitterly towards the end of August, 'except in the cafés and under the arcades of the Via di Po. The Ministers, excepting La Marmora, have no desire at all to have me as a colleague.'

In the meantime Cavour's one friend in the Cabinet, La Marmora, was trying to make D'Azeglio face the inevitable, but he had great trouble to do it. 'In a month,' said D'Azeglio, 'he will have the whole Cabinet upside down. I don't want the worry of it.' 'You are mistaken,' replied La Marmora, 'Camillo is a *gran buon diavolo*. And when he gets with us he will moderate.' At last D'Azeglio consented to bring his name before his colleagues, and they having consented, he sent for Cavour.

The day after their interview Cavour wrote as follows to D'Azeglio:

> Having carefully thought over what you said yesterday, I find no difficulty in agreeing upon all the points mentioned, except in regard to the Minister of Public Instruction. The more I have thought about it, the more I remain convinced that I should not be able to accept Mameli as a colleague. If you regard this larger change in the Cabinet as inopportune, I beg you not to hold yourself as in the least pledged towards me, and to appoint without delay a worthy successor to poor Santarosa.

'He begins badly, dear Alfonso, your *buon diavolo*,' said D'Azeglio to La Marmora, when he showed him Cavour's letter, but nevertheless he was persuaded to

[1] See Appendix B.

accept Cavour's condition. All that now remained was to get the consent of the King. The Premier sent Galvagno to sound him. When the King heard Cavour's name, he exclaimed, 'Don't you gentlemen know that this little man will kick you all out head over heels?' adding that Cavour's time would come, but for the present D'Azeglio had better submit a name more *simpatico*. Then La Marmora set to work to persuade the King. Seizing an opportunity returning from some army manœuvres, when Victor Emmanuel was in good spirits, he succeeded in spite of 'evident repugnance' in getting his consent to Cavour's appointment. Finally, Cavour writes on December 8th:

> After three days of painful hesitation I have ended by yielding and have accepted office. I have yielded above all to the wishes of the King, and still more to the pressure of La Marmora. Azeglio has been very good, so also has Galvagno. Up to now I have not seen Nigra.

Cavour's appointment was inevitable from the first, and D'Azeglio would have been far wiser to have faced the facts and offered him the post at once, instead of taking the line of least resistance and postponing the evil day until the last possible moment. The three months before the opening of Parliament would have given Cavour time to get thoroughly acquainted with his work, and saved him much unnecessary strain. Cavour's unpopularity with the Cabinet and the King was real enough. With the King he had scarcely a point of contact. Victor Emmanuel liked soldiers and sportsmen, and was not averse to courtiers. Cavour was neither the one nor the other. He had left the army more or less in disgrace, he hated Court functions, and as for being a sportsman he never even shot the snipe that swarmed in the ricefields at Leri. His business capabilities and interests only made matters worse. In the Cabinet the chief objection to Cavour was his masterful personality and his driving power. D'Azeglio drove his team with a slack rein, and the presence of Cavour was certain to upset the pace and bring confusion. He was equally certain to dominate the Cabinet, for none of them knew anything either of finance or industry, and they would have to submit to be dictated to on all such questions. But personal likes and dislikes had to give way before the fact that Cavour held the trump card. The conditions he had stipulated as necessary for his support of the Government, in his speech on July 2nd, had not been fulfilled, and if he was not offered a post in the Cabinet he would assuredly go into opposition and the Government would be defeated and have to resign. It was the nightmare of having Cavour in opposition that forced D'Azeglio's hand and made him offer Cavour the post, while on the part of Cavour the reason for his 'painful hesitation' was his uncertainty as to whether it would be better to become Minister of Commerce, the least important post in the Cabinet, or wait and turn out the Government and come in as President. The truth of this comes out in a letter that Cavour wrote to his bailiff at Leri, a man to whom he sometimes said things that he did not mention to more important people:

Torino, 10 Ottobre, 1850.

After three days of painful hesitation I have believed it my duty to yield to the pressure of the King, and more still to the gravity of the country's situation. At the point which things have reached, after the more than friendly explanations of D'Azeglio, it was a choice between joining the Ministry or turning it out. Now I believe that this latter alternative, if it might have been more satisfying to the *amour-propre* of its author, would have been highly detrimental to the interests of the country. In so doing I verily believe that I am sacrificing a part, if not all, of my future, to a sense of duty. If I have made a mistake, the worst that can happen to me is to find myself reduced, a little quicker than otherwise, to the position of a fertilizer of the Constitutional tree, which is the ultimate end of all Ministers.[1]

On October 11th, the *Risorgimento* appeared with this notice: 'This morning Count Camillo Cavour took

[1] Visconti, *Cavour Agricoltore*, p. 282.

the oath before His Majesty on appointment as Minister of Commerce and Agriculture.' But this was not his full title, for the Cabinet, determined to give him if possible enough to do, had added the navy to his other portfolios; and thus, with gloomy forebodings as to the future, and having thrown out Mameli to make room for him, D'Azeglio took this political cuckoo into the Cabinet nest.

III. MINISTER OF MARINE, COMMERCE, AND FINANCE

The Navy Estimates—Cavour's Economic Policy—Commercial Treaty with France—Trouble in the Navy—Commercial Treaties with England and Belgium—Appointed Finance Minister—The English Loan—Supplementary Treaty with France—The Political Situation—The Connubio—The Presidency of the Chamber—Split with D'Azeglio —Cavour resigns—Tour in France and England—D'Azeglio retires—Cavour becomes Premier.

At last, after two years' work as a private member, Cavour found himself in office. Another two years were to pass before he became the head of the Government, but in the meantime there was more than enough for him to do in carrying through the great economic reforms upon which he had set his heart.

At the moment when Cavour took office the hopes of Italy were at a very low ebb. The great effort of 1848 had ended in the reaction of the following year, when the old order had triumphantly reasserted itself. There was a French garrison in Rome; Leopold had returned to Tuscany with an escort of 18,000 Austrians; Modena had a garrison of 8,000. Lombardy and Venetia were once more under the iron heel of Radetzky, and Bomba was crowding the Neapolitan prisons with political suspects. Only in Piedmont was liberty still a reality, and Piedmont, twice defeated, and now weighed down by an indemnity to Austria, was financially exhausted. The future of Italy depended upon Piedmont's power of recovery, for she alone could provide the sinews of war for a national effort. At this critical juncture it was Italy's good fortune to find in Cavour, somewhat grudgingly appointed to the least important post in the Cabinet, the genius, who not only restored his country's prosperity, but who ultimately guided Italy to the goal of her ambition.

The first task to which Cavour had to give his attention was the preparation of the navy estimates which had to be presented early in the new year. In the two months at his disposal he made a close study of the whole question, and not content with the necessary financial provisions, prepared a scheme of reorganization which, had it been put in force, would have greatly improved the service. He soon saw that lack of discipline, independence, and a rigid caste system amongst the officers were the cardinal faults amongst the personnel. On this matter he wrote to the Admiral Commandant warning him that he would be expected to enforce rigid obedience from all the officers under him, and that disciplinary measures were at once to be taken if necessary, no matter how highly placed the offender might be, and that he could in this matter rely absolutely upon support from the Ministry.[1] When the estimates were presented in January, it was the first time for many years that the navy received proper attention, the estimates being usually tacked on to those of the army and passed perfunctorily through the Chamber. This time ten days were given up to their discussion. Cavour, who spoke two or three times each day, was a mine of information on the subject, and his suggested reforms were as interesting as they were thorough. Cavour was convinced of the need for radical reforms in the navy, but he was not quite sure of the line they ought to take; he was also aware of his own want of technical knowledge, and although the same could be said, with even greater truth, of the Chamber at large, he believed in the value of collective judgement even on questions where the opinion of technical experts might have been considered the only advice to follow. In the course of the debate every aspect of the navy was brought under review; pay and pensions, administration, naval construction and coast defence, training and equipment, gunnery and navigation, all alike were subjected to discussion. Among Cavour's suggestions was the transfer of the naval arsenal from Genoa to Spezia, and the creation of a great naval base at this

[1] Chiala, vol. v. Cavour to Admiral d'Auvare.

latter place. The reasons for this were partly strategic and partly commercial. He had great schemes for the development of Genoa, by linking it to the continental railway system, building docks, opening a transatlantic steamship service, and thus making Genoa the first commercial port in the Mediterranean. Hitherto, the fact that Genoa was a naval as well as a commercial port had prevented expansion and cramped both sides of marine activity. His next suggestion was the reform of the Reggimento Reali Navi, or Marines. This distinguished Corps was always regarded purely as a Regiment of the Line, and as such had a fine record of service. In peace times they garrisoned the coast defences, and provided the guards for the arsenal and naval establishments. Though supposed to form part of naval crews, professional jealousy prevented this whenever possible, since the Colonel in command disliked breaking up the regiment; and as Cavour pointed out, though at the moment they had three ships at sea, two in South American waters and one in the Mediterranean, not a single marine was on board. As to coast defence, the practice had grown up of using the less important forts as billets for those who should have been pensioned, and he mentioned one fort where the youngest member of the garrison was 72. Cavour now proposed to reduce their establishment, which exceeded the total number of enlisted seamen, and divide them into 'Guardiani' and 'Cannonieri'; that is, to form a special corps for coast defence and to train the rest as specialists in naval gunnery. He suggested building a Gunnery School ashore for this purpose, with a permanent staff, through which the Marines would pass for training. He was, however, undecided as to the respective merits of a special corps of gunners drawn from the Marines alone, and the desirability of passing equal proportions of Marines and of seamen through the same course of training. Unfortunately, the Piedmontese Chamber had no sea sense. Obsessed by fear of Austria, they looked east not west, and the idea of breaking up so distinguished a regiment met with strong opposition; Cavour, seeing that the reform could not be carried, had to be content with the appointment of a commission on naval gunnery. From gunnery Cavour turned to navigation, and put before the Chamber the case for the suggested suppression of the 'piloti' or 'Masters', as they were called in the British Navy. These men were the ships' navigators and formed a class to themselves. They provided the navy with a body of experts in their own line, but their very proficiency rendered it possible for an ordinary officer to attain the rank of captain, or even admiral, without being able to navigate his own ship. The question was difficult and technical, and after considerable discussion the Chamber accepted Cavour's suggestion that further studies should be made before a decision was arrived at. In view, however, of their possible suppression, he suggested that a naval school linked up with the University should be formed, at which naval officers should take a course in the theoretical side of navigation. Cavour's grasp of the whole subject, and the fresh and penetrating mind he brought to bear on naval problems, lifted the navy on to a fresh plane of public interest and no difficulty was experienced in passing the estimates.[1]

The demands of the Navy Office by no means absorbed all Cavour's energies, and during these months he had been preparing a series of measures that were destined to revolutionize the economic conditions of Piedmont. For many years Cavour had believed that his country was capable of great economic development if given opportunity and encouragement. Hitherto Piedmont had been, as it were, kept in a straight jacket, and Cavour was convinced that, if this was once removed and the country given air and freedom and exercise, it would develop rapidly to its full stature. The first step towards this desirable end was to sweep away the system of protection and introduce that of Free Trade.

[1] See Discorsi, vol. ii; Chiala, vol. v. Letters to Admiral d'Auvare. Gonni, *Cavour, Ministro della Marina*, cc. i and ii.

The method Cavour adopted was to negotiate commercial treaties with the different foreign governments. In these treaties he reduced the import duties as low as was compatible with the protection of home industries. His whole idea was to stimulate production by competition: to force the Piedmontese manufacturers to scrap out-of-date machinery and methods, to reorganize their businesses, to specialize on profitable lines of production, and learn to hold their own in the markets of the world, without the help of aid from the State. In doing this he had a political as well as an economic object. He wanted to win the support and sympathy of Europe, to advertise Italy, and bring Piedmont out of her isolation, and above all to point the contrast between the progress of constitutional Piedmont and the stagnancy of Austrianized Italy. To have cut off summarily the subsidies granted to various industries would have caused disorganization and widespread dislocation of trade. To have brought in a Free Trade Bill covering the whole trade of the country would have created a parliamentary opposition too strong to have been resisted. But it was, he believed, possible to induce Parliament to swallow piecemeal what it could not digest as a whole. Cavour judged rightly, and before July 1851 the Chamber had sanctioned a series of commercial treaties that practically abolished the protective system.

A week after passing the naval estimates Cavour brought in his first Bill, the Commercial Treaty with France.[1] The rigid protectionist policy of that country made it almost impossible for Piedmont to negotiate a profitable treaty. Cavour did his best, but the treaty was a poor one, in which the balance of advantage remained with France. But bad as it was, Cavour was determined that it should be accepted, even though he had to put the reasons on political rather than commercial grounds. Friendship with France, even at a sacri-

---

[1] This treaty had been initiated by his predecessor Count Santarosa, Cavour modified and completed it.

fice, was his motto. To any ordinary member newly promoted to cabinet rank, it would have been a painful ordeal to have had to introduce, as the firstfruits of office, so lame a treaty as that which Cavour brought before the Chamber on January 21st, 1851. But Cavour was of a different calibre. To him the treaty was the outcome of a fundamental principle, and as such worth the sacrifice it entailed. It was an integral part of a policy that he believed essential to the safety of the State. Far from trying to gloze over its defects, he adopted an attitude of perfect candour in regard to it, and openly admitted that the 'treaty fulfils neither the requirements of sound business nor the true interests of the countries concerned.' And then added, 'This treaty of mine is not a business proposition, it is an act of politics, and what we have to consider is whether, in our actual circumstances, it deserves the sanction of Parliament.'

Having made this confession, Cavour proceeded to build up, what was in effect a most brilliant defence of his handiwork, that would be difficult to equal as an example of how to present a weak case. As an example of his method we may take the clauses relating to the wine trade. A concession had been made to France reducing the excise duty from 16 lire to 10 per hectolitre. This was a real advantage to France and a clear loss to the Piedmontese exchequer; but Cavour first of all calmed the Protectionists by showing that 10 lire was still an effective duty, and did not spoil the market for the home producer; and then comforted the Socialist Left by pointing out that when the grape harvest was bad, as it was that year, and the people had to buy French wine, the reduction in the duty enabled the poorer classes to buy good wine at a price they could afford; so that the loss to the Treasury suddenly appeared almost as a national benefit! By such methods Cavour built up a cumulative defence which put a very different complexion on the value of the treaty, taken in its entirety. Finally, he dealt with the political aspect, pointing out the dangers of offending France by rejecting the treaty, and dwelling on the great importance both present and future of having her support and friendship. The speech was a personal triumph for Cavour, and though the debate continued, and he spoke several times on special points, there was no further doubt as to the final issue, and the treaty was accepted by a handsome majority.

While Cavour was thus piloting the treaty with France through the Chamber, two further ones, with Belgium and England, were almost completed. Both of these were of value, especially that with England, who opened all her ports throughout the Empire to Piedmontese trade, stipulating only that she should receive the treatment of the most favoured nation. In both, free-trade principles were much more pronounced, and their acceptance would consecrate the new commercial policy. On January 27th, Cavour wrote regarding them as follows:

> Thank you for what you say about the Treaty with France. In a few days you will see more discussions relative to the two treaties concluded with Belgium and England, which consecrate the principle of free trade. These treaties, both of which will certainly be completed—one is already signed—will be a great economic event. They will occasion very lively debates, and will perhaps rouse bitter opposition against me, the author of them. I don't care, I am prepared to face it, to push the country into the only path that can save it.[1]

Pressure of other business postponed the debate on these treaties until April, and in the interval Cavour had more time to devote to ordinary parliamentary business. A few days after the French Treaty was passed the estimates for the Ministry of Justice were introduced. The Left seized the occasion for a violent attack upon the reactionary tendencies of the Piedmontese magistracy. Count Siccardi, the Minister concerned, whose health was bad and amongst whose gifts, neither facility in debate nor strength of character were con-

[1] Bert, No. 318.

spicuous, let the Government down badly, and a defeat on the estimates looked more than probable. It was Cavour who once more came to the rescue and pulled the Government out of their trouble. After the debate D'Azeglio wrote to Sir Ralph Abercromby,[1] 'Cavour spoke very well indeed. Victory rested with the Government, and I congratulate myself every day more upon the acquisition of Cavour, who is a veritable *coq de combat*. A speciality we were in need of.'

While Cavour was engaged in preparing these measures for Parliament, as Minister of Marine his attention had been called by the Admiral Commandant to a series of breaches of discipline amongst the commanding officers both abroad and at home. The Piedmontese officers had been brought up in a very individualistic school. Admiral de Geneys, the creator of the navy, who had ruled it without let or hindrance from 1815 to 1839, used to tell his officers that 'rules and regulations were made for imbeciles.' Nurtured in this tradition, the Piedmontese commanders, once on the quarter-deck and out of sight of land, took little notice of the fact that they were under the orders of an admiral at Genoa or a general at Turin. But Cavour was not one to overlook disobedience to orders or to have his country's flag brought into disrepute. When the Marquis Incisa in command of the *Aurora* put in at Cagliari and stayed there contrary to orders, he found himself requested to explain his conduct, and this being unsatisfactory, he was forthwith tried by a Council of Discipline. A worse case was that of the Cavaliere Paroldo, commanding the *Eridano* stationed at Montevideo. From the Consul at that port Cavour received a report, the substance of which was that Captain Paroldo had been guilty of conduct unbecoming an officer, having got entangled in 'an amorous escapade' derogatory to his position, and, further, was accused of conniving at smuggling on the part of ships under his command. He was at once ordered home and court

[1] The British Minister at Turin.

martialled.[1] This case was hardly disposed of before a still more flagrant one arose. Amongst the senior officers holding important posts was Captain Count Persano, in command of the Corvette *Governolo*. Count Persano had had a distinguished career, more perhaps owing to his connexions and friendships and the use he made of them, than from any superlative merit. He was a close friend of Massimo D'Azeglio, and was in close touch with very influential circles. He was not popular in the service and he had a lasting feud with Admiral D'Auvare, of whom he was jealous. The *Governolo* had been selected this year as the ship upon which the students of the Naval School were to have their annual cruise of instruction, and Cavour, to save expense, took the opportunity of sending her to London with the national exhibits destined for the Great Exhibition of 1851. Count Persano was ordered to go straight to London, and having discharged the exhibits, to visit the naval ports on both sides of the Channel and then to return.

In leaving Genoa Count Persano ran his ship on the rocks at the mouth of the harbour, and for two days and a night she remained there, until having been lightened, she refloated. As soon as this took place Count Persano, without sending in any report, got underweigh and sailed straight for his destination, where he excited admiration for his seamanship by sailing up the Thames and taking up his moorings without a pilot. The accident at Genoa had of course created great excitement. There was no love lost between the mercantile marine and the Sardinian Navy, and the papers were full of scathing comments on the navigating abilities of the naval commanders, for the dangers of the rocks of Santa Limbania were a commonplace to every seaman. Cavour was furious, and after receiving the report of the admiral, which accused Persano of disobeying navigating orders and using disrespectful language to his superior officers, at once ordered that Captain Tholosano should be sent to London to take over the

[1] Gonni, *Cavour Ministro della Marina*, cc. ii and iii.

command of the *Governolo* from Count Persano, who was to return to Genoa and be court martialled. Count Persano's idea of discipline was elastic. It did not include returning for a court martial nominated by his enemy Admiral D'Auvare, until he had played all his cards.[1] He wrote at once to Massimo D'Azeglio for help, and then, in a sudden fit of anger, resigned his commission in the service. But he did not escape. D'Azeglio appealed to the King and tried to soften Cavour, but the latter was adamant. He refused either to accept Persano's resignation or to counter-order the court martial. But the influence of D'Azeglio and Persano's other highly placed friends was not without effect, and when he learnt from his correspondents that the court martial would probably let him off, he returned to await his trial. But it was only at the admiral's official request that he was spared being confined in a fortress immediately on his arrival, as Cavour had intended.[2] The court martial was held in due course. It quashed the charges of insubordination and negligence, but did not reappoint Persano to his ship. Although the sentence was light, Cavour was satisfied.[3] He was never one to bear malice, and soon after he offered Persano the command of a naval division, a post usually reserved for a rear-admiral. Persano made excuses, which Cavour accepted and the incident closed. The 'affaire Persano' made a considerable stir at the time. D'Azeglio even spoke of resigning over it, but Cavour's firmness had a good effect, and had he held the portfolio of the Marine longer, a different spirit would have prevailed.

[1] In writing to the admiral as to the personnel of the Court, Cavour added, 'I would desire to exclude any who may have private reasons for animosity against Count Persano.'

[2] Cavour to Admiral d'Auvare, March 8th, 1851.

[3] Cavour did not mince matters. When Persano asked permission after his trial to visit Turin, where he hoped to use his personal influence, Cavour, to whom the application was forwarded, replied, 'I am very glad Count Persano is coming to Turin. I wish to speak to him and let him know directly that it is I and I alone that have insisted on the court martial by which he has been tried, and to declare to him explicitly that, as long as I am Minister of Marine, I shall see that the laws of discipline are observed even by friends of the Prime Minister.' Chiala, v. No. 802.

About everything that Cavour touched there was always that quick grasp of essentials that is the basis of all sound reform, and it was a great loss to the navy when, in April 1851, his acceptance of the Ministry of Finance necessitated relinquishing his portfolio of the Marine. His outline of reorganization was scarcely more than sketched in before it had to be abandoned. His handling of the root problem of discipline is instructive. He was too wise to believe that, however necessary, a series of reprimands and court martials would effect a radical cure. His first step was to increase the funds allotted for the education of the seamen, and to recommend a special course of study for the officers. He wanted to have a weekly class for the students of the Naval School, at which the principles of the new democratic freedom should be taught, and a new tradition of loyalty initiated.[1] He suggested that the officers should mess together on shore. His idea of a theoretical course in navigation at the University, to be attended by relays of officers, was not only as modern in conception as it would have been valuable in practice, but was aimed at breaking down that exclusive spirit that made the naval officer a man apart. Equally sound was his idea of a gunnery school ashore, in which to train officers and men. But Cavour had no time to carry out his ideas, and when he resigned his portfolio the branch he had begun to bend sprang back to its old position.

On April 14th the debate on the commercial treaties with England and Belgium commenced. As Cavour anticipated, the opposition was strong, but it only seemed to spur Cavour to still more successful efforts. On this occasion, his chief adversaries were drawn from the Conservative Right, which hitherto had supported the Government except in its ecclesiastical policy. It was to Count Revel, their leader, that the defence of the

[1] It is instructive as to the state of things to note that the 'Professor of History,' to whom Cavour destined this important task, was a worthy old monk whose knowledge was confined to Greeks, Romans, and Assyrians!

existing system was entrusted. His main contention was, that, in adopting Free Trade they were deserting a tried and effective system to follow an abstract principle, an academic theory, which might well be disastrous and that once adopted could not be changed. To sacrifice at a blow, by reductions in duties, more than one-third of the total receipts, was madness. The benefits of the new system, if benefits there were, must be problematic and uncertain. Never would he vote for a treaty that he was convinced would be the ruin of the country he had sworn to defend.

When Count Revel sat down amid lively applause from the Right, Cavour rose. Though delivered on the spur of the moment, Cavour's reply was a masterly exposition of his economic creed. It was the imaginative quality of the speech, as well as the economic, that captured the Chamber. The obvious determination to drive the country into an industrial *Risorgimento*, by forcing them to scrap old methods and ideals, as the result of competition. He first explained why the Government had neither consulted the Turin Chamber of Commerce, nor submitted their proposals to a special Board of Inquiry as Revel had declared should have been done. Having been a member of the former body for twelve years, Cavour said, he was perfectly aware that they were a protectionist body, and therefore their verdict was known beforehand. As to an inquiry, the Government considered it useless and harmful. Useless, because all they could do was to estimate the costs of production, and their returns were certain to be based on the highest, rather than the lowest, scale of costs; harmful, because the results would have been similar to what had happened in France, where the Board of Inquiry recommended continued protection during the infancy of the industries concerned and in consequence they never grew up. Believing in the necessity of this reform, and of carrying it through quickly, the Government had no intention of allowing the protected interests time to organize themselves and add to the Government's difficulties. He then went on to consider the effect of the revised tariff on the principal industries affected, and passed in view the iron, cotton, and cloth trades.

Going into details of the iron trade he revealed the wasteful, out-of-date methods employed, and showed how the certainty of a profit, through monopoly, was the reason for the absence of any effort at improvement. Cavour knew most of the tricks calculated to impress the Chamber, and he realized the value of big figures. Taking up a statement made by the ironmasters that, from calculations made in France, the increase of cost to agriculture through a protected iron industry was only 7 centesimi per head, he caused a sensation by a rapid calculation based on the numbers employed in agriculture, showing that this meant a national tax on agriculture of nearly 2 millions of lire: 'Behold,' he said, 'the rather more than modest tribute agriculture pays to the iron industry!'

Turning to textiles, he took as the basis of his explanations a memorial forwarded to the Government by the trade, enumerating ten reasons why they could not compete with foreign goods without protection. Of these, only one, the extra cost of imported machinery, would Cavour admit as valid, and that he rendered nugatory by pointing out that the protection still given covered the additional cost of importation. As to the others, if they would organize and specialize they had nothing to fear from foreign competition.

Cavour next dealt with the question as to what was the actual loss to the Treasury entailed by his proposals, and how they expected to make up the deficiency. The amount was not 7 millions as Count Revel had estimated, but $5\frac{1}{2}$. It was impossible to give details as to how this amount would be made good. The Government believed that the reduction in the tariff would stimulate both production and consumption, and thus add to the wealth of the country and its taxable capacity. They believed it would greatly reduce contraband, and thus add to the Treasury receipts. Finally, he said, if their estimates of expanding trade proved false they would have to ask the country to surrender part of the increased wealth tariff reform had brought; which was an euphemistic way of saying that the deficit must be made good by extra taxation. Before closing his speech Cavour put the whole question to the Chamber on the broad ground of the economic tendencies of the age. The centre of significance in economic thought to-day, he said, was towards the betterment of the working classes. There were two schools of thought as to how this could best be achieved. The first was the Economic School, which believed in free competition based on the principle of liberty; the other was the Socialist School, that looked to State control of industry and the limitation of individual activity in the interests of the community.

> Reduced to their lowest terms [he said] the Socialist School maintain that the Government has a right and therefore a duty to intervene in the distribution and employment of capital; they maintain that the Government has a mission, a faculty, to substitute its own will—that it holds to be more illuminated—for the free will of the individual. If that is admitted as an unshakable truth, I do not know what one could respond to the working classes, or their spokesmen, if they should put forward the following argument: you believe it your right and duty to intervene in the distribution of capital, but why do you not intervene on the other element of production, wages? Why do you not organize labour?

Commenting on this speech Roberto D'Azeglio writes to his son:

> Camillo towers higher daily. It is certain that he is a very exceptional man, as you can see by his speeches in the Chamber upon all questions. These last discussions with Revel, armed at all points, who thought he would pulverize his adversary, have been truly luminous, admirable, without even having taken notes whilst his adversary read. He would be admired no matter where he was. I fear the Ministry will change its name.

The debate continued, but as before, Cavour's grasp

of the subject and his lucid and persuasive eloquence was the deciding factor, and when the voting took place the numbers for the Bill were 112 to 14 against.[1]

The country was now committed to a policy of Free Trade. Other treaties followed embodying and extending the same principles with Switzerland, the Zollverein, Holland, and later Norway and even Austria, all entailing an immediate sacrifice for a future benefit. The effects of Cavour's policy were soon felt both at home and abroad. A fresh activity became apparent in Piedmontese industrial life, and the old stagnancy began to disappear as the country realized that there was at last a driving force behind the Government. Abroad, the popular conception of Piedmont, sedulously broadcasted by Austria, as a dangerous little country alternately pugnacious and sulky, full of Mazzinians and republican hotheads, perpetually conspiring against the peace of Europe, was slowly dissipated as her commercial policy brought her out of isolation. Her energy, her free institutions and love of liberty, the bold stand she made against Austrian tyranny in Italy, began to be appreciated. These treaties were, in fact, the opening of a duel between Cavour and Austria for the support and good will of Europe, a contest that ended, through the genius of Piedmont's great statesman, in the discomfiture of Austria and the making of modern Italy.

But Cavour's task was only half done. It must be some years before the Treasury would experience the full benefit of the new measures, and in the meantime special financial provisions were necessary to tide over the period during which the diminished receipts would impoverish the exchequer. New taxation, and probably a big loan, would be required. But the trouble was that no one, not even Nigra, knew the full extent of the country's liabilities. Nigra, though honest and frugal,[2] had neither the commercial imagination nor the

---

[1] Discorsi, vol. ii. pp. 322 ff.

[2] On one occasion he found the Treasury empty and at once transferred 400,000 lire from his own bank to ensure the national solvency.

financial audacity to deal with the situation. Cavour made up his mind that Nigra must go, and that he must take the finances in hand himself. The whole position of the country would be imperilled unless a thorough financial stocktaking was carried through and the country told the truth about its position. When Cavour once made up his mind he was ruthless in his methods. He knew that Nigra was popular and had the confidence of the Cabinet, and that no ordinary appeal would be of any use; so, disregarding the predicament in which his unexpected action placed the Government, and giving as a reason Nigra's exasperating habit of sending a Treasury official (M. Arnulfe) to deal with financial questions in the Chamber, Cavour suddenly resigned.[1]

D'Azeglio, resentful of Cavour's methods and loyal to Nigra, would perhaps have accepted Cavour's resignation, but he was powerless. Cavour, as usual, was master of the situation. His presence as Minister in charge of the Treaties was vital; and Nigra, whom patriotism alone kept in office, cut the knot by resigning, and Cavour was offered and accepted the portfolio of finance. When about this time D'Azeglio, speaking of Cavour to Giuseppe Torelli, said, 'with this little man here I am like Louis-Philippe, I reign but I do not govern,' he was speaking very near the literal truth.

Cavour's appointment was announced to the Chamber on April 22nd. The next day, in reply to a question, he expressed his intention of making a full statement on the national finances at the earliest possible moment. Into this task he now threw all his energy, and a fortnight later, on May 8th, he made his eagerly awaited pronouncement.[2] His speech consisted of two parts; a history of the finances from 1847 to March 31st, 1851, and a programme of the measures that he would ask the Chamber to sanction to remedy the situation. The conclusion of the first part of his speech showed that the state was in debt some 68 millions of lire, with

[1] Chiala, vol. i. No. 149. Cavour to D'Azeglio.
[2] He was attacked by fever which delayed him some days.

a prospect of an adverse balance of some 20 millions on the next budget. To remedy this position, he proposed as a first measure to issue an internal loan for 18 millions. This amount would meet the needs of the Treasury for the next three, or possibly four months, and give them time to open negotiations to raise a big loan of 75 millions, if possible, in England. The reason why England was chosen was in order not to fall deeper into the clutches of Rothschild, who had already a big claim on the Piedmontese finances. His third proposal was to increase the capital of the Bank of Genoa and to permit an increased issue of paper. Cavour at once set to work to put his plans into action. The internal loan was floated, and to his great delight proved a signal success, bringing in double the amount anticipated. For the English loan his first task was to find the right man to negotiate it, and here one of Cavour's fine traits came out. Years before he had written to a friend, 'in politics there is nothing so absurd as rancour,' and he now gave a spontaneous proof of his adherence to that statement, by at once asking Count Revel, his most bitter financial adversary, to go as special Commissioner to England. Revel, with equal magnanimity, accepted, and within a very short time negotiations were afoot. In deliberately passing over Rothschild, Cavour ran the risk of offending a very dangerous opponent, but he was determined to free the national finances from the stranglehold of the Baron James. Cavour knew the value of speed, and if need be, secrecy, and he let no grass grow under his feet. The instant the Chamber had given their authorization, Count Revel left for London. The loan for 3½ million sterling was taken up by the House of Hambro. Two-thirds were soon subscribed, but the last million went slowly. On July 6th he wrote with satisfaction to Revel: 'Rothschild has sold everything, none of our rentes are now in his hands. The Baron James announced that we should fail. He even allowed himself a joke at our expense, saying, that the loan was "ouvert mais non couvert!"' Cavour had now all the money he required. He paid off the balance of the Austrian indemnity; liquidated the account with Rothschild; and found the money for the requirements of the railways.[1]

No sooner were his schemes of Finance under weigh than Cavour reappeared, as Minister of Commerce, with a Bill on Customs and Excise Reform. This Bill, which in his speech on future legislation delivered the previous July, he had declared to be essential to the country's welfare, was the complement of the commercial treaties. The debates were long and difficult, requiring great tact, endurance, and special knowledge on the part of the Minister in charge. For a fortnight Cavour wrestled with an avalanche of amendments in regard to sugar, wines, oil, cotton, hides, and other industries, whose representatives in the Chamber were clamouring for higher duties to keep out foreign competitors. His versatility, good humour, and sound judgement were never more fully displayed, while his firmness on matters of principle and readiness to compromise on non-essentials made the passage of the Bill unexpectedly rapid and easy. Two important Bills remained, an additional or supplementary treaty with France, and a finance Bill on the Bank of Genoa.

On the publication of the treaties with England and Belgium, France had at once taken umbrage at the terms accorded to England. Piedmont, it was true, had given more because she had received more; the advantages of an unrestricted trade with the British Empire being of far greater value to Piedmont than anything accorded to her by France. But France would not hear of getting less than England, though she had no intention of giving as much. A supplementary treaty had therefore to be negotiated, in which still further concessions were made for France's benefit. While the

[1] On Cavour's financial policy at this time, see Corti, *The reign of the House of Rothschild*, also Camozzini, *Cavour Economista*; Perrone, *Idee Economiche del Conte di Cavour*.

treaty was still *sub iudice*, Farini, one of Cavour's stalwarts, who now edited the *Risorgimento*, wrote to Castelli: 'we shall have a pretty lively discussion on the additional treaty with France, but it will be passed, because Cavour will make a Cabinet question of it and Cavour is now recognized as indispensable, even by his adversaries and those jealous of him, who are many both Left and Right. But he is such a man of heart, brains, and hard work, that I don't believe Europe to-day has his equal; he will triumph now and for a long time to come in spite of envy and anger.'[1]

Both the treaty and its author were attacked bitterly; once again Cavour had to press the political reasons to get it through, and his speech contained a notable passage that anticipated with remarkable clear-sightedness the political position a few years hence:

> Might it not happen [he said] that a position was created in which all Europe was involved? In which East and West found themselves in opposite camps? If this event, which is not probable but is not impossible, should arise, would the previous speakers who have spoken with such warmth, desire that we found ourselves in such unfriendly relations with France, that we had to trust, for fear of being attacked by France, upon the bayonets ranged across the Ticino? In view of such a possible situation arising, I believe it to be prudent that we, I will not say sacrifice, but consider as of secondary importance, economic considerations, and allow ourselves to be induced by political reasons to assent to this treaty; which assures the maintenance of cordial relations with France, and further assures us, that if European complications arise, we shall not have to try and make a political alliance, with a people with whom we are engaged in an economic struggle.

In spite of all Cavour's eloquence, however, things looked very black for the treaty. It passed, nevertheless, with a far larger majority than was anticipated, and the result was due at least in part to an unexpected development. Almost the last speaker was Sineo, one of the extremists of the Left, who made a bitter personal

[1] Castelli Carteggio, No. 63.

attack on Cavour, accusing him of arranging the treaty
to benefit his commercial enterprises. His accusations
were angrily repudiated by Cavour, and sympathy with
him affected the voting. The very next day, July 1st,
Cavour brought in the last important Bill of the session,
to increase the capital of the National Bank. The
Chamber was definitely hostile, and after a discussion,
which Cavour hoped had dissipated many wrong notions
and prejudices, he voluntarily withdrew it. The second
week in July the Commercial Treaties with Switzerland,
the Zollverein, and the Low Countries, were passed by
a weary and attenuated Chamber, and then the House
rose for the summer vacation.

When Parliament met in the autumn the probability
of a change of Government was in the minds of many
thoughtful people. D'Azeglio was sick and tired, and
it was clear that only with great difficulty could he take
his proper place. Cavour, on the other hand, holding
three portfolios, was in fact, with the exception of
foreign affairs, governing the country. It is probable
that after this date Cavour could, by going into opposition, have overthrown the Government at any time.
But the problem was not how to displace D'Azeglio,
but how to get a working majority. He was determined
not to do as his predecessors had done, and have to rely
on a scratch collection of votes for every measure; but
instead, to introduce as nearly as possible the English
system and become Premier as the leader of a majority
of the Chamber. 'I cannot govern,' he said, 'on the
point of a needle.' The meaning of this remark is clear
enough when we consider the position of parties in the
Chamber. These were four in number, the Right, under
Count Revel, which was the mainstay of D'Azeglio's
majority; the Right Centre, under Cavour, which likewise voted with the Government; the hydra-headed
Left, that systematically opposed them; and Rattazzi's
Centre Left party, which, although constituted as a
separate group, had hitherto voted consistently against

the Government, and was, in fact, almost indistin-
guishable from the Left pure and simple. Out of these
discordant elements, D'Azeglio, who had no party of
his own, had hitherto contrived to collect a majority.
At critical moments he had appeared in person and
thrown his chivalrous patriotism into the scale. The
margin of safety had been narrow enough, and without
the weight of his personal popularity, it would have too
frequently touched the danger-point. But this benefi-
cent influence once removed, and its place taken by the
provocative personality of Cavour, it was inevitable that
the margin would shrink still farther, and Cavour's
metaphor of the point of a needle was scarcely an
exaggeration.

Of all the combinations possible for Cavour, the only
one that was feasible, and that would effect his purpose
of obtaining a stable majority, was fusion with the Left
Centre. In the event of D'Azeglio's retirement from
the premiership three alternatives lay before the country.
A Government formed by Revel and the Right; the
substitution of Cavour for D'Azeglio with the Chamber
as it stood; or the formation of a new party by the fusion
of the two centres under Cavour. If the first of these
alternatives took place, the subsequent course of events
was not hard to foresee. Thanks to the loyalty of the
King, the Statuto was unlikely to be tampered with,
but it could be reinterpreted. A fresh concordat with
Rome would be made on the best terms the Vatican
would give, which was tantamount to a surrender.
The liberty of the Press would be curtailed as a concession to Austria and France. Austria would be quietly
reassured, all idea of *italianità* dropped, and Piedmont
would sink back into a more or less prosperous insignificance. Against this, the Left and Left Centre would
probably combine under Rattazzi; while Cavour, with
a party diminished by desertions, would remain as an
ineffective third party. The second alternative was
scarcely more hopeful. D'Azeglio's majority, fractional
and uncertain as it had been, was largely the result of

his personality. Cavour as President would at once lose votes from both Right and Left. He would struggle on for a time, but to keep a majority he would be forced to compromise, or he must resign. There remained the third alternative: fusion with the Left Centre. The dangers of this course of action were no less than the others. In the first place D'Azeglio would never consent to it; it would have to be arranged *sub rosa*, and D'Azeglio presented with a *fait accompli*, and the risk of his demanding Cavour's resignation at once must be faced. But apart from this, such a fusion would have an ill-omened significance. To many in Piedmont, and to all the world outside, Rattazzi was still the man of Novara, the democratic leader of 1849, who had brought disaster on his country. Fusion with his party, to the majority of Europe, meant fusion with the Left. It was idle to hope that France and Austria and the Conservative party in Piedmont would accept the statement that Rattazzi had stepped to the Right and not Cavour to the Left. In doing this Cavour would be running the risk of shipwrecking his own policy of friendship with France. But there was one great virtue in its favour: provided that Cavour could dominate and control it, the fusion gave him a solid majority independent of all other sections of the Chamber. It would enable him to make it impossible for the Right to govern, and ensure, at least, some years of power for his Government. But it was more than a clever manœuvre of party politics, it was an act of statesmanship; for in stretching his hand to the Left Centre, he would identify his policy with that large class of borghesia throughout Italy, in whom lay deepest the real spirit of *italianità*: and in so doing would draw to himself just those elements in whose co-operations lay the best hope for the unity of Italy.

To this policy there was one real obstacle, the distrust felt by the Left Centre as to the patriotism of Cavour. Hitherto Cavour had been more closely identified with the Right than the Left, and to understand the position it is necessary to appreciate the dividing line in political thought which separated the two sides in the Piedmontese Parliament. The common ground on which they met was loyalty to the Monarchy, the Statuto, and the independence of Piedmont. On these points, with the possible exceptions of a few republicans on the Left and extreme clericals on the Right, the Chamber was unanimous. The real dividing line between them was this: the Right were *traditionalists*, and the Left, to coin a word in view of what eventually happened, were *futurists*. The Right acquiesced in the fact that Piedmont was a small state and that Italy was divided. Their policy was the traditional one of their country, balancing the jealousy of France and Austria, and reaping what benefit they could from either. The utmost limit to which they would go was willingness to enlarge Piedmont but never to make Italy. Patriotic they were, but they thought in terms of Piedmont not of Italy. The Left, on the other hand, though they had no notion how it was to be done, nor even, perhaps, of the immensity of the difficulties in their path, thought and spoke in terms of Italy, not Piedmont. They still clung to the belief that the expressed desire of Parma, Lombardy, and Venetia, to be joined to Piedmont in 1848, gave them the right to regard them as lost provinces, a true *Italia irredenta*. In these two points of view lies the distinction between *municipalismo* and *italianità*, and the frequently expressed distrust of Cavour, which was a commonplace at this time, is to be explained by this same distinction. It was due to the uncertainty, as to whether his ultimate aim was to 'ingrandire il Piemonte' or 'fare l'Italia'. Common as this distrust of Cavour was, it had no real foundation in fact. But Cavour was above all else a realist, and the question of the unity of Italy presented itself to his mind as a concrete problem, bristling with difficulties; dependent, even for its partial realization, upon a series of possible opportunities which might or might not arise. Realist as he was, he held that the task of Piedmont at the

moment, as much for Italy's sake as her own, was to
fit herself to be in a condition to seize such opportunities
the instant they appeared above the horizon. But the
stupendous effort he was engaged in as a means to this
end, was held to be an end in itself, and he was believed
to be more interested in finance *per se* than in any
question of Italy's future. The difference between the
italianità of Cavour and the democrats was this: they
were like two people trying to put together a picture
puzzle of which the full design was unknown; but
whereas the democrats spent their time in staring at
the muddled pieces and trying to imagine the completed
picture, Cavour was fitting what pieces he could together, leaving to the future the inspiration that would
suddenly disclose the complete design.

The leader of the Left Centre, Urbano Rattazzi, an
adroit politician rather than a statesman, had long ago
seen the rising star of Cavour. After the disaster of
Novara he had separated himself from the extreme views
of the Left, as Cavour had done from the Right. In
fact the political position of both Rattazzi and Cavour
was the same. Their own following was too small to
bring them to power and they could join with neither
Right nor Left. Both, however, would achieve their
object if they joined each other. Foreseeing the mutual
advantage to be gained, the Left Centre had never
ceased to use the columns of their paper, *La Croce di
Savoia*, to flatter Cavour and insinuate the identity of
views and interests that underlay the apparent cleavage
between the two Centre parties. Despite the fact that
Castelli, Cavour's closest friend, had been urging him
to approach Rattazzi, Cavour up to the end of 1851 had
ignored the suggestion. Now, however, as the possibility
of assuming power drew nearer, a study of the position
revealed all the advantages of the scheme. The deciding
factor was Louis Napoleon's *coup d'état* in December
1851.

The political position of Piedmont after that event
was, in truth, precarious. With the advent of an

absolutist régime in France, Piedmont found herself
hemmed in on all sides by countries openly hostile
to her Constitutional form of Government, Belgium
in an analogous situation could rely upon England,
but Piedmont was without a friend. Already Louis
Napoleon had indicated to the Piedmontese Minister
in Paris that his country would be well advised to
restrain the excesses of the Press and get rid of the
undesirable *émigrés* who plotted in the safety of a free
country. But Austria and Prussia went much farther;
by means of an intermediary they warned Victor
Emmanuel and his Government that, refusal to har-
monize their political principles with those of the rest
of Europe, might entail serious consequences.[1] The
King replied in the brave and loyal spirit that always
characterized his political utterances, pointing out that
while willing and anxious to live on friendly terms with
his neighbours, and ready to do all he could, consistent
with his oath as a constitutional sovereign, to maintain
good relations with them, he was master in his own
house and intended to remain so. But both the King
and D'Azeglio realized that it would be advisable to
bring in a Press Law before Louis Napoleon joined in,
officially, with the suggestions of Austria and Prussia,
and D'Azeglio summoned the leaders amongst his
supporters to discuss the situation. At this meeting
Count Revel insisted on the necessity for a radical reform
of the Press; and Menabrea, one of the other leaders of
the party, was equally insistent on the need for a revision
of the franchise. The result of the Conference was the
Deforesta Press Law, but it had other consequences as
well, for it led directly to the Connubio.[2] Cavour, while
he supported the Press Law, fully recognizing its
necessity, realized that the effect throughout the country
would be disastrous. It would be interpreted as a
retrograde step and a concession to foreign pressure.

[1] Bianchi, *Stor. Doc.*, vol. vii. c. iii; Massari, *Vittorio Emanuele*, ii;
Chiala, vol. i. Introd. p. 217. Dispatch of D'Azeglio to London and Paris.

[2] The name by which the union of the two centre parties under Cavour
is generally known.

While it would put heart into the clerical and reactionary elements it would anger and depress the Liberals. Elsewhere in Italy, it would weaken trust in Piedmont and injure the constitutional cause. He foresaw that the situation might be so represented to D'Azeglio that, through weakness or want of foresight, he might embark on a course of action that might carry him farther than he meant to go. Moved then by this fear, and realizing that the danger could only be met by a corresponding strengthening of the liberal cause, Cavour made up his mind at once to approach Rattazzi.

Early in January 1852 Cavour met Rattazzi and Domenico Buffa at the house of Castelli. The programme was quickly agreed upon: Monarchy, the Statuto, Independence and Civil and Political Progress. It was then decided that on the occasion of the debate on the Press Law the new union should be publicly proclaimed. Rattazzi should first proffer his support to the Government, which Cavour would accept on the Government's behalf, and at the same time he would take the opportunity of definitely breaking with the reactionary section of the Right.[1]

The Deforesta Press Law was brought in on February 3rd, 1852. Its main provision was that all action taken against the Press for crimes against foreign Governments and Monarchs should in future be tried by Magistrates, and no longer be submitted to juries who would never convict. In regard to Press abuses concerning the internal affairs of the country no change was made.

In the course of the first day's debate both Rattazzi and Menabrea spoke. The latter, supporting the Bill, enlarged on the vices of the Press and let it be known that, for his part, the time had come 'to leap the barrier', in other words to control the Press and to narrow the franchise. Rattazzi, though he opposed the Bill, admitted that he did so with the greatest regret and definitely held out his hand to the Government. There

[1] Castelli, *Ricordi*.

was great excitement the next day to know what reply
the Government would make. They were not long left
in doubt. D'Azeglio, warned of what was going to
happen, did not put in an appearance, and Cavour,
speaking for the Cabinet, boldly accepted Rattazzi's
promise of support. 'A promise,' he said, 'that I accept
and value, since, if the honourable member employs
in defence of the Government, only a part of the great
ability he has hitherto shown in opposing it, the path
of the Ministry will be made very much easier.' He
then dealt with the Bill itself, emphasizing the dangers
resulting from unbalanced criticism of foreign states
and rulers, but at the same time insisting on the value
of complete freedom of the Press in regard to internal
affairs. Then he fulfilled the second part of his task,
remarking that after what he had said, the Chamber
would realize that he could in no way subscribe to the
opinions expressed by the Deputy Menabrea, and
therefore the Government resigned themselves to lose
definitely 'the feeble support hitherto given them by
the honourable Deputy and his friends.'

The day after Cavour's speech both Menabrea and
Revel replied. 'The Minister of the Finances,' said the
former, 'wishes to set sail for other parliamentary
shores. He is well able to do it, but I shall not follow
him. As regards myself, whatever Ministers sit upon
these benches they will find me faithful at my post. My
principles are never to yield to popularity nor to personal
considerations nor yet to political tactics'—to which
Cavour caustically replied that the Ministry had not the
least intention of 'setting sail for other shores.' No
manœuvre of such a kind was contemplated, but they
intended to sail 'in the direction of the prow not of the
poop.' It was, however, Revel who christened Cavour's
evolution with the name by which it has since been
known, in a passage of his speech where he expressed
his astonishment, when he observed that the Government had affected a *divorzio* with one section, while
at the same time contracting a *connubio* (marriage) with

another; and as the Connubio it has been known ever since. A curious feature of the Connubio was that Cavour did not join the Left Centre *con amore*; for its personnel he had small regard and for its political past nothing but contempt.[1] In explaining this fusion of parties it is usual to say that Cavour took a step to the Left and Rattazzi one to the Right, and so it was done. But there is no evidence to show that Cavour moved at all; he sacrificed neither principles nor programme, and he took great pains to emphasize the fact in the Chamber. The union was forced upon him, because only in this way could the Liberal movement neutralize the increase in reactionary power and influence, which the political conditions of Europe, due to the *coup d'état* in France, had brought into existence. It was the only way by which a party could be formed, which would keep Piedmont in the van of the movement for Italian independence and unity, and prevent the triumph of that spirit of *municipalismo* that regarded the continued division of Italy as inevitable and desirable, and asked for nothing better for Piedmont than proud poverty and political insignificance. Why then did not D'Azeglio demand Cavour's resignation when he found the Government pledged without his sanction or that of the Cabinet? There is no doubt that Cavour, with his penetrating grasp of political problems, saw much farther into the possible consequences of the situation than D'Azeglio. The postulates of the position, as Cavour saw them, were that there must be an immediate counter-movement to the forces of reaction—without the resignation of the Government. In the face of Prussian and Austrian pressure, the strength of Piedmont, at the moment, lay in the great trust placed in the personal character of D'Azeglio by France and England. If Cavour resigned, D'Azeglio must fall. His successor must be either Revel, whose name spelt

[1] See the Memoir of Galvagno on the Connubio, Chiala, vol. i. Appendix V; also Chiala, *Gouvernement Représentatif en Piémont*, for full account of the political causes; Brofferio, *Stor. Parl. Subalp.*, for the debate.

reaction, or Cavour, whose union with the Left Centre would be regarded as tantamount to a defiance of Austria and Prussia. It is this conviction that, whatever happened, the Government must not resign, that explains why Cavour did not offer to surrender his office nor D'Azeglio demand it.[1]

The position in which D'Azeglio found himself was embarrassing enough. He neither trusted nor wanted the men with whose support Cavour had presented him. He disliked and distrusted Rattazzi, but, as he remarked pathetically, 'if I am given votes without conditions I cannot refuse them.' All the same they proved useful. Their support ensured the passage of the Press Law, to which there was bitter opposition from the democrats, and this in turn smoothed relations with France and Austria and enabled the Government to come through what D'Azeglio described as a 'pretty warm corner.'

The firstfruits of the new grouping of parties appeared at the commencement of the new session in March, when Rattazzi's name was put forward for election as Vice-President of the Chamber. The Government nominated Boncompagni, but Cavour threw his weight on the side of Rattazzi and he was elected. A month later the President, Dionigi Pinelli, died, and once again the policies of Cavour and D'Azeglio clashed, this time more seriously than before. On this occasion Cavour did his utmost to persuade the Cabinet to support Rattazzi, and though D'Azeglio would not hear of it, Cavour so far succeeded that no official candidate was put forward, the members being left to vote for whom they wished. Cavour and Farini, now Minister of Education, worked for Rattazzi, while the rest supported Boncompagni. Once again Cavour triumphed and Rattazzi became President. The tension in the Cabinet was now acute. The King endeavoured to make peace. He induced D'Azeglio to withdraw his resignation, which he had tendered after Rattazzi's election, but the

[1] Chiala, *Lettere*, vol. v. No. 245. Letter of the Deputy Jacquemoud to Cavour.

position was impossible. A few weeks later Cavour, angered at the attitude of the Cabinet towards his new allies, resigned from the Government. The retirement of Cavour meant the fall of the Cabinet, which at once resigned. But the King refused to hear of another Prime Minister, and requested D'Azeglio to reconstruct the Cabinet, leaving our Cavour, Farini, and Galvagno.[1]

Though Cavour's methods were certainly not commendable from the English standpoint, his action viewed in its wider aspects was wise and statesmanlike. In spite of what had happened, he remained friends with D'Azeglio, and they talked matters over amicably. In the following letter to Salvagnoli at Florence Cavour puts the position with his accustomed clearness and lucidity:

> I thank you for your sympathy about my retirement from the Government. You may be certain that it will have no results harmful for the Constitutional cause, but rather that, ultimately, it will prove beneficial. In my opinion it was not simply useful, but indispensable, to consolidate strongly the Liberal party. That could not be done without drawing a veil over the past, and forgiving those that, more through ignorance than malice, misgoverned the country in 1849. D'Azeglio, who at first appeared convinced of this necessity, would not face the consequences of it, and so provoked a crisis which meant one or other of us must go. Foreign policy necessitated that I had to be sacrificed. I believe that D'Azeglio would have gladly resigned; as far as I could, I persuaded him not to do so, so he remained and I went, without ceasing to be both private and political friends. In his turn D'Azeglio will have to retire, and then we shall be able to constitute a cabinet frankly Liberal. In the meantime I am using my freedom to pay a visit to France and England.[2]

For a short time Cavour returned to his seat as a deputy, but his presence was more of an embarrassment than a help, and he wisely determined to take a good holiday abroad.

[1] Rendu, *Correspondance politique de M. D'Azeglio.* Letter dated May 24th, and Bert, No. 345 (written the same day), give the two points of view as to Cavour's action. See also Chiala, vol. i. Introd. p. 252 ff.

[2] Chiala, vol. i. No. 208.

Cavour had very definite ideas regarding the purpose of this visit. He wanted to study the political barometer; to estimate what chances there were of a liberal reaction in the West, and what degree of support a definitely Liberal Government in Piedmont was likely to receive. With this object in view he was anxious to meet as many of the leading men in France and England as possible; not only to discover their views and estimate their characters, but to dispel, if possible, the prejudices and wrong impressions that he believed existed regarding himself and his policy. From a study of his frequent letters at this time, it is easy to see that he did not think the present Government in Piedmont could last very long; and that, if he did not return and bolster it up, the time was not far distant when he would be called upon to form a Cabinet.

The chief difficulty that he foresaw was in the attitude of the King. The royal *entourage* was strongly clerical and reactionary. The old families who provided the Court Functionaries still lived in the Albertian tradition. 'The man of Novara' and all his associations stank in their nostrils, and it was therefore inevitable that the King's attitude towards the Connubio was prejudiced and resentful. The fact that Cavour was himself an aristocrat only made matters worse. Before leaving Turin Cavour had more than one interview with Victor Emmanuel, and the results were far from satisfactory. It was said that, at his first interview, the King dismissed him with the words, 'Signor Conte, you have 150,000 livres of *rente* and whatever happens it is all one to you, but understand, I have no mind to finish as my father did.'[1] He himself writing from London to Castelli says: 'The King was in a very bad humour with me, you may be certain of it, whatever may be said. At my last interview he was cold and constrained. I did not tell you because I knew it would hurt you. But I do not want to hide it from you any longer. He received me standing, close to the door, almost as if I had

[1] C. D'Azeglio, *Mémoires Historiques*, p. 450.

been some common person come to ask a favour. It is true that at the moment of my taking leave he had some remorse and embraced me. Quitting him like this, I have thought it wiser, despite your advice, not to write to him,' and in another letter he says, 'The King has not yet got over his prejudices regarding me. Time and the force of circumstances are necessary to enlighten him as to how much I have been calumniated by those around him.'

Cavour's study of the position abroad seems to have convinced him that not only was time in his favour, but that a definitely Liberal Government would have a fair reception if wisely led, and in spite of the solicitations of his friends he refused to return until he saw the crisis approaching.

In London he met Lord Malmesbury and Palmerston, both of whom preached prudence. 'The only difference between them is that the first is prudent from choice, the second from political necessity;' he had an interview with Disraeli, 'a man who will exercise a great influence upon the fortunes of this country.' He went to stay at Bowood with Lord Lansdowne, and later with Lord Minto in Scotland. He visited docks and arsenals and factories; spent an evening in the lowest quarters of London with the chief of police; and wrote home long letters full of criticisms of men and politics, shrewd comment and wise advice. On the pressing problem as to the attitude of the English Government towards Piedmont, he wrote:

The Tories are not hostile to us, on the contrary our antipopism makes them esteem us. The Minister of Foreign Affairs has spoken to me on this point in the most kindly and amiable way. One must not, of course, exaggerate the support they would give us if it came to fighting. But would the Whigs do more? That is what I am very doubtful about. The presence of the Tories in power has only one real inconvenience at the present moment: it creates a moral influence very regrettable and discouraging among our Liberal party, and gives audacity to the retrograde party.

Regarding the internal affairs of Piedmont, he found that his own work was absolutely unknown, and all the credit was given to D'Azeglio.

> I have convinced myself that the name D'Azeglio still exercises very great influence here. Ninety-five per cent. of political men in England know absolutely no other name than his: to him alone they attribute all the good that has been done in Piedmont. You will say that this is a mistake, an injustice, perhaps: but there it is, and one cannot rectify it without doing harm to the reputation of our country. Lord Palmerston, who has been kindness itself to me, nevertheless, said, in his own words, 'In England we put much faith in D'Azeglio, we have great confidence in him.'

On leaving London Cavour went north to Scotland; after a short visit, during which he lost his heart to Edinburgh, he turned south once more and crossed to Paris, where Rattazzi joined him. When, in the preceding May, the Piedmontese ambassador at Paris, the Marchese di Collegno, had announced to the Minister of Foreign Affairs the election of Rattazzi to the presidency of the Chamber of Deputies, M. Turgot had replied: 'I am sure that M. Rattazzi is as much a man of order as the rest of those who form the Cabinet at Turin; but,' he added, 'en politique on est l'homme de ses antécédents.' Europe only knows M. Rattazzi as the real chief of the democratic Cabinet of 1849, his election to the Presidency of the Chamber therefore will have a *détestable* effect; and what is worse is the fact that he was only successful at the third *tour de scrutin*, which is a proof that if he had been opposed by the Cabinet he would never have been elected. Europe then has reason to suppose that the Cabinet of Turin associates itself to-day with the men of 1849.'[1] It was to dissipate, if possible, this preconceived prejudice against Rattazzi, and less directly himself, that Cavour brought the new President of the Chamber to Paris and introduced him in person. To his friend Count Ponza

[1] *Diario politico di Margherita Provana di Collegno*, Appendix No. 7.

di San Martino, the future Minister of the Interior, he wrote on September 4th:

I am in Paris eight days, which I have employed receiving all kinds of people, from the Minister of Foreign Affairs to minor officials. I shall see Louis Napoleon alone to-morrow. From what I have seen here up to now, it seems to me that one can deduce that the French Government wishes us Liberal, so that we do not fall into the power of Austria: but would like us flexible in our international relations. But whatever may be the feelings of the Government, it will be guided by its own interests: we shall be either aided or sacrificed according as it will suit L. N. to oppose or be friendly with Austria. As you have said to me many times, it is upon France, above all, that our destiny depends. *Bongré, mal gré* we must be her partner in the great game that sooner or later must be played in Europe. Rattazzi has been much in society and has in general been judged very favourably. I believe that when he leaves, Paris will have learnt to judge him at his proper value, and that neither national nor foreign diplomacy will succeed in having him classed as a wild demagogue.

In another letter he adds, 'a few days ago M. Fould said to me that the President had remarked, "I am delighted to have met M. Rattazzi, a quarter of an hour's conversation was sufficient to destroy the erroneous opinion I had been led to conceive of him: I was told he was a *tête exaltée*: I have found him very reasonable." '

In another letter he says: 'While waiting, I profit by my stay here to let the men in the Government know the true state of things in Piedmont. I do not know if I have succeeded, but I do my best. The President asked Rattazzi and myself to dinner, and afterwards we had a private audience. On both occasions he has treated us with great kindness and spoke to us with great knowledge about Italian affairs.'[1] Cavour left Paris at the end of September, and after breaking his journey for a week at Geneva, arrived back in Turin in the middle of October.

Cavour returned to Piedmont refreshed in body and mind, with a knowledge of the men in England and

[1] These letters will be found in Chiala, vol. i.

France with whom he would have to deal, and a pretty
shrewd notion of the general lines of the policy they
might be expected to follow. How much the driving
force of his presence in the Government had been
missed may be gathered from the following extract
from *L'Opinione*, dated October 14th:

> It cannot be denied that business men and manufacturers are
> discouraged by the inertia that seems to have invaded the
> Government, which appears to have no knowledge of the real
> needs of the Treasury. It is an incontestable fact that during
> the Ministry of M. de Cavour the business of the country
> had taken an activity and extension unknown in the past.
> From whence came this movement, except from the con-
> fidence with which a foreseeing, enterprising statesman
> inspired the country? And is not the most striking proof
> of this fact the diminution of trade which followed the
> moment he left office? The magnificent schemes the Genoese
> had formed for the enlargement of the port, the transatlantic
> service, and so forth, have fallen into oblivion. Reproach
> them, and they will at once answer that they cannot risk
> undertaking great enterprises that require an immense
> amount of capital, unless they can foresee the charges that
> the needs of the Treasury will demand from them. One hears
> the same complaints at Turin. The development of the rail-
> ways, and the erection of new commercial buildings, depend
> on the solution of the financial problem. If that is much
> longer delayed the public wealth is bound to suffer, and may
> well produce a dangerous crisis as much for industry as
> for the Treasury.

D'Azeglio, on the other hand, worn out in body and
mind, was almost at the end of his resources. Owing to
lack of proper supervision, as he himself admitted, the
negotiations with Rome over the Civil Marriage Bill
had been mismanaged, and rendered a defeat in the
Chamber more than probable.[1] With an incapable
Finance Minister,[2] and Cavour in opposition, the posi-

---

[1] D'Azeglio to Rendu, November 1852.

[2] On his resignation Cavour had nominated his own successor, M. Cibrario,
as Minister of Finance, a part for which he was eminently unfitted. Cavour
was determined to be missed and not to have his plans interfered with, so
he chose a successor who was certain to initiate nothing.

tion would be hopeless. He must either submit to having the Government policy dictated by Cavour and the Opposition, or face a defeat in the Chamber and resignation. Under these circumstances he took the wisest course and resigned with his colleagues on October 22nd, recommending the King to send for Cavour. But the actual reason for D'Azeglio's resignation lay in the Civil Marriage Bill. The King had been unwisely drawn into it and induced to write a personal letter to the Pope. On receiving his reply, the King was more anxious than ever to settle the difficulties with the Church, and wanted D'Azeglio to withdraw the Bill or make a compromise, declaring he would 'never sign a Law that would displease the Pope.' The King thus inaugurating a policy directly opposed to that of D'Azeglio, the latter resigned, remarking that 'the hour of dying comes sometime to all, but the hour of dishonour should never come.'

The King summoned Cavour, who, when approached on the ecclesiastical position, told the King quite frankly that he would never countenance dictation from Rome, nor admit the Papal claims, and advised the King to send for Count Balbo. Cavour knew that once more he was master of the situation. He wrote to a friend:

> I have not been able to come to an understanding with the King: I depart for Leri. M. Balbo is charged to form a ministry. The *curés* of Savoy are very much pleased, but I doubt their joy will not be of long duration. For never has the anti-clerical feeling been stronger. I am sure of the loyalty of the King. The cunning of the priests and the weakness of D'Azeglio have led him astray. He misapprehends the feeling of the country. When he knows the facts, he will send the clerical party *au diable avant le temps.* . . .[1]

Cavour was right. Revel, La Marmora, Paleocapa, Dabormida, and half a dozen more refused to make part of the Cabinet with Balbo as Premier. The King had to recall Cavour, as he anticipated, and ask him to form

[1] Cavour to de la Rive, Chiala, vol. i, No. 237.

a Cabinet without conditions attached; to meet the King half-way, Cavour undertook not to make the Civil Marriage Bill a Cabinet question, and with that proviso he formed his Cabinet.

Three members of D'Azeglio's Cabinet kept their portfolios. La Marmora at the War Office, Boncompagni as Minister of Justice, and Paleocapa as Minister for Public Works. Cibrario became Minister of Public Instruction, a much more congenial post, while Cavour took the Presidency and the Ministry of Finance. Two new members were introduced; Count Ponza di San Martino as Minister of the Interior, and General Dabormida at the Foreign Office. Cavour first suggested Rattazzi for the Interior, but the King vetoed him, and he had to wait a little longer before he entered the Cabinet. On November 5th, 1852, the great Ministry took office and a new chapter opened in the history of Italy.

IV. THE BEGINNING OF THE GREAT MINISTRY

The Situation in Piedmont—The Budget—The Rising of February 6th at Milan—The Austrian Decree of Sequestration—Action of the Government—The Austrian Note and the Reply—The Memorandum—Action in Parliament—The Shipping Subsidy—Attack on Cavour's Palazzo—The Bank Bill—Cavour dissolves Parliament.

THE change of Government in November, 1852, was both necessary and timely. D'Azeglio's work was finished. For three years, despite great physical disabilities, he had kept the ship of state on an even keel by the honesty of his diplomacy and the sterling value of his personal character. During this period, Cavour, leaving to his chief the foreign policy of the country, had effected an economic revolution in the country's industries, and set Piedmont on the path of progress and prosperity. But he had done more than this. He had recomposed the parties in the Chamber so that for the first time the Government had a solid majority in Parliament, and in consequence a prospect of some years of undisturbed power.

The training Cavour had received thoroughly equipped him for his task. He had held four portfolios, finance, industry, agriculture and the navy, and had fitted himself through long years of thought and study for that of Foreign Affairs. During the four years it had taken him to rise to the premiership he had had few advantages. He had fought his way to power by sheer strength of will, ability, and hard work, obstructed at every step by hostility and envy. He became Premier not because he was popular but because he was indispensable. Cavour came to the Presidency with a programme and an objective, the Independence of Italy. This involved two things, the expulsion of the Austrians, and the preparation of the Italian people to govern themselves when the moment came. It was not to be merely a change of rulers but an obliteration of boundaries. The one objective must be the work of foreign policy, the other of internal policy, and both can be seen developing year by year until they coalesced in the Kingdom of Italy.

The situation of Piedmont when Cavour assumed the helm of state was sufficiently disquieting. The non-committal support of England and the vague conditional friendship of France, were weak reeds to lean upon in the face of the determined hostility of Austria and Rome. For Piedmont was faced with a deliberate conspiracy between these latter powers, directed, not merely against her legislation or her policy, but against her Constitution. From their point of view the position was intelligible enough. Piedmont was the only Constitutional State in Italy. As such, she not only prevented that unity of subjection to Austria which was the aim of this latter power, but she undermined Austria's influence in every other Italian state. To Rome she was equally objectionable, Piedmont's vindication of the supremacy of the civil power being a constant threat to the Papal dominance in the Peninsula.

> The difficulty lies [wrote Sir James Hudson[1] to Lord Clarendon] in the policy which is to be pursued by Piedmont in regard to the Court of Rome. The Court of Rome demands the withdrawal of the civil marriage Bill; this might be possible, but M. de Cavour sees that the public opinion of Piedmont is bitterly hostile to the pretensions of Rome, which demands the repeal of the Siccardi Laws, the re-establishment of the Foro Ecclesiastico, and the restoration of the exclusive privileges of the Roman Church in Piedmont. The immediate action of the Pope upon the mind of the King, and the Pope's letter, let the King see very clearly that if the Civil Marriage Bill is not withdrawn he must expect his excommunication by the Church.[2]

Even more explicit is a dispatch written a few months later in which he says 'the difficulties raised by Rome and the complaints she utters are not against the

---

[1] Sir James Hudson succeeded Sir Ralph Abercromby almost simultaneously with Cavour's appointment as Premier.

[2] F.O. 67, vol. 186, No. 100.

Siccardi Laws, the Civil Marriage Bill, or the repartition of the Church revenues; these are simply questions used as weapons against the Constitutional system of government in Piedmont. If they were all conceded to-morrow Rome would find as many other subjects of grievance. She will never rest until she has destroyed the Sardinian Constitution.'[1]

A further source of difficulty between Piedmont and the other continental Powers was the excesses of the Press. The recent Press Law, which enabled any foreign Power to take action in the Law Courts, made no difference. The Austrian Minister demanded that, whenever an article considered offensive to his country appeared in a Piedmontese paper, the Government should spontaneously, and without waiting for a demand from Austria, instantly publish a counter-statement. The French and Prussian Ministers were scarcely less peremptory in their demands. At any time the irritation might lead to a joint *démarche* which might precipitate a crisis. Cavour, however, found a staunch natural ally in the British Minister, who fought the battle of freedom for the Press amongst his diplomatic colleagues. In one of his dispatches he describes a colloquy with the Prussian Minister, in which he put the case for Piedmont in the following terms:

A sovereign without guards, save that afforded by the loyal affection of his people: a people with merely a preventive police: industry everywhere: security of life and property: an increasing revenue: Government with a large Parliamentary majority: full employment and high wages: symptoms of prosperity, of content, of sound rational progress, the law respected, the Press free, and the prisons empty. I begged him now to turn to the rest of Italy. He would find bloated war establishments without a foreign enemy, crippled revenues, discontented populations: military law, barbarous executions: secret societies aiming at the lives of Sovereigns: the prisons gorged, spies, brigandage, poverty, and general discontent.[2]

[1] F.O. 67, vol. 195, No. 128.   [2] F.O. 67, vol. 172, Nos. 5–6.

It was natural that an intimacy should spring up between so staunch a defender of Piedmont and Cavour, and in this fact lies the value of Sir James Hudson's dispatches, for they reflect in substance the mind and views of Cavour himself. The British minister was under no illusions regarding the aims of Austria and he took care that his government should know the unvarnished truth.

> To meet Count Buol's views [he wrote] the Piedmontese constitution must be so diluted as to be palatable to Austria: the Press placed under censorship: the present government driven from power and replaced by a cabinet chosen from the Clerical-Ultramontane party. Piedmont will not accept these conditions. She possesses a young king who said to his mother not many days ago, when she with a mother's fondness spoke to him of danger: 'Mother, the princes of our House have been accustomed to mount their horses when they had to choose between death and dishonour, they died as became them, honourably. Do you expect your son to do less or to die less honourably than his ancestors?'[1]

The difficulty of this situation lay less in the probability of trouble in Piedmont than in the possibility of its reaction abroad. Cavour knew that he could depend upon the loyalty of the King, without which during these years even his genius could scarcely have saved Italy. He had a solid majority in Parliament, and the country was with him. But if to the pressure of Austria and Rome was added a clerical triumph in France, the position might become desperate. The balance lay between Napoleon's need for clerical support and the value of a 'spirited foreign policy,' as a counter-attraction to clerical intrigues. If Napoleon felt constrained to propitiate Rome, Piedmont might be the victim, but if the spirited foreign policy was to be preferred, friendship with Piedmont might be of value. Cavour's policy, then, was directed to cultivate good relations with France, to avoid all provocation of Austria and Rome, and to concentrate on the progress

[1] F.O., vol. 193. No. 58.

and prosperity of Piedmont. This latter had a many-sided value. By heightening the contrast between the Kingdom of Victor Emmanuel and the rest of Italy, it focused the eyes of Italian Liberals on the virtues of Constitutional government. It won the approval of England, and coincided with Napoleon's ideas of law and order, at the same time being a constant source of irritation to Austria, though one at which she could hardly take umbrage.

Cavour was no religious persecutor, and he had far less animus against Rome than many of his contemporaries. He told the King quite plainly, when he was first offered the Presidency, that he could not consent to a repeal or alteration in the Siccardi Laws, that he was aware of a difficulty which had sprung up between Piedmont and Rome since he had quitted office, namely, the law respecting civil marriage and the question of the more equal distribution of Church property in the Sardinian States, and that, for his part, he approved of neither of these measures. He was prepared to abide by the decision of the Senate in regard to the former, and not attempt to force it upon that body, and to check any measure tending to introduce legislative action in regard to the latter, but farther than this he would not go.[1] Both La Marmora and Dabormida said that Cavour had, in this, conceded more to Rome than they were prepared to approve. The King, however, had told him this was not sufficient to satisfy Rome, whereupon Cavour had advised the King to send for Count Balbo, which he did. The second time Cavour was sent for he gave no pledges beyond promising not to make the Civil Marriage Bill a Cabinet question. But as a constitutional minister, Cavour could not override a clear expression of the country's will, and the determination to resist the pretensions of Rome was both widely spread and deep seated. He was eventually compelled by public opinion to introduce measures

[1] F.O. 67, vol. 186. No. 105. Confidential report of Hudson to Lord Clarendon.

affecting the Church, of which he realized the need, though he disliked the general principle upon which they rested. But it has to be admitted that the financial needs of the State contributed considerably to overcome his scruples. At the moment of his accession to power, however, he felt that the country's chief need was a period of rest from controversy, in which to complete the reorganization of the administrative and financial machinery of the State.

Early in the new session Cavour, in his capacity as Minister of the Finances, introduced the Budget for 1853. As in previous years there was once more a large deficit. The total indebtedness of the country being 39 millions of lire, of which 17 millions was on the year's working. To meet this situation Cavour proposed to raise a loan of 2 millions, to save 7 millions by economies and taxation reform, and impose fresh taxation which was estimated to produce a further 6 millions.[1] Though Cavour spoke hopefully of balancing the Budget in the course of the next two years, he must have realized that the system he was pursuing rendered this almost impossible. Although the national trade was expanding (the receipts had increased another 5 millions during the year) it was not growing fast enough to make up for the loss imposed by the reduced customs receipts. In addition to this, the need for the investment of capital in temporarily unremunerative public works, railroads, canals, docks, and roads, which was a vital part of Cavour's system, swallowed up the receipts faster than they came in. Nothing more clearly reflects Cavour's *italianità* than his system of finance. If he had been thinking only of Piedmont, his anxiety to balance the Budget could have been easily effected by cutting down the army and postponing his expensive public works. To have done this would have been to sacrifice Italy's hopes to Piedmont's financial soundness. It would have meant surrendering the leadership of Italy and dropping

[1] *Discorsi*, vol. vi. p. 26. The new taxes were: on private and public vehicles, on movables, and an extension of the *gabelle*.

back into insignificance. As it was, he gambled upon the future, kept Piedmont in debt, in order that, when the opportunity came, her army would be fully equipped and ready, with good roads and railways behind it and the foundations laid for a future era of prosperity and expansion. This interpretation of his intentions could not of course be mentioned in public, everything was put down to the needs of Piedmont, and this kept alive the widely felt doubt regarding Cavour's patriotism, and helped to sustain the charge of *municipalismo*. After the Budget came ten days of vigorous debates on the new taxes, all of which Cavour steered successfully through the Chamber. A week later, on December 16th, he had to take in hand the ungrateful task of supporting in the Senate the Civil Marriage Bill, of which he did not approve. This Bill had been introduced by the Government on April 9th, 1850. In the preceding June, after Cavour had resigned, it was passed by a large majority in the Chamber of Deputies, and now came up for discussion in the Senate. Cavour, speaking late in the debate, made the case for the Bill unmistakably clear. The Government asked that the contract of marriage should be put upon the same footing as it was in France and England, Holland and Belgium. The law upon matrimony in Piedmont was medieval; far behind that, for instance, which existed in Naples.

When the Senate proceeded to vote on the first article (which contained the substance of the Bill) the numbers on either side were equal, and the casting vote of the President being given against it, the clause was rejected, whereupon the Government withdrew the Bill. Cavour must have been thankful for so good an excuse, not only to fulfil his pledge to the King, but to take at least one bone of contention out of the mouth of the clericals.

Cavour's absorption in parliamentary reform was, however, rudely broken early in the new year (1853) by a much greater danger than difficulty with the Church. In January 1853 the Sardinian Government got wind of a Mazzinian conspiracy at Milan. Anxious to avoid all charge of complicity, Cavour took severe measures. The Austrian frontier was picketed with troops, with orders to stop all unauthorized persons. Numerous arrests of suspected persons were made at Genoa, including a young Sicilian, afterwards to be Prime Minister, Francesco Crispi.[1] On February 6th the rising took place, ending in an immediate and complete failure, though it cost the lives of some Austrian soldiers.[2] At first the Austrian Government behaved with studied moderation. Piedmont was thanked for the steps she had taken and the tone of Count Strassoldo's proclamation was unusually calm and reasonable.

This attitude of the Austrian Government caused some perturbation in Turin, for the harm done to the Italian cause abroad by these foolish and useless outbreaks would be doubled by a policy of mildness on the part of Austria.[3] But Austria did not belie her reputation for severity. Ten days later, in the name of the Emperor, was issued an edict sequestrating the goods of all Lombard and Venetian *émigrés*—whether or not they had since obtained another nationality—on the ground of their undoubted complicity in the outbreak of February 6th.[4] To realize the full significance of this decree and the thoroughness of its illegality, it is necessary to recall the terms of the treaty signed between Piedmont and Austria after the campaign of Novara in 1849.

On that occasion it had been the first care of the Piedmontese negotiators to safeguard the position of the numerous Italians in Lombardy who had fought under the Sardinian flag. The terms, therefore, of the treaty included an amnesty for all so inculpated, with the exception of eighty-six individuals mentioned by name.[5] Nearly all of those who were thus excluded, having left the country, their position was regularized

[1] See Bianchi's *La politique du Comte de Cavour*, Letter No. xi.
[2] A full account will be found in Tivaroni, *L'Italia Austriaca*, c. i. § 4.
[3] See Massari, *Il Conte di Cavour*, p. 90.   [4] Text in Zini, vol. iii. documenti.
[5] The Government made this amnesty a *sine qua non*. Bolléa, *Lettere del Risorgimento*, E. D'Azeglio to Alessio di Tocqueville.

by permission to demand the right of emigration in conformity with the Austrian civil code. As many of them, having escaped from Austria, did not think it necessary after the event to ask for the right to emigrate, the Emperor on 27th of December 1849 issued a decree by which all such should be 'considered and treated as being freed from the rights and duties of Austrian nationality.' In other words, they became foreigners, whose goods and possessions in Austria were protected under the Article 33 of the civil code. As the result of this many of the most prominent and well-known Lombards now became naturalized Piedmontese subjects. The effect then, of the decree of February 13th, 1853, was to reduce to penury a large number of Piedmontese subjects, by a law which not only broke the pledged word of Austria in the treaty of 1849, but the personal word of the Emperor himself as given in the rescript of December of that year.

The publication of the decree of sequestration fell like a bombshell on Piedmont. Its unfairness, illegality, and vindictive spirit were plain to all. But the nation remained calm and restrained, despite the provocation to an outburst of anger and a display of bellicose spirit, for which it is not unlikely Austria hoped. The first act of the Government was a dispatch to Count Adrian di Revel, the Sardinian Minister at Vienna, pointing out the illegality of the procedure, and requesting to know definitely, whether or not the sequestration applied to those who were now Sardinain subjects. While awaiting the reply, the Government approached Count Francesco Arese, a close personal friend of Louis Napoleon, and one of those who were most severely hit by the Austrian decree, to lay the case for Piedmont before the Emperor. At the same time, Cavour bethought himself of Massimo d'Azeglio, who was in London selling his pictures, and whose influence with English men of state he knew to be very great, and wrote to him begging him to use his influence with the English Government.[1]

[1] Chiala, vol. ii. No. 253. 'Austria in striking at our citizens has aimed at

On March 9th the reply of Count Buol was presented to the Government by the Austrian Minister, Count Apponyi. It was an angry document, full of vague and unsubstantial charges against Piedmont and the policy and behaviour of its Government. The decree, said Count Buol, was 'issued by the Emperor in the plenitude of his power and in the incontestable interest of the preservation of his Empire,' and he continued, 'we recognize to no foreign Government the right of demanding from us proofs of the culpability of individuals among the *émigrés*, since it is not a question of the execution of a judicial decree, but of a measure of public safety, justified by notorious facts and applied to possessions situated within the domains of the Emperor.' In regard to the general conduct of the Piedmontese Government was the following angry paragraph:

> The Sardinian Government, which has received the emigrants and accorded to them its protection, to-day raises its voice in their favour. May we not be allowed to ask what this Government has done to stop or to paralyse the activity employed by these emigrants to our detriment? Has it put a bit upon this abominable Press, directed by them, and which at bottom is nothing but a constant appeal to revolt? Has it lent us its help to seize the threads of the plots woven unceasingly by these refugees? Has it, before this last outbreak, expelled those that we have pointed out as the most dangerous among them? Far from it. It has pushed its partiality for the *émigrés* up to the point of openly violating the treaty of extradition made with Austria, refusing peremptorily to surrender to us those among them who were accused of the crime of high treason.

On receipt of this note, the Piedmontese Government, after full discussion, forwarded to Vienna a second note. In this, after expressing his surprise at the manner in

discrediting our Government in the eyes of Italy and Europe. It would achieve this end if after repeated and vain efforts we should remain with our hands in our pockets. We cannot allow the constitutional and liberal principles of which we are the last defenders in the south of Europe to be vilified. Driven to extremes we shall either act with vigour or resign. England cannot stand by and see our country reduced to such a choice of extremes. The help of England will prevent this.'

which Count Buol avoided the point at issue, General Dabormida reviewed in detail the legal aspect; after which he firmly rebutted the vague charges made against his Government, instancing the Press Law, of which Austria could always avail herself for redress; and pointing out that the refusal of Piedmont to surrender culprits was due to the fact that the treaty did not embrace those accused of political crimes.

Count Buol's answer to the second Piedmontese note was largely a repetition of his first reply. Insisting that it was a measure of public safety, regarding which no other nation had any right to interfere, he characterized the emigrants, amongst whom were many of the best known and respected names in Lombardy, as 'felons lying under the accusation of the crime of high treason.' He admitted he could not tell the innocent from the guilty, so that the only way of dealing with them was to punish all alike, adding that 'the last rising at Milan has given the Imperial Government the right to seize all those upon whom fall grave suspicion of complicity.' No evidence of any kind was adduced, but in its place angry abuse and insinuations. It was the defence of an exasperated bully.[1]

But by far the most trenchant criticism of the Austrian notes came from Sir James Hudson, who, with undiplomatic directness but with perfect accuracy, summed them up in a letter to Lord Clarendon in these words:

These notes declare broadly and distinctly that, if Piedmont does not perform the office of a police agent for Austria, she shall be crushed. The supreme will of the Emperor and the safety of the Austrian Empire is the sole ground put forward for the conduct of the one state towards the other. There is a broad hint that a change of Government in Piedmont; a radical alteration of the Constitution; the destruction of the liberties of the Piedmontese Press, may soften the blow which Austria declares she is ready to deal at Piedmont: but, even with these conditions, it is clear that the part

[1] The text of the Piedmontese notes will be found in Zini, *Storia d'Italia*, vol. iii.

subsequently assigned to Piedmont is that of police agent to Austria. Under these circumstances I see no hope of an amicable settlement of the difficulty which has been created by Austria, who has rendered it impossible for Piedmont to retreat with honour from the position and the rank she holds amongst the states of Europe.[1]

On receipt of the second note from Count Buol, Cavour saw plainly that there was no hope of any withdrawal on the part of Austria. To prolong the controversy was useless. An admirable memorandum stating Piedmont's contentions in full, moderate in tone and lucid in arrangement, was drawn up by Cibrario and sent to Count Revel at Vienna, with orders to present it and then to return to Piedmont, leaving the Legation in the hands of a chargé d'affaires. Copies were then circulated to the Powers through the Piedmontese diplomatic agents, with a covering letter stressing the principal points to be emphasized.[2] There can be little doubt that Austria's action in this matter was the joint work of Vienna and Rome, and that its true object was to sting Piedmont into reprisals, and thus open up a situation in which, to avoid a declaration of war, Cavour and the National Party would have to resign power and make room for a Government under the influence of Austria. Hudson put the situation with his usual frankness:

Antonelli has attempted to cajole Cavour in negotiation and he has miserably failed. Rome is stopped, checked by Piedmont: she applies to Austria for assistance, and it is granted. Austria is in her turn astonished to find a mere handful of men bar her progress and pretensions successfully. She cannot understand how it is that a government is found in Italy, over whom threats, women, and money has no influence: who are insensible to fear and deaf to personal favour: who think ribbons are best seen upon women, and money in the pockets of those who work honestly. What I dread is not the

[1] F.O. 67, vol. 193. No. 35.

[2] Text in Zini. See also Bianchi, *Stor. Doc. Diplom.*, vol. vii. c. iv. § 2. Lord Clarendon characterized it as a document 'not less remarkable for the moderation of its language than for the soundness of its principles and the able marshalling of its arguments.'

act of sequestration, but the feeling of hate for this country (Piedmont), which must grow from the failure of this great blunder. The strength of the Cavour or Constitutional party is that its maintenance is a question of national existence. Austria knows that if she can destroy Cavour's government she can reign supreme in Italy.[1]

Cavour's handling of this question of the sequestrations, his first essay in European diplomacy, was masterly. It was dealt with promptly, firmly, and with perfect dignity. He stopped it before it degenerated into a war of 'notes' and closed it with an unanswerable statement of his case. If he failed in his immediate object of saving the innocent victims of Austria's anger, he achieved his ultimate purpose of putting Austria utterly in the wrong in the eyes of Europe, and raising Piedmont still higher in general esteem. 'Austria,' Cavour said to a friend, 'has made a grave mistake. She has raised public opinion against herself throughout all Europe. Thinking to do us an injury she has rendered us a great service. Have no doubt; we shall profit by it: we shall cross the Ticino all the sooner.' No higher tribute could well be paid to Piedmont's attitude throughout than the brief note of Hudson to Lord Clarendon:

> I am bound as the Queen's minister at this Court to declare to your Lordship that having attentively followed the proceedings of the two countries on this question, there is not one word in General Dabormida's exposition of his case which is not borne out by facts: and that the conduct of Piedmont, of her Sovereign, her Government, and her people, has been open, honest, and loyal towards Austria.

Looked at in relation to Cavour's policy as a whole, this incident has a genuine importance. Cavour saw clearly that the preliminary condition for the realization of Italian independence was the moral support of Europe. He had to reverse the accepted axiom that Austria was benefiting Europe by policing Italy. He had to win Europe to the true view that Austria was a brutal

[1] Clarendon Papers, Hudson to Cavour, April '53.

tyrant. On the material side, the prosperity of Piedmont
was a first proof, but even stronger was that which was
now revealed, namely, Austria's scorn of legality, utter
lack of justice, and want of self-control. Metternich
spoke truly, when he remarked a few years later, 'There
is only one statesman in Europe, that is M. de Cavour,
and he unfortunately is against us.'

The attitude of the Chamber of Deputies during these
anxious weeks was an object lesson in their constitutional
development. A few years before, such an occasion
would have been an opportunity for awkward questions
and wild patriotic speeches, but now they quietly continued their work without raising the least difficulties
for the Cabinet. But they still had their part to play.
When the Memorandum had been delivered, and
Sardinia's protest registered by the recall of their
Ambassador from Vienna, Cavour moved in the
Chamber the appropriation of 400,000 lire to be used
as compensation for those suffering from the sequestration of their property. In a tone of quiet dignity he
wound up the short debate with these words:

> No one of the speakers on the Bill before the Chamber having
> offered any criticism of it, is a fresh proof that, when one
> deals with questions affecting the honour, dignity, or inde-
> pendence of the nation, every difference of opinion that may
> exist in this Parliament, disappears immediately. I need not
> then defend this Bill. I need only congratulate the Chamber,
> as I might also congratulate the country, on the unanimity
> of opinion shown during these last few days, both in the
> Capital and in the provinces, upon this measure.

The final expression of the National feeling came,
appropriately enough, from the King, when shortly
afterwards, on the recommendation of his Prime
Minister, he raised Count Carlo Borromeo and the
Marquess Giorgio Pallavicino—two of the leading
Lombard émigrés—to the dignity of Senators of the
Kingdom.

Before the session closed Cavour brought in and
passed a Bill to subsidize a transatlantic steamship

service. He took the occasion to review the progress of the country, and his speeches, both in the Chamber of Deputies and in the Senate, throw much light on the policy of economic regeneration that he had been all along pursuing. It is a very shallow view of Cavour that regards him as so many of his contemporaries did, as an unimaginative business man immersed in finance. From first to last Cavour's work was essentially creative, and beneath the technical mastery of facts and figures a deeper spirit is plainly discernible. It was not merely that Cavour was fascinated by the 'romance of industry,' his true motive force was deeper still. From the outset he had determined to free his nation from that medieval spirit that paralysed industry, and kept the masses of the people in obsequious poverty beneath an ignorant landowning class and a narrow and bigoted clergy. To do this in a poor country, such as Piedmont, it was necessary to adopt a daring system of finance: to place foreign loans and attract foreign capital; to use the national income for capital expenditure rather than for paying his bills. And the soul of the nation rose to meet him. In his last speech of the session, delivered in the Senate on this question of the transatlantic shipping subsidy, he put this policy with an eloquence and potency that lifts it almost into the region of romance, closing his speech with these words:

When, after our glorious but unfortunate struggle, we found ourselves in a most difficult condition, faced with an enormous adverse balance, it was then that the two roads lay before us; that of strict economy, of establishing an equilibrium by means of little savings—and the one we follow now. You have chosen this latter; and, while with one hand you give a favourable vote to the new taxes, you have had the courage, the boldness, to sanction reforms that tend to diminish still further our receipts: it appears almost insane; yet the fact has shown the wisdom of your policy. As I have said, you might have postponed to a time more opportune, these new projects and extraordinary expenses: you have done the opposite: you have imposed on the Government the duty of carrying out quickly the works already undertaken. You have sanctioned many new taxes: you have spent millions upon the new railways of Novara and Susa during the last year. This year you have been still more daring. You have sanctioned schemes for the two most perilous and difficult railways in Europe: you have voted ten millions for new roads in Sardinia: you have offered a guarantee of $4\frac{1}{2}$ per cent. to one of the most costly of our railway undertakings: after this, will you stop before the expenditure of some hundreds of thousands of lire? After having spent hundreds of millions to make Genoa one of the great commercial centres of Europe, will you refuse some half million of lire to assure to her the commerce of America? You will not, I trust, render yourselves guilty of this anomaly; you will, I hope, give your vote for one further step on the road you have hitherto trodden; a road replete with difficulties, surrounded by obstacles and not devoid of dangers, but one which, if we follow with energy, prudence, wisdom, and firmness, will for certain lead this courageous nation to noble destinies.[1]

A long and arduous session ended early in July. One hundred and forty-two bills had been presented, one hundred and twenty-four passed, and two rejected. 'The temper and the diligence of the House,' wrote Sir James Hudson, 'were beyond all praise; the members were never seduced from the proper sphere of their action into disputations upon politics. The Chamber of Deputies has given during the last session abundant proof of their love of order, of the country, and of their sovereign.'

Cavour, tired out with the work of the session, went to recuperate at Pesio, and later went for the autumn to Leri. He was far from idle, busying himself with the next year's Budget, as we can see by the numerous short notes to officials at Turin. The summer of 1853 proved a season of sore trial to Piedmont. First came an outbreak of the dreaded cholera; then the disease known as the *crittogama*, struck the vines; and then the harvest failed. Bread prices began to soar, and with the inevitable suffering came unrest and discontent. Cavour was advised by well-meaning friends to buy

[1] *Discorsi*, vol. vii. p. 621.

up the corn supply and establish a Government monopoly, or else to follow the procedure of the King of Naples and fix a price for corn. Cavour had his own solution, but it was not that of his friends. He sent for Antonio Scialoia, the late professor of political economy at the University, and said to him, 'Do you know what they advise me to do to lower the price of bread? Either to establish a monopoly or decree a fixed price? What do you advise?' 'I say,' answered Scialoia, 'that in this case it is necessary to proclaim absolute free trade in corn.' And Cavour, rubbing his hands, as he always did when pleased, remarked, 'At last I have found a man who in these matters thinks the same as I do.' Twenty-four hours afterwards, Cavour reduced the tax on imported corn to ten *soldi* per hectolitre.[1] But Cavour had plenty of enemies only too ready to exploit the difficulties of the situation. Reds and Blacks alike stirred up trouble. While the Reds went about spreading the most iniquitous calumnies, attributing the shortness of bread to Cavour and his friends, who, they said, bought up the corn for private speculation; a view supported by such papers as *La Maga* and Brofferio's *Voce del deserto*; the Blacks passed on to Vienna and Paris garbled stories of the unrest and revolutionary spirit in the country. Hübner, the Austrian Ambassador in Paris, recounted these rumours to Drouyn de Llys, who in turn passed them on to England. Lord Clarendon promptly wrote to Sir James Hudson to make a tour of the country, and report. On his return he wrote in reply:

> I have been unable to discover any traces whatever of such ideas on the part of this Government and people. I have seen great content under privations amongst the labouring population: great industry in commerce and manufactures: great loyalty to the Crown and perfect confidence in the working of the constitution and in the uprightness of the King's Ministers. I notice that the extreme factions both red and black are exceedingly active, and both are working for a like

[1] Chiala, *Lettere*, No. 300. vol. ii and note.

purpose, the subversion of the present Government. After carefully reviewing the present condition of the country and the conduct of its Government, it is my duty to acquaint your Lordship that I consider the language used by M. Drouyn de Llys, as false in substance, and as unjust as it is unwarranted.[1]

Not long before, the King had said to the Duc de Guiche, the new French Minister, 'The Austrian Government presses upon Piedmont by all imaginable means. Her agents surround my throne and urge me to overturn the Constitution. . . . If Piedmont loses her institutions, the National Party disappears with them, and that of Austria takes their place at once, with the firm intention of delivering Piedmont and her King, who becomes a crowned vassal, over to Austria. This shall never happen while I am living.'

The combined efforts of Reds and Blacks against Cavour at last produced a result. On the evening of October 18th, while Cavour was busy at the Ministry of Finance, an excited crowd of hooligans attacked Cavour's Palazzo; the timely arrival of a picket of carabineers soon drove off and dispersed the crowd, but their temper was ugly, and had Cavour been at home he might have shared the fate of Prina.[2] Congratulations on his escape, and protests against the outrage, were showered upon Cavour, who treated the incident with his usual calmness and courage. It was just at this time that Cavour made his first change in the Cabinet. A year of office had dissipated all fear of revolutionary tendencies in Cavour's policy, and, as Boncompagni was anxious to resign his post, Cavour invited Rattazzi to join the Cabinet as Minister of Justice, his predecessor taking his place as President of the Chamber of Deputies. The change was not without influence on the policy of the Cabinet, for Rattazzi brought ecclesiastical measures once more to

[1] F.O. 67, vol. 195. No. 109.

[2] A hated Austrian Finance Minister, murdered by the mob at Milan in 1814. See Tivaroni, *Italia durante il dominio Francese*. 'To share the fate of Prina' became a byword.

the forefront of the Cabinet's programme, by preparing a long-talked-of measure on the repartition of the Ecclesiastical revenues.

The winter session opened in November, but after sitting only eight days Parliament was dissolved and a general election announced. The immediate cause of this was the defeat in the Senate of a Bill to enlarge the powers of the National Bank, that having passed the Chamber of Deputies earlier in the year, now came up before the Senate. The Bill was of importance, though its immediate application was perhaps not necessary, for it was the corollary to the new economic system. Cavour realized that if there should be a rapid extension of trade, as he hoped, cheap and easy credit was an essential of success. He proposed therefore to transfer the functions of the General Treasury to the National Bank, by opening a current account in the name of the Government into which all unemployed sums were to be paid; in return for which benefit the Bank was to keep at the disposal of the Government a sum of not less than 15 millions of lire. The sole right of note issue was, in future, to be held by the National Bank; the Bank was to open a branch to be known as the 'Bank of Sardinia' in that island. The main contention of the Committee in moving its rejection was that the Bill established a banking monopoly and was a betrayal of the principle of liberty of commerce of which Cavour had been so strong a supporter. Cavour opened his defence of the Bill with a brief history of banking operations in the country. He recalled the founding of the banks of Genoa and Turin, followed by their amalgamation as the National Bank, which in turn had been followed by permission to double the capital, on condition of opening two branch banks at Nice and Vercelli. We now have, he went on to explain, a bank with a capital of 32 millions. Such a bank could, without the least danger, issue notes for 60 millions which for some years to come would be ample for all the needs of the country. Comparing the value of large banks with

small, he pointed out the value of the former in times of
crises and difficulty.   In any ordinary commercial crisis
a strong bank could always assist a weak one.   In times
of national crisis there were only two remedies, to raise
the bank rate or to borrow from abroad; if this latter
was necessary a big bank could get money where small
banks could not.   Dealing with the objections to the
proposed functions of the Bank as the General Treasury,
that it gave too much power and influence to the Direc-
tors, while putting the Government to some extent in
its hands, Cavour explained that this could not happen.
The system of national accountancy was fixed by law.
The taxes collected in the provinces must be paid into
the Provincial Treasuries, which, after making the
necessary disbursements, kept the surplus unless ordered
by the Minister of Finances to send their balances to
the General Treasury; so that the amount of the
Government's current account at the Bank would be
entirely in the hands of the Finance Minister.   The
system thus differed from that of England and Belgium,
where all taxes were paid direct into the National Bank.
The advantages were, economy, by doing away with the
expenses of the General Treasury, a more rapid circulation in the country, and the fact that surplus sums would
be earning interest instead of being locked up in the
Government strong room.[1]   Cavour's gift of lucidity
was never more fully displayed than in this speech, nor
his power of ready and convincing reply.   When the
success of the small banks in Scotland was urged in
favour of complete liberty, Cavour, analysing the cause,
showed that it was due, not to their circulation which
was exceedingly small (he gave the figures), but to the
fact that they were saving-banks, and made their profit
by clever use of their deposits, and added that, such
banks he would always promote and encourage.
Cavour's arguments, however, could not save the Bill,
which was thrown out by 32 votes against 28.

[1] Cavour attributed the monetary crises taking place at this time in
America to the law which immobilized vast sums of gold kept as a reserve.

The reason for this adverse vote is uncertain. Roberto D'Azeglio, writing to his son, declares that many of the senators felt themselves unqualified to express an opinion on so technical a subject: that Cavour's speech made a very favourable impression, but that, when they saw all the *gros bonnets* of finance against them they thought there must be some great unknown danger and voted against the Bill. Farini, on the other hand, attributed the Government's defeat to political motives. Writing to Castelli, he says, 'the opposition to Cavour in the Senate is political: real friends there he has few, enemies many. The Chamber of Deputies is old and tired; if it is spurred into action, it will drag itself along but it will do no really valuable work. I believe that to this evil one must bring a prompt remedy, and the only efficacious one is the immediate dissolution of Parliament.'[1] There was truth in both these points of view. Cavour's economic views were opposed by those who knew little about them, simply because he was the author of them. Clericals and reactionists in the Senate voted against him on principle. But Cavour had also opponents of a more worthy kind. Behind the adverse vote of the Senate lay the economic beliefs of one of the most learned economists in the country, Francesco Ferrara, the Professor of Political Economy at Turin University. In the columns of his paper *L'Economista* with its motto *Libertà per tutto e in tutto*, he fought what he considered the monopoly policy of the Government with unmeasured language and unyielding persistance, and the rejection of this Bill was one of the fruits of his labours.[2]

Cavour was annoyed and disappointed over his defeat. Believing, as he did, that, with the oppressive weight of taxation laid on the country, an increased rapidity of circulation of wealth, such as he believed would follow from his bank policy, was of vital importance, he decided

[1] Chiala, *Lettere*, vol. v. p. 305.
[2] G. Prato, *Francesco Ferrara a Torino*.

to interpret the decision of the Senate as a challenge to the policy of the Government, and make an appeal to the country. On November 20th Parliament was dissolved.

This decision, which came as a great surprise to the country, was not new. As far back as August Rattazzi had written 'the idea of dissolving the Chambers certainly deserves to be taken into consideration, especially now that peace seems assured for some time. The moment would be opportune, for it is certain that the election would result in a big Government majority.' The Parliament had been elected in the autumn of 1849 and had only another year to run. The full effect of the new taxes, which would certainly militate against the Government, was not yet felt in the country. The moment was propitious, the reason sufficient, and Cavour acted at once. Cavour's decision met with success. The Government's firm handling of the sequestration question had gratified the country, and the good results of its economic policy were evident on all sides. The country responded to the call and returned a still larger majority for the Government.

The reforms effected during the three and a half years Cavour had held office were a striking tribute to his genius. The army had been reorganized and strengthened, nearly every department of state had been modernized: important laws had been passed relating to the judicature, and above all was the revolution in the economic and industrial condition of the country. Addressing the Chamber of Deputies on May 8th, 1850, on the state of the national finances, Cavour had said: 'We have, then, to provide 167 millions: the ordinary revenue is estimated at 90 millions, revealing a deficit of 77 millions.' In the estimates for 1854 the revenue was estimated at 122 millions, and the expenditure reduced to 147 millions, leaving a deficit of 25 millions, a reduction of no less than 52 millions of the indebtedness of the State, and Cavour had actually anticipated establishing an equilibrium in

1855! It was a wonderful achievement and one for which Cavour might justly claim full credit. The preliminary task that Cavour had set himself was achieved just in time, for the 'European complication' from which he hoped at last to draw real benefit for Italy was opening before him in the Crimean War, and Piedmont was ready now to play its destined part.

V. THE CRIMEAN ALLIANCE

Cavour's Attitude—Opinion in the Country—The King—Position of Austria—First Suggestions—Dabormida's Attitude—Cabinet Opposition—The matter drops—Difficulties in the Country—Negotiations renewed—England proposes Alliance—The Secret Articles—Austrian Convention of December 2nd—Struggles in the Cabinet—Alliance without Conditions—Discussion of Treaty in the Chamber—La Marmora in London and Paris—The King's Review—The Contingent sails.

WITH the opening of 1854 the Crimean War began to cast its shadow across Europe. It came as no surprise to Cavour. As long ago as 1835 he had written while on a visit to England, 'if Russia encroaches much farther upon Turkey, it will only have the result of stirring up the Government here to contain this ambitious power within reasonable limits by force of arms.' In introducing his commercial treaty with France in 1851 he had repeated the warning, envisaging a European situation in which the West was arrayed in arms against the East. Foreseeing this possibility, his policy had always been one of friendship with England and France, especially the latter. 'It is above all upon France that our destiny depends,' he had written to his friend Castelli in 1852, 'for good or ill we must be her partner in the great game that sooner or later must be played out in Europe.' It is not, therefore, surprising that in his own mind Cavour was already planning an alliance with the Western Powers in the struggle that was looming in the distance. But the crux of the problem lay in the attitude adopted by Austria. If she joined Russia, as Cavour hoped rather than expected, the war would probably become European, and in the event of victory Italy might easily recover her freedom.[1] But if she joined France and England, what could Piedmont do? Could she fight alongside Austria, and if she did, what reward could she gain? The answer to this lay in the field of international diplomacy.

[1] Mayor, No. 79. Cavour to Hambro. 'If Austria declares for Russia and the war becomes general; then we must perforce take part in it.'

In this idea of participating in the coming struggle Cavour was almost alone. The notion of taking part in a war against Russia was something quite outside the orbit of the average Piedmontese mentality. In their opinion there was only on: country to fight, and that was Austria; and only one place to fight in, and that was Lombardy. To send troops out of the country was suicidal. Then there was the expense; the fact that they had no quarrel with Russia; and above all, that there was nothing to gain by it. It was hardly surprising that, when Cavour's audacious plan was first made known, the Cabinet, the Parliament, and the majority in the country, were all against it.

The path of Cavour at the opening of 1854 bristled with difficulties. The reasons why Piedmont should remain neutral were only too painfully obvious. She was small, she had no direct interest in the quarrel, and she was in no financial condition to stand such a strain. All of such reasons Cavour appreciated, and all of them his wider vision discounted. The instinct of the statesman told him that now was the day of salvation, and he never swerved from his determination to bring his country into the ranks of the combatants. He converted the Cabinet, Parliament, and the country; he risked his own political future; he hazarded the destiny of his native land; and all equally in a venture in which success remained a matter of pure conjecture until the very last moment. But he never hesitated, and in the end his audacity was more than justified.

Cavour's first step was to sound the King. As early as January 1854, three months before war was declared, Cavour said to Victor Emmanuel, 'Does it not seem to Your Majesty that we ought to find a way to take part in the war that the Western Powers are about to declare on Russia?' To which the King replied in his abrupt way, 'Certainly, and if I cannot go myself I will send my brother!'[1] Assured of the Royal support, Cavour next looked out for a suitable channel through which

---

[1] Massari, *Vittorio Emmanuele II*, c. xxxiv.

to let the Ministers of the Allied Powers know his own attitude and that of the King. In February he went to Genoa for the opening of the completed railway from Turin, and while there opened his mind to a certain Count Toffetti on the subject. Count Toffetti was a distinguished Milanese and a friend of Sir James Hudson, the English Minister, who in 1848 had been sent by the Provisional Government to endeavour to win the King of Naples to make war on Austria. Unconnected in any way with the Piedmontese Government, he was an admirable unofficial agent for Cavour's purpose.[1]

In the meantime, in preparation for war, both sides were pressing Austria for an alliance, but without success. Her position was in truth one of great difficulty, and the tortuous policy she pursued was conditioned by her situation. Her natural sympathies were with Russia. As far as political tradition and methods went, Austria was Russia's local representative in Europe, as her own provinces as well as Italy had good reason to know. In 1849, a Russian army had saved the Hapsburg Empire from disruption, and if personal gratitude had any weight, Franz Joseph would now help a friend in need. But Austria could not do as she liked. She had her interests both in Germany and in Italy to consider. One factor in the situation was the attitude of Piedmont. The relations between them were little less than an armed neutrality, and Piedmont's army was not to be despised; for if Austria had good reason to scorn her leadership in the past, she had a great respect for the fighting qualities of her troops, and Piedmont kept her powder dry.[2] Austria dare not join Russia, for the moment she had fully committed herself

[1] Massari, *Cavour*, c. xxi. *Diario Politico di M. Provana di Collegno*, April 18, 1854. 'The object of the last journeys of Hudson to Genoa were conferences with Toffetti, who thinks that Piedmont should send an army to the East in the pay of France and England.'

[2] La Marmora to D'Azeglio, April 1853. 'We can put 70,000 men and 120 guns in the field in a fortnight, and the men are far better instructed and much more disciplined than they were in 1848 and 1849.' Chiala, *Lettere*, vol. ii. p. 29, note.

and sent an army to the east, Piedmont would for
certain join the allies and invade Lombardy, with or
without French and English help; and even a double-
headed eagle was not prepared for a war on two fronts.
But if Austria dare not join Russia, she would not fight
against her. No inducement the allies could offer would
compensate Austria for the enmity of her great eastern
neighbour, whose influence over the Slav population in
the Hapsburg monarchy was incalculable, and whose
anger at such duplicity and black ingratitude was not to
be lightly esteemed.

Austria, approached by France early in the year,
threw the blame for her hesitation to join the allies on
Piedmont. The position in Italy was too uncertain and
the attitude of Piedmont was threatening. Napoleon
replied with an official note in the *Moniteur* which, after
alluding to the success of the negotiations at Vienna,
added that matters were complicated by the fear of
revolutionary troubles in Greece and Italy 'which are
in direct opposition to the interests of France . . . the
Government cannot allow that if the flags of Austria
and France unite in the East, any one should attempt
to divide them on the Alps.'[1] When Turin asked for
explanations, France replied that the remarks in the
Moniteur had references to the 'revolutionaries.'[2] But
Cavour was not deceived. Then Lord Clarendon
sounded the English Minister in Tuscany, and received
the same reply, adding, that Marshal Radetzky had even
spoken of the occupation of Alessandria as a guarantee.
Then he wrote to Sir James Hudson expressing the
hope that Piedmont would not 'take advantage of the
war for selfish purposes.' The English Minister
promptly requested an audience and had a long talk
with Cavour. Without consulting his Cabinet, but
knowing that the King agreed with him, Cavour
offered to send a contingent of troops to aid the allies

[1] *Moniteur Universel*, February 22nd.
[2] Drouyn de Lluys to the Duke de Guiche, March 6th. See Matter,
Cavour et l'Unité Italienne, vol. ii. p. 286.

if Austria declared war on Russia. Hudson drew up
the results of the interview in a dispatch, but before
sending it submitted it to the Foreign Secretary.
General Dabormida thoroughly disagreed with Cavour's
suggestion. The Prime Minister, he said, was only
expressing his own opinion; the matter had never been
brought before the Cabinet and he could not agree to
the contents of the dispatch.[1] So Hudson burnt it, and
in its place he wrote a private letter to Lord Clarendon
in which after acknowledging his Lordship's letter he
went on as follows:

> I determined to speak frankly and fully to Cavour. I said
> that I thought the time had come when he ought to enable
> Her Majesty's Government to set at rest all those Austrian
> apprehensions, and more especially, as an explicit declaration
> on his part, would enable Austria to march against Russia
> if she was so disposed, and would deprive her of the excuse
> of not marching if she were false. I said, your army is
> 45,000 strong, too many for peace, and too few for war in
> Italy; Austria suspects you (ungraciously and unjustly), if
> you were asked to diminish your army by a third at this
> moment you would decline under existing circumstances,
> and I agree with you. But supposing, as a guarantee for your
> conduct in Italy (Austria having declared war against Russia),
> you were invited to send one-third of your army to the
> Danube to fight by the side of the allied army, would you do
> so? Cavour replied: Yes, and if you desire it, you shall reduce
> your question to writing and I will answer it.[2] I took this
> step in order that there might be no mistake upon the subject.
> I think after this, we ought to hear no more of Austria's
> 'not being able to concentrate her troops for the purpose of
> acting against Russia because she fears revolutionary move-
> ments in the neighbourhood of Lombardy.' (Mr. Scarlett,
> No. 25, 11 Mar.) At all events, here is the Duke of Genoa

[1] Bianchi, *Stor. Doc.*, vol. vii. c. 5.

[2] On a separate page Hudson gives the question and answer:
Hudson: Que ferait le Gouvernement de Sardaigne dans le cas où l'Autriche
ayant déclaré la guerre à la Russie il serait invité par l'Angleterre et par la
France à prendre part à la guerre d'Orient?
Cavour: Mon opinion personnelle est que dans ce cas le Gouvernement
du Roi devrait accéder à la motion qui lui serait adressée et envoyer de 12
à 15,000 hommes à l'Orient.

Clarendon Papers, April 14th, 1854.

and 15,000 good bayonets at your Lordship's orders if you think proper to demand them. Austria would, of course, on her side engage not to molest Piedmont during the àbsence of the contingent. I told M. de Cavour that he was quite at liberty to tell the French Minister, and he said he would do so.

The significance of this incident should not be missed. Though the question had not been discussed by the Cabinet, Cavour had sounded various members as to sending troops to the East, and had found nothing but opposition. Determined, if possible, to get his own way, he fell back on the line he had so often found succeed with D'Azeglio, of presenting the Cabinet with a *fait accompli*; that is, he hoped, as the result of Hudson's dispatch, to have a definite request for a contingent to lay before the Cabinet at its next meeting, believing that they could not reject it. This plan had been spoilt by the cautious diplomacy of Dabormida, and in consequence, nearly a year was to pass before the treaty was an accomplished fact. This is probably the meaning of the remark Cavour made to his niece, the Marchesa Alfieri, when in the spring of this year she one day asked him, 'Why don't you send 10,000 men to the Crimea?' 'Ah,' said Cavour with a sigh, 'if every one had your courage what you have just proposed would be already done.'[1]

Cavour brought up the general question of participating in the war a few days later at a Cabinet meeting, but he was supported only by Cibrario, the Minister of Education. La Marmora was dismayed by the expense; Dabormida made the raising of the sequestrations an essential preliminary condition; other members urged the foolishness of dividing their forces in the face of the enemy and taking part in an unnecessary war fought at a distance; to some the idea of being the ally of Austria was unthinkable. All regretted 'the precipitation' of the President of the Council. Very little secrecy appears to have surrounded the deliberations of the Cabinet; perhaps Cavour was anxious for the matter

[1] de la Rive, *Le Comte de Cavour.*

to be discussed in public, for on April 20th we find the
following note in the Diary of the Marchesa di Collegno:

> To-day Collegno spoke to Dabormida and learns from him
> that the proposal of Hudson to send Piedmontese troops to
> the East was rejected by the Cabinet. Cavour and Cibrario
> were the only members who from the first were very favour-
> able to it, but fortunately they changed their minds. La
> Marmora, Paleocapa, and Rattazzi were strongly opposed to
> it, so also Dabormida. They proposed to strip Piedmont of
> her army and send them like Swiss in the pay of foreign
> Powers, and this to please Austria! Austria demanded also
> the citadel of Alessandria, but this even England opposed.
> Collegno breathes more freely to-day now he is assured that
> such an enormity will not be sanctioned. The Lombards
> were favourable to it, who knows why?

This account, which coming from Dabormida must
be accepted as substantially correct, is valuable as
revealing very clearly two of the chief objections levelled
at Cavour's scheme. First, the question of the subsi-
dizing of the troops; and secondly, the accusation that
they were being sent abroad on the demand of Austria.
As to the former, it seems undeniable that at first
Cavour was willing to let France and England find the
money. For four years Cavour had worked desperately
hard to restore the finances. To establish an equilibrium in the Budget was a triumph very near his heart.
In the King's speech at the opening of Parliament he
had spoken of the 'nearly restored finances,'[1] a phrase
he had defended by the bold prophecy that it would be
realized in 1855. Now, he saw ahead a fresh mass of
debt, hopeless deficits, and more taxation. It is scarcely
to be wondered at that he looked eagerly to shifting the
new burden on to other shoulders. But he quickly
saw his mistake. When he first broached the subject to
La Marmora, the latter asked him, 'Where will you find
the money?' and when Cavour replied, 'We must look
to England for it,' La Marmora was up in arms at

[1] The qualifying adverb was the suggestion of the King, Cavour having
spoken of the 'restored finances.'

once.[1] The mere suggestion of the army being used as mercenaries roused the old Piedmontese pride. The army was furious; officers sent in their papers; and Cavour realized that such a condition would prejudice hopelessly the very cause he had at heart, and at once determined to shoulder the financial burden. The second accusation, that the army was to be sent abroad to calm the suspicions of Austria, was even more difficult; it was one of those statements which it was impossible either to prove or to disprove; there was just sufficient ground for its truth to justify its repetition by those who wished to believe it. Cavour denied it, and as far as possible ignored it. The position he took up was that, the instant Piedmont was invited by France and England to join the alliance, with the necessary guarantee against attack by Austria in the absence of the army, he would use all his power to ensure acceptance of the offer, regardless of the attitude of Austria. He hoped the invitation would come before Austria made up her mind to join the alliance, but he did not think it likely; and while waiting, he bent all his energies on converting public opinion to recognize the value of participation in the war. For this, time and free discussion were necessary, and Cavour wisely ceased to press the question for the time being, and allowed the negotiations to be conducted by the slow and prudent method of his Foreign Minister, reserving the use of his personal influence for the moment when a decision became imperative.

The position at the end of April, at which date the first phase of the negotiations may be said to have closed, was this: the allies knew that Cavour and the King were willing to join the alliance and send a contingent of troops, once the attitude of Austria was clear, but that the rest of the Cabinet was against them, and opinion was divided in the country. On the other hand, Cavour was aware that no direct request would probably

[1] Massari, *Alfonso La Marmora*, p. 143. See also his speech in the Chamber in Brofferio, *Storia del Parlamento Subalpino*, vol. vi. p. 737.

be made until the Austrian policy was decided, but that the Sardinian offer was being kept warm by the allies until they saw their way to make use of it.

A policy of prudent reserve and watchfulness was indeed necessary, for the situation was difficult enough.

> The political skein gets more and more tangled [Cavour wrote to a friend], the assassination of the Duke of Parma will make things worse. The Austrians are restless: they send us legions of spies, who would like to make trouble on our borders. They will not succeed. Watch the intrigues of Napoleon. They have been directed lately to the South of Italy especially. Murat's nephew Count Pepoli stayed two months at Genoa, where he conferred with Pepe and other Neapolitans. Yesterday he left for Paris.[1]

In another letter he writes:

> Thank you for the daguerreotype portrait of our friend Mazzini. It may help us to receive him as he deserves, if ever he thinks of paying us a second visit. I am not uneasy regarding him, for we are in a position to checkmate all his plots. Dabormida has written to you about Garibaldi. If he comes simply to revisit his family and children we shall not disturb him in the least; but if he thinks of coming here in the interests of Mazzini we shall not tolerate his presence for a minute. If Garibaldi has warlike intentions it is not to Piedmont that he should direct his steps but in the direction of Naples and Sicily. I know that they expect him in those quarters.[2]

On March 27th war against Russia had been declared by France and England, and on April 12th they signed their Treaty of Alliance, which concluded with an invitation to all the powers of Europe to join with them against Russia. The formal notification reached Turin in May, and on June 2nd Dabormida handed Sardinia's reply to Sir James Hudson and the Duc de Guiche. Correct in form and cold in tone it expressed the Government's appreciation of 'the disinterested devotion with which the Allied Powers pursue in common

---

[1] Cavour to Count Oldofredi, March 29th. Mayor, *Lettere*, No. 81. The Duke of Parma was assassinated on March 26th.
[2] Cavour to Emanuele d'Azeglio, April 4th. Mayor, No. 82.

the triumph of a sane and liberal policy.' Sardinia's reply was printed in the *Moniteur*, and Drouyn de Llys, commenting on it to Villamarina, the Sardinian Minister, said:

> We are quite satisfied with the reply of your Government. It is well that for the moment Piedmont preserves a prudent reserve. But do not neglect to prepare yourselves quietly to face the eventualities that may arise. If Austria joins us frankly and definitely, when she is fully committed and has given solid guarantees, Piedmont will then be able to consider whether she cannot see her way to give us active assistance, in order to have her vote and her share of compensation in the final settlement. If Austria only comes half-way, so much the worse for her, Sardinia will have a favourable opportunity to take a good revenge.[1]

The attitude of France towards the Sardinian alliance was never very satisfactory. She was much more anxious to keep Piedmont from proving an anxiety to Austria than she was to see Sardinian troops in the fighting line. Her policy seems to have been, to keep Piedmont quiet with promises and expectations until after Austria had signed the alliance, and then to ask Piedmont to join, and ship as much of her army as convenient to some safe place like Constantinople as part of an 'army of reserve.' In this way Austria would have an easy mind concerning her Italian provinces, and Piedmont, though flattered by participation in the war, would win no laurels, make no undesirable friendships with England, and remain as dependent as before on France.

Victor Emmanuel, no less than Cavour, was impatient at the cautious and non-committal attitude of his Foreign Secretary, and a few days after the dispatch of the Sardinian reply to the allies, he took a hand in the diplomatic game in person, and invited the Duc de Guiche to come and see him. At this interview the King was blunt and to the point. He was determined, he said, to join the alliance. It was the only reasonable

[1] Text in Massari, *Vittorio Emanuele.* See also Bianchi, *Stor. Doc.,* c. vii.

thing to do. If he could, he would send 30,000 men, but
that was impossible. 'I shall laugh at Austria once my
troops have fought with yours, but do not compromise
me either here or with France,' he added.[1]

The Chamber of Deputies rose for the summer recess
in July, and Cavour, freed from parliamentary duties,
had more time to appraise the situation. The country
was struggling with great difficulties. As he wrote to
Baron Hambro, 'I am wrestling with every possible kind
of trouble. After the food shortage, the *crittogama*;
after the *crittogama*, the war; after the war, the cholera.
This succession of disasters has slowed up and almost
stopped the economic movement that manifested itself
with such energy, and has nearly paralysed my resources. In truth I may say that for two years I govern
in adversity.'[2] Genoa was suffering from the allied
blockade of the Black Sea and her trade with Odessa
was dwindling. The cholera was raging in various parts
of the Kingdom and how to deal with it was a desperate
anxiety. In his spare moments Cavour was studying
medical treatises and sending for information on sanita-
tion. There was difficulty in Savoy as well. The failure
of the vintage had been a severe blow. The new Victor
Emmanuel railway was not doing well, and the work
that Cavour had hoped would absorb the unemployment was at a standstill. All this led to trouble and
discontent with the Government. The hesitations of
Austria, and the consequent inevitable delay in taking
a decided line of action, was giving time for intrigues
to develop. Mazzini was in Bellinzona in May, and his
presence was always a sign of trouble. Republicans and
Murattists were active at Genoa, and at any time some
foolish outbreak might prejudice all Cavour's schemes.
He could do nothing but wait. Both France and
England knew his determination to join the alliance,
but he had first to be asked to do so. 'The best method
of cutting short the very awkward questions arising in

---

[1] Massari, *Vittorio Emanuele*, gives the full text of this interview also
reproduced by Matter.   [2] Mayor, *Nuove Lettere di Cavour*, No. 167.

this country,' wrote Sir James Hudson, 'is to demand the Piedmontese contingent, and as a natural consequence, to make Austria restore to their Sardinian owners their sequestrated estates in Lombardy.'[1] But England was waiting for France, and France for Austria, and Austria was waiting to see how the war went before she decided on which side of the fence to come down. The chance of being asked to join the alliance before Austria came in was growing more and more remote: 'the negative reply of Russia renders the alliance of Austria with the Western Powers daily more probable. It would be useless to try and prevent it,' Cavour wrote early in September. Then Austria added insult to injury in the matter of the sequestrations, by ordering the administrators of the confiscated estates to contribute handsomely out of the revenues of the *émigrés*, to what she cynically termed a 'voluntary loan.' Cavour thought of another protest and even of reprisals, but wiser counsels prevailed. 'For the moment we are constrained to an energetic note upon the new Austrian iniquity sent to Paris and London, repeating that only the absolute necessity of so doing compels us to put up with this fresh insult.[2] With such irritation existing between them it seemed impossible that Sardinia and Austria could fight side by side. But Cavour's instinctive sense of the greatness of the opportunity overrode even the hateful situation of fighting with, instead of against, Austria. Later, in September, he opened his mind once more to Sir James Hudson: 'The time has come,' he said, 'when the public interest of Europe renders it necessary to make common cause with the Western Powers. If Austria marches with France and England, Piedmont will march by the side of Austria to Moscow if necessary. This is no idle boast. There are many Piedmontese still living who marched to Moscow in 1812. The Piedmontese of 1854 will, in a given case, march there again in your cause.'[3]

[1] Clarendon Papers.   [2] Cavour to Count Oldofredi, *Lettere*, vol. ii. No. 320.
[3] Clarendon Papers, September 15th.

The events of the war, however, were soon to put a new value on the Piedmontese alliance. France was more or less indifferent. The Piedmontese contribution was too small to outweigh her position as a hindrance to the chance of winning Austria. But the attitude of England was different. In the middle of September the allied armies had disembarked at Balaclava. The English army was barely half that of France, and the heavy losses suffered at the battle of the Alma, and later at Balaclava and Inkerman (Nov. 5), made the need for reinforcements urgent. In continental warfare it was the inherited tradition of England to supplement the smallness of her own army by hiring the troops of the secondary powers. To raise an army on a cash basis had certain advantages over the orthodox method of alliances. It did away with awkward problems of compensation afterwards, and obviated difficulties from exigent representatives of the smaller Powers at the Peace Conference. This was her policy now, and it is not surprising to find Lord John Russell writing in November to Lord Palmerston:

> Could we not engage some ready made and disciplined force? Might we not get six thousand men from Portugal, ten thousand from Spain, and ten thousand from Piedmont, to be taken on British pay, with their own officers just as they are, but to be under the orders of our own Commander-in-Chief?[1]

No doubt the official concerned with transport and supply was endeavouring to purchase salt pork and biscuits on much the same lines.

In the meantime, whilst events in the field were driving England to close with Cavour's offer of a contingent of troops, opinion on the alliance was crystallizing in Piedmont. The Parliamentary Right under clerical influence was against it.[2] The opposite wing

[1] *Later correspondence of Lord John Russell.*

[2] Hudson, in a letter to Clarendon, mentions that the Pope said to Bevilacqua, 'Io sono un Turco: Io prego per la mezzaluna,' and when Bevilacqua asked why he did not let the faithful know, he replied, 'Perchè non sono libero,' referring to the Russian sympathies of the political section of the Sacra Consulta. *Clarendon Papers.*

even more so. Hatred of the 'man of December,' and the inconceivable position of fighting beside Austria, made the Left irreconcilable. But the masses in town and country, the political centre party, and the more far-seeing minds throughout the country realized the prestige Piedmont and Italy would gain in fighting beside France and England, and favoured the alliance. Cavour had given up all idea of a subsidy, La Marmora had been won over, and the army was beginning to understand that the stain of Novara might yet be wiped out in the Crimea. But the problem of the sequestrations was still a formidable stumbling-block.

The successes of the allies in October and November at last decided Austria on which side of the fence to come down, and on December 2nd she signed a convention with France. It was a typically evasive document, repeating the four points upon which agreement had been reached in April, and stipulating in addition that, if peace was not in sight by the end of the year, the three Powers 'should deliberate without delay upon the most effective means to obtain the object of their alliance.' News of the signature of the Convention reached Turin the same day. It was a severe blow to Cavour, but he determined to make the best of it: 'the alliance of Austria with France and England,' he wrote, 'appears an accomplished fact, we must resign ourselves to it, and try to draw all possible advantage from it.' By Austria's adhesion a new situation was in fact created. As long as Austria remained neutral there was always the chance, however remote, that circumstances might drive her into the arms of Russia. Piedmont never altogether abandoned this hope, and one of the reasons why Cavour was so anxious that Piedmont should be invited to join the alliance, while Austria's line of action was still undecided, was the possibility that Piedmont's alliance with France and England might help to bring about this desirable end.[1] But when

[1] As late as July 12th, 1855, Victor Emanuel wrote to La Marmora: 'The war in the Crimea will last all this year, and next year we shall make

Austria joined first, all hopes that Piedmont would enter on her own terms must be abandoned, and with this went the chance of seeing the Italian question on the agenda of the Conference, and also the likelihood of obtaining any increase of territory at the expense of Austria or her ducal satellites. On the other hand, it made it imperative for Piedmont, with or without conditions, to follow suit, for an alliance of France and Austria was the most dangerous combination possible for the safety of the political edifice in Piedmont.

But if Cavour anticipated that the participation of Austria would render the assistance of Piedmont unnecessary in the eyes of the Western Powers he was mistaken, for it had just the opposite effect. On November 29th, three days before Austria entered the alliance, Sir James Hudson received a private letter from Lord John Russell, written on November 26th, warning him that a contingent of Piedmontese troops was going to be asked for and requesting information as to the reception of such a demand, without however mentioning the approaching convention with Austria. In his reply Hudson said:

> As to the Piedmontese contingent I imagine there will be no difficulty in securing it. The main condition will naturally be some explanation on the part of Austria as regards the sequestrations. But an *amende honorable* is so easy that I cannot conceive that there would be any difficulty on the part of the Cabinet of Vienna, if they are honestly bent on joining with us in the war against Russia. The trouble lies with Austria and France, who have no wish to see Piedmont take an active part in this war. I received your letter on the 29th. On the 2nd December we received news here of the signature of a treaty between France, England, and Austria. I can scarcely reconcile this treaty with the warning held out in your letter of an intention to demand the contingent. I have my own doubts as to Austria and France ever permitting it. I beg you to believe that the 'difficulty will not be here, but an attempt will probably be made by some dextrous

it where we have made it before.' *Biblioteca di Storia Italiana Recente*, vol. iv.

diplomatic *escamotage* to persuade our Government that it is so.[1]

In spite of the English ministers' difficulty in reconciling Austria's adherence to the treaty with a request for Piedmontese support, the latter was genuine, and it was only due to an unfortunate postal error that the Piedmontese Government did not receive the request simultaneously with the information of the Austrian convention with France. For, three days before it was signed, Lord Clarendon had written to Sir James Hudson instructing him to sound the Piedmontese Government as to its willingness (1) to furnish a contingent of troops to be placed under the orders of Lord Raglan and to be paid by England, or (2) to adhere to the treaty of April 10th and provide a contingent at their own expense. This letter unfortunately went astray and did not reach Turin until December 13th.[2] On its arrival Sir James Hudson at once showed it, together with that of Lord John Russell, to General Dabormida, and a Cabinet Council presided over by the King was held the same day. To the first request, that Piedmont should furnish troops to be paid by England, the Cabinet replied by a firm and dignified refusal. 'The Sardinian Government,' the Foreign Secretary wrote, 'could not consider under any circumstances a loan of troops; it is therefore indispensable that an offensive and defensive treaty shall be signed between the Western Powers and Sardinia.' The next day (Dec. 14th) the second proposal was considered, and it was decided to adhere to the treaty of April 10th and provide a

---

[1] Russell Papers, December 8th.

[2] F.O. 67, vol. 201. Telegram from Hudson dated December 13th. 'Your letter of the 29th only arrived this morning,' and attached is this Memo. 'It is not known in the Italian Department to what this refers, but if to a private letter of Lord Clarendon, it would, unless there had been any orders for its being sent on specially from Marseilles, have been forwarded by the Consul there, according to his instructions, at the first opportunity, and it is understood that unless dispatches for Italy are sent on by special messenger there is often much delay in reaching their destination. F.O.' This is followed by an indignant letter from Hudson giving in detail the time taken by the dispatches during the year, usually 8 days to 14; the ordinary post took 3½ days.

contingent of 15,000 troops—on certain conditions. Two conventions were drawn up, one political and the other military, and handed to the two Ministers to forward to their respective governments.

The following is the text of the political convention:

The Sardinian Government desires to adhere simultaneously to the offensive and defensive treaty of April 10th between the Governments of France and England, at the same time it will sign a convention by which it undertakes to furnish a contingent of 15,000 men, on conditions to be fixed, and of which the first is the loan of two millions sterling at 3 per cent., payable after the war on conditions to be determined hereafter.

The two Western Powers declare that they will, at the conclusion of peace, take into consideration the services rendered to the coalition by the Sardinian Government and the sacrifices made in men and money.

By this treaty the Sardinian Government enters the European Concert; takes part in the negotiations, and sits at the Congress held for the re-establishing of peace and restoring the European equilibrium.

Secret Articles

Art. 1. The two Western Powers undertake to employ all their efforts to have the sequestrations upon Sardinian subjects, decreed by Austria on Feb. 13th, 1853, removed.

Art. 2. The high contracting parties will upon the re-establishment of peace take into consideration the state of Italy.

One other condition was made, on the initiative of the King, that Sardinia should be assured that the convention between Austria and France contained no secret clause detrimental to Sardinia.

In his covering letter Hudson did his best to minimize the importance of the secret articles.

The first [he writes] merely engages England and France to use their best endeavour to induce Austria, about to become an ally, to give up that ridiculous mountain in labour—the sequestration question. The second simply mentions Italy in such a way as will enable Piedmont to quiet nine-tenths of the unruly spirits who will be set in motion, if no mention is made of Italy in an instrument of which Piedmont is a party. These articles, in the present condition of the Peninsula, are in my opinion absolutely necessary to defeat the aims of demagogues and revolutionaries of one sort or another.

Lord Clarendon found the Sardinian proposals 'fair enough,' but thought that there would be difficulty in adopting the secret articles. 'We cannot,' he said, 'compel Austria to be just and we should frighten her to death by promising to take the state of Italy into consideration at the end of the war.' At Lord John Russell's suggestion they were sent on to Lord Cowley in Paris, after reading his comments Lord John wrote, 'I agree with Cowley that if Austria hesitates now, it will be good to throw her over. We have Sardinia at our elbow and for my part if on Jan. 15th Austria is not our Ally, I should accept the Sardinian offer.'[1]

But the acceptance of the Sardinian offer, together with the secret articles, to which from this correspondence England seems about to give a favourable answer, was stopped by France. Drouyn de Llys, at the prompting no doubt of Austria, wrote to Lord Clarendon opposing the secret articles and suggesting that Piedmont should be asked simply to adhere to the treaty without condition. It was a clever move, placing Piedmont in the awkward position of either refusing to join the alliance or of coming in without any assurance whatever. The first alternative would be a signal diplomatic victory for Austria, the second would throw an overwhelming responsibility on Cavour.

While this exchange of notes on the fate of Sardinia's offer was taking place, dispatches from the Piedmontese Ministers in Paris and London had made clear to the Sardinian Foreign Secretary the determined objections of both powers to the secret articles. He struggled bravely. In two admirable dispatches, dated December 21st,[2] he put the case for their adoption with force and point. 'We are small,' he wrote, 'and it is only

[1] Clarendon and Russell Papers.   [2] Bianchi, *Stor. Doc.*

too true that the interests of the small are easily placed
in the background. But we ought, all the more perhaps,
to cling to our honour and dignity, for if we once allow
it to be compromised we shall with difficulty find a
chance of recovering it.' But strong and reasonable as
Piedmont's case was from her own point of view, it was
hopeless from that of France and England. How could
they sign two secret articles with one ally aimed directly
at another? Their acceptance was impossible. That
Cavour expected their rejection is seen from his readiness to sign the treaty unconditionally. He would have
been glad enough to have had them, but he was too
clear-sighted not to see how different they looked from
Paris and London. What he was really anxious about
was whether the allies understood and appreciated the
greatness of the sacrifice Piedmont was prepared to
make on their behalf, or whether it was just a matter
of obtaining cannon-fodder.[1]

On January 1st Hudson had an interview with
Dabormida, and read to him Lord Clarendon's dispatch, but no progress was made. 'As long as the
Austrian sequestrations existed,' he said to Hudson,
'it was impossible for the Sardinian Government to
hope to be able to carry public opinion with them, or to
procure the necessary authorization for sending her
army into the Crimea, or for maintaining that army
during the war. In short, unless the sequestrations are
taken off the Government cannot send an army to the
East.' The next day Hudson wrote to Lord Clarendon:

> I regret to say that the King and his Ministry make the with-
> drawal of the sequestrations a *sine qua non* for the dispatch of
> the Piedmontese army to the Crimea. This Government
> cannot admit the Austrian doctrine that, the sequestrations
> are an internal question with which other European nations
> have nothing to do. They say, and I believe every publicist
> in Europe agrees with them, that it is a question of treaty
> stipulations and international law, and as such requires
> redress . . .[2]

[1] See Cavour's letter to the Countess Rasini. Mayor, No. 207.
[2] Clarendon Papers.

On the same day as this was written, the Duc de Guiche returned to Turin from Paris, primed with verbal instructions from Drouyn de Llys, and the last stage of negotiations was entered upon.

On January 7th another fruitless Conference was held, at which the obstinacy of the Foreign Secretary and the indecision of Rattazzi once more prevented any result being reached. After this meeting Cavour was forced to recognize that, if the treaty was to be signed, Dabormida, and possibly Rattazzi, would have to be replaced. On the same day Victor Emmanuel sent for the French Ambassador, and equally with Cavour, expressed his dissatisfaction with the way things were going.

> I know everything, absolutely everything, and I am very dissatisfied [said the King]. I can make nothing of all these hesitations and conditions. I find them stupid; if we act frankly and openly we shall do far better. As for me, my opinion is either to carry through the alliance without conditions or to have nothing to do with it. The Emperor and I have exchanged assurances of friendship: he has my word and I have his: we are incapable of deceit, and that is enough for me. If we are beaten in the Crimea we shall get along somehow, and if we win, well! that will be better for the Lombards than all these articles they want to add to the treaty. Patience: you know what I told you: if these will not go through with it I will take others that will. But it has not yet come to that; for both the country and the Chambers are of my opinion.[1]

Equally with the King, Cavour was prepared to sign the treaty without reserves or restrictions, but up to now he had made no attempt to force his views either on the country or the Cabinet, leaving the negotiations loyally in the hands of his Foreign Minister. But the moment was approaching when he would have to act, for his patience was nearly exhausted. At this critical moment Cavour's hands were strengthened from an unexpected quarter. It was common knowledge in

[1] Massari, *Vittorio Emanuele.*

Turin that the question of the sequestrations was the stumbling-block, and realizing the danger to the country of a rupture in the negotiations, Achille Mauri, in the name and with the full support of the leading men amongst the *sequestrati*, wrote to Cavour begging him not to allow their personal troubles to jeopardize the well-being of the country. Cavour was touched and pleased with this act of generosity which made it easier for him to override, in the wider interests of the nation, the patriotic but obstinate determination of his Foreign Minister.[1]

On January 9th, the Cabinet met once more to consider the position, and decided that, if necessary, they would send La Marmora to Paris to learn at first hand the disposition of the French Government. The same evening, the Ministers of France and England were asked to call at the Ministry of Foreign Affairs, where they found Cavour, La Marmora, Rattazzi, and Dabormida awaiting them. The discussion turned on a fresh suggestion from Dabormida arising out of Lord Clarendon's last dispatch. The Government, he said, was prepared to sign the treaty without the secret articles provided that the substance of them was embodied in a confirmatory note 'un note reversale,' and signed by the Powers. Both ambassadors objected: Hudson 'strongly recommended the Sardinian Government not to insist upon a measure, which must inevitably produce a persistence on the part of Austria in that very state of things which the Government of the King was desirous to remove', and on the question of mentioning Italy at the Peace Conference after the war, he insisted that Great Britain and France 'must reserve to themselves the unfettered right of acting at the time and in the manner they think most expedient.'[2] De Guiche opposed the idea even more strongly, and as, when first mentioned, this solution had been favourably received, Dabormida was both astonished and irritated

---

[1] Bersezio, *Il regno di Vittorio Emanuele II*, vol. vi. p. 270.

[2] F.O. 67, vol. 205.

at the apparent *volte-face* of the two ambassadors.[1] So
heated did the discussion become, notably between
Dabormida and de Guiche, that Cavour, doubting
whether the French Minister truly represented the real
attitude of the Quai d'Orsay, cut short the discussion
by announcing the Cabinet's intention to send the
Minister of War to Paris. This raised a still stronger
protest from the Duke, who declared that such a step
was useless and a slight on his powers as Minister of
France, finally going so far as to say that La Marmora
would be 'badly received' in Paris. The Duke's protest
made a great impression, and when it was supported
by Hudson, the idea was given up. A deadlock seemed
to be reached, and de Guiche, seeing no further use in
prolonging the discussion, remarked that after all it
was natural that Piedmont should desire to remain
neutral.

> There is no question of neutrality [Cavour rejoined at once],
> by the very fact of this discussion we have abandoned
> neutrality, but to justify signing the treaty in the eyes of the
> public, the King's Government requires to see in writing
> those assurances of sympathy already given by the Western
> Powers. Could we not insert, by way of compromise—not
> in the treaty but in a protocol which would precede it—the
> reasons we have put forward for our attitude of reserve?

After some consideration Hudson and de Guiche
acceded to this proposal, and withdrew into an adjoining room. When they had drafted the protocol they
returned and read it to the four Ministers. It was at
once accepted by Cavour and La Marmora, Rattazzi
hesitated, and Dabormida 'preserved a moody silence
and offered no observations upon it.'[2] It was now long
past midnight, the discussion had lasted four hours,
and Cavour brought it to a close. But his own work
was not finished. It was, he knew, the moment for

---

[1] According to Matter this was due to a private letter of Lord Clarendon's
to Hudson in which occurred the sentence 'in any case it is not necessary to
make these expressions of sympathy and unofficial promises the object of
a solemn and public declaration,' vol. ii. p. 306. I have not come across
this letter.

[2] This is Hudson's account. *Clarendon Papers.*

a final decision. He at once made his way to the Palace, and gave a full account of what had taken place to the King. The moment had come, he said, to decide. His own decision was taken; either acceptance of the protocol and treaty, or resignation. Victor Emmanuel did not hesitate an instant, in full accord with Cavour, he signed the treaty, and at four in the morning everything was finished. Dabormida resigned, and the King entrusted the portfolio of Foreign Affairs to Cavour *ad interim*. 'This morning,' wrote Hudson the next day, 'we were invited to call at the Ministry of Finance, where we found the President of the Council, who informed us that the King had been graciously pleased to accept the resignation of General Dabormida, and that he himself took his place: that the Sardinian Government accepted the protocol, acceded to the treaty of April 10th, and was prepared to send 15,000 men to the East.'[1]

The credit for the Sardinian alliance in the Crimean War, which was to prove the first step on the road to Italian emancipation, must be given to Cavour. His audacious brain conceived it, and his patience, resourcefulness and determination, carried it through. He might have written concerning it, what he said of the commercial treaties with the same two countries: 'They will occasion very lively debates, and will perhaps rouse bitter opposition against me, the author of them. I don't care. I am prepared to face it, to push the country into the only path that can save it.' As it was, he wrote to Count Oldofredi, 'I have assumed a tremendous responsibility. It does not matter, come what may, my conscience tells me I have fulfilled a sacred duty.'

The treaty signed, the next matter was ratification. Copies were at once sent to Paris and London, and after an untoward delay on the part of France, which

[1] The fullest account of the last stages of the negotiations is to be found in Massari, *Vittorio Emanuele II*. The resignation of Dabormida caused a reshuffling of offices. Cibrario succeeded Dabormida at the Foreign Office and Lanza was brought in as Minister of Public Instruction.

caused some uneasiness at Turin, were returned signed and sealed on January 25th. The next day Cavour presented them to the Chamber of Deputies, and the debate on their acceptance commenced on February 3rd. The discussion expressed in miniature the feelings of the country. The Left, like the Press that supported them outside, fulminated against the treaty. 'The war ruins our maritime commerce,' exclaimed Farina, 'it paralyses the industrial development of our country and is the source of every kind of economic ruin.' Brofferio declared the treaty 'neither just, rational, useful, nor necessary.' The thought of fighting beside Austria was more than some of the Left could stomach: 'the day our tricolour waves unfurled beside that of Austria,' cried Biancheri, 'it will be needful to drape it in mourning, lest the unavenged blood of our brothers with which it is already stained should be contaminated by so impure a contact.' This kind of oratory, however, carried little weight. A fine defence of the treaty was made by General Durando, a speaker whose voice was not very often heard. In an interesting historical sketch of Piedmontese statesmanship, he showed that the growth of the country was not due to a deliberate and sustained policy of acquisition, but rather the result of their Princes taking part in European struggles outside their own country; an ingenious argument for participation in the Crimea. He was very good on the dangers of neutrality, and closed his speech with a telling peroration. 'Remember,' he said, 'that in a war of this magnitude, if, when Europe opens her arms to you, you repulse her; if you adopt a policy of doing nothing; if you proclaim yourself neutral (in which nobody will believe); you may, perchance, live politically, but your sons and your grandsons will die unhonoured at the foot of the Alps and with them will be buried the last hopes of Italy.' The speech made a great impression.[1]

[1] *Diario Politico di M. Provana di Collegno*, February 3rd. 'General Durando made a speech in favour of the treaty that roused the Chamber to delirious enthusiasm. It was decided *séance tenante* to print 13,000 copies for distribution to the troops.

Revel, who followed, approved the treaty, remarking that far from censuring the Government for subscribing to the alliance, he approved it strongly. 'Had I been upon the Ministerial bench,' he added, 'I should not have done otherwise.' But he spoilt his support, and created a vexatious and heated digression, by remarking that Piedmont found herself in the hard necessity of embarking upon a great war, 'thanks to the too revolutionary policy of the Government.' More precisely, thanks to the *Connubio* of Cavour and Rattazzi. Together with Count Solaro della Margherita he regretted Piedmont had not accepted a subsidy instead of a loan, which he did not think would have been derogatory to the dignity of the country. The speech of Cavour, which was awaited with great interest, was somewhat spoilt by having to reply to Revel, and in the process having to rake up old animosities. He began by giving an account of the negotiations, stressing the effort made regarding the sequestrations; he then passed on to deal with the motives of the allies in inviting Sardinia to join the alliance; far from there being any compulsion as Revel had suggested, their relation with the allies had throughout been most friendly, and to add point to this, he quoted from a letter of Lord Clarendon to Sir James Hudson, in which Sardinia was referred to in very flattering terms.

> You can assure Count Cavour [the letter ran] that the treaty is popular in this country, not only in all the great cities, but almost one might say in the villages—popular to a degree that one could scarcely credit, amongst a people that as a rule do not interest themselves in foreign countries. There exists throughout England as much admiration for the wisdom and courage which Sardinia has shown in difficult circumstances, as sympathy for the successful efforts she has made to establish a reasoned liberty.[1]

---

[1] Hudson wrote the next day apropos of this letter: 'the effect on the House was the happiest possible, and enraged the two extreme parties to such a pitch that M. de Revel, who always passes for a sober, reserved, and talented man, quite lost his head. Menabrea was heard to say, if we don't break down this treaty this Government will last for the next five years.' Hudson to Cavour.

Cavour next dealt with Sardinia's interest in the struggle, and showed how her interests, as well as her political institutions, would be adversely affected by a Russian victory, and that both duty and interest prompted her to join the allies. He then came to the real problem: having been asked to join, what ought they to do?

There were only two alternatives, either acceptance or neutrality. Now the only conditions for a safe and effective neutrality [he said] lay in being so placed that remaining neutral could do no possible harm to either belligerent. But this was impossible for Sardinia. To remain neutral but armed, as the opponents of the treaty suggested, with a view to opportune intervention in their own interests, was at once to be of genuine assistance to Russia. To do this would not only mean losing the sympathies of the Western Powers, both during and after the war, but also sacrificing the sympathy of Liberal Europe. And even so, neutrality was not always a safe path for a small power, however good its intentions. Venice was neutral in 1797, but that did not save her from Campoformio. Piedmont had in fact no alternative, the alliance was an absolute necessity.

He then dealt with the financial and economic aspects of the treaty, leaving the military side to La Marmora. He brought his speech to a close with an answer to the question, How can the alliance help Italy?

I reply [he said] in the only way that it is given to us, or perhaps to any one, in the actual conditions of Europe, to help Italy. Experience of the past years and even centuries has shown how little Italy has benefited from all her revolutions, plots, and conspiracies. Far from helping her, they have been one of the greatest calamities that have afflicted this fair land. And not only, gentlemen, through the great number of individual sacrifices they have occasioned; not only because they were the reason or pretext for greater rigours; but specially, because these repeated conspiracies have had for effect to lessen the esteem, and up to a certain point the sympathy, that the rest of Europe feels for Italy. Now, gentlemen, I believe that the first condition for the betterment of the state of Italy, the one that exceeds all others, is to raise her reputation, to act so that all the nations of the world, both governors and governed, render justice to her qualities. But for this two things are necessary: first to prove to Europe that Italy has the political sense sufficient to govern herself properly, to school herself in liberty, that she is in a condition to be able to adopt the most perfect form of government known; and secondly, to show that her military valour is equal to that of her ancestors. You have rendered in the past this service to Italy, that you have shown by your conduct for the last seven years that the Italians know how to govern themselves with wisdom, prudence, and loyalty. There lies before you an equal, if not a greater, service; it is for our country to show that the sons of Italy can fight with true valour on the field of glory. I am certain, gentlemen, that the laurels our soldiers will win on the battlefields of the East, will do more for the future fate of Italy than all those who have thought to regenerate her with the voice and with the pen.

It was a fine convincing speech and satisfied the Chamber, and what little doubt there was as to the fate of the treaty vanished after Cavour had spoken. The final ballot showed 101 ayes against 60 noes. Even less opposition was met with in the Senate, where Azeglio sponsored the treaty, though he did not expect much from it. 'I spoke for the Treaty,' he wrote to his nephew in London, 'and would do as much again, but it is nothing very gay.'

No time was lost when once the treaty was passed in putting it into execution. La Marmora left at once for Paris and London, to find out to whom the Piedmontese contingent was to be attached and what was to be their destination. He found Napoleon planning to take over the supreme command in person and the formation of an army of reserve at Constantinople, of which the Sardinian troops were to make part. This plan suited neither La Marmora nor Cavour, both of whom were anxious to see the Piedmontese in the fighting line. At the moment there were conversations proceeding at Vienna, with a view to bringing about an early peace, and though expectations of a successful result were small, it encouraged a tendency to hold back the departure of the Piedmontese contingent until the issue was decided. Passing on to London, La Marmora interviewed Lord Clarendon, and notes that 'he did not speak of hopes of peace from the Conference, but it was evident to me that they wish to delay our departure in the expectation that peace may be realized. He disapproved fully, and with good reason, of Napoleon's plan to go in person to the Crimea.' He then had a long talk with Palmerston, who was plainly very anxious, without prejudicing the independent position of the Piedmontese troops, to get them attached to the English army and under the orders of the English commander-in-chief.

> With much finesse and delicacy [La Marmora writes] the Prime Minister made it clear that, in consideration of the fact that England was providing our transport, and further had given us a loan to meet our expenses, we were expected to reinforce the English army. Finally, he asked me whether we preferred to be with the English or the French. I endeavoured to explain as well as I could that under no circumstances were we to be considered as simply auxiliaries of the English army; that what was said by the English papers, and especially the remarks of Lord Aberdeen, had somewhat wounded our national *amour-propre*; that according to the terms of the Convention, the Piedmontese were to make part of the allied army and be under the orders of the commander-in-chief without being part of either the French or English army. 'Have you any difficulty in working with the French?' he asked me. 'To us it is a matter of indifference,' I answered frankly.[1]

This delicate problem was left open, and was ultimately settled by the good sense and tact of the commanding officers in the Crimea. As the weeks passed the situation changed. Napoleon was dissuaded from going to the seat of war in person, and the army of reserve at Constantinople did not materialize. After a good deal of diplomatic exchanges the destination of the Piedmontese troops was settled by a telegram to Hudson: 'It has been

[1] *Biblioteca di Storia Italiana Recente*, vol. iv. pp. 110–12.

arranged between the French and English Governments that the Sardinian army should go direct to Balaclava and that they should take part in the operations in the field.'[1]

On La Marmora's return from Paris and London he was actively engaged in the organization of the Expeditionary Corps. In order that the whole army might share in the campaign, a battalion was drawn from every line regiment, a squadron from each regiment of cavalry, and every artillery brigade provided a battery, which together with the necessary complement of engineers and administrative services, made up a force of 17,795 men, 4,404 horses, and 36 guns. When all was ready the troops were assembled at Alessandria, where the King reviewed them and presented the regimental colours. Among the King's *entourage* that day was Sir James Hudson, who described his impressions in the following words:

> I accompanied the King to Alessandria last Saturday to assist at the Benediction and distribution of the standards to the regiments going to the Crimea. The whole thing was right royal, loyal, and soldierly, and it would have done your Lordship's heart good to have seen the quick earnest devotedness of the King, the troops, and the people. I never witnessed a more touching sight, and the King could not trust himself to deliver the speech he had prepared, and General Durando read it. I saw tears in the King's eyes. I afterwards dined with the King and his one regret was that he could not accompany his soldiers to the war.[2]

A week later the troops began their embarkation, and on April 26th La Marmora left with the last contingent, bearing with him the hopes of Italy.

[1] F.O. 67, vol. 201. Clarendon to Hudson, April 19th, 1855.
[2] *Clarendon Papers.*

VI. THE STRUGGLE WITH THE CHURCH
NOV. 1854—MAY 1855

The Ecclesiastical Problem—Cavour and Antonelli—The State of the Church in Piedmont—The Attitude of Cavour—Provisions of the New Bill—The Attitude of the King—The Debate in the Chamber—Public Excitement—Death of the Queen Mother—Death of the Queen—Death of the Duke of Genoa—State of the King—The Papal Allocution—Debate renewed—Speeches of Rattazzi and Cavour—The Bill passed by the Chamber of Deputies—The Debate in the Senate—The Calabiana offer—Resignation of Cavour and the Cabinet—Attempts to form a New Government—Popular Excitement—Letter of D'Azeglio—Cavour recalled—The Bill becomes Law.

A PIEDMONTESE Cabinet was always in the difficult position of having to face a double problem in the Government of the country, the civil and the ecclesiastical; its task was complicated by the fact that, on all ecclesiastical questions, the divisions cut diagonally across the line of political cleavage, so that the support the Government could rely on for their civil legislation was untrustworthy in all matters effecting religious problems. The Left, for instance, which normally opposed the Government, invariably supported it on any Bill which tended to weaken the power of the Church; whereas the Right, which not infrequently voted with the Government on civil bills, was its strongest opponent on all ecclesiastical measures; and even Cavour's own centre party was not altogether to be trusted when problems concerning the Church were brought forward. Outside Parliament it was the same; there was no class in the country from the nobility to the peasantry that was not divided differently on religious questions to what it was on political.

Nor were the difficulties limited to internal affairs. It was the recognized policy of Rome to appeal to the Catholic Powers to bring pressure to bear on any country whose policy endangered the privileges or interests of the Church, and the Piedmontese Cabinet had always to be prepared to justify its actions to the Catholic world, and be ready to meet protests and pressure from Vienna or Paris. The action of Austria in the matter of the sequestrations, for instance, was generally regarded as taken in response to an appeal from Rome to create a diversion and relieve the pressure on the ecclesiastical front. For these reasons measures affecting the Church were always an unpleasant and controversial business. They split the country, aroused bitter passions, and were enveloped in an atmosphere of animosity that strained the national temper to the utmost. Moreover, it was so easy to impute vindictiveness and the spirit of persecution to the authors of such legislation that, the importance of the issues at stake was apt to be obscured, and it is only by a survey of the real position that the action of the Government can be fully understood.

But in studying the problem of Church and State in Piedmont there is one misconception which has always to be avoided. The struggle was in no sense a revolt against the Catholic Faith. On all spiritual questions, on all points of faith and morals, the supremacy of the Church remained untouched and uncontested. There was no decay of religious fervour, no lessening of the spiritual power of the clergy, no diminution in worship. Piedmont was devoutly Catholic and remained so throughout the struggle. It was in fact a revolt not against the Catholic Faith, but against that survival of medievalism, which the nation now recognized as incompatible with progress and modern ideas. With unerring insight Rome put her finger upon the source of the trouble when she denounced the Constitutional Government of Piedmont as the arch-enemy. There could be no room in the medieval system of Rome for government by the people, and it was the medieval system almost in its entirety that had persisted in Piedmont, and it was the granting of the Statuto that had made the struggle inevitable.

But what Rome did not realize was that the demand for constitutional government in Piedmont was a reaction of the human spirit against that hateful system of

secrecy, espionage, obscurantism and repression, for
which Rome herself had been directly responsible. For
thirty years since 1815 Rome had exercised undisputed
supremacy in the counsels of Piedmont.[1] A series of
devoted kings had lavished upon her power, influence,
and wealth. During these years it was calculated that
not less than one hundred millions of lire had been
bestowed upon the Church in gold, lands, and endowments. Everything she suggested was carried out. Her
Jesuits conducted the education of the country; her
bishops controlled the universities; her lawyers and
law-courts took cognizance of every case wherein the
Church's rights and interests were even indirectly
concerned; her censorship controlled the publication
of every book and journal, prevented the freedom of the
Press, and the entrance of all undesirable literature from
abroad. Offences against religion, from sacrilege to
fasting and church attendance, found their corrective
duly enshrined in the pages of the penal code. The
secular arm stood ready at her slightest behest to enforce
her law and discipline. It was the perfectly governed
State as Rome conceived it, wherein the Church
directed and controlled, in what she believed the true
and highest interests of men, the machinery of civil
Government. It was Rome full fed and unfettered,
directing how Christians should be educated and exert-
ing all those influences and restrictions that she believed
best for them—and thirty years in which to produce
a result.

And that result, what was it? A nation sunk in
poverty and ignorance, exasperated, revengeful, bent
on the abolition of the whole hateful system and the
inauguration of a free and Constitutional Government.
However one may respect or value the spiritual influence of the Church of Rome at this time, there can be

[1] It should be remembered that the twenty years of Napoleon's rule had
much lessened both the wealth and power of the Church, and that at the
restoration in 1815 Victor Emanuel I had not only restored all the privileges
and wealth the Church had possessed before the Napoleonic era, but had
largely increased her wealth, a practice followed by his successors.

nothing but condemnation for the effects of her political influence. She initiated and encouraged a system as vicious as it was disastrous. By identifying herself with all the worst practices of absolutism, and working hand in hand with all the repressive machinery of the State, she intensified the hatred in which the whole system came to be held. The growth of Socialism and Communism, which she attributed to the civil power, was the work of her own hands, the result of driving underground every aspiration towards liberty and persecuting every semblance of free thought or speech. The verdict of an intelligent community as to the source of the evils that oppress it, may err as to the guilt to be attributed to individuals, but as to the general causes, it seldom makes a mistake; and the fact that the first demands of the populace when freedom came within sight, were for the abolition of those very institutions and practices considered most essential by the Church, press censorship, military police, and education by the Jesuits, is alone sufficient to indicate correctly to whom the poverty, ignorance, and discontent of the people was to be attributed.

In 1846, at the close of thirty years of Papal predominance, came the election of Pius IX to the chair of St. Peter. His momentary aberration into the paths of liberalism rendered constitutional Government in Piedmont a certainty, but very soon, under the reactionary pressure of the Sacred College, he reverted to Rome's traditional policy and threw all his weight on the side of Austria and absolutism. What followed may be summarized in the words of D'Azeglio:

> The bishops elected under the old order, and in accord with the Austro-autocratic absolutists, published pastoral letters against the Government and the Constitution, and in various other ways commenced war. The Government was defenceless. It armed itself with the Siccardi laws. That party, that will not allow peace in Italy as long as the Piedmontese Constitution exists, inspired the conduct of Rome. An accord was rendered impossible or at least indefinitely suspended.

Rome will not yield as long as the hope of revolution in Piedmont remains.[1]

In the face of this bitter and determined opposition the diplomatic attitude of the Government was both patient and conciliatory, but as determined as Rome herself on the matter of reform, by agreement if possible, but if not, without it. This is how D'Azeglio describes what took place:

> We found ourselves faced with the alternative of setting the country on the path of reform, and so keeping faith with the King and the State, or of throwing the country into a grievous series of disorders and contentions by violating the most solemn of oaths. How many high-minded men have we not sent to Rome, that she might know our true conditions better than by mere dispatches? In how many ways have we not implored—I blush to say it—implored—in order that Rome might renounce with a good grace what it was no longer possible to preserve? That through her the State might not have to face incalculable dangers. How did she reply? No, No, and always No! Let the State be ruined, let it be torn by factions and tumults—what does it matter to us? No![2]

The advent of Cavour to the premiership brought Rome an opponent whose intellect was as subtle and whose will was as firm as her own; with a mind unmoved by the emotional appeal of Catholicism and impervious to the fear of ecclesiastical censures. He bore Rome no bitter hostility; he would much rather have worked with her than against her, and if only she would have left politics alone he would have given her a liberty almost excessive in its generosity.[3] But in the long struggle which now commenced between Cavour and Cardinal Antonelli, there was a fundamental opposition in principles, training, and outlook that rendered an accord impossible. Both were statesmen, and on the plane of diplomacy they fought like two skilled fencers, but although Cavour was a professing

---

[1] A. Colombo, *Carteggi e Documenti inediti di Emanuele D'Azeglio*, Appendix, No. 8.

[2] Zini, *Storia d'Italia*, vol. iii. Documenti, No. 113.

[3] Artom, *Cavour in Parlamento*, Introduction.

Catholic all his life, his subconscious mentality was Protestant. On his mother's side he came of old Huguenot ancestry, intensified by a century and a half of Genevan Calvinism, and while the Catholic fervour of his father's family was transmitted unimpaired to his elder brother the Marquis Gustavo, Camillo was sadly tinctured with the mentality of his mother's family. Brought up in the social and economic teaching of English political thinkers, a student of the rationalistic philosophy of Bentham, Cavour was a firm believer in the force of facts, and till the last he held a touching belief that Rome would be open to the persuasive power of reason. Opposed to him was a man, of whom it is sufficient to say that he was by birth a Neapolitan peasant, and that nothing in his subsequent training and development altered the view-point of his early years. That two such minds should find a common denominator regarding the function of the Catholic Church in relation to the State, was wellnigh impossible.

On assuming the presidency of the Council, Cavour, immersed in finance, seemed desirous of giving ecclesiastical questions a wide birth. He speedily withdrew the Civil Marriage Bill, and made no mention of any coming legislation. But Cavour soon found that it was impossible either to ignore or placate the clerical hostility. The incessant intrigues of the camarilla at Court, the obvious complicity of Rome in the matter of the sequestrations, the chronic opposition to all government measures, together with the insistent demand of public opinion, convinced him that action would have to be taken, and the entry of Rattazzi into the Cabinet was almost a pledge to this effect. In the meantime the report of the Commission that had been appointed to take a census of the clergy, and make an inventory of the resources of the Church, came to hand. This document exposed a state of things that more than justified Government legislation.

In a country whose total population was less than

five millions, the census revealed the presence of 23,000 ecclesiastics[1] of one kind or another. There were 41 bishops and archbishops,[2] 1,313 canons, 2,774 parishes, and above 8,500 in monastic establishments. This provided a bishop for every 106,000 inhabitants and a priest for every 214. The wealth of the Church afforded even more striking figures. The estimated income from lands and endowments, apart from all that was received in fees, dues, and collections, was upwards of 17 millions of lire, or one-thirteenth of the national revenue.[3] The income of the thirty bishops and archbishops on the mainland exceeded a million lire a year, giving an average of over 30,000 lire each. At least one archbishop had an income of 100,000 lire a year. To estimate the real value of these figures they must be compared with those of other classes in the country. Fortunately from Cavour's letters and Budget speeches we are able to draw some comparative figures. The following table shows some relative amounts:

The Archbishop of Turin	100,000
The Bishops (average)	30,000
Cabinet Ministers	15,000
The Treasurer General (3 clerks to pay) . .	12,000
The President of the Court of Cassation . .	12,000
The Director of the National Bank . . .	10,000
The Counsellors of State	8,000
Commandant-General of Marine . . .	8,000
Vice-Admiral	8,000
Intendant General (highest Civil Servant) . .	7,500
Read-Admiral	7,200

The evidence produced by the Commission was all

[1] The significance of this figure will be realized by the English reader by noting that, if the Church of England to-day was staffed in the same proportion there would be 280 bishops and 161,000 clergy, whereas the actual numbers are 40 bishops and 17,000 clergy. Further, taking the population of greater London at 7½ millions, if the entire bench of bishops and all the active parochial clergy were concentrated there, on the Piedmontese basis there would still be a shortage amount to 20 bishops and 17,000 clergy!

[2] Belgium with a population of 4½ millions had one archbishop and five bishops.

[3] An equivalent proportion in England to-day would give the Church of England an income of 60 millions instead of 6.

that was needed to convince Cavour of the necessity of legislation. Though he had been urged by individuals and parliamentary groups, as well as by communal and provincial petitions, to bring in a Bill of this kind, his hatred of compulsion and persecution had made him refuse, but now he hesitated no longer. The fundamental concept of Cavour's policy during these years was to make Piedmont, as the nucleus of a future Italy, a prosperous, modern, constitutional State based on Liberty. But he saw now that things had reached a point when further progress was rendered almost impossible until the wealth and political power of the Church was curtailed. It was useless to hope for further development so long as a power, hostile to every act of the Government, unscrupulous in its methods and political in its aims, was permitted, unchecked, to use its vast wealth and influence to bring about, if possible, the restoration of medieval absolutism. It was a situation which had had to be faced by nearly every Catholic country in Europe, and Cavour made up his mind that the time had come to face it in Piedmont. As he wrote to Villamarina in Paris: 'With the best will in the world it is impossible to come to an understanding with Rome. Rome will acquiesce in our liberty and our independence far more readily, than in those laws that introduce in a moderate measure in this country, conditions that have existed for the last half-century in all other Catholic countries.'[1] But he refused to gratify the predatory instincts of the Left by any measure of confiscation, though he was ready to abolish the useless Orders and reduce the exorbitant salaries of the bishops, for the benefit of the poor clergy and relief of the State. The Bill which was laid upon the table on November 28th, 1854, contained the following provisions. The first clause read:

> All the religious Orders are declared abolished, with the exception of the Sisters of Charity and those of St. Joseph, and those Orders and Communities dedicated to public

[1] Chiala, *Lettere*, vol. ii. No. 247.

instruction, preaching, or the care of the sick, which are mentioned by name in the list, approved by Royal decree, and published simultaneously with the present law.[1]

The Bill further decreed that no Order or Congregation could henceforth be constituted in the Kingdom except by special legislation; the number of Regular Orders was limited; the Chapters of all Collegiate Churches, with certain exceptions, were suppressed together with the simple benefices. With the funds thus accruing to the State, an Ecclesiastical Bank was to be established to provide life pensions for the dispossessed members, and to supplement the stipends of the poor clergy. Further funds for this purpose were to be realized by reducing the salaries of the archbishops to 18,000 and the bishops to 12,000 lire, and by imposing an *ad valorem* tax on the richer benefices for the support of the poorer ones.

While this measure was in preparation, negotiations were once more opened with Rome, but with no better success than before. Then the King, desperately anxious to bring the quarrel to an end, sent a personal embassy, consisting of his old preceptor, Monsignor Charvaz, Archbishop of Genoa, and the Bishops of Annecy and Maurienne, to try and come to an agreement with Rome. But while still negotiating the new Bill was brought in, and the bishops at once wrote to the King a severe letter, which ended with these words:

> The law is based on principles that the Church can never admit and has always rejected. It presupposes that the State can suppress at its will religious communities and that it is master of the possessions of the Church. No compromise is possible on such principles, which are plainly contrary to Catholic doctrine, and in consequence all official intervention on our part would now be useless and out of place.[2]

This letter was followed a few days later by one from

---

[1] 334 convents containing 5,506 persons were suppressed by the Bill, leaving 274 houses containing 4,050 persons. See Thayer, *Cavour* (vol. i. p. 358), reproduced from Brofferio, *Stor. Parl. Subalp.*, vol. vi. appendix; also Zini for details and figures.

[2] Chiala, *Lettere*, vol. ii. Introd. p. cii.

Mons. Charvaz. The poor King, who was destined to be the storm centre in the coming struggle, writes with an unhappy sense of premonition to La Marmora:

> Since I saw you this morning I have received another letter from Mons. Charvaz full of severe reproaches: I see plainly that the matter is going to be serious, and that I am the one who is going to have all the unpleasantness; for you others, when you are in a fix, I know very well what you do, but I remain in the sauce.

When the Bill was presented at the opening of the session, it was prefaced with an introduction which was read to the Chamber. To minimize as far as possible the controversial religious element, Cavour insisted on regarding it as a financial measure, due to the *indefettibile necessità* of removing from the Budget the annual subsidy of a million lire towards the stipends of the poor clergy; and of devising means to replace it by a repartition of ecclesiastical revenues and the suppression of useless religious Orders and Communities. It was then submitted to a Committee for examination, who reported to the Chamber on December 28th. In making his statement, the reporter, Carlo Cadorna, laid stress on the inequalities of the clerical incomes. The salaries of the archbishops, he said, were almost as large as those of all the Belgian bishops combined, and twice as large as that of the Archbishop of Paris, while, on the other hand, there were hundreds of deserving parochial clergy whose stipends were less than 500 lire annually. The debate began on January 9th. It opened with the enumeration of the petitions received in favour of the Bill, signed by more than twenty thousand citizens, together with separate petitions from 117 Communal Councils and 32 special delegations, demanding the confiscation of ecclesiastical wealth, reductions in the number of bishops, the abolition of the convents, and the extension of military service to the clergy. On the other side were petitions, or rather protests, signed by the bishops of Savoy, and another from those of Piedmont. The Right demanded that the

Bishops' protest should be read, to which the Left objected, saying that, if one side was heard the other should be also. Cavour, however, supported the Right: 'I am convinced,' he said, 'that if the protests of the bishops were published they would furnish the supporters of the Bill with their most valid arguments, and provide a proof of the absolute indispensability of this reform. I demand,' he added amid the applause of the Chamber, 'that they be read immediately.' And read they were. It was a clever move, for the violent language and provocative tone used by the bishops did their cause more harm than good. The Bill they said was unjust, illegal, anti-catholic, and anti-social. It was characterized by ingratitude, cynicism, violence, and immorality. It was injurious to the Church, the King, and the nation. After this the debate proper began.

The first speaker was the President of the Chamber, Boncompagni, who, after vacating the chair in favour of Lanza, spoke in favour of the Bill, dealing chiefly with the legal aspect. The Bill involved two questions: the first was whether the State had any right to change or dispose of the goods of the Church; if it had, the second question then arose as to whether the Bill was wise and just in the use it was making of this right. If, on the other hand, it had no right to interfere with church property, then it was an act of unjustifiable violence, and indefensible. The bishops maintained, and they were later amply supported by the Pope, that the Church was a true *imperium in imperio*, that the goods and persons of the Church were sacred, and could be no more touched by the State than could the persons and goods of another nation. That even the paying of taxes was, so to speak, an act of grace, and in no sense a duty or a necessity. Boncompagni, on the other hand, maintained that the State had as much right over Church property as over any other, with which, for the benefit of the State as a whole, they could deal as they thought fit; and that therefore the State was perfectly within its right in presenting this measure before the Chamber. The first speaker against the Bill was Cavour's brother, the Marquis Gustavo. Consumed with anger at the iniquity of the measure, he was specially severe upon his brother and the hypocrisy of calling the Bill a financial measure, when in reality it was an act of spoliation. 'To kill a man,' he said angrily, 'because one has a right eventually to his possessions, is a thing so outrageous that no one could be found to defend it. To extinguish an association, whether it be of value to humanity or only harmless, simply because when extinct you can seize its wealth, is a thing immoral and illegal despite all the forensic subtlety directed to establish the legality of the measure.' The Marquis was followed by a tremendous oration from Brofferio. Treating the question historically, Brofferio went back to the Donation of Constantine—a gift from the civil power—the source of all the Church's wealth, and claimed that what the State had given it could take back. Then across the ages he traced the iniquities of Rome, her greed, her persecutions, her fatal love of calling strangers into Italy from Pepin to Napoleon III. With an unsparing hand he laid bare her condemnation of those, the pioneers of knowledge, whose beliefs traversed the doctrines of the Church. It was a grim indictment. For three days the battle raged, speaker after speaker denouncing in turn the Government or the Church. On the third day the last speaker was the old Count Solaro della Margherita, for eighteen years Charles Albert's Foreign Minister, a *cattolico del baldacchino*:

> the proposed law [he declared] is more than an insult, it is a wound to the Church; it is more than an insult to justice, it is a betrayal of this nation. The Romans, though Gentiles, respected the virtue of the Vestals; but now, in a Catholic country, there is no respect for virgins consecrated to the service of God. To go through so long a series of injuries is a task too grievous. I prefer to exclaim with an ancient writer that, the enormity of the crime is beyond the power of the

tongue to express 'vincit officium linguae sceleris magni-
tudo.'

The Chamber was tolerant, but its good temper was
taxed beyond bearing when the speaker declared the
Bill a 'sacrilegious robbery' and there was a storm. The
speech was too violent to influence the Chamber, yet
in the days that followed, many must have remembered
the words of the old Count, whose loyalty to his King
and his Church were beyond dispute, as he exclaimed:
'Oh may it please God, whose avenging arm still holds
the chastisement of man, to spare from any ill this our
dear country! But if upon us should fall any of those
calamities that form the human lot, how many will say,
and perchance with truth: This unjust law has been the
cause, we have provoked the anger of Heaven!'

But it was not alone within the walls of the Palazzo
Carignano that the battle raged. The Press on both
sides fulminated against their adversaries, and while
the pulpits shook with denunciation of the Government,
the cafés and the Circolo Nazionale re-echoed to the
cry of 'Down with the Priests!'[1] In town and country,
in the streets, and wherever men assembled, the
struggle was rife. Cavour was alarmed lest the very
morale of the country should suffer from such violence.
Engrossed as he was at the moment, with the final
negotiations over the Crimean alliance, he had little
time to spend in the Chamber, and he did not speak on
the Bill until much later. But amid all the excitement
and passion of those days, there was one place only
where it deepened into tragedy, and one brave heart
alone that wrestled with a burden of sorrow that few
are called upon to bear. And that heart and that place
was the King within his palace. For within those walls
three persons lay dying, his mother, his brother, and
his wife.

On the fourth morning of the debate the Chamber

---

[1] Treitschke, *Cavour*. 'On all sides the cry was heard, 'war to the Priests,
the State must possess the goods of the Church, for they belong to the
people!'

met as usual, only to be notified of the death of the Queen Mother, and adjourned for ten days. Maria Teresa, the widow of Charles Albert, was one to whom life had been a tragedy. An Austrian Princess, the daughter of the Grand Duke of Tuscany, she had known but little happiness in her married life; devoted to good works and to her religion, the struggle between Church and State had broken her heart. Her epitaph has been written in the words 'a mother of the poor, a most virtuous and devoted wife, and a most unhappy woman.'[1] The Chamber assembled again on June 22nd, only to hear the announcement of the death of the Queen and her infant son, and again to be adjourned. The nation was horror-stricken, and a deep wave of sympathy swept across the country for their loved and afflicted King. But of all the tributes of sympathy, there was surely none more touching in its honest simplicity than the words of Sir James Hudson written in a private letter to Lord Clarendon, in acknowledgement of a letter of condolence from Queen Victoria and Prince Albert:

> and indeed, my Lord [he wrote], never did a sovereign, from his steady, manly virtues, deserve more thoroughly this gracious need of sympathy; and never did bereaved husband stand more in need of consolation, for he dearly loved and respected his departed Queen. I can assure your Lordship that I never beheld a more touching spectacle, than the universal sympathy and sorrow of high and low upon the loss of one as beautiful as good, as gracious as she was charitable, the deceased Queen Marie.

Yet once again, a fortnight later, the Chamber met, this time to receive the announcement of the death of the King's beloved brother, the Duke of Genoa, whom so short a time before he had destined for the command of the troops in the Crimea.

It would, perhaps, have been too much to expect from the clergy in the circumstances, that they should regard the disasters to the Royal Family under any other

---

[1] *Diario Politico di Margherita di Collegno.*

aspect than as a visitation from God for the injuries inflicted on His Church. But in spite of all they could do to influence an ignorant and superstitious people (and they did not hesitate to make known their interpretation even to the King himself), the country remained firm in its determination. 'The King is not to be intimidated,' wrote the British Minister, 'the people in general are so devoted to their sovereign and to his house that they are quite prepared to share with their prince whatever odium the Court of Rome may think proper to attempt to heap upon His Majesty.' Nevertheless, Victor Emmanuel could not be insensible to the pain that the struggle with the Church had caused to his wife and mother, and the thought spurred him to use the first opportunity to come to terms with Rome. But if there was a streak of superstition in the religion of the King, it was more than counterbalanced by his magnificent sense of loyalty to the constitution, and his clear sense of duty as a constitutional monarch. His proud title, 'Il Re Galantuomo', was not bestowed in vain. Surrounded as he had been from the first day of his reign, with an unceasing and insidious propaganda, designed to induce him to violate his oath, in the spirit if not in the letter, his absolute loyalty to his Ministers remained unshaken. The character of the King was curiously simple. The almost elemental quality of his tastes and passions was akin to that of his own peasantry, and the same might be said of his religion.[1] But, as is often found in characters of this type, there went with his simplicity a native shrewdness that stood him perhaps in better stead than an intellect of finer fibre. The innuendoes and suggestions of courtiers and ecclesiastics dropped harmless from the King's armour of simplicity, while his natural quickness and sound common sense divined their purpose much more rapidly than they expected. The conjunction of a character of this kind, with the wide knowledge, the grasp on

[1] 'He had,' said an Anglo-Italian friend who knew him well, 'the piety of a brigand.'

reality, and the penetrative intellect of Cavour, formed a very powerful combination.

On January 22nd the Pope, in a secret Consistory, pronounced an allocution on the Piedmontese Law on the Convents, as it was usually called.[1] After recalling to the minds of his venerable Brothers 'the zeal, solicitude, and forbearance of the Church,' regarding previous Piedmontese ecclesiastical legislation, the Holy Father characterized the Bill under discussion as 'repugnant to national, divine, and social law, greatly adverse to the good of human society, and above all, favourable to the most pernicious and grievous errors of socialism and communism.' 'In truth,' he went on, 'we cannot find words with which to express the grief we so deeply feel, at seeing so many incredible and horrifying misdeeds already committed against the Church and its venerable rights.' Then, after deploring the losses suffered by the Church, he added, 'and therefore we raise anew our voice with apostolic liberty, and do reprove and condemn not only all the single decrees already promulgated by that Government to the detriment of religion, the Church, and the rights and authority of this Holy Chair, but also the law recently proposed, declaring all alike absolutely null and void.' Not content with this wholesale condemnation, he descended to individuals, and 'most seriously warned all those in whose name the laws already promulgated have been ordered or carried out, and also those others who should dare to be favourable to the law lately proposed, or should approve or sanction it, that they attentively meditate on the punishments and censures which by the apostolic constitutions and canons of Sacred Councils (especially that of Trent Sess. 23. ch. xi) were established against robbers and profaners of sacred things, and the violators of ecclesiastical power and liberty, and the usurpers of the rights of the Church and the Holy Chair.'

In addition to this allocution, a number of documents

[1] Text in Zini.

and extracts from the correspondence with Piedmont were circulated amongst the members, copies of which were obtained by the Government. Together, they form a remarkable presentation of the claims made by Rome and show the irreconcilable nature of the two points of view. The following are brief extracts from the documents:

The Church is of a superior order to Civil Society.

A State cannot be given or receive a Constitution that has the effect of subjecting the persons and goods of ecclesiastics to all the Laws of the State. Equality of Law cannot be applied to ecclesiastical persons and property.

The State cannot permit the public exercise of non-Catholic religions. The erection of a Protestant Church, permitted in Turin and Genoa, was a memorable outrage against the Catholic Church; it has raised the indignation of the faithful, was an injury to the Church, and tends to humiliate it.

A State cannot pass a law to regulate the civil status of its members without first putting itself in accord with the Holy Father.

The liberty of the Press is not reconcilable with the Catholic religion in a Catholic State.

The appeal *per abuso* ought to be abolished.

The State has no right to require that the provisions of Rome, outside matters of faith, are subject to the royal *exequatur*. This is an injury done to the Church, an abuse of the civil power, a null act, condemned by the supreme authority of the Church.

Bishops and clergy that refuse obedience to the Civil Law (as that relating to the abolition of the Foro Ecclesiastico or the Sardinian tithes) and that urge resistance to such law, do their duty.[1]

The most staunch adherent of the Papacy might well demand that such claims as these, when carried out in practice, should at least benefit and content those who lived under them. That if the Church were thus above the State, and in a condition of 'untouchability', her

[1] Brofferio, *Stor. Parl. Subalp.*, vol. vi. appendix No. 2, gives five pages of quotations and summaries of these documents. See also the letter of Cavour to Villamarina. Mayor, *Lettere*, No. 225.

subjects should be at least as happy and prosperous as those ruled by a less divine institution. In other words, that the States of the Church should be a model for other rulers. But alas, what were the facts? These are the words of D'Azeglio:

> For many centuries the Pope has governed three millions of subjects. Over them he exercises in all its fullness a double authority, the temporal and the spiritual. What has been the result? Four armies were required to put him upon his throne, and two foreign powers are necessary, and always will be necessary, to keep him there.[1]

It is not needful to stress the point unduly, but it was known to all that the Papal subjects were the most wretched, the most ignorant, and the most discontented of all the States of civilized Europe.[2]

Enough has been given to reveal the attitude of Rome, but it is interesting to observe, as showing the difference in point of view, that whereas Cardinal Antonelli had these documents circulated as his defence, Cavour, having read them, also had them circulated as his justification.[3]

The interrupted debate on the Law on the Convents recommenced on February 15th. It would be tedious as well as unprofitable to attempt to give any synopsis of the whole discussion, and it will be sufficient to follow the advice of Cavour himself who wrote to Villamarina on February 19th: 'I am sorry not to have ordered last week that you should be sent a *résumé* of the discussion on the Law on the Convents. It shall be begun to-day. In the meantime, I must impose upon you as a penance for my sin, the task of reading *in*

---

[1] Risposta di M. D'Azeglio alle accuse di slealtà e violata fede contenute nella esposizione del Card. Antonelli sulle trattative col Governo di Sardegna per le riforme ecclesiastiche. Text in Zini, *Documenti*, vol. iii. p. 484.

[2] It was a moot point amongst civilized rulers as to whether the palm for misgovernment should be given to the Pope or the King of Naples.

[3] Cavour to Villamarina. Mayor, No. 225. 'You will receive copies of several documents published by the Pope. I advise you to study them. They will furnish you with conclusive arguments to demonstrate the impossibility of coming to any understanding with Rome. Have a translation made of the famous project of Cardinal Santucci for the use of M. Drouyn de Llys. This alone is sufficient to justify us.'

extenso my speech and that of Rattazzi. You will find there pretty well all the arguments used in favour of the law, arguments to which no reply has been given as yet.'

The function of Rattazzi was to deal with the legal aspect of the Bill and to prove that the State was within its rights in introducing it. The difficulty, he said, was to find the owner of these monastic establishments. In the case of a civil association, the property belonged to the members in their corporate capacity, and at any time that the association was dissolved the property or its value could be divided amongst the members. But in ecclesiastical corporations the members took a vow of poverty and could own nothing. The fact was that the owners were fictitious persons created by the State, and what the State had created it could destroy. And again, if these establishments were dissolved, to whom did the property belong? It was impossible that it could be shared by the members as they could not own anything, the only possible owner was the State.[1] The State, therefore, had the right to resume possession of what was, in fact, their own property. He then went on to point out the practical danger to the State from the difference between civil and ecclesiastical property. The possessions of civil persons were perpetually changing hands. They were accumulated at one time and dissipated at another. Civil property was, in fact, fluid. But ecclesiastical property never changed hands. It increased but never diminished; it was held in perpetuity, yet under conditions by which those who used it did not own it and could not alienate it. The result was the gradual absorption of the wealth of the State in the hands of the Church.

The consequence will be [he added] that property thus held will become an insuperable obstacle to any steady progress; in the course of centuries, property will be entirely concen-

[1] Boncompagni had dealt with the point that there was no record that the State had ever recognized the ownership of the Church as such: nor had any law ever been passed handing over property to the Church in perpetuity.

trated in the hands of ecclesiastics; and that, in fact, has happened in many states, and amongst others, in the Kingdom of Naples, where at one time four-fifths of the entire kingdom was in the hands of the Church, until a law was passed that not only stopped further acquisitions but put the property of the Church upon the market.[1]

The following day Cavour spoke. On important measures, such as this, he always chose his moment for intervention with care. The Chamber had by now had a surfeit of violent language and denunciation and was prepared to listen to reason. His tone throughout was most moderate; he seemed anxious to impress the Chamber with the conviction that the Bill before them was a reasonable measure of reform and not an attack on the Church. That it was necessary, desirable, and opportune, and a matter entirely within their jurisdiction. He began by remarking that he thought after the legality and justice of a measure of this kind had been so amply demonstrated by those best qualified to express an opinion, it was desirable, in order that the Chamber could form an adequate judgement, that the material and political effects should be indicated by the Government. The purpose of the Bill was, he confessed, largely financial. Its adoption would benefit the country in various ways. It would save the taxpayer a million of lire by removing that sum from the Estimates. It would meet many public needs by providing buildings for barracks, hospitals, schools, and prisons, at present occupied by small bodies of the monastic orders. But besides these direct financial results the indirect economic effects would be even more valuable. The monastic orders had, he believed, arisen to meet a real social need, and in their time had been of great value to civilization. Their preservation of Art and Literature in the Dark Ages, their contributions to agriculture, their life of poverty and asceticism had all been of genuine value in the times that were passed. But to-day they had outlived their purpose and

[1] Brofferio, *Stor. Parl. Subalp.*, vol. vi. c. iii.

their utility. The world had changed, the monks had not; he would go so far as to say that in these days they were not only useless, but actually harmful, to the best interests of society.

> The claustral habit of abstention from work [he said] exercises a very bad effect upon industry, it renders labour less respectable and less respected, but even worse is the rule of life followed by the Mendicant Orders. The regular progress of society requires two conditions: increased production and growth in knowledge. Now can it be said, gentlemen, that the mendicant orders, for all that they contributed to the emancipation of the lower classes in the Middle Ages, contribute anything to-day to the progress of the people? Certainly not. To live by begging rather than work is to-day considered by all liberals and reformers as a social evil that requires an efficacious remedy. It is easy to see the contradiction involved between proclaiming the need of reforming pauperism, of expelling from the minds of the lower classes that fatal idea of supporting life by means of begging, and at the same time maintaining institutions that up to a certain point regard begging as an honourable profession. You condemn with one hand what you favour with the other. You are aware how strong is the force of association of ideas, and I repeat, that as long as the idea of begging is associated with that of sanctity, this deplorable custom will have an inevitable force against which legal enactments will break themselves in vain.

Before leaving this aspect of the question, Cavour, to estimate the effects of the religious orders upon society, drew a contrast between Spain and Naples, where they flourished, and England and Prussia, where they were abolished. Then, turning to Switzerland, he declared that a study of that country, canton by canton, would reveal with almost mathematical certainty, from their degree of prosperity, the presence or absence of monastic Orders. 'The prosperity of the Swiss Canton,' he declared, 'will always be found to be in inverse ratio to the number of begging friars the Canton contains.'

Cavour then passed on to deal with a number of criticisms of the Bill that had emerged during the debate, as to its character and probable effect, and then finally came to the question of its general political opportuneness. This he dealt with under three heads: in regard to Rome, to foreign countries, and to internal conditions. On the first of these he repeated much that has already appeared in his letters and speeches; that the attitude of hostility on the part of Rome was consonant with her policy all over Europe; that it would have been impolitic on the part of the Government to introduce the measure at this particular juncture, if there had been any sign of improvement in the relations between the two Courts in the near future. But there was not. The introduction of the Law could scarcely make matters worse, its non-introduction would not have made them any better. In regard to foreign countries, Cavour announced that the measure had been received with favour in the Press of nearly every country, including even a number of journals printed in Vienna, and he considered the moment exceptionally opportune from the fact that Europe was far too much occupied with other matters to trouble its head about Piedmont's internal affairs. Then he came to the question of the effect of the Law on Piedmont itself.

It had been said by several speakers that in the present condition of the country, engaged as it was in a European War, it was most inopportune to introduce so contentious a measure. This, said Cavour, would have been an argument of great weight had the country been previously in a state of profound peace. But that was not so. The country had for years been agitated on this question, and if the Government had not brought in this Bill, it would not have lessened the bitter opposition of the ultra-Catholic party, but simply provoked a liberal agitation as well. Then he went on:

> As long as there is inscribed in the Budget a million of lire for the clergy, when the country knows that the income of the Church exceeds 17 millions; as long as you maintain this army of 8,000 and more monks, do not hope to see peace reign in the country. There will always be a large majority

who will insist on the cancellation of this sum and demand the reform of the religious orders. Make this reform and peace will return. And why? for this very simple reason. Because experience shows that the effects of this reform will be very different from what its opponents anticipate; it shows that this reform is without real inconvenience to the clergy themselves, and instead of injuring, it promotes the interests of religion. Make this reform and you will have peace.

The fate of the Bill in the Chamber of Deputies had never really been in doubt, but in this speech Cavour marshalled the case for the Government with a clearness and simplicity that made it irresistible. And when the voting took place the Bill passed with 116 against 36.

Cavour was now allowed a short breathing space before the Law was due for discussion in the Senate, but it was a time filled with unpleasant forebodings. Cavour knew far too much concerning the strategy of Rome to be unduly elated over the success in the Chamber. Rome regarded the struggle in the Chamber of Deputies as a reconnaissance in force, for the real battle was to be fought in the Senate. From Cavour's private correspondence, we can see not merely his private opinion as to the fate of the Bill, but the desperate effort it had required to keep the Cabinet together while the Crimean alliance and the Law on the Convents were before the country. In March he writes as follows to Count Teodoro di Santarosa:

The Ministry [I write it to you under the seal of absolute secrecy] has been for a month or more in a state of permanent crisis. First the question of the treaty, then that of the Convents, has placed the Cabinet twenty times and more upon the edge of resignation. Now, we have at least provisionally retaken our line of march, and it is pretty certain that for some time at least there will be no ministerial changes.[1]

Later in the same month (neither letter has an exact date) he writes again to the same correspondent:

The Committee in the Senate appears hostile to the Law on

[1] Chiala, *Lettere*, vol. ii. No. 343.

the Convents. If the Commission they nominate pronounces against it, it is probable that the Government will resign and its place will be taken by Revel, who has sensed office for a long time. I do not think it would be desirable to create a batch of Senators to overcome the opposition in the Senate. The Law on the Convents is not so popular, it is fought by too many people, to justify using extreme means to make it pass. Revel will obtain from Rome, or the clergy, the sacrifice of the 900,000 francs inscribed in the Budget, and thanks to this, he will be able to exist for a time. Keep the most absolute secrecy about all this.[1]

It is plain from this letter that Cavour did not expect the Bill to survive the discussion in the Senate, and that he had some inkling of what was going on behind the scenes. The fact was that, in the handling of the Bill, Cavour had made a tactical error. By insisting of its character as a financial measure he had laid himself open to a *riposte*, of which the clerical party quickly took advantage. If they should offer to relieve the State of the financial burden, the *raison d'être* for the Bill as a financial measure at once disappeared. It would, of course, be tantamount to a ministerial defeat, the Government would resign, and the situation for which the Church had so long worked would be created. Moreover, the Right coming into power on such conditions would be bound hand and foot to the bishops, for their existence as a Government would have been paid for in hard cash by the Church. The success of this plan depended first on the King. Would he be willing to purchase a fictitious religious peace at the cost of handing over the country to a Government paid for by the clergy? And secondly, would the country stand it? It was a delicate, even a dangerous, situation. The truth seems to have been that the fate of the Law in the Senate was so problematical that the Bishops determined to draw up a counter project of their own. For the success of their plan the consent of both Rome and the King was necessary. Negotiations were at once

---

[1] Chiala, *Lettere*, vol. ii. No. 245.

opened with the Papacy, while all possible pressure was brought to bear upon the King. Victor Emmanuel was in a pitiable state. The reaction after all he had been through had brought him to the edge of a nervous breakdown. 'He has explosions of grief,' wrote Constanza D'Azeglio, 'that are heart-breaking.' In such a condition the task of the bishops was easy. They had a clear field, for neither Cavour nor any other member of the Cabinet was a close personal friend of the King. In an interview with Monsignor Calabiana, Bishop of Casale, the King begged him to help him out of his difficulty, and the bishop consented. Torn between his duty as a Catholic and a Constitutional Sovereign, the King wavered first to one side, then to the other. At one time declaring that he would never sign the Law on the Convents; at another saying the opposite.[1] Cavour, aware of what was going on, though without knowledge of the actual proposal, could only await developments, while doing his best to encourage the King to stand by his oath if the Law was passed. On April 23rd, the discussion on the Law commenced in the Senate, and on the 24th the King received a letter from the Episcopate containing the following proposal:

> As the principal object of the proposed law, according to the literal expressions of the Minister of Finance in his report on the Bill, is to find the means of meeting the charge of 928,412 lire provided by the Government for the support of the parochial clergy, the undersigned, duly authorized, declare that, if the law is at once withdrawn, the episcopate consents that the said sum shall be raised upon the ecclesiastical resources on the mainland, and guarantees the consent of the Court of Rome for the same.

The King, without considering the full implications of this offer, at once welcomed it with the liveliest satisfaction as providing an admirable solution of the difficulty, and having sent for Cavour, gave him the 'very gratifying news', and showed him the bishops' communication. When Cavour read it, he must have

[1] See Treitschke, *Cavour*.

realized the mistake he had made in treating the Law
as a financial measure, thus obscuring the vital political
principle that underlaid it; for he had not only given
the bishops the chance to render the Bill unnecessary,
by offering to provide the money, but had left the
impression on the mind of the King that the financial
problem was the true purport of the Bill. Cavour at
once discerned the full significance of the proposal. If
Parliament accepted it, which he did not believe to be
probable, the Government would have to resign and
be replaced by one that would work with Rome and
the bishops. Cavour's knowledge of the temper of the
country on ecclesiastical matters had long ago convinced
him that this was the one thing the people would not
stand, and he foresaw a struggle between the King and
the nation. He expressed his adverse opinion as to
accepting the offer to the King, but added, that if His
Majesty wished it, he would raise no difficulty to having
the proposal brought before the Senate, reserving,
however, his own freedom of action. The King insisted,
and after a hurried interview with the President it was
arranged that it should be introduced in the form of an
amendment on April 26th.

On April 25th, the day after his interview with the
King, Cavour spoke in the Senate in favour of the Law.
With his knowledge of the proposal that would be put
forward the next day, his words had a special significance, and were addressed as much to the nation and
the King himself, as to the Senate. The difference in
tone between this speech in the Senate and that previously delivered to the Deputies, is very marked. In
this latter, he seemed almost anxious to minimize the
importance of the Law, treating it as a moderate measure
of internal reform; but when he came to address the
Senate he sounded a warning note of a very different
quality. He commenced his speech by summing up
the attitude of the opponents of the Bill in these words:

Gentlemen, the various speakers who have risen to oppose
this Bill, using more or less excited language and carrying

into the discussion an unusual warmth, not to say passion, have condemned it, as contrary to religion and the rights of property; as leading to the application of fatal socialistic and communistic doctrines; as violating formally sanctioned pacts; and finally as odious, revolutionary, and ruinous.

After dealing with a number of legal and economic points relating to the law of property and mortmain, he came to the main object of his speech, which was, to drive home the danger of provoking a deadlock between the King and the country by insistence on a reactionary rather than a progressive policy. The Bill had been fought by a number of speakers as a revolutionary measure of danger to the State, and in defence of this proposition they had used the French Revolution as a parallel. The reforms of 1789, they said, had been introduced by comparatively moderate men, but the result had been their overthrow by the extremists, with all the horrors of 1793. To this argument Cavour replied, with a greater historical accuracy and a point that could scarcely be missed, by remarking that the events of 1793 were to be imputed 'not to the unhappy statesmen of 1789 but rather to those who refused every reform from the commencement of the reign of Louis XVI; to those proud prelates and courtiers who accused Turgot and Malesherbes, as we are now being accused, of being revolutionaries and innovators.'

But the parallel was not sufficiently exact to suit Cavour, and after dwelling on one or two subsidiary points, he brought his speech to a conclusion with the following note of warning:

It has been stated by certain speakers that, as a necessary and inevitable consequence of this law, a great upheaval in the country must ensue. This has been used by some as a warning, by others as a threat. To these I will reply by the lessons of history.

I will begin by declaring that I have too much trust in the sense and patriotism of the episcopate and the national clergy to believe that this danger could be realized. But if it should happen, if this agitation should unhappily exceed a certain limit, I would remind the Senate that it would not

be the first time that fatal struggles have taken place between
the principles of liberty and progress and that of reaction,
cloaked beneath the mantle of religion. In the seventeenth
century in England the reactionary party, led by the Jesuits,
commenced a bitter war on liberty and progress, and the result
of that struggle was the fearful catastrophe that dragged to
irreparable ruin the old and venerated line of the Stuarts.

In times nearer to us in France, after the restoration, a
monarch not less enlightened than prudent succeeded in re-
establishing peace and harmony between the new times and
the old; but when to this monarch another succeeded, who,
having surrendered himself to a party that, under the pretext
of favouring religious interests, fought all progress and
liberty, another struggle broke out that resulted in the ruin
of the old throne of the Bourbons. I trust, gentlemen, that
made wise by the lessons of history, such events will not
take place amongst us, nor do I believe that our venerable
clergy desire to imitate the examples I have brought before
you.

There was no mistaking the warning conveyed by
Cavour's words, and it is probable that they had their
intended effect on the mind of the King, in steadying
him from any tendency to reverse the policy of the
country. The next day, the Bishop of Casale, Monsignor
Calabiana, submitted the proposal of the bishops to the
Senate, as a mark of their 'devotion to the King and
loyalty to the Government.' Immediately the Bishop
had closed his brief speech, Cavour rose and suspended
the sitting, giving as his reason that 'it would be impossible for me and my colleagues to give an immediate
opinion on this very serious proposal until the Cabinet
has thoroughly examined it and also learnt the attitude
of the King towards it.'

That evening the Cabinet met and examined the
proposal and found it unacceptable; then, to give complete freedom of action to the King, the Government
resigned.

The rapidity and decisiveness of Cavour's action was
prompted by that political instinct that never failed him.
He saw at once that the reputation both of himself and

his party would be hopelessly prejudiced in the eyes of the nation if he touched the proposal of the bishops. To delay action would create suspicion, whereas prompt resignation would make his position unmistakably clear. But if Cavour anticipated that the clerical influence with the King had gone so far as to induce him to pledge himself to offer the Presidency to Count Revel and the extreme faction, he was wrong. The first choice of the King fell on the Senator Desambrois; when he refused, the King sent for Boncompagni, the President of the Chamber of Deputies; when he refused also, he turned to General Durando, who had recently succeeded La Marmora as War Minister in the Cabinet. Durando undertook to try to form a Government, though he would not commit himself regarding the acceptance of the bishops' proposal.

In the meantime, the country grasped the situation with extraordinary rapidity. The rumour spread that the country had been sold to Rome, and the blame was laid on the King. It was right, in so far, that the King's support of the proposal of the bishops had obliged him to accept Cavour's resignation, and would force him to accept a Cabinet that was in favour of it, if he could find one; but it was wrong, if it impugned his loyalty to his oath or the Constitution. During these weeks the King suffered bitterly. The clerical camarilla that surrounded him spared him nothing: 'They tell me,' he said, 'that God has punished me: that he has taken my mother, my wife, and my brother because I have consented to these laws; they threaten me with still worse; but do they not know that a sovereign who would win happiness hereafter, must try to make his people on this earth happy?' As the days passed and no decision was reached, the attitude of the populace became more and more threatening. Not since 1848 had Turin witnessed similar scenes. The piazza before the palace was filled with a silent expectant crowd; troops made their appearance; a single tactless order and anything might have happened. But the crowd was orderly and the military tactful and no incident occurred. Durando, to quiet public opinion, issued a proclamation which appeared one morning on all the walls of the city. It was promptly torn down and trodden underfoot. In the meantime, efforts were made in all directions to piece together a Cabinet. Villamarina was sent for from Paris as a possible Foreign Minister. All kinds of leading men were approached, and all refused. When Victor Emmanuel sought advice he was told to recall Cavour. Massimo D'Azeglio, deeply moved at what he considered the King's surrender to the clericals, talked of joining the crowd on the piazza; twice he was refused an interview with the King, and then in despair wrote him a noble letter begging him to retrace his steps from the dangerous path he had chosen. This was what he wrote:

Your Majesty:

In Spain it was forbidden to touch the King under pain of death. There was one whose clothes caught fire; no one dared to touch him and he was burnt to death. But I, if I was to risk my head, or even to lose utterly your favour, would consider myself the most vile of men if at a moment such as this I did not write to you, since I have not been permitted to speak to you in person.

Your Majesty, believe an old and faithful servant, who in serving you has never had a thought but for your welfare, your good name, and the country's good; I say to you with tears in my eyes and kneeling at your feet, *go no further on the road you have taken.* There is still time. Retake the former one. An intrigue of monks has in a day succeeded in destroying the work of your reign; in agitating the country; imperilling the Statute; besmirching your name for loyalty. There is not a moment to lose. The official declarations in the last appeal have not solved the question. It is said that the Crown seeks new lights. Let the Crown say that these lights have shown the proposed conditions to be inacceptable. Let them be considered as if they had not been, and things will retake their normal and constitutional course as before. Piedmont will bear anything: but, to be put again beneath the priestly yoke, no, per Dio!

Consider the intrigues of the monks with the Queen in Spain, to make her sign a shameful concordat, and see where it has led! These intrigues ruined James Stuart, Charles X, and many another. Your Majesty, believe me these things I mention have happened; it is not of religion but of self-interest that they think. Amedeo II fought Rome for thirty years, and won. Be firm, and your Majesty will win likewise. Do not be angry with me, this act of mine is that of a *galantuomo*, a faithful subject and a true friend.[1]

AZEGLIO.

Cavour with grim determination kept himself apart. He knew that this was a matter the King must fight out for himself. There could be no half-measures now. It was Church or State, subjection or independence. Once settled, the road would be clear.

The letter of D'Azeglio, echoing as it did Cavour's speech in the Senate, made the King pause. News of the exasperation of the public reached him. The National Guard, called upon to give cheers for the King, had maintained an ominous silence. Hard things the public were saying about him came to his ears. He realized that this state of things could not go on. Durando could neither get a Cabinet together nor find a line of accommodation with the bishops. The King lost patience and sent this message to the clericals: 'I will wait until three o'clock for their proposals, if they have not come by then, I shall recall the *bestia nera*.'[2] Three o'clock came and no reply. Victor Emmanuel sent for Cavour. The crisis was over.

Cavour once more in the saddle, things quickly reassumed their normal course. But the position was still delicate.

The ship of state is refloated [he wrote], but will it reach port? It is still uncertain, for we have more than one danger to avoid. But it has become possible, thanks to the obstinacy of the bishops who have refused the offer of Durando, which was most moderate. These gentlemen thought themselves certain to be able to force the King, by sheer obstinacy, to nominate a Ministry from the Right. They deceived them-

[1] Chiala, *Lettere*, vol. ii. p. 145.
[2] More familiar in its French form of *bête-noir*.

selves. The King desired an honourable compromise, and
in that he was right; but he never had any idea of putting in
power a party that the country will not have at any price.

The Senate retook their discussion of the Bill, and, after
a last effort of the clericals to postpone a decision for
four months had been defeated, a solution was found
in an amendment of Desambrois, which Cavour
accepted. The amended Bill was in due course presented to the Chamber of Deputies. Cavour wound up
the final debate with these words:

> In constitutional Governments, the parties in opposition,
> that do not bear the burden of responsibility, I do not say,
> can, but ought naturally to propose the *desirable*; the parties
> that share the weight of responsibility, whilst they recognize
> the *desirable*, try to attain the *possible*.
> Now, gentlemen, we believe that for us it was not possible
> to carry a better measure. I trust therefore that we shall be,
> at least in part, absolved from the charges brought against us.
> I conclude by saying that the Ministry has done its utmost
> to promote the solution of this great question. It is of
> opinion that if it is not the best possible, it is, however, such
> as to give satisfaction to all moderate people, those who
> desire progress, yet without its attainment having to be
> bought by too great sacrifices.

When put to the vote the Bill was carried by 95 to
23. The next day the King signed it, as Cavour wrote
to La Marmora 'with a good grace that has made me
quite forget the *mauvais quarts d'heures* that this
wretched Law has caused me.' Then, worn out, he
started for Leri, writing on his arrival to his friend de la
Rive:

> After a bitter struggle, a struggle carried on in Parliament,
> in the salons, in the Court and the street alike, rendered more
> painful by a series of tragic events, I felt myself at the end of
> my intellectual powers and have been obliged to come here
> and try to retemper my forces by some days of rest. Thanks
> to the elasticity of my fibre, I shall soon be fit to take up
> business again, and before the end of the week I expect to be
> back at my post where all the difficulties, which a political
> position that gets wider daily involve, await me.

The Law on the Convents was the coping-stone on the edifice of the new Piedmont. After five years of strenuous reform Piedmont had become a modern state freed at last from the medievalism of the past. The first great task to which Cavour had bent his energies was accomplished and he could now turn to the wider field of foreign policy. Henceforth, though he still remained Minister of Finance, his work lay in the Foreign Office, carrying to its destined end the work inaugurated by the presence of La Marmora and his little army in the Crimea.

VII. THE CONGRESS OF PARIS

WHEN the Law on the Convents was at last upon the
Statute Book, Parliament rose for the summer vacation.
Before the session ended, however, Cavour took the
opportunity to complete the Cabinet, and relieve him-
self of the burden of two portfolios. Deforesta became
Minister of Justice, Lanza of Education, while the
Foreign Office was nominally handed over to Cibrario,
though Cavour retained the direction of policy.

The Crimean War was a struggle between the great
Powers, into which, in a somewhat surprising manner,
one small Power had contrived to enter. This fact,
which angered Austria, was regarded with sympathetic
indifference by France, but was useful to England.
None of the high contracting parties, however, proposed
at first to take much notice of their small ally. She had
refused to let her soldiers be paid for as mercenaries,
which is what would have suited England best, since
it would have removed any future liabilities, and had
insisted on being treated as an ally in all respects on
an equal footing. In spite of this they held Conferences
without consulting her, and gave her politely to understand that, the honour of temporarily sitting beside them
in the same coach was ample reward for the losses and
expense she incurred on their behalf. As to her position
at the Peace Conference, her allies intended it to be that
of the small boy informed by his elders that he cannot
come to the dinner party, but he may come down to
dessert, but he must sit still and not talk. Cavour,
however, was determined that the Piedmontese delegate

should not only sit as an equal with his allies, but that they should listen to what he had to say. In other words, Cavour had made up his mind that, at the Conference called to settle the affairs of Russia, the delegates should talk about Italy, and he had set himself the task of so connecting the two in the minds of the Powers that, a Congress commencing with the neutrality of the Black Sea, should, as a logical sequence, end with the condition of the Papal States.

In the summer of 1855 the question as to the length of the war was already exercising the mind of Cavour. He did not want it to end too soon. It would be disastrous if peace came before the Piedmontese troops had won their spurs. Though it seemed unlikely enough, he still clung to the hope that the equivocal attitude of Austria might cause a breach, and that Piedmont might yet fight Austria instead of Russia. In the meantime, however, his chief preoccupation was to prevent the claims and interests of Piedmont from being overlooked; to clear up the difficult question of her status at the final Conference, and to prepare the policy to be adopted by Piedmont when it came. Reviewing the situation as a whole, it was evident that the chief difficulty in the way was the attitude of Austria. As long as their present strained relations existed, Austria would systematically veto any attempt of Piedmont to obtain territorial compensation, and do her best to exclude her, if possible, from participation in the Congress. Moreover, by the Convention of December 2nd, which Austria had signed with France, the allies had pledged themselves to take immediate steps for further action, if peace was not in sight by the new year, and a Conference had already been arranged to be held at Vienna in March. To this Conference Piedmont had a right to send a representative, but Austria had ignored her, and France and England had taken no notice of the fact. It was not likely that Austria, on her own initiative, would invite Piedmont, with whom for two years now diplomatic relations had been suspended, to send a delegate to Vienna, and neither of her allies would risk offending Austria from an excessive sense of loyalty to Piedmont. Thus, from every point of view, good relations with Vienna seemed desirable, and Cavour determined to make an attempt to re-establish them. For this purpose he invoked the aid of France, and the French Ambassador at Vienna, Bourqueney, approached Count Buol, who admitted that Piedmont had a right to be summoned to the Vienna Conference and agreed to talk the matter over with the Marquis Cantono, the Piedmontese chargé d'affaires. But the olive branch held out by Cavour was not destined to be accepted. At his interview with the Piedmontese chargé d'affaires, Count Buol at once raked up all the smouldering embers of discontent; the Press, the quarrel with Rome, as well as the sequestrations. Determined to keep the breach open, Count Buol insisted on terms that Cavour could not and would not accept with honour, and after two months of fruitless negotiation the attempt at reconciliation was dropped.[1]

Cavour, with a loyal spirit that did him credit, in writing to France and England to explain the impossibility of a *rapprochement* with Austria, added, that, anxious not to cause difficulties for his allies, he would accept the situation and acquiesce in the non-representation of Piedmont at the Vienna Conference.[2]

But the efforts of Vienna to discredit Piedmont had other results, for they opened the eyes of France and England to her power for mischief-making in Italy, and strengthened Cavour's contention that there would be no peace until Austria was driven out. In pursuance of her policy towards Piedmont, Austria soon found another opportunity for interference, this time in Tuscany. The Prime Minister of the Grand Duke, Baldasseroni, had recently accepted, with the accus-

---

[1] Bianchi, *La politique de Cavour*; Chiala, *Lettere*, vol. ii; Mayor, No. 235; Bianchi, *Stor. Doc.*

[2] Bianchi, *Stor. Doc.*, vol. vii. c. vi.

tomed politeness of diplomacy, the appointment of a certain Count Casati to the Sardinian Legation at Florence, then occupied by the Marquis Sauli. This young man was the son of that Count Gabrio Casati who had been President of the Provisional Government at Milan in 1848. As soon as the Austrian representative at Florence, Baron von Hügel, heard of this appointment he determined to make trouble. As the result of his representations to the Grand Duke, Leopold informed Baldasseroni that the nomination was unacceptable, and that he refused to receive Count Casati at Court. The Prime Minister, who, like the Grand Duke himself, was completely under the thumb of Austria, at once hastened to the Piedmontese Minister and demanded the recall of Count Casati, whom he said, as an Austrian Archduke, Leopold could not receive. The Marquis Sauli promptly refused, and referred the matter to Turin. Not content with this, and urged on by von Hügel, Baldasseroni wrote personally to Cibrario requesting not only the recall of Count Casati but that of the Marquis Sauli as well! The reply of Cavour to this rude and unnecessary request was to recall the entire Legation to Turin. Things were in this condition when Count Buol felt it necessary to interfere. Having sent for the Marquis Cantono, he informed him that Austria was greatly interested in the quarrel between Sardinia and Tuscany, and that, if the former did not take the initiative in having the matter settled, the Imperial Government would feel obliged to intervene as in a matter in which she was directly interested.[1] In putting forward this arrogant claim Count Buol overreached himself, and Cavour was the last person to miss an opening when it was offered to him. The note the Piedmontese chargé d'affaires received in reply to his communication was short, but very much to the point:

Since Count Buol has so far exceeded the bounds of prudence and moderation as to use such language, you will explain

[1] Cantono to Cibrario, October 3rd.

to him that his remarks were as offensive in their form as inadmissible in their substance. Among other things you will ask him if, in spite of European Treaties and International Law, Tuscany has ceased to be an independent state; it will be your duty to read this dispatch to Count Buol, and if he persists in his threatening attitude, at which we have been greatly astonished, you will give him to understand that his threats will not have the least influence upon the actions of this Government. Having discharged this duty, you will take a holiday, for which permission is herewith accorded.[1]

But the Marquis Cantono hesitated to present so incisive a document and consulted his French and English colleagues, who advised that he should write to Turin for further instructions. Cavour had anticipated this line of conduct, and in order that Count Buol should reap the full benefit of his mistake, posted a copy of the dispatch to him direct! Count Buol read the dispatch, and knowing that he was in the wrong, took the first opportunity of explaining away his remarks and let the matter drop. Soon after, Austria having withdrawn her support, Tuscany requested the return of the Piedmontese Legation, which was duly accorded, Count Casati being appointed in the interval to the Paris Legation. As the result of this incident Piedmont's relations with Austria became worse rather than better.[2]

While Cavour was thus engaged the thoughts of the nation were engrossed with the Crimea, waiting daily for news of a victory from the East. Every one realized, and none more fully than Cavour, that the fate of Italy was in the haversacks of La Marmora's soldiers. The letters that Cavour wrote to the Piedmontese commander during these months are a revelation of the poignant anxiety that filled his mind and the intensity with which he longed to hear that the Piedmontese troops had been in action.

During these weeks the destiny of Piedmont seemed in the eyes of Cavour to be engaged in a desperate race between peace and victory. Which would come first?

[1] Cibrario to the Marquis Cantono, October 9th, 1855.
[2] See on this affair Bianchi, *Stor. Doc.*, vol. vii. c. 6. § 4.

News of battle or a suspension of hostilities? Cavour had gambled with the fate of his country, and the strain as he stood and watched the ball of fate rolling was cruel.

At length, on August 11th, the Piedmontese troops went into action on the Tchernaia and fought valiantly, as Cavour knew they would. The next day came the telegraphic dispatch, and Cavour proudly writes to the Countess La Marmora as follows:

> MADAME,
>
> The Minister for War has to-day received the following de-spatch from Alfonso:
> This morning the Russians attacked the lines of the Tchernaia with 50,000 men.
> The telegraph will tell you if the Piedmontese are worthy to fight beside the French and English.
> We repulsed the Russians to the cry Viva il Re! Viva la Patria! The Piedmontese have fought splendidly. General Montevecchio is dying. We have lost 200 men. The Russian losses are considerable. The French despatches will tell the rest.

The country received the news with unbounded relief and enthusiasm. The strain had been prolonged, and the reaction gave rise to wild hopes of future victories. La Marmora became the national hero, to whom Cavour at once wrote in terms that reveal the deep pride he felt in the army and its commander:

> I cannot delay expressing to you the immense satisfaction with which the entire country has received the news conveyed in your telegraphic despatch, in which, in terms so noble and expressive, you announce the brilliant feat of arms on the Tchernaia, where for the first time our troops have had the chance of showing of what they were capable, when they fight under a leader worthy to command them. The news has raised the spirit of the nation and reconciled every one to the policy of the alliance. The King is enchanted and bids me compliment you in his name.

The allies gave full credit to the bravery of the Piedmontese troops, and at last the spectre of Novara was laid, and the little country could hold its head high once more before friends and foes alike.

The importance of the battle on the Tchernaia has been obscured by the dramatic events that followed, for scarcely a month later came news of the capture of the Malakoff and the fall of Sevastopol; the military value of the former struggle, however, and the worthy part played by the Piedmontese may be gathered from a letter from Lord Clarendon, in reply to the congratulations of Piedmont on the fall of Sevastopol:

> Her Majesty's Government regret that the gallant army of the King under the command of General La Marmora, who is daily acquiring fresh titles to esteem for the great military talents he displays, should not have taken an active part in that day which will be for ever memorable, but they had already gloriously contributed to the fall of Sevastopol by defeating the Russians on the Tchernaia, and thereby frustrating the plan of general attack which is now known to have been meditated by the Russians.[1]

From Cavour's point of view, however, the political results were of even greater importance. The country became not merely reconciled to but enthusiastic over his foreign policy, the financial burden was borne almost with cheerfulness, and the tone of the whole country was retempered by a much needed tonic. Abroad, it threw Piedmont into a sudden prominence, and a wave of enthusiasm for Victor Emmanuel and his people swept across Europe. It sealed the alliance by the closest of all bonds, and threw up into an unenviable notoriety the time-serving policy of Austria; above all, it strengthened Piedmont's claim to a position of equality in the Conference which the fall of Sevastopol now brought much nearer. Cavour was not slow to take advantage of the new popularity of his country. It decided him to settle quickly the proposed visit of Victor Emmanuel to Paris and London and set him again to work on plans for Piedmont's future.

In spite of all Cavour's arguments and all the pressure

[1] *Clarendon Papers.*

he could bring to bear upon the Cabinets of London and Paris, he could get no guarantee of equality of status for the Piedmontese representative at the Conference. After much correspondence Napoleon went so far as to say that 'the Piedmontese representative should take a direct and personal part in all discussions which concerned his country's particular interests. Beyond this, the French and English delegates would take care to keep the Piedmontese representative daily informed of all matters of general interest discussed by the Congress. Finally, the plenipotentiary of the King of Sardinia should sign the treaty containing the conditions of peace'. The answer from London was identical. But Cavour would not take 'No' for an answer, and continued to press his case with persistence. The part played by the Sardinian troops at the Tchernaia raised the prestige of Piedmont, but neither France nor England could see their way to create a precedent by which a secondary power should be raised to the status of a great power. Such an action might in the future lead to unexpected results, and might enable Austria, for instance, with her influence over the secondary states of Germany and Italy, to have a preponderant voice in every future Conference. But time worked in Cavour's favour. La Marmora, recalled from the Crimea to take part in an imposing military council of the allied generals in Paris, created a good impression. Then Victor Emmanuel went to Paris and London in the autumn, and came through the ordeal with credit, despite the nervous strain which his gauche manners caused to his staff. Fortunately, at Windsor he behaved, said Cavour, 'like a perfect gentleman.' Cavour accompanied him, and though politically the visit was a disappointment and all hopes of a guarantee for territorial compensation for Piedmont disappeared, Lord Clarendon formed 'a very high opinion indeed' of him. But it was at Paris on his return journey that Cavour's hopes at last received some small encouragement. In a conversation that he had with Napoleon, the latter asked him, What can we do for Italy? Cavour requested permission to submit his reply in writing, and on his return sent it to Walewski in the form of a letter of six pages.[1] Like all Cavour's writings and speeches, it is so lucid and concise that it is difficult to quote from, the texture being so close that it must be given *in extenso* or reduced to headings. He started from the following standpoint:

> Austria having taken so large a part in the late events, and by a diplomatic fiction being considered as having rendered a signal service to Europe, it is necessary to take as a starting-point, at least for the moment, that one will not demand from her any territorial sacrifice in Italy. It is upon this basis, unfortunate for us, but one which as a practical man it is necessary to accept, that I indicate the benefits which this country might expect from the decided and benevolent action of the Emperor.

Put in their shortest form Cavour's suggestions may be summed up as follows:

1. To induce Austria by friendly pressure to render justice to Piedmont and to keep the engagements made with her by
   (*a*) removing the decree of sequestrations,
   (*b*) by permitting the junction of the Piedmontese and Lombard railway systems,
   (*c*) by regulating the vexatious police system which harassed the commercial and personal relations between Lombards and Piedmontese.
2. By forcing the King of Naples to cease scandalizing Europe by conduct contrary to all the principles of justice and equity.
3. By a thorough reform of the Papal States in the Romagna: this is to be done by
   the removal of the Austrian troops: by putting the Romagna under the rule either of the Duke of Modena or the Grand Duke of Tuscany. If

---

[1] Cavour asked D'Azeglio to write it, but the consequent brochure did not satisfy Cavour, it was too long and wanting in conciseness, so he wrote the reply himself. D'Azeglio was not pleased.

this is not practical, then, to secularize the administration completely, rendering it entirely independent of interference from Rome, with an administrative centre at Bologna or Ravenna, without however removing the State from the Papal power.[1]

Cavour did not entirely leave out the claims of Piedmont to consideration, remarking that, if the Romagna was bestowed upon Modena or Tuscany, this would lead to a 'territorial revision in which Piedmont would be able to find a just compensation for the sacrifices she had made.' The simplicity and moderation of these proposals, so carefully designed to avoid the veto of Austria, ensured a good reception both from Walewski and Napoleon, and provided Cavour with a basis for an Italian programme at the Congress, always presupposing that the Italian question could be brought upon the agenda.

On January 16th the Czar accepted the proposals of Austria as the basis of a Conference and peace now became assured. In France the news was received with general enthusiasm. The bells were rung and the streets illuminated, stocks went up five francs, and Paris delightedly anticipated the pleasures of an International Congress. England was less demonstrative; she was fully prepared to continue the .war unless her peace terms were accepted. In Piedmont the news caused consternation.

> Peace is deplorable for us [wrote Cavour to La Marmora], I am in despair about it, but not being able to stop it one must accept it, and try and draw all possible advantage from the bad position in which this crafty trickster Austria has placed us. The news has been received with general grief. Liberals of all shades are in dismay over it, and the *codini* themselves are not too pleased about it. The King after an angry outburst has accepted it with resignation.

It now became urgent to appoint a representative. To the general surprise Cavour refused to go himself

[1] Chiala, *op. cit.*, No. 415. Also in Zini.

and induced the Cabinet to appoint D'Azeglio. The only explanation of this is that Cavour expected failure, and rather than risk his own political future, he wished to send D'Azeglio, who had nothing to lose. D'Azeglio accepted, but when he found out, almost by accident, from the Duc de Guiche, that he would not be on an equality but be treated as a secondary Power, which Cavour with a great lack of candour had not told him, he indignantly refused to go, and Cavour was compelled to take his place.[1] But things turned out better than Cavour expected. Though neither England nor France would accept the responsibility of establishing a precedent, the very high opinion they had of Cavour, and a genuine sense of loyalty to their ally, prepared them to make an exception in this particular case. Thus, though the position of Piedmont was never exactly defined, before the Congress opened, Cavour's persistent and skilful diplomacy had in fact assured his position, and amongst all the parties concerned, not excepting Austria, the right of Cavour to sit as an equal amongst equals was tacitly admitted. This is a fair inference from the following letter from Lord Clarendon to Hudson, dated Paris, February 23rd:

A meeting was held two days ago at the Foreign Office here, to settle the mode of procedure to be followed at the Conference, and I expressed my regret that Count Cavour had not been summoned. A long conversation then took place respecting the *locus standi* of Sardinia, in which Count Buol took the principal part, but I must do him the justice to say, in a most respectful and friendly tone towards Sardinia. He argued that we should be erecting Sardinia into a first-rate Power, which would disturb the settled order of things in Europe, and create a precedent which might be inconvenient hereafter; that, moreover, the very treaty about to be negotiated, might entail obligations as well as charges upon Sardinia which might be onerous for her to fulfil, such as maintaining vessels to watch the Danube. There was truth as well as fairness in some of Count Buol's observations, but I main-

[1] See Castelli, *Ricordi*, for the inner history of Cavour's appointment as plenipotentiary.

tained that, without having any wish to give to Sardinia a European importance to which she did not herself pretend, she must at the approaching Conference be treated on a footing of perfect equality. I said that Sardinia had behaved towards us with chivalrous boldness: she had at once accepted our invitation to join the Western Alliance, and had launched into the war without inquiring about conditions or caring for consequences; that we would never abandon our friend or permit any slight to be put upon her because we might not stand in want of her at the moment. No formal proposition was definitely made about interfering with Sardinia, and all that Lord Cowley and I would admit was that, if Count Cavour considered that any particular question did not concern Sardinia, he would be at liberty to attend the Conferences or not as he thought fit, while that particular question was under discussion.[1]

If this letter had been written in time to be read to Cavour before he left for Paris, it would have given him great satisfaction, but he left Turin on February 13th. The substance of it was, however, repeated to him by Lord Clarendon in person at their first meeting.[2] It is in fact a complete justification of the bold course adopted by Cavour in joining the alliance regardless of safeguards and guarantees, and it is pleasant for the English reader to find that England, at least in the person of her Foreign Secretary, appreciated the audacity of that act, and that the trust that Cavour at all times reposed in the honourable conduct of England was not misplaced.

Cavour left for Paris, however, before these opinions were expressed, and his state of mind was one of deep depression. What worried him was the problem as to whether he could rely as surely on the support of France and England as he could on the opposition of Austria and Russia. The Italian question he knew was, after all, a side issue, though he had done his best to make it appear as an obstruction in the very centre of

[1] *Clarendon Papers.*
[2] See letter to D'Azeglio in No. 63 in Bianchi's *La politique de Cavour.*

the mainline to peace. Could he make the Conference
see it? Would his position be such, and his influence
of sufficient weight, to have it brought up in despite of
Austria? Determined that it must be everything or
nothing, he wrote his own instructions in the name of
Cibrario, in which it was clearly stated that, if his
position was not entirely satisfactory, 'the plenipoten-
taries of Sardinia are instructed to retire from the
Congress, and M. de Cavour, after having protested,
will leave Paris.' On the eve of departure he wrote to
Villamarina, who was the second representative, 'it is
possible, it is even probable, that the present mission
will be the last act of my political life. I am glad to
finish my career beside you, persuaded that you will
assist me in my last moments with the affection of which
you have given so many proofs.' But on his arrival
in Paris his gloomy forebodings were speedily dissipated. 'The question of our admission to the Conferences without restrictions,' he wrote, 'was settled in
our favour without difficulty. Walewski was perfectly
explicit in our first meeting. But every doubt was removed by the Emperor, who said to Clarendon, "I
could not conceive how it could be otherwise." The
only word of reserve was uttered by Clarendon, who
said, "you have too much tact to take part in matters
that do not concern you at all. You will assist at their
discussion and think of something else." "But," he
added quickly, "in truth I cannot imagine what the
question would be that did not interest you." The
principle vindicated, there remains the substance, this
is the difficulty!'

Cavour came to the Congress with an extra resolution
in his pocket, which it was his firm intention to affix
to the Agenda of the Conference, a resolution that
might have been worded that 'in the opinion of this
Conference the condition of Italy is dangerous and
deplorable and the cause of it is Austria.' He was
determined that before they separated the delegates of
the Powers should understand the true condition of

Italy, the dangers that such a state of things created, and hear in outline at least, the remedies demanded by the situation. In the general discussion that he hoped would be provoked, concrete proposals designed to free one or more Italian provinces from the tentacles of the Austrian octopus might emerge, and as a result some territorial compensations for Piedmont's sacrifices in the war might be forthcoming. But Cavour was under no illusion as to the improbability of obtaining anything tangible for Piedmont. In his case it was no question of the Prime Minister of a small Power trying to gratify the vanity of his country by enlarging the boundaries of the State. Cavour had a wider knowledge of European problems than any delegate at the Conference, and with his European outlook he knew the difficulties of his own proposals better than any one else. He put forward his schemes for territorial changes in Italy partly because his political position at home might be endangered if he returned absolutely empty-handed; and partly because he held it to be a duty to rescue any scrap of Italian soil from the brutal dominance of Austria. But his real object was to impeach Austria before the assembled Powers, to justify the claim of Italian nationality, and erase the cynical dictum of Metternich that Italy was 'a geographical expression'. This, he knew, in the state of European relations was the utmost that was possible.

Now the difficulties of the task that Cavour had set himself were enormous. In the first place it was entirely outside the scope and purpose of the Congress; in the second place the delegates had no instructions to deal with such a question and had no desire to do so; and in the third place it would be certain to stir up animosities which might split the alliance of the Western Powers into fragments. The Austrian delegates could be relied on to veto any and every proposition that Cavour put forward. The representatives of France would do the same, for Cavour found Walewski systematically anti-Italian and Bourqueney 'more Austrian than Buol'. Lord Clarendon, though genuinely sympathetic towards Italian aspirations, and holding very strong personal views as to the abominable government of the Papal States and Naples, was very firm on not upsetting the settlement made by the Treaty of Vienna; while Napoleon was only too willing to throw over this latter, but was equally anxious not to offend Austria, and mortally afraid of hurting the feelings of the Pope, whom he desired as godfather to the Prince Imperial, who was born during the Congress. Russia was not interested, except in so far as she supported the King of Naples, whose methods of government were abhorrent to the rest of the Conference, Austria excepted.

At the moment the Congress opened, the results of Cavour's diplomacy had reached this point, that Lord Clarendon had consented to speak on the Italian question if it was brought up, and Napoleon had expressed himself as sympathetic towards bringing it up, but did not see how it could be done. Both of them, however, would have been quite satisfied if the Italian question had been indefinitely shelved and the Congress had closed without any mention of Italy. Cavour, in fact, had to lift the dead weight of the entire Conference. It was Cavour *contra mundum*, and the story of how in the face of the apparently insuperable obstacles he contrived to get the problem of Italy discussed, is a record of skill and pertinacity rarely surpassed. From the start friendship with Clarendon and pressure on Napoleon were the two cardinal points in Cavour's diplomacy. Throughout the Congress Cavour led a kind of double diplomatic life; an inner life of intense effort concentrated on making Napoleon add the Italian question to the agenda of the Conference and on urging Lord Clarendon to speak strongly on behalf of Italy, and an outer life spent in the Conferences and amid the social life of Paris equally concentrated on creating a sympathetic atmosphere for Italy and inoculating the world of diplomacy with her real needs and difficulties.

We are fortunate in having in the letters written by Cavour to Emanuele D'Azeglio, the Sardinian Minister in London, an intimate record of Cavour's diplomacy during the Congress.[1] They were written chiefly for the ear of Lord Palmerston, and were intended to keep him informed, from the Italian standpoint, of how things were going. The occasional use of the phrase 'échauffez Palmerston' reveal their purpose, though the process was not so effective in the hands of D'Azeglio as the corresponding process of 'warming up Clarendon' was in the capable hands of Cavour himself. Yet if Cavour was sincere in what he said, he did not like the role of diplomat, though he had very great aptitude for it nevertheless. To great quickness of perception and an intuitive sense of what was passing in the mind of his adversary, he added the chess-master's gift of calculating all the moves upon the board. He was outspoken and candid, though he had great powers of secrecy and self-control, together with a ready tongue that could be equally incisive or humorous, and he could turn aside an awkward question or relieve a tense situation with masterly skill. But he was no rash talker and knew all the value of silence. His energy and activity was unceasing, and to great mental and physical strength he added, thanks to what he called his 'elasticity of fibre', a recuperative power that after the most exhausting labour enabled him to rise perfectly refreshed after four or five hours of sleep. In society he appeared as an admirable talker, full of anecdote and quick repartee, distinguished by a *brio* and lightness of touch that deceived people as to how much there was beneath.

Cavour made friends very quickly, and once in Paris he was soon on good terms with the majority of the delegates. He quickly won over the Russians, and later was on friendly terms with the Prussians, whilst from the first his relations with Lord Clarendon were most cordial. The Austrian and the French delegates were his chief opponents, but the cause of Italy was not

[1] Published by Bianchi under the title *La politique de Cavour*.

without its highly placed friends. Napoleon himself
had been under the spell of Italy from the days of his
youth; his uncle, Jerome, the Princess Matilde, and
Prince Napoleon, were also warm supporters of her
cause. Benedetti, the secretary of the Conference,
Corsican by birth and Italian by sympathy, dropped
more than one hint of value to Cavour before the Congress ended. But Cavour had his own inner circle of
influence with the Emperor. There was Count Arese,
an old and intimate friend of his exile, who since
Napoleon's accession had been the normal channel of
private information, and now for the first time appears
the name of one who, from this time onwards, was to be
the intermediary between Cavour and Napoleon in their
most secret correspondence, Dr. Conneau. Three days
before the Congress opened Cavour writes to Count
Arese:

> The excellent Conneau, after leaving a card on me, returned
> yesterday morning early and told me at once in a tone of real
> satisfaction that, according to your expressed desire, he had
> asked and obtained permission from the Emperor to act as our
> intermediary, and said he was prepared to receive and trans-
> mit all communications that I thought necessary to send to
> the Tuileries. Conneau requested secrecy, which I promised,
> so that no one in Paris or Turin, yourself excepted, will know
> of this precious channel of communication for bringing our
> desires before the Emperor.

Having established his lines of communication,
Cavour could now go forward. He had arrived in Paris
on February 16th. On 21st he had his first interview
with the Emperor, of which the above appears to have
been the firstfruits. Then he interviewed Clarendon.

> Clarendon has been perfect [he writes], he told me about the
> Conference yesterday with Walewski and Buol. He com-
> plained about my not being invited to it. Buol, he said, raised
> the question of my being admitted on a basis of perfect
> equality, but on his declaring that England would not allow
> the status of her ally to be called in question, Buol no longer
> insisted. Clarendon is very well satisfied with Buol, who is
> much more anti-Russian than Walewski. He does not trust

this latter, but has full confidence in the Emperor, who treats him with the greatest distinction and gives him his complete confidence.

Three days later the Congress opened. Writing the next day to D'Azeglio Cavour has these words:

The first seance of the Conference has passed off very well. Walewski as President was very amiable and polite, but weak. He never feels certain from one moment to another that he will not be caught out by my neighbour Brunnow, who is one of the most crafty individuals I have ever come across. The said Brunnow is very clever with his pen, and I performed a service to the English delegates by warning them to be very careful of the words they use, of which, perhaps, they do not always grasp the exact significance. Orloff affects a very bluff and hearty manner, but for all that at bottom he is just as crafty. The Russians speak with horror of the Austrians. Orloff loves the French, respects the English, but scorns the Austrians. I don't think he is acting. His eye is ferocious when he speaks of these gentry.

During the early sittings Cavour was discretion itself. Speaking very little but when necessary giving his opinion in a few words, always to the point and on the Liberal side. But he missed nothing, and watched with quiet amusement the rival diplomats measuring swords and jockeying one another for the lead. 'In the second sitting which took place yesterday,' he writes on February 29th, 'Brunnow has been still more crafty than in the first. He tried quite simply to put us out of court by means of a double-edged reservation. But Clarendon snubbed him sharply. The Russian swallowed the rebuke and on the advice of Orloff withdrew his reservation. Brunnow finesses too much and over-reaches himself. With all his sham bluffness Orloff is much the cleverer of the two. Bourqueney read what is called 'the elucidation of the four points', but the phlegmatic Ali, the Turkish delegate, remarked that the ideas were more muddled at the close of the debate than at the commencement.'

The first two sittings of the Congress were sufficient

to prove to Cavour that the real work of the Conferences was done in secret behind the scenes, and that the
debates were only a solemn form, the substance of which
had been previously settled elsewhere. In short, that
all parties were doing exactly what he himself was
engaged in.

> There have been all kinds of pourparlers during these recent
> days [he writes] between the different plenipotentiaries,
> especially between the Russians and the Anglo-French.
> They are, I believe, very nearly in accord in spite of their
> apparent rivalry. The Russians will yield on nearly all points
> provided that they get that bit of Bessarabia that it was
> proposed to take from them. The Emperor is entirely in
> favour of this concession, and Clarendon, who on the first
> day rejected it with hauteur, now begins to say that the ques-
> tion of Bessarabia is in essence an Austrian question, that
> England has only a small interest in it, &c. To me it is
> plain that unless he gets positive orders Clarendon will end
> by yielding. As things are, it is much the best thing to do,
> for neither France nor the Emperor are prepared to make war
> for a scrap of Bessarabia.

One of the critical questions was the fate of the great
fortress of Kars which the Russians had taken from
Turkey and did not want to give back. England, on
the other hand, was as determined that it should be
restored as she was that the Åland Islands should not
be fortified by Russia. The debate on these points took
place the first day of March and Cavour gives us the
following account of it. It may be mentioned that Lord
Clarendon, when excited or pleased, had a trick of
rubbing his chin, as Cavour himself used to rub his
hands; Cavour sometimes called him 'l'homme du
menton chatouilleux':

> The height of the storm, the fifth point, is passed. Peace,
> which was very probable, now becomes certain or pretty
> nearly so. England has obtained the non-fortification of the
> Åland Islands and the restitution of Kars. Clarendon was
> very fine upon the Kars question. He declared that England
> would have fought for twenty years rather than yield on this
> point. He rubbed his chin and overturned his chair in

assuming *une pose dramatique*. His attitude calmed Orloff,
who was getting angry—

and then he adds the significant words:

> Peace being now assured I am going to drop my attitude of
> reserve and take Clarendon, whom up to now I have left in
> peace, seriously in hand. To-morrow we assist at the opening
> of the Chambers. Tuesday will settle Nicolaieff, and Wednes-
> day, I pounce upon the English plenipotentiaries.

Napoleon was already surrounded with a network of
influence and suggestion calculated to keep the need
for doing something for Italy continually before him;
but it was also necessary to have definite proposals to
put forward, and these occupied much of Cavour's
thought. In the scheme that he had originally suggested
in his letter to Walewski,[1] the central point had been
the Romagna, which he had proposed either to divide
between Tuscany and Modena or to secularize completely, whilst preserving the nominal suzerainty of the
Pope. But Cavour soon discovered that, at the moment,
this plan was impracticable. The birth of an heir to
the throne, which was expected during the Congress,
and the determination of the Empress to have the Pope
as her child's godfather, made Cavour's plan impossible.
To despoil the Pope of his estates or even to take the
management of them out of his hands, as a reward for
a favour bestowed, was hardly a proposition to be
seriously entertained by the Emperor. Cavour, therefore, devised an alternative. This was to appoint the
Duke of Modena to the throne of the proposed united
provinces of Moldavia and Wallachia, transfer the
Duchess of Parma to Modena, and join Parma to
Piedmont. When first mentioned to the Emperor he
was warmly in favour of it. 'The Emperor has said to
me,' Cavour writes as early as February 26th, 'that
as soon as the chief questions are settled and peace is
assured with Russia, he will raise the Italian question,
and propose squarely to send the Duke of Modena to
the Principalities, translate the Duchess of Parma to

[1] See p. 192.

Modena, and cede Parma to Piedmont.' But when this plan was put before Clarendon he preferred the original idea; 'he would like better,' wrote Cavour, 'manger un morceau du Pape.' But on examination the second plan was found almost as difficult of execution as the first. The Duke of Modena was an Austrian Archduke, and the Austrians were exceedingly unpopular in the Principalities., 'All the Moldo-Wallachians who come to see me,' Cavour writes, 'declare they would prefer a Russian prince or a Phanariote to an Austrian Archduke, in the second place I don't think in the present mood of the Russians that they would accept a cousin of Franz Joseph, a fanatic Catholic, and a humble servitor of the Pope to boot.' So Cavour had to cudgel his brains to find a third solution. The crux of the problem was how and where to remove the Duchess of Parma so that her duchy might come to Piedmont. The Duchess was a widow of thirty-eight with a son eight years old. It was obvious that a woman could not be sent to rule at Bukarest or Jassy. She would have to be married. But to whom to marry her was the problem. The only person who seems to have occurred to Cavour, whose knowledge of the European matrimonial market was doubtless not as extensive as that of the commercial market, was the Prince di Carignano, a cousin of Victor Emmanuel and an ardent Catholic. So he writes to D'Azeglio in London proposing to marry the Duchess of Parma to the Prince, send them to Bukarest, and trusting there will be no issue from the marriage, declare the young Duke of Parma heir-presumptive. 'It has at least the advantage of being more dramatic than the other solutions,' he adds. Before long even this solution was seen to be hopeless.

But the rock upon which Cavour's hopes were wrecked, in regard to transferring an Italian princeling to the Principalities, was the opposition offered to their union into a single State, and the determination of Turkey to retain her suzerainty. Cavour and Napoleon were strongly in favour of union. They held that dis-

united both Principalities would be under Austrian
influence and would rapidly become a battleground for
Austrian, Russian, and Turkish intrigues, and be, in
fact, worse off than at present. Austria and Turkey,
backed at first by England, were opposed to union. The
first two, because their influence would be greater over
two weak states than one compact one, the latter,
because in her opinion a single State would be dominated
by Russian influence. Although Cavour realized the
possibility of benefit to Italy if a prince was to be
appointed, it was not on this ground that he defended
so strongly the principle of union.

> The Union of the Principalities is required in the best interests
> of both countries; if they are not united and formed into a
> strong and compact state, they will remain as in the past,
> plunged in corruption and disorder. All the Wallachians
> and Moldavians who come to me declare that union is the
> principal benefit they expect from the Congress. It will be
> a veritable shame if Europe leaves these two countries a prey
> to anarchy and the intrigues of Russia and Turkey. I cannot
> conceive the motives that keep Clarendon in uncertainty,
> unless it is the tales that Lord Stratford writes to him, who
> wants to establish an ultra-liberal régime with full liberties,
> a weak central Power and strong Chambers, just as if he was
> dealing with an old Anglo-Saxon stock. For Heaven's sake
> persuade Palmerston that it will be a crime of lèse-civilization
> if he sustains the status quo and opposes himself to the just
> desires of the whole Roumanian population.

Cavour fought hard for union. He insisted that the
Nationals should be consulted and begged Lord Clarendon to ask those in Paris for their opinion. He suggested making use of Lord Shaftesbury and Exeter Hall
to bring pressure to bear on Lord Palmerston and the
English Government. 'It would be truly desolating,'
he wrote, 'if Lord Palmerston is faithless to the Liberal
principles that he has proclaimed all his life in Parliament, on the only occasion he has had of putting them
into practical application.' But though England came
round, the Congress was beaten by the obstinacy of

Turkey and Austria, and no definite union was proclaimed, and in consequence no prince was required to occupy the throne. The problem was solved the year following by the independent selection of the same man as their ruler by both States.

The debates on the union of the Danubian principalities dragged on day after day; Turkey and Austria always obdurate and a settlement getting less and less likely. At last, Walewski suggested a special commission to deal with it, and the proposal was accepted. But when the names of those selected were read over, Sardinia was left out. Cavour said nothing at the moment, but promptly raised so many objections and difficulties that the matter was left over to the next meeting. That evening Cavour let Clarendon and the Emperor know what had taken place, and the next meeting was stormy. Clarendon was furious, 'fit to break windows,' Cavour said. The Emperor sent Bourqueney (to whom Cavour attributed the omission of Sardinia) to request Count Buol to include a representative of Sardinia on the panel, but Buol refused. The situation was saved by Cavour, who, satisfied that the rights of Sardinia had been sufficiently asserted, calmed down Clarendon and quietly withdrew his claim to representation. The reason for his action was that he foresaw that on this particular question he would have had to take sides against either France or England, and thereby prejudice their joint action later on behalf of Italy. But Count Buol was soon made to pay for his mean attempt to slight Sardinia. At the same sitting the question of the navigation rights on the Danube was on the agenda. Buol with a great show of candour proposed to add, to the clause that declared the navigation of the river free to all nations, the words, 'save the acquired rights and existing conventions.' It was just one of those points where Cavour's special knowledge was of value. No one saw anything exceptional in the phrase, and all were prepared to pass it without comment, when Cavour asked 'if by that he intended to preserve the monopoly of the steamship navigation previously granted to certain companies?' Buol, after hesitating, said, 'Yes.' This reply had an electric effect on the Conference and above all on Clarendon, who broke out in strong denunciation of Austrian rapacity, and after a long opposition Buol was forced to refer the matter to Vienna for reconsideration. It was an effective *exposé* of Austrian ideas of freedom.[1]

The Congress had now been sitting for nearly three weeks, and despite all Cavour's efforts the likelihood of any material change in the governments of Italy, or any territorial compensation for Piedmont, seemed more remote than ever. One plan after another had met first with qualified approval from Napoleon and then had been quietly laid aside as impracticable. Cavour realized it as inevitable, and decided to evacuate his advanced positions and concentrate on his main line of defence, a discussion on the condition of Italy. In anticipation of this necessity he had written to his friend Castelli begging him to go at once to Bologna and ask Marco Minghetti to prepare a memorial signed by men of repute upon the true state of the Romagna, and then to come to Paris as quickly as possible.

Minghetti arrived in Paris with the memorial on the 10th of March. He found Cavour 'more irritated than confident', and the position having changed and his previous work not meeting the case, Minghetti was set to work to draw up two fresh notes, one to prove that the reforms promised by the Papacy since 1831 had never in the least particular been carried out, and another, in which was to be embodied a full plan for the administrative reform of the Legations. They were written in two days, and on the 13th of March were sent to Lord Clarendon and on the following day to the Emperor. Cavour was in a feverish state of strain. The work of the Congress was drawing to a close, a few more sittings and peace would be signed, and not a

[1] See the amusing description of this incident in the letter of Count Oldofredi to Massari, Appendix C.

word as yet of Italy. On the 16th the Prince Imperial was born, and Cavour, his notes, and even Italy, were forgotten in the orgy of paternal pride and excitement. For some days the proud father was quite incapable of business, the sittings were suspended, and Cavour, irate and impatient, had to curb himself as best he might.

In the interval of waiting until the Imperial father returned to his normal condition Cavour redoubled his efforts to 'échauffer Clarendon.' The British Plenipotentiary at last began to respond. He sent for Sir Edmund Lyons for consultation, who on hearing of Cavour's plan, remarked that there would be some difficulty in making the Pope swallow the pill in preparation. Clarendon repeated this opinion to Cavour, who replied, 'certainly, if you only intend to use compliments and caresses to succeed; what is necessary is that Napoleon takes the Pope by the nose and you hold him by the chin,' at which, he adds, 'Clarendon rubbed his own and laughed much.' On March 19th Cavour obtained an audience with the Emperor, with him came Lord Clarendon, by now infected by Cavour's enthusiasm and strength of purpose. The Emperor began by expressing his desire that the Congress before it closed should take into consideration not only the condition of Italy but the desirability of 'revising existing treaties.' This, of course, meant the Treaty of Vienna. This suggestion alarmed Lord Clarendon, who, however, turned it cleverly by remarking that this would result in drawing together Austria, Russia, and Prussia, and reconstituting the former alliance of the North. Then the Emperor proposed that the excesses of the Belgian Press and the Swiss refugee question might be coupled with the Italian question, but here again Lord Clarendon countered the proposal by remarking that while he deplored the excesses of the Press he would be unable to counsel repressive measures. Clarendon's attitude on this point was of real value to Cavour, for the Piedmontese Press was an old source of complaint both at Vienna and Paris, and a discussion would have offered to Count Buol a fine line of attack on Piedmont. Then the Emperor suggested that the questions of Greece and Italy might be jointly considered. This pleased both Cavour and Clarendon, whereupon Napoleon promised to instruct Walewski to add these two questions to the agenda. At last the question of Italy was to be brought forward! The idea of the Emperor in thus coupling together Greece and Italy was that both countries being occupied by foreign troops it would introduce the Italian question in a manner less irritating to Austria. Napoleon proposed, moreover, to suggest to the Conference that as peace was now a reality all foreign occupations should cease. Both Clarendon and Cavour gladly acquiesced in this suggestion, and to stimulate Walewski Cavour put in hand a note on the subject.

It was a masterly stroke on Cavour's part to induce Lord Clarendon to accompany him to this audience with the Emperor. For Cavour represented a State of very small importance, whose claims could easily enough be brushed aside for political reasons, if later other influences had been brought to bear on the Emperor; but this could not be done when his word was given to both Piedmont and England. Further, it pledged Lord Clarendon to take a leading part. For Cavour to have spoken on behalf of Italy was to be expected, and would have carried little weight, but a denunciation by England's representative was a very different matter, and Cavour was now assured that the lead would be taken by Lord Clarendon. The weak point of the position was the passive resistance of the French representatives to the policy of the Emperor, for neither Walewski nor Bourqueney was prepared to say a word against Austria or to condemn the government of the Papacy.

The Congress was now rapidly drawing to a close. Every one was anxious to see it finished. The delegates were tired and fractious. The English quarrelled with

the Prussians over the preamble, the Turks and the
Russians fell out over the Christian populations in
Turkish hands, and Buol, whose arrogance and unpleasant manners made him generally disliked, finally
exasperated Walewski over the evacuation of the Principalities. Cavour, always alive to an opportunity, seized
the moment when Walewski was annoyed with Buol
to hand him a note-verbale on the Italian question.
Caught at the right moment, he received it with a good
grace and promised to speak to Buol with energy on
the matter. On March 30th the Peace was signed.
'The drama is finished,' wrote Cavour, 'and the curtain
falls without having revealed any denouement materially
favourable to us. The result is sad but not discouraging.
Thanks to us, opinion in regard to Italy is singularly
improved. It will end by changing the facts that
politics believes it must respect.'

Just at this moment when the friendship of Clarendon
was of such vital import to Italy, Cavour was fortunate
enough to be able to do him a good turn and at the
same time to put the arrogant Buol in his place. Bourqueney had informed Buol that, as soon as peace was
signed, the delegates should present themselves at the
Tuileries to announce the fact to the Emperor. Cavour
got wind of this and informed Clarendon, who agreed,
and announced that he would move a motion to that
effect the next morning. But Bourqueney intended this
role to be played by Austria not England, and invited
Buol to move the resolution. Cavour heard of Bourqueney's little plan from the Prussians, and at once told
Clarendon, who came down early on purpose, and when
Buol arrived he found that Clarendon had forestalled
him. The Emperor was gratified, for after thanking
the Congress, he addressed some special words of
thanks to Lord Clarendon.

After the signing of the treaty the Italian question
suddenly came to the front. Palmerston, Clarendon,
and the Emperor all commenced to show a real interest
in Italian problems. The Emperor said to Clarendon,

'Propose to the Congress that the Duchy of Modena is decreed reversible to Parma and Parma given to Piedmont.' Palmerston devised a variation of Cavour's last plan, and wrote suggesting that King Otho was removed from the throne of Greece and the throne offered to the Prince di Carignano, who was to marry the Duchess of Parma and hand over that Duchy to Piedmont. Cavour welcomed all these suggestions, for they showed an interest in Italy, but he realized them as impracticable, for over all alike hung the veto of Austria, and as he knew, Napoleon, in the last instance, was unprepared as yet to break with the Empire of the Hapsburgs.

During the last days of the Congress the result of Cavour's tireless efforts on behalf of Italy began to appear. The network of suggestion with which the Emperor was surrounded had converted the Italian question almost into an obsession, so much so, that even as he strode up and down his room during the anxious hours when he awaited word of the birth of the Prince Imperial, he was heard muttering, 'certainly something must be done for Italy.' The academic interest in Italian questions with which Lord Clarendon had come to the Congress had, under the fostering care of Cavour, become a suppressed fury of indignation against the policy of Austria and her satellites throughout the Peninsula. The Russians, who had arrived scornful and bitter against the part taken by Piedmont in the war, had been completely won over. Cavour's demand for the immediate raising of the naval blockade upon the conclusion of peace had delighted them, and Cavour was able to write to Cibrario, 'as to the Russians they have been very explicit. Count Orloff shows us the greatest friendship, and Brunnow lavishes the most kind phrases upon us. Yesterday, Orloff said to me when shaking hands, "I have written to the Emperor this morning that we have every reason to be gratified with the Sardinian plenipotentiaries!" ' It was the same with the Prussians, 'at least we have won the friendship and sympathy of the Prussians,' he writes in the same letter; 'Baron Manteuffel, though a very reserved man by nature, gives us every evidence of esteem and good-will. His colleague, Count Hatzfeldt, goes much farther, and talks of the identity of our interests *vis-à-vis* to Austria and the causes of complaint she gives to both alike, in a manner that positively suggests making advances towards us.' All this had an immediate as well as a future value, for it at least ensured a benevolent neutrality and no active opposition when Cavour took the field against Austria. Of his personal popularity and the deep impression his statesmanlike qualities had made upon the delegates there is not the least doubt. Thiers, who was certainly in a position to know, said to Minghetti, 'Is it nothing to sit as an equal with the great Powers? Is it nothing to be represented by a minister held in high esteem and praised by every one? He is the Benjamin of the Plenipotentiaries, and on every side I hear eulogies of his great ability; if you want more you are insatiable.' Thiers spoke with astonishment of the prestige Cavour had acquired, though to the last he did not believe his influence could be so great as to be able to bring up the Italian question before the Congress closed.

At length, on April 8th, the Italian question emerged. Walewski had received his instructions from Napoleon, and however ungrateful the task, it had to be carried out. To render it as palatable as possible to his friends the Austrians, he sandwiched the Italian question between the occupation of Greece on the one side, and the iniquities of the Belgian Press on the other. In opening the subject, the almost casual tone that he adopted, made it clear that he was anxious to impress the Conference with the fact that the matters discussed were of small importance, and that the debate itself was strictly unofficial. It seemed desirable, he said, before the Conference broke up, that the Plenipotentiaries should exchange ideas upon a number of matters that required solution, and upon which it might be useful to have the opinions of the delegates to prevent possible

future complications. Then after touching briefly on
the abnormal condition of Greece, and the desirability
of altering it, he came to the problems of Italy. The
States of the Church were, he said, likewise in an
abnormal condition. It had been found necessary, on
the invitation of the Pope, that France should occupy
Rome and Austria the Legations. France was ready to
evacuate Rome as soon as it could be done* without
compromising the interior tranquillity of the country,
and he hoped that Austria would be prepared to do the
same. Then, dealing vaguely with the general conditions
of the country, he invited the Conference to say whether
it was not desirable that certain Governments in the
Peninsula should be advised to display a greater spirit
of clemency towards their people. Having thus touched
with the lightest possible hand upon the brutal methods
of Austria and her satellites, and on the iniquitous rule
in the Papal States, he passed on to Naples. The conduct of the King of Naples Walewski denounced with
a warmth that contrasted strongly with his gentle
handling of Austria, but there was a reason for it, and
having bitterly censured the Neapolitan Government,
he brought his speech to a close with a tirade against
the excesses of the Belgian Press. Cavour has recorded
his opinion of the 'gigantic incapacity' of Walewski as
President of the Conference, but his handling of the
Italian question on this occasion was clever enough and
admirably adapted to the end he had in view, to prevent
anything definite resulting from the discussion and
thus to defeat the object of Cavour. He declined to
condemn the policy of Austria, which was Cavour's
prime objective; he put the French occupation of Rome
on an equal footing with the Austrian occupation of the
Legations, thus rendering Cavour's task of denouncing
Austria much more delicate and difficult; and finally,
by his censure of Naples, he exasperated the Russians,
and Russian support was the deciding factor in obtaining
any practical result from the discussion.

The first speaker was Clarendon. He began with a

few sentences on Greece and the Belgian Press, deploring the excesses of this latter but making it clear that, as a minister of a country where the Press was free, he would countenance no repressive measures. He then turned to Italy. He was well up in his subject, not only having carefully studied the information so freely provided by Cavour and Minghetti, but having had the personal testimony of Sir Edmund Lyons, as well as that of Sir James Hudson. He began with the Romagna. The Austrian occupation was tending, he said, to become permanent; he recognized that as things were it would be dangerous to evacuate them at once, but it was all the more necessary for the Powers to take steps as quickly as possible to make this situation, which upset the European equilibrium, cease. Then, warming to his subject, he went into details of the misgovernment of the Papal States, which he bluntly characterized as the worst Government in the world. It is well to remember that this Government was as much, if not more, Austrian than Papal. It had, he said, all the very worst features of absolutism; arbitrary power, excessive taxation, corrupt administration, and military brutality. 'He charged,' wrote Oldofredi, 'like Lucan at Balaclava.' Passing on to the condition of Naples, he declared that it was the duty of the Powers to protest vigorously against the system of this insensate Government. 'There can be no peace without justice,' he went on, 'and the King of Naples must be forced to amnesty his political prisoners.' The policy of King Ferdinand was a positive danger to the tranquillity of Europe, and he must be compelled to change it, and though, personally speaking, he did not believe in interfering in the internal affairs of other States, in this case, Congress or no Congress, such conduct would have to be put a stop to.' And Cavour murmured *sotto voce*, '*et bientôt, mon cher.*'

Lord Clarendon's speech was a bombshell. All Walewski's efforts to minimize the importance of the issues involved, all his attempts to veil in diplomatic generalities the realities of the situation, were rudely torn asunder, and for once a European Congress heard the plain unvarnished truth. Buol was furious, Cavour triumphant. Cavour summed up the speech by saying, 'it would have been impossible for any Italian statesman to have formulated an indictment of the Roman Government more powerful or more accurate than that of the Foreign Secretary of Great Britain'.[1]

When Lord Clarendon sat down Buol spoke. He expressed his astonishment (and well he might!) that at a Congress called to make peace between the allies and Russia a subject so alien to their purpose should have been introduced. He had neither the necessary instructions to discuss the subject nor sufficient powers to deal with it. To the suggestion that he could ask for instructions from Vienna, he replied very abruptly, that, as he did not consider the Congress competent to treat of the questions put forward by the President, he would not only decline to ask for instructions, but would advise the Emperor of Austria to refuse to give them if such a request should be made to him. All the attempts of Walewski to persuade the Austrian Plenipotentiary to adopt a more conciliatory attitude failing, it was obvious that no result of a practical kind could be forthcoming. The Russian delegates, angered by the indictment of their protégé at Naples, took their cue from Buol and declared they had no instructions to deal with questions outside the terms of peace. The Prussians followed suit, though Baron Manteuffel declared that Prussia was always ready to discuss matters affecting the peace of Europe, and then tried to drag in the question of Neufchâtel.

It was now the turn of Cavour. When he rose to speak the atmosphere was electric. Angry words had come from both sides, and it needed but a further indictment of Austria, such as was to be expected from a representative of Piedmont, to cause an explosion. And no one present was so well equipped to do it.

[1] Cavour to Cibrario. *Politique*, pp. 150 ff., April 9th.

Cavour, a master of irony, with a caustic tongue that knew only too well how to lash his opponents into fury, had at that moment every inducement to win a personal triumph over Austria. But Cavour's political tact was unfailing. He had no desire either to create a scene or to score a triumph over Count Buol. The vigorous onslaught of Lord Clarendon needed no further support to render it effective, and Cavour was too wise to blur its incisive outline by any rhetorical effort of his own. His language and his tone was as moderate as his presentation of his case was convincing, and he contented himself with driving home, from the Piedmontese standpoint, the views that Lord Clarendon had already expressed.

He recognized at the outset of his speech the right of Austria to refuse to discuss the question of Italy, but at the same time, he held it to be of vital importance that the Powers assembled in Conference should express their formal opinion on the subject. He emphasized the character of the Austrian occupation in Northern and Central Italy, and its increasing tendency to assume a complexion of permanent occupation, and he pointed to the state of siege existing at Bologna, as incontrovertible evidence that the presence of Austria made matters worse rather than better; maintaining a state of things contrary to the Treaty of Vienna, destructive of all political equilibrium in Italy and constituting a veritable danger to Piedmont. The Powers could not by their silence sanction such a state of things. Piedmont, above all, menaced on every side by Austria, must protest most strongly against the existing régime in Italy. And he brought his speech to a close by demanding that the opinion expressed by the plenipotentiaries of Great Britain and France, as well as the protest of Sardinia, should be embodied in the protocol. When speaking of the Austrian occupation, Cavour was interrupted by Baron Hübner, the second Austrian plenipotentiary, who in an angry tone asked, 'And what about the French occupation of Rome and the Sardinian troops at Mentone?' Cavour replied that Italy desired the complete evacuation of all foreign troops from her soil, but that there was a wide difference between an isolated detachment of French troops in Rome and the military occupation of half Italy by Austria. 'As to the principality of Monaco,' he added, 'Sardinia is ready to withdraw the fifty men at Mentone, and abandon the Prince to the affection of his subjects, provided that she is not held responsible for the ducking in the Mediterranean to which he will indubitably have to submit.' And the Conference broke into a peal of laughter.

After Cavour had finished the sitting soon came to an end. No propositions were brought forward and no practical proposals were made. Italy was left as she was. But Cavour had at least pinned down the Conference to one practical point, his demand that the protest of Sardinia and her allies should be embodied in the protocol. To this Buol strongly and obstinately objected, and the matter was left over until the next sitting. It was a small compensation, but at least, if it was admitted, the state of Italy would be registered in black and white for all to read.

The significance of the sitting of April 8th was far greater than its practical results would indicate. That it should have been held at all was a veritable triumph for Cavour. But more than that was the impeachment of Austria. Austria, whose whole policy since the outbreak of the war had been based on appearing at the Conference as the arbiter of Europe, found herself at the close disliked, if not hated, by every country represented, and actually put in the dock by her despised little neighbour Piedmont. At the next sitting the question of embodying Cavour's protest in the protocol was at once brought up. Cavour himself expected its rejection. But Walewski was firm and Buol had had time to reflect. The unpopularity of Austria was too obvious to be ignored, and Buol decided that discretion was the better part of valour. 'Buol,' said Clarendon, *a mis de l'eau dans son vin*, and the protest was duly inserted.[1]

The effect of the sitting of April 8th on Cavour's plans for the future was somewhat unexpected, for it caused his hopes of armed support for the Sardinian cause to veer suddenly from France to England, mainly as the result of Lord Clarendon's speech. In this he committed one of the few errors of political judgement of which he can be justly accused. His first verdict was correct enough. 'Lord Clarendon,' he wrote the next day to Rattazzi, 'convinced, I believe, of being unable to arrive at any practical result, judged it was his duty to employ *extra-parlamentare* language.' This was probably the truth. Perceiving, as Cavour did, after Walewski's opening speech, that the attitude of France, Austria, and Russia would block any concrete proposals, Lord Clarendon let himself go and gave vent to his personal opinions and feelings: for no responsible statesman, who hoped for any definite proposals as the outcome of the discussion, would have used such provocative language as did Lord Clarendon. Immediately after the sitting Cavour asked for an interview, and he has left the following detailed account of what transpired, written the day after:

> Yesterday morning I had with Lord Clarendon the following conversation:
> My lord, what took place at the Congress proves two things: 1st. That Austria is determined to persist in her system of violence and oppression towards Italy; 2nd. That the efforts of diplomacy are powerless to modify her system. From this follow consequences excessively painful for Piedmont. In the face of the irritation of political parties on the one side, and the arrogance of Austria on the other, there are only two lines of action to be taken; either to come to terms with Austria and the Pope or to prepare for war with Austria in a not far distant future. If the first of these alternatives is to be preferred, I shall have on my return to Turin to advise the King to call to power the friends of Austria and the Pope.

[1] An Italian translation of the Protocol of the sitting of April 8th is given in Mistrale, *Da Novara a Roma*, vol. 5, Documenti, No. 78.

If, on the contrary, the second hypothesis is the best, my friends and I will not recoil before the necessity of preparing a terrible war, a war to the knife, *une guerre jusqu'avec les couteaux*. Here I stopped. Lord Clarendon without showing either astonishment or disapproval, then said: 'I believe you are right, your position becomes very difficult. I believe that a rupture is inevitable, only the moment for speaking of it aloud has not come.' I replied: 'I have given you proofs of my moderation and prudence. I hold that in politics it is necessary to be exceedingly reserved in words and excessively decided as to action. There are certain situations in which there is less danger in a policy of audacity than in an excess of prudence. With La Marmora I believe we are in a condition to commence the war, and for the short time that it will last you will be obliged to help us.' Lord Clarendon replied with great vivacity, 'Oh, certainly, if you are in a difficulty you can count on us and you will see with what energy we will come to your aid.'

Whether or not the actual words here imputed to Clarendon are exact, matters little. What is clear is that, taken in conjunction with what he said at the Conference, the impression Lord Clarendon left on the mind of Cavour was that England would support Sardinia with arms if it came to war with Austria. It is possible that Cavour, in his own mind, argued that a level-headed, responsible statesman of the calibre of Lord Clarendon would never have taken the strong line that he did without knowing that the Cabinet and public opinion were behind him. It would have been a reasonable line to have taken, and Cavour's intimate knowledge of English constitutional history would have supported him in his view. This was where Cavour made his mistake. Lord Clarendon had spoken personally rather than *ex cathedra* as the spokesman of the Cabinet, and thus left on the mind of Cavour a wrong impression. Did Cavour, carried away by one of those fits of optimism to which he was at times subject, always more favourable to an English than a French alliance, see visions of bagpipes and busbies in the streets of Genoa? At any rate, so much significance did he attach to Lord

Clarendon's words and general attitude that he wrote as follows to Rattazzi:

> I am certain that England, disappointed over having had to make peace, would welcome the opportunity for a new war, specially one that would have for its object so popular a cause as Italian freedom. Ought we not to use so favourable an opportunity to make one supreme effort on behalf of the destinies of our country and the House of Savoy? But as it is a matter of life and death, it behoves us to walk with the utmost caution; that is why I believe it of value to go to London and talk to Palmerston and other leaders of the Government. If these share Clarendon's point of view it will be necessary to make ready quietly, float a loan of 30 millions, and on the return of La Marmora send Austria an ultimatum she cannot accept, and begin the war. The Emperor will certainly not oppose such a war, in his heart of hearts he desires it. He will certainly help us if he sees England enter the lists.

After interviewing Clarendon, Cavour had a long conversation with the Emperor, who gave him the very best advice. After expressing in very decided terms his dissatisfaction with Austria, he said to Cavour: 'Go to London, come to an understanding with Palmerston, and on your return come and see me.' And this Cavour did.

The Congress broke up on April 16th. During the last few days Cavour had long conversations with Prince Napoleon, Clarendon, and the Emperor. The general position in which the Congress closed could not be summed up better than in the prophetic words of Napoleon to Cavour: 'Austria will give way on nothing. She is ready to make war rather than consent to your obtaining Parma; at the moment I cannot present her with a *casus belli*; but make your mind easy, I have a presentiment that the actual peace will not last long.' Before leaving Paris Cavour presented a last memorandum to France and England, in which, after once more exposing the actual conditions of Italy, he warned the Western Powers that, thus threatened, Sardinia at any moment might be forced 'by inevitable necessity to adopt extreme measures of which the consequences were impossible to foresee.'

Cavour crossed to London on the 19th. He had a most cordial reception. He dined with the Queen and talked freely with Prince Albert. Palmerston, who had just lost his stepson, could only give him a short and unsatisfactory interview. 'I have seen many political people,' he wrote to Rattazzi, 'all declare themselves as favourable to our cause. The Tories seem not less decided than the Whigs. The most enthusiastic are the zealous Protestants headed by Lord Shaftesbury. If these were in power they would start a crusade against Austria.' But it took Cavour but a very brief time to realize the true position, and the hopes of active English support raised by Lord Clarendon quickly faded. There was sympathy, but sympathy without soldiers. Cavour returned to Paris keenly disappointed, but the visit had had its value, for it dissipated once for all the vision of English troops in Italy. He stayed but a short time in Paris and was back in Turin on the 29th.

Cavour arrived in Piedmont in a very similar state of mind to that in which he had reached Paris ten weeks before, feeling that everything depended upon his first reception. Now, as then, his doubts were soon dissipated. He went at once to see the King, who not only received him most warmly, but with his own hands bestowed upon him the Collar of the Annunciata, the highest Order in the Kingdom. On May 6th he made his eagerly awaited statement before the Chamber of Deputies. In a moment of depression Cavour had written to Rattazzi, not to be surprised if an adverse vote in the Chamber sent him back to his ricefields at Leri. But there was no real danger of this taking place. The common sense of the Piedmontese told them that there was no alternative to Cavour, and the private letters of Oldofredi and Minghetti, revealing the real part he had played at the Conference, filled the hearts of those who read them with a just pride in their representative. 'He was and is,' Oldofredi had written to Massari, 'the most eminent man here; he is the lion of the Conference.' But his speech to the Deputies was very difficult. It was destined to be read not only in Piedmont but in every capital in Europe. His real work could not be explained in public, and he had little enough to show for all his efforts. He commenced with an outline of the work of the Conference, paying handsome compliments both to the loyal support of his allies and the benevolent attitude of the Russian delegates. He touched on the liberty of the Press apropos of Belgium, and sounded a note of warning to those who had ears to hear, in a passage where he said, 'I maintain that the liberties of the Press, even when extended to its utmost limits, has few dangers for the internal affairs of a country, but regarding foreign relations, it has many dangers and very few advantages.' He forestalled criticism on coming back without any territorial compensation (for which he had worked so hard) by declaring that no sensible person had ever expected it. If the war had been continued and its sphere enlarged, then, perhaps, such a compensation might have been expected, but in the actual circumstances it was impossible. Then, with a hint that, if Italy wanted freedom she would have to fight for it, he added:

> The great solutions are not carried into effect with the pen. Diplomacy is powerless to change the condition of a nation. At most, it can but sanction completed facts and give them legal form. What benefit then has Italy obtained from the Congress? We have gained two things, first, that the anomalous and unhappy condition of Italy has been proclaimed to Europe, not by demagogues, or revolutionaries, excited journalists, or party men, but by representatives of the greatest nations in Europe; by statesmen at the head of their countries' Governments; by distinguished men accustomed to consult the dictates of reason rather than the impulse of emotion. That is the first fact, which I consider of the greatest value. The second is that these same powers have declared that, not only in the interests of Italy herself, but in the interests of Europe, a remedy must be found for the evils from which Italy is suffering. I cannot believe that the

sentiments expressed and the advice given by such nations as France and England can remain for long, sterile of results.

Then he came to the climax of his speech:

Truly if from one side we may congratulate ourselves on this result, on the other, we have to recognize that our position is not without difficulties and dangers. It is certain, gentlemen, that the negotiations conducted in Paris have not improved our relations with Austria. We have to confess that the Plenipotentiaries of Sardinia and Austria, after having sat for two months side by side, and after having co-operated together in the greatest political task of the last forty years, have parted without any personal animosity but with the profound conviction that the political position of the two countries is farther than ever from any common accord, the political principles of the two countries being irreconcilable. This fact, gentlemen, it has to be admitted, is grave; this fact may arouse difficulties and dangers, but it is an inevitable, a fatal, consequence of that loyal, liberal, and decided system initiated by King Victor Emmanuel when he ascended the throne, of which the government of the King has always sought to be the interpreter, and to which you have always lent a firm and consistent support. Nor do I believe that in face of these difficulties and dangers you would wish to advise the King to change his policy. As a result of the policy pursued during these last few years we have taken a great step forward; for the first time in our history the Italian question has been brought forward and discussed before a European Congress, not as at Laybach and Verona with a view to aggravating the evils of Italy and rivetting more tightly her chains, but with the manifest intention of bringing some remedy to her wounds and of expressing strongly the sympathy felt for her by the Great Powers. The Congress over, the cause of Italy is now carried before the bar of public opinion; before that tribunal which, in the memorable words of the French Emperor, must deliver the final verdict and proclaim the ultimate victory. The struggle may be long, the fluctuations of fortune, perchance, many; but we, trusting in the righteousness of our cause, await with confidence the final issue.

With this speech closed the prelude to the last act of the long drama of the *Risorgimento*. The quick intelligence of the Italian people perceived at once its true significance and the greatness of the end that had been achieved. From all over Italy came testimonies of gratitude to Piedmont's Premier. Tuscany sent him a bust inscribed with the line from Dante, 'Colui che la difese a viso aperto.' The Romans and the Neo-politans sent him medals struck in his honour, and the Milanese subscribed for a statue, to be erected at Turin, representing a Piedmontese soldier defending the Italian flag. At last, after eight years of struggle, Cavour's greatness was recognized throughout Italy.

VIII. FROM PARIS TO PLOMBIÈRES

Cavour's Memorandum—Sounds European Opinion—Daniele Manin—
Garibaldi—La Farina and the National Society—Results of the Con-
gress—European Situation—England and Austria—Sequestration
Decree raised—Franz Josef visits Milan—The Sequel—Cavour's
Domestic Policy—Fortification of Alessandria—New Naval Base at
Spezia—The Mont Cenis Tunnel—Mazzini's Plot at Genoa—Difficulty
with the Emperor—Fall of Rattazzi—The Elections of November—
Precarious Government Majority—Orsini's Attempt on Napoleon—
French Demands refused—Victor Emmanuel and Napoleon—Orsini's
Letters—Published in Piedmont—The New Press Law—The Pre-
liminaries to Plombières—Cavour meets Napoleon—Goes on to Baden
—Letter to the King.

ASSURED in his own mind of the sincerity of Napoleon's
professions of friendship for Italy, and of his determination to fight Austria on her behalf if the opportunity was forthcoming, thus obtaining the twofold
result of winning Italy's freedom and destroying the
settlement of 1815, Cavour on his return from Paris
felt equally certain of the moral support of England and
the neutrality of Russia and Prussia. The task that lay
before him was to turn these personal beliefs into facts.
To procure definitely the alliance of France, and to
assure himself of the diplomatic isolation of Austria.
His first step was to print his memorandum of April 16th
and a full text of the final debate in the Chamber, and
send copies for distribution to all the Piedmontese
Legations. To each he wrote an official letter in which
he made clear the position and the policy to be followed.
Referring to the very firm and decided language of the
Memorandum[1] he wrote:

> In speaking as I have done, I have had in view, above every-
> thing, to preserve to Piedmont and the moderate-liberal party,
> the influence and the prestige they have acquired in Italy.
> If we had lowered the flag we had raised in Paris, the
> Mazzinians would have seized it, and the moral influence of
> the revolutionary party would have completely gained the
> ascendant. In acting as we have done we are masters of the
> situation. We shall not use our position to push the country

[1] Text in Zini, vol. iii. No. 126.

towards revolution. On the contrary, we shall strive to maintain calmness and order in all parties throughout the peninsula, so as to give time for the policy of moderation advocated by France and England to produce its effect.[1]

Towards Austria the attitude of Piedmont was equally clearly defined, 'Our intention is neither to provoke Austria nor to incite trouble in other parts of Italy; but simply to show ourselves decided to oppose by every means in our power her policy of penetration and dominance.' Anxious to know how this attitude was received in Europe, Cavour made use of the journey of General Dabormida (to congratulate the Emperor of Russia on his accession), to sound the courts of Europe. He visited Vienna, Warsaw, Berlin, London, and Paris, and from each place sent back dispatches to Cavour.[2]

Count Buol was unusually friendly, Austria having decided in view of her equivocal position in Europe to adopt a policy of conciliation towards Italy, in order to obtain if possible the support of England, and, perchance, France. At Warsaw, the Emperor Alexander said to Dabormida, 'tell your King that I count upon his friendship, that friendship which has lasted so long a time between our two dynasties, and he can count upon mine.' Prince Gortchakoff said, 'Be prudent and our friendship will not fail you.' Equally satisfactory was the tone at Berlin. In London, Lord Palmerston asked him bluntly if Piedmont meant 'to alter the map'. Both he and Lord Clarendon showed some reserve, and refrained from committing themselves and distrust of Russia was evident in their attitude.[3] Both here and in Paris the note sounded was 'prudence'. 'It is necessary to wait,' was Napoleon's dictum. But, taken as a whole, the visit revealed to Cavour a sympathetic attitude, and confirmed him in the line he had taken. This conduct, however, caused intense annoyance at Vienna, though Buol concealed it from Dabormida. 'I have for some

[1] Cavour to Jocteau. Mayor, No. 309. See also Nos. 311–14.

[2] Chiala, *Lettere*, vol. vi. pp. 16 ff.

[3] 'Russia will do anything,' Palmerston said, 'to break the Anglo-French alliance.' Clarendon added that both Russia and Austria were 'incorrigible'.

days been aware,' wrote the British Ambassador at Vienna to Lord Clarendon, 'of the extreme irritation produced here by Count Cavour's Memorandum and the note of April 16th, followed up by the debate in which sentiments very hostile to Vienna were expressed. The language of Count Cavour has been of a description to give deep offence not only to the Austrian Government but to the whole Austrian nation.' And Count Buol declared to the Ambassador that, 'if Sardinia sends a single soldier into Parma or into the Roman States, or into any district, in short, occupied by Austria, it is immediate war, whether or not Sardinia be supported by allies.'[1]

Cavour's primary object was the French alliance. But he saw its possible dangers as clearly as he saw its advantages. He had no intention of substituting French for Austrian predominance in Italy, nor of allowing her to remain in Italy once the Austrians were expelled. To prevent this it was essential that on Italy's side the war, when it came, should, as far as possible, bear a national, and not a Piedmontese, aspect. If Italy showed a united front under the banner of 'unity and Victor Emmanuel', she could speak with an authority that Napoleon would be obliged to respect. His next step, therefore, was to set in action all those forces that made for unity under the Monarchy of Savoy.

As a practical proposition, Cavour's vision of a united Italy at this time did not pass the Garigliano. The Kingdom of Naples was under the peculiar patronage of Russia, and Russia's friendship was essential, to prevent Germany from attacking France or sending active support to Austria. The Government of Naples was so bad that a revolution in the north was certain to produce a similar reaction in the south, and, if that took place, no Government in Europe was likely to step in to save the Neapolitan Bourbons, provided that her present methods remained the same. So leaving Naples on one side, Cavour bent all his forces to strengthen

[1] Seymour to Clarendon, May 21st. F.O. 167, vol. 88.

the acceptance of Victor Emmanuel in the north and centre of Italy.

Amongst those whose voice had still a great influence in Italy was Daniele Manin, the hero of the defence of Venice in 1848–9. Since then he had lived in retirement at Paris. In 1854 he had broken a long silence with a letter, in reply to some remarks of Lord John Russell in the House of Commons advising Italy to keep quiet under Austrian rule and concern herself with internal reforms. 'We want to be masters in our own house,' wrote Manin. 'We do not desire Austria to improve her Government in Italy, but to go.' Later the part taken by Sardinia in the Crimean War and her representation at the Congress of Paris drew the old republican to the thought of unity under the House of Savoy. Cavour visited him in Paris, and was able to write that Manin 'had declared himself an ardent supporter of our policy'. It was at this time that Manin wrote in a famous letter to Lorenzo Valerio: 'Convinced that it is above everything necessary to make Italy, the republican party says to the House of Savoy—*Make Italy and I am with you, if not, no!*' To the Constitutionalists, it says, strive to make Italy and not merely to enlarge Piedmont: be Italian and not Piedmontese, and I am with you, if not, no!' Convinced of the wisdom of Cavour's policy, Manin raised the banner of Italian unity, with its watchword, 'Victor Emmanuel King of Italy.'

Before long Cavour won over another valuable supporter to his cause, Garibaldi. After his almost mythical adventures in 1849, Garibaldi had returned to America. There he watched and waited,

> . . . fain
> To fly, but forced the earth his couch to make
> Far inland, till his friend the tempest wake.

In 1855 he was back again in Europe, and in the first months of 1856 he bought his rocky home at Caprera. In August he came to Turin and had an interview with Cavour. Cavour gave him hope, ard authorized him

to give that hope to others, and Garibaldi left him full
of faith in the prospects of Italy, and reconciled to the
thought of monarchy and Victor Emmanuel. The
adhesion of these great names to his policy was a
genuine triumph for Cavour, but one of even greater
practical value came soon after. The National Society,
with its indefatigable secretary, La Farina, had for some
time been working on parallel lines to Cavour.[1] Giorgio
Pallavicino, for eighteen years a prisoner in the Spiel-
berg and the bosom friend of Daniele Manin, was the
President of the Society, but he had little faith in
Cavour, 'to think of making Italy with Cavour,' he had
written, 'is absurd.' But he was won over by Manin,
and in the autumn of 1856 the affairs of Naples brought
the Society in touch with Cavour. For some years there
had been Murattist intrigues in Naples. Lucien Murat,
the son of Napoleon's Marshal, was being put forward as
an alternative to Bomba. The attitude of Napoleon
towards his candidature was characteristically obscure.
At one time he repudiated it, and at another he seemed
to give it his support. Cavour made up his mind, in his
anxiety not to offend the Emperor, that if it was supported in earnest by France, he would not oppose it.
To the Count Gropello, the chargé d'affaires at Naples,
Cavour wrote: 'You will not oppose the support being
given to Murat, without however favouring it. Murat
is a bad solution, but as it is the only one that might
be successful, it will be necessary to submit to it with
a good grace.'[2] But at the same time he kept his
minister in England, not only informed of what was
going on, but gave him instructions to keep the matter
before the English Cabinet.[3] It was while matters were
in this state that La Farina wrote, asking to know what
was Cavour's policy on this question.[4] Cavour's reply

[1] 'Unity, Independence, and Victor Emmanuel' was the watchword of the
National Society. See Bolton King, *History of Italian Unity*; Thayer,
Cavour; La Farina, *Epistolario*.
[2] Cavour to Gropello, Chiala, vol. vi.
[3] *La politique de Cavour*, Letters 99–100, 111.
[4] Chiala, *Lettere*, vol. ii. No. 476; also No. 580.

was to invite his correspondent to visit him the following morning at 6 a.m. At this interview Cavour laid all his cards upon the table. He had faith, he said, that Italy would become a single kingdom with Rome for her capital, but he did not know whether Italy really desired this solution of her problems. None of his political friends agreed with him, nevertheless, if Italy showed herself ripe for unity, he believed that the opportunity to achieve it was not far off.

This interview with La Farina throws much light on Cavour's subsequent policy. The position was very intricate and difficult. Open agitation against the *status quo* was the one thing Europe would not sanction, besides, it was to play the game for Austria and invite effective repression. To do nothing, and leave Italy to decide for herself when the crisis came, meant that at the critical moment an upheaval of republicans, federalists, unitarians, and autonomists would throw Italy into chaos, and possibly lead to the maintenance of the old system for the sake of law and order. It was vital that the country should have one policy and one cause as a rallying-point, and that a scheme of Government should be prepared to replace the actual system, at once and effectively, when the repressive hand of Austria was removed. So Cavour feigned ignorance of the organization that was going on through the National Society, while in fact he knew all about it. 'Come and see me whenever you like,' he said to La Farina, 'but come before dawn so that no one sees you or recognizes you. If I am asked questions in the Chamber, I shall deny you like Peter, and say, 'I know him not!' Henceforward, the two met almost daily, and thus Cavour directed and controlled the work of the Society in conjunction with his foreign policy. As to the original cause of the interview, La Farina seems to have convinced Cavour of its danger, and by the simple expedient of arousing Palmerston's suspicions, Cavour quickly put an end to the hopes of Lucien Murat. In thus focusing the aims of the Italian Liberals on a single solution of the national problem, Cavour was not only simplifying the issue before the country, but was undermining the position of his one serious opponent, Mazzini, and his vision of a republic.

While Cavour was thus mobilizing public opinion in Italy in favour of monarchy under the House of Savoy, Napoleon was endeavouring to prepare opinion in Europe for the acceptance of his Italian policy. The Congress had resulted in a definite feeling of hostility to Austria on the part of France and Russia, a continuance of distrust of Russia on the part of England, and a joint sense of sympathy for Italy on the part of all the Powers except Austria. As the inevitable outcome of these tendencies England drew towards Austria, while Russia approached France. Germany was the uncertain factor, Prussia tending towards hostility to Austria, while the smaller Powers supported her. A fortunate offer of mediation on the part of Napoleon, in the dispute between Prussia and Switzerland over Neufchâtel, brought Prussia nearer to France. With Russia, Napoleon had little difficulty. The Czar would have welcomed an alliance, but France, forced in such a case to choose between Russia and England, held back from breaking with England. Napoleon, however, met the Czar at Stuttgart in June 1857 and cleared the way for a more definite policy later, while to allay the resulting irritation at the Court of St. James, he visited the Queen at Osborne the following month.

As the result of Napoleon's diplomacy the position of Austria approached isolation. Her one friend was England, but even her friendship was not very wholehearted. Though Palmerston was not above bullying a weak power or bluffing a strong one, as he had shown in the case of Greece, and of France in 1840, he liked no one to do the bullying but himself. Austria's treatment of Italy angered him, for he had a real sympathy for Italian aspirations, a feeling which he shared in common with the nation as a whole. In consequence, the difficulty of trying to keep the friendship of both

Austria and Italy led to a policy of blowing hot and cold that was very confusing to both his friends, so that, with the constant changes from support to blame and back again, Cavour scarcely knew whether England was on his side or not.[1]

But beneath all these diplomatic manœuvres lay the real problem, whether or not the settlement made at the Congress of Vienna in 1815 was to continue to be the basis of European diplomacy. In spite of the breaches that had been made in its original symmetry, the settlement of Vienna was still the corner-stone of the European system. The ideas and principles that then determined the rearrangement of Europe were still kept in all their first freshness as the Magna Charta of Austrian diplomacy. To them she owed her possession of Lombardy and Venetia and her right of intervention elsewhere in the Peninsula. She stood, now as then, rigid and unprogressive, upholding the ideas of a past age by means of an obsolete political system. Austria might break, but she would never bend, and from this uncompromising traditionalism her chief strength was drawn. Facing her across the Ticino stood Sardinia, the mouthpiece of Italian aspirations, the embodiment of the ideas of the future, as Austria was of the past. The continental champion of nationality, democracy, and constitutional Government, the adoption of any one of which would have rent the Austrian Empire into fragments. Twice she had fought Austria for liberty and twice she had been defeated, and now she stood ready again, but this time with a menacing shadow behind her that bid Austria pause. Round these two protagonists of autocracy and democracy were grouped the rest of Europe. Napoleon, no lover of democracy, was, however, bent on the destruction of the 1815 settlement and the freedom of Italy from Austrian influence, to achieve which he was prepared to support the new idea of nationality. Germany, with one half

[1] See Cavour's letters to Em. D'Azeglio at this time in *La Politique de Cavour*.

leaning on Vienna and her system, and the other waiting to raise the same banner as Italy. Whilst England, with her genius for compromise and love of the illogical, was trying to reconcile two incompatible principles. Upholding the Vienna Settlement (not because of its merits but on the ground of the sanctity of treaties) and at the same time supporting Italy's desire for freedom and nationality. Under these circumstances the policy of Cavour was directed to keeping open the breach with Austria, without, however, driving her to extremes; to drawing closer the bonds with France and endeavouring to extend the support given to him by Lord Clarendon to the British Government as a whole.

Cavour had left Paris convinced that there was only one solution of the Italian question and that was war with Austria. From now onwards he had no Piedmontese policy apart from the thought of Italy. His parliamentary measures were designed on this basis, and there was nothing he desired less than well-meant attempts to patch up a peace with Austria. Piedmont, in his opinion, was simply the detonator destined to explode the Italian shell. Cavour's point of view was never fully understood in England, who persisted in believing that a little goodwill on both sides was all that was required to re-establish friendly relations between Austria and Piedmont. The English Government now set to work to bring about the one thing Cavour dreaded more than anything else, a policy of conciliation, emanating from Vienna. The efforts of England met with unexpected success. In response to her representations Franz Joseph decided on leniency. He raised the sequestration decree imposed on Piedmontese subjects, decided on a personal visit to his Italian provinces, and named the Archduke Maximilian as Viceroy. All of these measures were admirably calculated to win the goodwill of his Lombard subjects and the hearty approval of Europe. It was, however, too late. The iron had entered too deeply into the soul of Lombardy and Venetia for any such palliatives to be effective. But the policy perturbed Cavour. Pressed in his turn, Cavour agreed to adopt a more conciliatory attitude and sent apposite instructions to the Marquis Cantono at Vienna,[1] and even considered sending a special envoy to compliment the Emperor on his arrival at Milan. But once again all attempts at a real *rapprochement* failed.

The day before the Emperor's entrance into Milan the Austrian police seized and expelled as an undesirable a certain M. Plezza, who was, as a matter of fact, a distinguished Piedmontese Senator visiting friends. Victor Emmanuel was furious and at once refused to send an envoy to Milan. To stimulate the annoyance of Austria, the official journal, the *Gazzetta Piemontese*, on the day of Franz Joseph's arrival, inserted in its columns two items of news particularly objectionable to Count Buol's susceptibilities. It announced that 7,000 livres had arrived from Lombardy as a contribution to the fund for presenting 100 canon to the new fortifications at Alessandria, and that the Milanese were sending a sum of money to Turin with which to erect a statue to the Piedmontese army. Once more the banderillos of Cavour exasperated the Austrian bull into charging, and drove Count Buol to make another of those diplomatic mistakes that merely strengthened the position of Piedmont without benefiting Austria.

But, diplomatically, Cavour kept up his tone of conciliation. He took no notice of the incident concerning M. Plezza, and wrote to his chargé d'affaires at Vienna regarding the raising of the sequestrations that 'the principal cause of the interruption of diplomatic relations between Sardinia and Austria having ceased, the King's Government finds no difficulty in renewing them . . . nothing is now required except to nominate our representative at Vienna, immediately Vienna has appointed her minister at Turin.'[2] But Count Buol had a genius for doing the wrong thing. On his return from

---

[1] Cavour to Cantono. Mayor, No. 427.
[2] Cavour to Cantono, February 4th. Bianchi, *Stor. Doc.*

Milan, stung by the attitude of Piedmont to the Emperor, he dispatched to Count Paar, in charge of the Turin Legation, an angry note to be read to Cavour, enumerating once more the provocations of Piedmont; the Press, the fortifications of Alessandria, the proposed statue; denouncing in general the conduct of the Government and closing with the words 'it will be for Count Cavour to indicate to you what means he intends to employ to efface these painful impressions and what are the guarantees that he can offer us against the indefinite prolongation of a state of things diametrically opposed to the relations we desire to see exist between the two countries.'[1] Cavour described the tone of the dispatch as 'violent and menacing,' and wrote concerning it, 'it is possible, even probable, that Count Buol, counting upon English support, has believed he would intimidate me. He has thought that seeing me deprived of the support of England I should not dare to resist. He deceives himself strangely if he believes me timid and *anglomane* up to this point.'[2] When the facts were known Cavour found strong support both in London and Paris. 'Buol,' wrote Lord Clarendon, 'has committed *une grosse bêtise* and Cavour must be very grateful to him for having so thoroughly played into his hands.'[3] Cavour's reply, firm and reasonable as it was, did not satisfy Vienna, and Count Buol withdrew the Legation from Turin; Cavour followed suit, and diplomatic relations ceased between the two countries. This incident tested the loyalty of both his allies, and Cavour rejoiced to find them still firm in his support. But nevertheless he found it hard work to dissipate the distrust of England. In the Autumn of 1856 the widowed Empress of Russia took a villa at Nice. The visits of Victor Emmanuel and Cavour, the presence of various Russian Grand Dukes, soon spread rumours of an alliance between the two countries. There was no truth in these reports, but Cavour had difficulty in

[1] Text in Zini, vol. iii.   [2] Cavour to Em. D'Azeglio, *Politique*.
[3] Clarendon to Em. D'Azeglio, March 26th. *Politique*.

allaying the Russophobe suspicions of Palmerston and Clarendon.

Cavour had one advantage in the diplomatic struggle not always granted to statesmen. He knew personally the men with whom he had to deal. The Congress had at least done this for him and it was a genuine help. When Lord Clarendon, for instance, in response to pressure from France, complained in one of his dispatches of the excesses of the Sardinian Press, Cavour, knowing that their views and their difficulties were similar, wrote to his Minister in London, 'tell Lord Clarendon that I am as angry with the Press here as he was with the articles in *The Times* during the Congress.' One can imagine how his Lordship rubbed his chin and smiled at this incorrigible Piedmontese. Another of Cavour's difficulties came from the double channel of diplomacy issuing from Paris. Walewski and Napoleon held different views on Italy. Sometimes they coincided and sometimes they did not. In the first case they had to be taken seriously, whereas, in the second there were always possibilities of manipulation. This fact also complicated the English dispatches which, if inspired through the Hübner-Walewski channel, had an importance much less than when they expressed the Emperor's views. Shortly after the rupture with Turin, Buol suggested to Walewski that Austria, France, and England should send Sardinia a collective note demanding that she should undertake formally to respect existing treaties. This, of course, meant that Cavour should promise to do nothing to alter the territorial arrangements in Italy, which was the central purpose of all his diplomacy. Walewski consented and approached Lord Clarendon, who, looking at the matter not from the standpoint of Italy's future but from that of the sanctity of treaties, also consented. This little plan failed, however, thanks to Napoleon, who when it was brought before him would have nothing to do with it. 'I realized from the beginning,' he said to the Marquis di Salmour, 'that Sardinia could never consent to what England desired, that we should send her a collective note; for if any one was to demand of me that I should declare in writing that I would never attempt to obtain the Rhine frontier, I should certainly not consent, though I have not the least intention of doing so.' And then he added a phrase that the verdict of history hardly corroborates: 'Je n'aime pas la politique tortueuse, je vais droit au but.' Napoleon's conduct on this occasion earned the genuine gratitude of Cavour. It revealed, not only how true a friend to Italy the Emperor was, but that apart from him there was little help to be expected for the furtherance of Cavour's schemes for Italian unity.[1]

The rupture of diplomatic relations with Austria decreased rather than increased Cavour's difficulties. It saved him from the constant complaints of Vienna and enabled him to pay more attention to his foreign and domestic policy. Abroad, there were two questions left over from the Conference that had to be settled: the delimitation of the Bessarabian frontier, and the union or separation of the Principalities. On both questions England and Austria were opposed by France and Russia, and Cavour definitely supported France in favour of the union of the Principalities, but did not agree with either side on the question of the frontier.

I am exceedingly sorry [he wrote to his Minister in London] to find myself in disaccord with the English Government on the question of the Principalities and to be unable to share their views (I will not say passions) on that of Bolgrad; but I cannot follow a line contrary to the principles that I have always professed. We cannot be Liberals in the West and Absolutists in the East. You can assure the Government, however, that we will do nothing to create new difficulties. As to the influence of Russia upon us it is a tale invented by Austria. We desire to be on good terms with this Power and cultivate happy relations with her, but, in all great political questions, we shall never forget that Russia represents a principle directly opposed to that upon which our policy rests.

[1] *Carteggio Cavour-Nigra*, vol. i. No. 6. Salmour to Cavour. *Politique*, Nos. 132, 136.

I should be grieved if our conduct should lose us the sympathy of men that I respect as much as Lord Palmerston and Lord Clarendon; but I prefer rather to submit to this sacrifice than to lose their esteem.[1]

Cavour held firmly to his principles and came out of the protracted negotiations without losing the goodwill of either of his allies.

The Sardinian Parliament met for the first time since the summer of 1856, the first week of the new year, and the nature of the measures Cavour introduced indicates clearly enough the policy he was adopting towards Austria. It would scarcely be accurate to say they were provocative, but they were designed with a complete disregard for Austrian susceptibilities, and on a scale that envisaged Italian, rather than Piedmontese, requirements. In his defence of them he admitted quite candidly that they were the logical outcome of the 'wisely progressive' policy consistently pursued by the Government, which had, he declared, won for Piedmont the sympathy of Italy and the esteem of all Europe, but there was no disguising their military significance. The first of these was an Appropriation Bill for five millions of lire for the fortifications of Alessandria. It was opposed by the Right partly on the ground of expense and partly as tending to provoke Austria. But a measure of internal defence had the full sympathy of the Chamber, and it passed without difficulty. Five years before Cavour had had a desperate struggle to procure money for the defence of Casale, eventually succeeding only by a majority of four votes in each Chamber. How far the country had changed in the interval was indicated by the fact that this time only fourteen adverse votes were recorded. A little later, Cavour brought forward a bill for the transference of the naval base from Genoa to Spezia, and the building of docks and warehouses at Genoa. This measure sanctioned the expenditure, spread over a number of years, of no less than fourteen millions. The grandiose

[1] Cavour to Em. D'Azeglio. *Politique.*

nature of the scheme, together with a failure to realize
the benefits that it would produce in the trade of the
country, provoked a strong opposition to the measure.
In his defence, Cavour, after relating the history of the
measure which dated from 1850, passed in review the
whole trade of the country, showing the striking
increase in all branches that had taken place under the
new free-trade system. He then insisted with great
force on the absolute necessity of having at Genoa a
port that could not only deal with the repairs of the
mercantile marine but could handle the cargoes of the
largest modern vessels. He pointed out how impossible
this was as long as Genoa was also the naval base of
the country; that there was no room for both in the
same port; and that in Spezia they had an ideal situation
for the requirements of the navy. The Bill was passed,
but only by a majority of twenty. Before the session
closed Cavour introduced the third Bill, to meet the
expense connected with the piercing of the Mount
Cenis tunnel and the Victor Emmanuel railway that
was to pass through it. Cavour's imagination had long
been captivated by this immense undertaking. Both
as an engineer and a statesman it interested him deeply.
He regarded it as the *chef d'œuvre* of the country's work,
and as far back as 1847, in an article he had written in
a French magazine, he had waxed lyrical over the
prospect of undertaking it. In spite of all opposition
Cavour carried it through, and in September Victor
Emmanuel in person fired the first mine.[1]

In the debate on this Bill a number of deputies had
not unnaturally advocated caution. With all the expenses already incurred, to go slow in so tremendous
an undertaking was not an unreasonable suggestion.
But Cavour would not consider such a course. In a
remarkable passage at the close of his speech he
said:

I trust, Gentlemen, that in your last session you will not

[1] See *Discorsi*, vol. x.

belie your reputation. I trust that you will always follow a frank and resolute policy. If you adopt the proposals of the deputy Moia, you will inaugurate an absolutely contrary system. I should be very grieved at it, not only because it would ruin this stupendous undertaking, but, because, such an attitude would be a fatal augury for the line of policy that Parliament will pursue in the future. We have the choice of two roads: we have chosen that of resolution and boldness: we cannot remain half-way: for us it is a vital condition, an unavoidable alternative: to progress or perish.

It was remarkable that Cavour should thus as it were identify the very life of the nation with an undertaking of this kind, which might be called simply a commercial speculation. But Cavour, in his own way, had an idealism as lofty as that of Mazzini or Garibaldi. It had not the moral purity of the one nor the appealing directness of the other, yet it had a nobility of its own. To Cavour the nation's effort, seen in such material things as railways, docks, and commerce, had, one might almost say, a spiritual value as an interpretation of all that was highest in the national character. Cavour realized that the salvation of Italy could never be won by her material, but only by her moral, force. The prestige of Piedmont, the appeal she made to Europe, lay not in her power but in her progress. In the sacrifice the little country was prepared to make on behalf of liberty, good government and material prosperity; in her willingness to bear excessive taxation for the sake of the future; Cavour saw both the greatness of Piedmont and the salvation of Italy. In a time of profound peace, with a balance in the Treasury, such a programme as Cavour now put forward might have been termed excessive; but, with a chronic adverse balance, and facing the prospect of a desperate struggle with Austria, the audacity of his plans were extreme. But Cavour believed the nation was behind him. He knew that weakness would be fatal, and with a courage and skill not easily paralleled, he urged Piedmont forward without pause or hesitation.

He was playing a hazardous game. Outside his own country, unknown to his Cabinet or to Parliament, he was preparing for a future revolution everywhere in Italy.[1] In Piedmont he was the champion of law and orderly progress. When at the opening of the session the extreme Left denounced his failure to support the rising of Bentivegna in Sicily during the previous autumn, he replied: 'neither our words nor our policy tend to excite or support useless disorder or vain attempts at revolution; as long as we shall be at peace with the rest of Italy we shall never employ revolutionary means nor try to excite tumults or rebellion.' This was the attitude it was necessary to assume in the eyes of Europe—until the moment was ready—and even then the risings in Italy must have every appearance of being spontaneous. Above all Piedmont must be orderly.

With such a policy, one can realize the burst of anger with which Cavour learnt of the Mazzinian rising which took place in Genoa on the last two days of June. The defections brought about in the ranks of his followers, through the success of Cavour's policy and the activity of the Società Nazionale, urged Mazzini to make one last attempt to achieve his own solution of the Italian problem. Combining two separate plans, he devised a simultaneous descent on the coast of Naples and a rising at Genoa. On June 25th a band of devoted revolutionaries, under the command of Carlo Pisacane, a Neapolitan Duke, embarked on the *Cagliari*, a steamer plying between Genoa and Sardinia. Having seized the vessel at sea, they touched at the island of Ponza, where they released and armed some hundreds of Neapolitan prisoners, mostly common criminals. Landing at Sapri, in the Gulf of Policastro, they tried in vain to raise the peasants. After some aimless wandering they were met and routed by a battalion of Neapolitan militia. Half the small band was killed, and the rest fell into the

---

[1] This was the task of the National Society of which Cavour was the *deus ex machina*.

hands of Bomba's police, reserved for a worse fate. Carlo Pisacane himself was slain.[1]

The rising at Genoa, the idea of which was to seize the forts and send arms and men to Pisacane, was an even greater fiasco. The Government acted with vigour, a few scuffles, and the loss of some innocent lives, dissolved the whole effort in a few hours. Cavour might well have tempered the severity with which he treated all who were adjudged accomplices of Mazzini's ill-starred attempt, but the need to make it clear to France and England that all such efforts would be repressed with the full strength of the Government, urged him to make an example of all who could be connected with the revolt.

Both abroad and at home the results of this attempted rising reacted disastrously on Cavour. To forestall, if possible, further reproaches from England, he wrote to D'Azeglio in London, with what looks like intentional exaggeration: 'It appears now without any doubt that the great European revolutionary party, *of which the head-quarters are in London*, had decided to bend all their efforts to seize Genoa and make this town the citadel of anarchy—I regret that among those arrested was an Englishwoman.' France was a much more important and difficult matter. The fundamental condition for a war in support of Italy in the mind of Napoleon, was that it should in no way be connected with revolution. His own throne was too insecure for him to risk the possibility of bringing about another 1848. At first Napoleon, when he heard of the rising at Genoa, showed a genuine anger, and permitted Walewski to use strong words. Cavour, however, pointed out that the attempt, far from showing that Italy, and especially Piedmont, sympathized with revolution, proved just the opposite. If the whole strength of the movement could do no more than this, as a practical

[1] Io non vedeva più fra mezzo a loro
Quegli occhi azzurri e quei capelli d'oro
Eran trecento, eran giovani e forti
E sono morti.   *La Spigolatrice di Sapri.*

proposition its power was negligible. Napoleon shortly
after went to Plombières and there talked over the
question with a close friend of Cavour's, the Marquis
di Salmour.[1] He soon became more reasonable, and
on his return to Paris he wrote to Villamarina, 'nothing
is farther from my mind than to cause embarrassment
to Count Cavour. He can count upon my desire to
support his government by all possible means. If at
times I find it necessary to make some *représentations*
he should regard them as advice from a friend.'[2] Thus
Cavour weathered one more storm successfully.

But it was in Piedmont itself that the events of Genoa
caused most embarrassment to the Government. The
Ministry, and especially Rattazzi as Minister for Internal
Affairs, was accused of want of foresight and vigour, and
of disregarding the warnings it had received from well-
informed quarters. The Clericals and Extremists went
farther, accusing Rattazzi of closing his eyes and ears
deliberately, out of sympathy for Mazzini and his fellow
conspirators. Even by his friends and supporters
Cavour was discreetly urged to make use of the situation
to drop Rattazzi. The Connubio was still remembered.
Cavour absolutely refused, and even made a point of
being seen in the companionship of his much-abused
colleague. Finding their efforts all in vain, the Right
determined to combine with the Clericals and oust the
Government at the approaching general election.
Cavour underrated the danger, and scarcely realized
how many arguments existed that could be used against
the Government. The Clericals had never forgiven or
forgotten the Law on the Convents, and taking orders
from Rome, they worked with a thoroughness and lack
of scruple against the Government that revealed the
deep-seated nature of their resentment. If we may
believe Cavour himself, full use was made of that power
of spiritual intimidation which Rome knew so well how
to use. At the last moment the Clericals and Extremists

[1] *Carteggio Cavour-Nigra (CCN.)*, Nos. 6 and 7.
[2] *CCN.*, vol. i. No. 12.

suddenly nominated a host of their own special candidates, so that for 204 seats there were nearly 1,000 contestants. The elections were fixed for November 15th, and on the eve of the poll Costanza D'Azeglio described the situation in these words, in a letter to her son:

> Here we are in a state of excitement of which I have never seen the like. The Piedmontese, thanks to the elections, have dropt their national character. Every one seems possessed of a devil. Every one wants to be a deputy. There are 204 seats and there are more than 700 candidates without counting those who will be put forward at the last minute. At Turin we are fairly quiet, but in the provinces it is 'une bacchanale incroyable.' The papers are veritable defamatory pamphlets, that I can no longer bear to read.[1]

When the results of the election were known it was found that the extreme Left had nearly disappeared, and its place was taken by a solid block of Clericals and Extremists of the Right, numbering about sixty. Though this still left Cavour with a working majority, the varying *nuances* of the Liberal majority caused him much uneasiness. At first Cavour considered the position as a real defeat, and doubted if he could succeed in carrying through his programme, but a study of the position revealed possibilities, and he set to work to repair the damage as far as possible. Soon after the Chamber met it adopted and passed a motion excluding the clergy, and a bevy of successful canons found their political career cut suddenly short. Then a big effort was made over the by-elections, necessitated by the success of popular members in more than one constituency, and when the personnel was finally determined, Cavour found himself better placed than he expected.[2]

But in order to win over the doubtful supporters a sacrifice was required, and Rattazzi was the victim selected. So Rattazzi resigned, Cavour became Minister of the Interior as well as of Foreign Affairs, and Lanza took over the Finances. Determined to keep the Liberal

---

[1] *Mémoires Historiques.*   [2] See Chiala, *Lettere*, vol. vi. pp. 80–90.

principles of the Government in the forefront of his programme, Cavour put the following sentence into the address from the Throne: 'I do not doubt to find once again in you, the same strong and loyal help in applying and developing those liberal principles upon which, *now, in a measure immutable*, our national policy rests.' These words particularly pleased the King, who remarked, 'That is good, that is just what I think, I may have to abdicate, but I will never change.' They were greeted with great applause when delivered. Cavour's acceptance of the Home Office was due to his anxiety not to introduce a new member into the Cabinet and thus give a handle to rumours that he was leaning to the right or left. It was a fortunate choice, for the new Parliament had scarcely opened before the need for a strong hand at the Home Office became painfully apparent.

Suddenly, on January 15th, Cavour received news that an attempt to assassinate the Emperor and Empress on their way to the Opera had been made in Paris the evening before. His first thought was 'Let us hope they are not Italians.' A little later came the details—and the names, Orsini, Rudio, Pieri, Gomez—all Italians. Cavour's heart sank, for he knew the storm that was about to break upon his head. But worse than that was, what effect would this have on Napoleon's intentions regarding Italy? For Cavour knew well enough that it was not on France, but on Napoleon, that the chances of redemption for his country rested. He had not long to wait for the storm to break. First came a note from Walewski written 'in a very benevolent spirit but exceedingly bitter against the *emigrati* and the Press.' Then a few days later, the new French Minister, the Prince de la Tour d'Auvergne, arrived with a formal dispatch, demanding that the journal *L'Italia del Popolo* should be suppressed and a solemn disapproval given of the Mazzinians and all their works; that the editor of *L'Unione* should be expelled from the country, together with all dangerous foreigners; finally, that the law relating to crimes against Sovereigns should be amended and strengthened.[1]

Walewski sadly misunderstood the position, policy, and character of Cavour, if he imagined that he would submit to having his country's laws dictated from the Quai d'Orsay. The honour and independence of Piedmont was as dear to Cavour as to his King, and he answered Walewski in a tone there was no mistaking. To all the French demands Cavour replied with a firm and determined, No. He would apply the full rigour of the law, increase the surveillance of the refugees, but he could not alter the fundamental laws of the Kingdom which would be equivalent to a *coup d'état*.

> Charles Albert died at Oporto rather than bend his head before Austria [he wrote]. The young King will go and die in America, or fall, not once but an hundred times, at the foot of our Alps, before soiling the untarnished honour of his noble race; and we, his ministers, will follow him. We are enemies of revolution, we hold assassination and those who preach it in as great horror as you; but we are Liberals, because we believe that liberty alone will save Italy, and Liberals we shall remain; if we must lose your precious friendship and fall into isolation, at least we will fall flag in hand and with our honour intact.

But while Cavour refused to be dictated to by France or any one else, he was too practical minded not to see the dangers of his position. An article in an obscure journal, *La Ragione*, excusing regicide, gave him his opportunity. It was at once prosecuted and as promptly acquitted by the jury empanelled to try the case. Cavour immediately prepared a bill to revise the jury system, and thus do what France required, by another road. He worried Mazzini's journal to death by confiscation and prosecution. On the refugees at Genoa his hand fell heavily, and the expulsions soon ran into three figures, and by a special clause in the new bill he arranged for the prosecution of journals publishing objectionable articles against foreign states and rulers,

---

[1] Walewski to De la Tour d'Auvergne, January 22nd, 1858.

by means of a simple agreement between Piedmont and
the Foreign Secretaries of other countries. By making
these steps known in the right quarters he pacified
Napoleon.

While Cavour was thus dealing with the diplomatic
side of the difficulty, the King sent his first aide-de-
camp, General Della Rocca, to Paris to felicitate the
Emperor on his escape. On February 5th he had a
long audience, and immediately on its conclusion wrote
to the King a letter in which he reproduced the words
of the Emperor as nearly as he could remember them.
'What I say to Piedmont,' said Napoleon, 'I am saying
to Belgium and to Switzerland, and also to England,
who is a great Power. I should be without blood in
my veins if I tolerated assassins on my frontiers and
allowed my neighbours to preach assassination in their
Press. England and France have an equal interest in
alliance, but if nothing is done there, friendship will
soon cool, and from coolness to hostility, my dear
General, you know, there is but a step.' Then, after
expressing his affection for Victor Emmanuel and his
friendship for Piedmont, he went on, 'but, if nothing
is done there, if you cannot find means to muzzle the
Press, to protect morality and religion, if you have no
police, well, my friendship will cool and I shall be
forced to a close alliance with Austria.' Then, after
pointing out that Piedmont's only chance of help lay
in France, that England was useless, and there was no
one else, he emphasized that Piedmont must do 'everything that is necessary, everything that I have a right
to expect,' and ended with the words, 'read the papers
and see the addresses that I have received from the
army. I have had to suppress the strongest of them.
I have only to raise a finger, and my army, and the
whole of France, will march enchanted to whatever spot
I point out as the home of the assassins.'[1]

The underlying note of menace conveyed by the
General's letter aroused all Victor Emmanuel's pride.

[1] *CCN.*, vol. i, No. 13.

As Cavour put it, 'the blood of the Comtes Verts, of Emmanuel Philibert, and Victor Amadeus that runs in his veins, has revolted at the *inconvenant* language of the Emperor. After having proved a faithful ally and a devoted friend, he scarcely expected threats and menaces to be used towards him.'[1] There was no mistaking the tone of the King's reply to Della Rocca. 'Notwithstanding the personal compliments of the Emperor,' he wrote, 'his words, as repeated in your letter, reveal something that approximates to reproach and menace (things to which I am little accustomed), especially when the Emperor speaks of allying himself closely with Austria against us *if we do not at once obey his will.*' Then, after remarking that he was afraid della Rocca had not faithfully reported the words of the Emperor, 'for I know,' he said, 'by experience the nobility and loyalty of his heart, and that he always sees very clearly into things,' he dealt briefly with the four points of the letter: the Press, the Police, the Émigrés, and England. On the first three he repeated much of what had been said by Cavour, on the last he added: 'We have certainly been friends with England, when our policy required it, but we have no close alliance; the Emperor ought to know how little, personally, I love England, its policy and its Lord Palmerston. I have only one true friend, that is the Emperor himself.' But it was in the last paragraph that Victor Emmanuel expressed his true feelings:

after what I have said, my dear della Rocca, the Emperor should be convinced of my good intentions, and understand that what he desired has been done before he requested it. If he requires a policy of violence here, I shall lose all my influence, and he, the sympathy and affection of a generous and noble nation. Don't be an imbecile, dear General; tell him all that from me, and, *if the words that you transmit to me are the actual words of the Emperor*, tell him, in the terms you think best, that one does not treat a faithful ally in such a way; that I have never tolerated compulsion from any one;

[1] Cavour to Villamarina, February 6th. Chiala, ii.

that my path is that of untarnished honour, and that to this honour I hold myself responsible to none but God and my people; for 850 years my race has held its head high and no one shall make me lower it; yet, for all that, I have no other wish than to be his friend.[1]

This letter left Turin on February 9th, and in his covering letter to the Marquis Villamarina Cavour wrote: 'I do not think any harm would be done if Della Rocca committed the indiscretion of reading it to the Emperor; only he must take care not to let it out of his hands, for fear that the Emperor might take a copy of it, for it contains a sentence about England that I regret, but it cannot produce difficulty as long as it does not provide a written proof of the King's small sympathy for perfidious Albion.' The effect of this letter must have astonished both the King and Cavour. Instead of arousing anger and bitterness in the mind of Napoleon, it seems to have clenched once for all his determination to help Italy. When Napoleon heard the proud words of the King he exclaimed: 'Now that is what I call courage! Your King is a brave man, I love his answer. Write to him at once, put his mind at ease as to my intentions and express to him my regret at having caused him pain,' and before Della Rocca left Paris Napoleon said to him, 'assure your King that in case of war with Austria I will come and fight beside my faithful ally, and tell Cavour to put himself in direct communication with me, we shall certainly understand one another.'[2]

Other forces were at work to persuade Napoleon to commit himself definitely to come to the help of Italy. The small but influential group of Italian patriots, Conneau, Bixio, Madame Cornu, and the rest, urged him in this direction. Napoleon must also have known that in the opinion of many competent observers the moral and political condition of France was such that only a successful war could re-establish the Imperial

[1] *CCN.*, vol. i. No. 16.
[2] Della Rocca, *Memorie di un Veterano.*

prestige.[1] From another quarter it was urged that England was the villain of the piece. Isolating France by diplomacy, allying herself with Austria, repeating the policy of Pitt towards Napoleon I, and in consequence, only by overthrowing Austria in Italy and binding Italy to France could safety be assured.[2] All these arguments no doubt had their effect; but it was the indomitable spirit of Victor Emmanuel and Cavour that precipitated all the vague ideas suspended in the mind of Napoleon, and solidified them into a policy of action. A successful war against Austria, fought in alliance with Piedmont, might mean three things dear to the Emperor: the destruction of the Treaty of Vienna, the cession of Savoy and a new frontier on the Alps, and a possible union by marriage with the oldest reigning House in Europe.

The decision to carry out this scheme appears to have definitely matured between January 14th, the date of Orsini's attempt, and February 25th, the date of the opening of his trial, and Victor Emmanuel's letter seems to have been the deciding factor; for in no other way can we explain Orsini's two letters to the Emperor and the use he made of them. In the ordinary course of events the trial and execution of Orsini would have scarcely interested the Emperor, and certainly no letter from him would have been read in court and then published. But having once made up his mind to ally himself with Piedmont, Orsini assumed in the eyes of Napoleon a certain importance, as a means towards popularizing his Italian schemes. So he sent Pietri, his Prefect of Police, to interview Orsini in prison, and convince him that Napoleon, far from being an enemy of Italy, was the best friend she had. In this he succeeded, and either Orsini himself or his counsel, Jules Favre, drew up an appeal to the Emperor on behalf of Italy,[3]

---

[1] Salmour to Cavour. *CCN.*, No. 6. Nassau Senior to Lord John Russell. (*Later Correspondence of Lord John Russell.*)

[2] Salvagnoli to Cavour, January 16th.

[3] M. Paléologue in his *Cavour* maintains that the style of the letter is that of Favre.

and Napoleon gave him permission for it to be read in Court and then published. It created, of course, an immense sensation, with its final appeal, 'Let not your Majesty disregard the words of a patriot standing with his foot on the scaffold. As long as Italy is not independent, the tranquillity of Europe and of your Majesty is a mere chimera: deliver my country, and the blessings of 25 millions of citizens will follow you through posterity.' In due course Orsini was condemned, though the Empress and even the Emperor would have been willing to spare his life.

The impression produced on Cavour by these events was one of dismay.

> The effect produced here is immense [he wrote] and elsewhere in Italy the effect will be still greater. It has transformed the assassin into a martyr . . . the position taken by Orsini, the work of the Emperor himself, renders our task an hundred times more difficult. How can we fight successfully the doctrine of regicide, when in France they endeavour to make it interesting by means much more efficacious than articles in the Press? The King is very upset over this unhappy publication and for the embarrassment it has created for his Government.[1]

Cavour, not guessing the Emperor's intention, failed to perceive the advertisement it gave to the cause of Italy in France, and the possibilities it opened for the creation of a public opinion favourable to French intervention in Italy. But the incident was not closed. In return for the publication of his letter Orsini consented to write a second in condemnation of political assassination, to which he had, he said, by a 'fatal aberration,' been drawn. Word reached Cavour that Napoleon wanted this to appear on the Piedmontese official journal. He could scarcely believe it, and sent to Paris for confirmation, only to receive the reply 'publish.' Cavour replied, 'we will publish Orsini's letter and statement, but note that, it is a direct assault upon Austria, not only on the part of Piedmont but also of the

[1] Chiala, *Lettere*, vol. vi. p. 196.

Emperor.' In due course the letter appeared with the following heading sanctioned by Napoleon: 'The Italian patriots may rest assured that it is not by crimes condemned by all civilized societies that they will be enabled to obtain their just desires; to conspire against the life of the only foreign sovereign who nourishes feelings of sympathy for their misfortunes, and who alone can yet do something for the welfare of unhappy Italy, is to plot against their own country.' Napoleon had strange ways of reaching his ends, and the publication of Orsini's letter was his answer perhaps to the words of the Papal Nuncio when he heard of the outrage, 'Behold the fruits of the revolutionary agitation fomented by Cavour!' and equally was it a reply to the suggestion of Hübner, 'does not your Majesty think that the moment has now come for an intimate accord between France and Austria to compel Piedmont to stop the patronage of the emigrants and the excesses of the Press?' Napoleon was right in his judgement, for the letter of Orsini raised hopes in Italy and increased her trust in France.'[1]

Cavour had now to occupy himself with the Bill on the Jury system. Its chances of success were not increased by what had happened in England, where Palmerston's Conspiracy Bill had been rejected and he himself thrown from power and replaced by a Tory Government. With this example of independence before them, the Left were more than ever determined to oppose the measure. To the Right the Bill was congenial, but whether they would support it was doubtful, for they were opposed to the general policy of the Government. Apart from the merits of the measure the Bill had a special interest which did not escape the notice of the Chamber. Six years previously, under pressure from Napoleon after the *coup d'état*, another Press Law had been brought in. It was the occasion of

[1] The King's comment was 'La lettera Orsini è un affare che va bene: Una volta si diceva i morti non cantano più, tutto cambia: che tempi!' *CCN.*, i. 28.

the now famous *connubio*. On that occasion, Cavour had
stretched a hand to Rattazzi, while he had sacrificed
Menabrea and his supporters to the susceptibilities of
the Left. Now, again under pressure from Napoleon,
a second was introduced, but this time Cavour stretched
a hand to Menabrea and his following, having just
sacrificed Rattazzi to the susceptibilities of the Right.
It was also noticed that the two scapegoats demanded
by the political exigencies of the moment, Menabrea
in the one case and Rattazzi in the other, had, on each
occasion, supported the measure.

Cavour had no difficulty in passing the Bill. His own
party and the support of the Right ensured success.
Cavour himself was recognized on all sides now as
indispensable. The country was expectant. The
significance of the Orsini incident had not been lost,
and a ministerial crisis was the last thing the country
desired. But Cavour met one great difficulty in the
debate. The Chamber wanted information, just that
information which Cavour could not give. On his
side he was anxious that the Chamber, and through
the Chamber, the country, should know that great
possibilities about which he could not talk, lay immediately ahead. He wanted them to understand
without his telling them. This is how he did it. Cavour
had spoken of 'national aspirations,' which being
translated, meant 'war with Austria,' as the aim of the
Government, and referring to the speech of the Marquis
Costa de Beauregard, he spoke as follows:

The honourable member, who, I believe, has not been a
diplomat, questioned me with complete frankness. How do
you intend to achieve this aim, what means will you employ?
he asks. You speak of diplomacy and moral influence, but
how can these obtain your end? the honourable member will
forgive me if I tell him he is somewhat indiscreet. It is
obvious that a Minister of Foreign Affairs does not come here
to say what, in all eventualities, his line of action would be.
I have said on a solemn occasion that the function of diplomacy was to give legal sanction to completed facts. I had,

indeed, forgotten one thing, that is, that while diplomacy can prepare events, it cannot complete them. To do that one does not require the Minister of Foreign Affairs—but one of his colleagues. The honourable member will excuse me if I go no farther. (Bravo! Bene!)

The Bill was passed on April 29th. The debate was scarcely over before those events at which Cavour had hinted in his speech were drawn appreciably nearer. During the previous autumn Cavour had received from Paris proposals for the marriage of the Princess Clotilde, the King's eldest daughter, to Prince Napoleon. The offer had been politely refused on the ground that the Princess could only marry an heir to a throne.[1] Now the first week in May the proposal was again put forward, but this time coupled with two others; alliance with France in a war against Austria and the formation of a kingdom of Upper Italy. Such a proposal was a very different matter, and Cavour regarded it as of such supreme importance for the future of the country that he would neither deal with it through the usual diplomatic channels nor even commit his reply to writing. By the hand of his private secretary, Costantino Nigra, he sent to Paris a note requesting that, as his presence at the Tuileries would create 'immense suspicion', it would be best if the Emperor would send Dr. Conneau to Turin to discuss the proposals submitted to him. On May 15th Dr. Conneau wrote that he had interviewed Napoleon, who, after confirming the three points put forward in Prince Napoleon's communication, emphasized the necessity of finding an adequate *casus belli*. To clear the position he had stated the conditions under which his assistance would not be forthcoming, (i) if it was a war purely between Italian powers, (ii) if it partook of the nature of a revolutionary uprising or a Mazzinian conspiracy, (iii) if the cause he was asked to support was that of Lombard subjects who had become naturalized Sardinians. Further, he

---

[1] *CCN.*, vol. i. p. 99. Letter of Villamarina to Cavour, September 12th. See Chiala, vol. ii, Cavour to Rattazzi, September 15th.

warned Cavour not to offend Russia by his attitude towards Naples; assured him that he would give Austria no opportunity for friendly overtures; and fixed the spring of 1859 for the outbreak of hostilities, leaving to Cavour the task of finding or making a plausible *casus belli*.[1] The visit of Dr. Conneau took place the last days of May, and in the interval Cavour was busy with parliamentary work. The vast credits already passed by the Chamber necessitated a loan for forty millions. The debate lasted from May 14th to 29th, when the loan was sanctioned. On June 2nd, Cavour wrote to Villamarina that he had seen Dr. Conneau passing through Turin on his way to Florence; that he had reason to believe from what he had said that Napoleon would like to talk to him about the state of Italy, and that, as he proposed to spend some weeks in Switzerland when the session closed, he would be very happy to pay the Emperor a visit. The second week in July he left Turin for Geneva, and there received a letter from Napoleon's aide-de-camp that the Emperor would be charmed to see him at Plombières any day before July 24th, when he was due to return to Paris, and on July 20th the meeting took place.

The first interview began at 11 a.m. and lasted until 3 p.m. Napoleon commenced by saying that he had decided to support Sardinia with all his forces in a war against Austria, provided that a non-revolutionary cause, which would justify the war in the eyes of diplomacy, and especially of public opinion in France and Europe, could be found. Cavour then suggested, first, the trouble arising from the Treaty of Commerce with Austria, and then Austria's illegal expansion of power in Italy. Neither of these reasons satisfied Napoleon. They then examined together the map of Italy and finally found in Massa-Carrara a promising centre in which to foment the necessary rebellion. Sardinia was to provoke an appeal from the inhabitants, demanding annexation to Piedmont. The King would thereupon

[1] *CCN.*, vol. i. Nos. 29, 38.

address a threatening note to the Duke of Modena, who, relying on Austria, would probably reply in a similar tone. Victor Emmanuel would then occupy the Duchy and war would commence. After deciding that Naples should be left strictly alone, and that the Pope should be left in peaceful possession of Rome and the country round it, they passed on to the object of the war and the final settlement of Italy. Austria was to be completely driven out of the Peninsula and the country divided into a confederation of four powers. The Kingdom of Upper Italy, embracing North Italy from the Alps to the Adriatic with Romagna and the Duchies added, under the House of Savoy; a Kingdom of Central Italy composed of Tuscany and the greater part of the States of the Church; Rome and the Patriarchate, and the Kingdom of Naples. The Duchess of Parma was to be offered the throne of Central Italy, and the Pope was to be the President of the Confederation, which was to have a constitution based on that of Germany.

Having settled the future of Italy there came the question of the price to be paid. Napoleon demanded the cession of Savoy and Nice. Cavour, after stressing the severity of sacrificing the cradle of the race, agreed to surrender Savoy, but pointed out that to cede Nice was to infringe the principle of nationality, the people being Italian. At this the Emperor, after thoughtfully caressing his moustache several times, remarked that this was, after all, a secondary question which they could deal with later. The military aspect was next dealt with. France would provide 200,000 men and Italy half that number. To carry out their programme the complete defeat of Austria would be necessary and peace might have to be signed at Vienna before Austria would yield her Italian provinces. As to finance the Emperor agreed to furnish Piedmont with material, and facilitate the raising of a loan in France.

At this point the interview was broken off for an hour, Cavour being instructed to return at four o'clock, when the Emperor proposed to take him for a drive. Seated beside Napoleon, who drove his own phaeton and pair of American horses, the conversation was resumed. 'For three hours,' wrote Cavour, 'the Emperor drove me through the valleys and forests that make the Vosges one of the most picturesque parts of France.' No sooner were they out of the streets of Plombières than Napoleon broached the subject of the marriage of Prince Napoleon to the Princess Clotilde. On this subject Cavour had received precise instructions from the King. Unless Napoleon made it a *sine qua non* of the alliance he was not to engage the King by any definite acceptance. To these instructions Cavour strictly adhered and on his return to Plombières nothing definite was settled. Napoleon expressed his keen desire for union with the House of Savoy, did his best to whitewash his cousin's past and insisted on his good qualities; his ability, his sound judgement, and his good heart. Cavour on his side urged the extreme youth of the Princess, who was only fifteen, and the unwillingness of the King to force a marriage upon her. The interview ended on their return to Plombières.

Immediately after leaving the Emperor Cavour dispatched a cipher message to the King, and then, moved by a sudden inspiration, departed himself for Baden. On his arrival he at once supplemented his dispatch to Victor Emmanuel with a long account of his meeting with the Emperor. After detailing in full what had passed, he added some pages of comment, mostly regarding the proposed marriage. He sought to impress upon the King that this was, in fact, the key to the whole situation; that although the Emperor had not made it a *sine qua non* he would be deeply hurt if the proposal was refused, and his attitude towards Piedmont would certainly be adversely affected. The proposal was not new. He pointed out that the alternatives to the Prince, since the Hapsburgs and the House of Lorraine were out of the question, were not many, and must be sought, either amongst the little courts of

Germany or in Portugal. If not the heir to Napoleon, the Prince was only separated from that position by a child of two years old. In fact, that the alliance, though it had its difficulties and drawbacks, was one that the King might well accept without hesitation.[1]

Having dispatched this letter Cavour turned to the business in hand. In the course of the next twenty-four hours he saw the King of Würtemberg, the Prince of Prussia, the Grand Duchess Elena of Russia, Manteuffel, and the Russian diplomat, Balan. The result, especially with the Russians, was eminently satisfactory: 'If one can rely on what was said to me by the Grand Duchess Elena and Balan,' he wrote to La Marmora, 'we can depend for certain upon the armed support of Russia. The Grand Duchess said that if France supported us, Russia would compel the Government to do the same.' Balan said: if you have a *chasseur de Vincennes* on one side of you, you can count on having a soldier of our Guard on the other! Prussia, however, was uncertain, in spite of the resentment generally felt towards Austria. After this brief and satisfactory visit Cavour turned homewards and was back in Turin by the first of August.

Ten years before, Cavour had written 'revolutions which have not their *point d'appui* in Paris are abortive.' Upon this *point d'appui* Cavour had since concentrated as the centre of his own plans for a revolution in the conditions of Italy. Now it was offered to him, and on the strength of Napoleon's word he returned to Turin to set in motion every active force that he could command to rouse the national spirit to seize its opportunity, for such a chance might not come again for a generation.

[1] *CCN.*, vol. i, Nos. 51 and 52.

IX. FROM PLOMBIÈRES TO WAR

Cavour and the National Society—Nigra sent to Paris—First Negotiations—
Prince Napoleon meets the Tsar at Warsaw—The King and the
Princess—First French Proposals—Peace Pressure on Napoleon—
Cavour and Hungary—The Speech to Hübner—The King's Speech
from the Throne emended by Napoleon—Its Effects—Lord Malmes-
bury's Efforts for Peace—Marriage of Princess Clothilde to Prince
Napoleon—Lord Cowley's Mission to Vienna—Cavour's War Loan—
The Volunteer Movement in Italy—Difficulties of Napoleon—Cavour
orders Partial Mobilization—Napoleon proposes a Congress—Cavour
refuses to disarm—Napoleon supports him—Last Efforts—The
Austrian Ultimatum—War.

CAVOUR returned from Plombières with nothing but
a verbal agreement with the Emperor, and in consequence, with the knowledge that if Napoleon failed him
there was no means of redress and no policy but submission. But he never seems to have doubted his own
ability to provoke Austria to attack and thus fulfil the
condition laid down by Napoleon for the intervention
of France, and he forthwith set to work to carry out his
side of the preparations for war. The essence of the
task before him lay in the accomplishment of two things:
first, to turn the pact made at Plombières into a signed
treaty; and secondly, to find an adequate *casus belli* that
would justify Napoleon in fulfilling his share of the
bargain.

Cavour was convinced that the success of the plan
made with the Emperor hung on the marriage of the
Princess Clothilde to Prince Napoleon. A refusal would
wreck the whole design. 'I am certain,' he wrote to
La Marmora, 'that the Emperor attaches to this
marriage the very greatest importance and that upon
it depends, if not the alliance itself, at least the final
issue. It would be a most lamentable error to ally oneself with the Emperor and at the same time to offend
him in a way he would never forget,' and he begged
La Marmora to support his energetic words to the
King on this point and allow no scruple of 'rancid
aristocracy' to ruin the formation of Italy.[1] Some time,

[1] Chiala, *Lettere*, vol. ii. No. 532; *CCN.*, vol. i. No. 52.

however, must elapse before a decision on this vital question could be reached, and Cavour in the meantime threw himself into the task of organizing all the available military resources in order that the army might, if possible, reach the 100,000 men which he had undertaken to provide.

Cavour was anxious that the army should contain as large a proportion as possible of Italians from outside Piedmont. The only method by which this could be done was to raise a supplementary force of volunteers. The ideal leader for such a force was ready to hand in Garibaldi, and Cavour lost no time in putting his plan into execution. He interviewed La Farina, and all the resources of the National Society were requisitioned to rouse the country and organize a force of volunteers. He summoned the leaders of the national party, Minghetti, Garibaldi, Pepoli, and others, and urged them on the same path. It was all done with the utmost secrecy, but during the months following Plombières, everything was made ready for an influx of the youth of Italy into Piedmont the moment the signal was given. To La Farina was also entrusted the task of preparing the rising in Massa-Carrara, and in October a detailed plan was sent to Cavour and approved.[1]

Cavour in his own mind had fixed the beginning of May 1859 for the opening of hostilities, and he eventually proved to be only a week wrong in his calculations. But an extraordinary nicety of adjustment was required. A movement such as he was now initiating would gather momentum, and after a certain point could with difficulty be arrested. To be attacked too soon would mean disaster, and once ready, he could not keep his new army in prolonged inaction. It was this question of time that proved one of his critical anxieties, for the difficulties experienced by Napoleon made it almost impossible for him to keep pace with Cavour. There came a time when the delay that Napoleon craved for meant possible disaster for Cavour,

[1] Chiala, *Lettere*, vol. ii. Appendix VIII; *CCN.*, vol. i. Nos. 123–5.

and only great skill and good fortune, combined with a real loyalty on the part of the Emperor, prevented Cavour's plan from collapsing in utter failure.

While Cavour was thus engaged he received a note from the Emperor asking him to send a confidential agent to confer with him in Paris. Cavour at once sent Count Costantino Nigra, his private secretary. Few statesmen have been so fortunate in their choice as Cavour, and few have been so well served, for Nigra presented the views of his master with a tact and a fidelity which was in itself remarkable, and at times with an audacity which would have scarcely been possible to an official ambassador. As Nigra himself recognized, his obscurity was one of his chief assets, for he passed unnoticed where a more important personage would have created rumour and suspicion.

Nigra had his first audience with Napoleon on August 31st. He found the Emperor preoccupied with two points, the *casus belli* and the question of time. He was not entirely satisfied with the Massa-Carrara project. He asked for information regarding the Austrian fortification of Piacenza, and remarked that if Austria pursued her proposal to incorporate her Italian provinces in the German Confederation, this would provide a satisfactory opening. Then smiling, he added, 'I almost wish that M. Panizzi, who is travelling at this moment with Sir James Hudson in Austria, was arrested and ill-treated by the Government. It would be very unpleasant for the Director of the British Museum, whom I esteem, but it would have an excellent effect in England and suit our plans exactly.' On the question as to the time for the commencement of the war he was less satisfactory. He did not believe it possible to be ready by the spring. It was necessary to float a loan and there was scarcely time. It would be better he thought to postpone it until the spring of 1860 or at the earliest the late summer of 1859. The winter would give them the advantage of having the Tyrolese Passes blocked with snow and thus cover their left flank.

When the interview was over Nigra wrote a full account to Cavour.[1]

Shortly after this the Emperor went to Biarritz, where Cavour's reply, dated September 17th, reached him. The idea of postponing the war for a further twelve months by no means suited Cavour's plans, and his letter was mainly an argument against it. From the political point of view he emphasized the fact that thanks to the 'cleverness and wisdom' of the Emperor, the political atmosphere in Europe was particularly favourable at the moment; then, making use of current rumour, he dwelt on the risk of a *rapprochement* between Austria and Prussia or Russia, due, if time was given to them, to the diplomacy of England in the one case, and to the Empress of Russia in the other. As to Italy, delay was equally dangerous. With time, the policy of conciliation pursued with such persistence by the Archduke Maximilian might prove successful; delay might dissipate the splendid spirit that at present animated the Liberals throughout Italy, and offer a further opportunity to the Mazzinians or the so-called party of action for another revolutionary movement. Cavour doubted whether he could control the situation indefinitely. As to the military side, the cessation of hostilities during the winter, while it would enable the allies to consolidate their gains, would give time to Austria to draw upon her great reserves.[2]

Cavour's letter reached the Emperor on September 23rd, and the same day he summoned the Prince Napoleon to Biarritz and entrusted him with an immediate mission to the Czar at Warsaw. Nigra had his second audience with Napoleon after his return to Paris at the end of September. He found Cavour's arguments, the Emperor said, 'very just and weighty,' and once more acquiesced in the original time-sheet. He was still uneasy as to the cause for war. He impressed upon Nigra that in his opinion the successful issue of the struggle depended to a large extent upon having a just

[1] *CCN.*, vol. i. No. 75.   [2] *CCN.*, vol. i. No. 90.

cause. They must have public opinion, not only in France and Italy, but above all in England, on their side, if they did not want this latter Power as an enemy. The Prince's mission, he went on, had for its object to induce the Czar to hold Germany in check by threatening hostilities, if she showed any inclination to go to the help of Austria. He then brought up the question of the marriage and made it clear that both the Empress and himself were most anxious to see it realized and attached very great importance to it, and he added, that he proposed to write direct to the King on the subject. The Emperor closed the audience by requesting Nigra to remain in Paris until the result of the mission to Warsaw was known.[1] The Prince returned on October 6th and at once informed Nigra that he had been successful. The Tsar was prepared to bind himself with a treaty to keep Germany quiet, if France would be responsible for England, and even to declare war, if necessary, and put troops and his fleet at Napoleon's disposal. To clench the matter the Baron Roncière de Noury was at once sent to St. Petersburg.

Victor Emmanuel and Cavour were delighted at the news from Paris. Cavour was especially pleased with the Emperor's attitude towards the marriage. It had not been all plain sailing with the Princess. When the marriage had first been proposed to her by the King she had refused to consider it, and Cavour, who had no sentiment at all on the subject, was in despair. But later, when she realized the political significance of the union, she changed her attitude and only stipulated that she should meet her future husband before any contract was signed. The King and Cavour accepted the condition. Once reassured that there was no likelihood of a definite refusal, Cavour was in no hurry. The signing of the treaty was to be the pre-condition of the marriage. Nigra was, therefore, instructed to let the Prince know that there were difficulties, which would probably not be removed until after she had seen the

[1] *CCN.*, vol. i. No. 100.

Prince in person. He thus kept open a line of retreat in case the treaty failed to materialize.

All, however, went well up to the end of October, but with November the difficulties began to appear. On one side or both there was a leakage of information and diplomacy began to bestir itself. Then Salvagnoli, the Florentine statesman, paid a visit to the Emperor at Compiègne and roundly proposed the formation of a Kingdom of Central Italy to be formed by joining Parma, Modena, and Bologna to Tuscany, together with the island of Corsica, having Florence as a capital and Prince Napoleon as King; in return, Sardinia was to be ceded to France. Though Napoleon ignored the suggestion, and, moreover, remarked that he would never think of raising any member of his family to a throne and thus commit the error of the First Empire, Cavour was angry that counter propositions of such a kind should be put before the Emperor.[1] But worse was to follow. On November 25th Cavour received a long letter from Nigra detailing an important interview he had had with Prince Napoleon. As soon as the result of the mission to Russia was known, the Prince had said to him General Niel would be sent to Turin. The avowed object of his journey was to be the marriage, but he would, in fact, be empowered to conclude everything. He would bring with him five documents for signature. A public and a secret treaty, a military and a financial convention, and another relative to the marriage. The principal clauses of these documents were as follows:

The treaty which could be made public would contain the offensive and defensive alliance between France and Sardinia, the cession of Savoy and Nice to France, and an undertaking on the side of Piedmont to pay all the expenses of the war; this treaty would have a preface declaring the independence of Italy and the principle of nationality. The secret treaty would define the extent of the new Kingdom of Upper Italy which

[1] *CCN.*, vol. i. No. 143.

was to embrace Piedmont, the Austrian Provinces, the Duchies, and the Papal States north of the Apennines up to Ancona; a guarantee for the temporal sovereignty of the Pope, without, however, any mention of the extent of his dominion, and a clause to regulate in common at the peace the rest of Italy according to the results of the war and the attitude taken during the war by the said States. By the military convention, the Emperor in person was to assume the supreme command. The French army and 40,000 Piedmontese under General La Marmora was to operate on the left bank of the Po, and the rest of the Piedmontese army under Victor Emmanuel would act on the right bank and occupy the Duchies and Legations. Genoa was to become the French depot during the war under a governor nominated by the Emperor.

Nigra did not fail to protest against the severity of these terms. On the question of the payment of the French army by Piedmont he remarked that, either France came into Italy as the auxiliary of Piedmont— and a paid auxiliary—in which case she had no claim to the supreme direction of the war, or she came as the principal party interested, and then, she ought to pay her own troops. When the Prince said that without this clause the war would be unpopular, and it would be said that France came into Italy simply for the benefit of Piedmont, Nigra replied that she came for her own interests; to consolidate the Empire by a successful war and to procure, by enlarging Piedmont, a useful and devoted ally—to say nothing of getting Savoy and Nice. As to the military arrangement, he told the Prince that his King was not one to stand still and see others fight. He was capable of leaving his generals on the right bank and plunging alone into the thick of the fighting across the river.

When Cavour received this outline of the French proposals he got somewhat of a shock. He comforted himself, however, with the thought that 'a work so great as we have undertaken could never be achieved without meeting immense difficulties, which it is necessary to envisage with calmness and courage and overcome by wisdom, cleverness, and determination.' In his instructions to Nigra relative to these suggestions he laid stress on preventing a visit from General Niel before the Prince arrived in person. This would ruin everything. The Prince must come first, or at least they must come together. As, to paying the expenses of both armies, it was impossible. If they did so all the popularity of France would vanish. He could undertake, he thought, to feed the French army, but to do more than that would be to sow a germ of destruction in the heart of the tree they sought to raise. Equally impracticable were the military arrangements. What would Italy say, what would Europe say, above all, what would France say, if, while the French troops stormed the Mincio, the King was content to watch them through his glasses from the other side of the river?[1]

The negotiations thus opened proceeded steadily until the arrival of the Prince at Turin in the following January, when the final modifications were made and the treaty signed. Not the least harassing to Cavour was the financial question. He had hoped to raise the necessary money by a loan in France, guaranteed by the French Government, but both the Prince and the Emperor assured him that this was impossible. It was, in fact, all the Emperor could do to raise money for himself, owing to the opposition of the banking interest to war with Austria, so the 50 million loan that Cavour required had to be floated in Italy, where it met with a splendid response and was covered without difficulty. Then came bad news from Russia. The Czar imposed conditions: two years for preparation; the revision of the Treaty of Paris of 1856, and an assurance that there would be no disturbance in Poland. These terms put all idea of active Russian intervention out of court, and though fresh negotiations were opened, any prospect of greater value than benevolent neutrality on the part of Russia disappeared.

[1] *CCN.*, vol. i. Nos. 150–3.

Besides these difficulties Napoleon was beginning to experience the pressure of diplomatic Europe. 'As soon as I was alone with the Emperor,' wrote Nigra on December 15th, 'he said to me that the nearer the fatal epoch approached, the greater and more numerous became the difficulties. From one side Germany and Prussia, warmly supported by Austria and England, and on the other side this latter Power dreading every combination that might infringe the settlement of 1815 to which her honour was pledged.' His own entourage was no less averse to his plans. 'Every one around the Emperor,' Nigra continued, 'excluding neither the Empress nor Fould nor the Minister for War, nor even General Niel himself, is terrified at the idea of war with Austria.'[1] Napoleon's method of calming Europe was to keep his own Foreign Secretary, known to be strongly pro-Austrian, in ignorance of his plans, so that his denials of warlike intentions could have all the weight of sincerity. But this could not last for ever, and before the end of the year Walewski was told the truth, and another strong opponent of war was thus let into the secret. But in spite of all these obstacles the Emperor held firm: 'I could well have wished to have had a year clear before me,' he said at the same audience, 'before venturing on the execution of our plans, but I have decided to hasten the moment of action since that is what you desire and what the actual condition of Italy demands.' Walking back together to the Palais Royale that night after the interview, the Prince said to Nigra, 'assure M. de Cavour that as far as our plans depend upon the will of the Emperor everything will be settled easily enough, but as to that that is outside his power, it will be necessary to do the best we can with our common forces.'

Nigra returned to Turin a few days before Christmas and there was a momentary lull in the negotiations, but not for long, for Cavour, acting on a hint dropped by the Prince that 'it was necessary for him to return before

[1] *CCN.*, vol. i. No. 170.

the first day of the new year,' sent him back the last days of December. He brought with him two letters from Cavour and the King to the Emperor, the burden of which was the same. After a warm invitation to the Prince to come to Turin about the 15th of January, the King continued: 'The excitement of this nation is *au comble*, and I do not know if one will be able to restrain the Lombards, from some hasty action until the time that your Majesty desires to commence operations. Austria knows more than is generally believed, and when the marriage is announced, that Power will regard it as morally a declaration of war, and then I shall have to be prepared for all eventualities,' and he then asked that the Emperor would have ready at some convenient point a force of thirty or forty thousand men which could at once be sent into Piedmont. In this request, Napoleon, after some hesitation, acquiesced, and two divisions were sent to Marseilles ready for immediate embarkation.

Before 1858 ended, three outstanding difficulties in Europe were, for the time being, successfully closed. The double election of Colonel Couza at both Jassy and Bukarest settled the vexed question of the Principalities, Wallachia and Moldavia at last coalescing in the new Kingdom of Rumania. The trouble between the German Confederation and Denmark over Holstein was ended by the submission of Frederick III to French and Russian pressure, and on December 23rd the measures proposed by the Confederation were suspended. Lastly, the joint action of Russia and France was, for the third time, successfully employed in Serbia, where the proposed intervention of Austria on behalf of Turkey's protégé Alexander Karageorgevic was checkmated. The settlement of these troubles was most opportune for the designs of Napoleon, and left the road clear for the opening of what Cavour called 'the greatest drama of modern times.'[1]

But Cavour did not confine his machinations against

[1] See Debidour, *Histoire Diplomatique de l'Europe*.

Austria to France and Italy. He was already in relations with the Hungarian General, Klapka, whom he had interviewed in Turin and sent on to Napoleon. He had an agent ready to proceed to Belgrade, where there was still a possibility of trouble for Austria with the Serbs. He was also meditating action in the Principalities, where anti-Austrian feeling was very strong, and where the new ruler, Colonel Couza, was a close friend of France. Even if these movements failed, the mere knowledge of their existence would embarrass Austria and fan Cavour's policy of exasperation. But for the moment, these activities were held up out of deference for the difficulties of Napoleon, and Cavour's policy was rather one of restraint than of provocation, nevertheless the end in view always remained constant. In May 1856 he had written to a friend 'in three years we shall have war, the real one . . .', and now, with four months to run, he became more precise. Lord Odo Russell, on his way to Rome in December, had an interview with Cavour at Turin. Cavour remarked that he would have 'an interesting winter,' for war would be declared against Austria. Lord Odo answered that Austria had only to adopt a policy of delay to exhaust Piedmont's resources, and if Piedmont was the aggressor she would lose the sympathy of Europe. Cavour agreed, but pointed out that if Austria was the aggressor the sympathy would be on his side, to which Lord Odo remarked that Austria would never commit so stupendous a blunder. 'But I shall force her to declare war against us,' was the reply of Cavour. Incredulous, Lord Odo sarcastically asked when he expected to perform that diplomatic prodigy: 'about the first fortnight in May' was the reply. On leaving him Lord Odo noted the date in his diary. It was wrong: Austria declared war on April 29th.

In spite, however, of all the secrecy that had been observed, the fact that Napoleon and Cavour were meditating war with Austria on behalf of Italy, was an open secret in all the Chancelleries of Europe at the

close of 1858. On the 1st of January Napoleon received
the Diplomatic Corps. After speaking politely to the
Papal Nuncio, he passed to the Austrian Ambassador,
Baron Hübner, to whom he remarked, 'I regret that my
relations with Austria are not as good as I could wish,
but I beg you will write to Vienna that my personal
sentiments towards the Emperor remain the same.'
There was possibly no particular significance in these
words in the mind of the Emperor, but they spread
through Europe like wildfire, and everywhere were
interpreted as the first overt sign of war. Cavour was
surprised. 'It seems,' he said, 'that the Emperor wants
to go forward.'[1] But although he wrote to Prince
Napoleon that the Emperor's words to Hübner had
caused immense excitement in Italy, he did not pay
much attention to them, for he was, at the moment, in
an agony of apprehension lest the visit of the Prince,
and in consequence the signing of the treaty, should be
postponed. In a few days, however, he was reassured.
The Prince was to depart on January 13th, with full
powers, and General Niel was to accompany him. This
matter satisfactorily settled, Cavour could return to the
other problem that was causing him anxiety.

The Piedmontese Parliament was due to meet on
January 10th, and the speech from the Throne was a
matter of anxious concern to the Cabinet. The words
pronounced by Victor Emmanuel must have the
sanction of Napoleon, for the tone of the two allies
must correspond. So on December 31st Cavour forwarded the first sketch of the speech to Nigra with
instructions to obtain the opinion and comments of
Napoleon. The closing words of the discourse were
as follows:

> Comforted by the experience of the past, we await, prudent
> and decided, the eventualities of the future. Whatever they
> may be, they will find us, strong through concord and firm

[1] To E. D'Azeglio in London he wrote: 'the Emperor after having recommended precedence for eight months has opened the year with an outburst
(*algarade*) that recalls the style of his uncle on the eve of declaring war.'

in our determination, treading in the steps of our Magnanimous Predecessor, ready to complete the great Mission entrusted to us by Divine Providence.

The manuscript was returned with the last paragraph cancelled by the pencil of Napoleon, with the following words in the margin, 'I find this too strong and I should prefer something like the following,' and then in the pen of Mocquard was a paragraph containing the words:

If Piedmont, small though it is in territory, counts for something in the Councils of Europe, it is due to the greatness of the ideals it represents and the sympathies it inspires. This position, without doubt, creates for us many dangers, yet, while we respect treaties, we cannot remain insensible to the *cris de douleur*[1] that reach us from so many parts of Italy!

When Cavour read the Emperor's emendation, he was as puzzled as he was pleased.

I have received the Emperor's notes upon the speech [he writes to Nigra on January 7th]. He finds the last paragraph too strong, and proposes by way of substitution, another, in which it is a question of 'cris de doleur' rising from all parts of Italy. But this is 100 times stronger! What the devil does he mean? Truly I don't yet know what we shall make of it. Tell the Prince that this allusion to cries of grief will produce an immense effect.

Cavour, the King, and Rattazzi all set to work on translations, with the Cabinet acting as adjudicators, and the King won, and his version was incorporated in the speech, which was then sent off once more to Paris for the Emperor's inspection. On January 8th Cavour wrote to Villamarina: 'Nigra will have told you that, under the pretext of softening our speech from the Throne, the Emperor has added two or three incendiary phrases. I hesitated for a moment to insert

[1] The origin of this famous phrase is interesting. In May 1833, after his adventure with the Italian patriots, Napoleon wrote a brochure entitled *Onore Militare*, advocating that the armies of the various states should act together, *prestando orecchio al grido di dolore che sale da ogni parte della penisola.* Napoleon sent it to Mazzini for publication in *La Giovane Italia*, but he would not print it. Mazziotti, *Napoleon III e l'Italia*; Luzio, *Studi e Bozzetti*.

them, but the King had more courage than I had, he declared that he would not be more timid than his Imperial ally. We hurl the bomb on Monday.' Cavour was very worried, and the time was so short that it was doubtful if the Emperor's reply would arrive before the opening of Parliament; to add to his troubles he received a telegram on the evening of the 8th from Nigra, saying, 'Emperor frightened by news from Turin; if the discourse is bellicose a loan will be utterly impossible.' So the next day Cavour wrote that, if he heard nothing, he should advise the King to suppress the last paragraph containing the 'grido di dolore' phrase, and he added that the rumours that Napoleon had heard were exaggerated, Lombardy was very excited but amenable to advice from Turin. 'At moments of crisis,' he went on, 'it is necessary to dominate the position; one obtains results in proportion as one uses an iron energy and knows how to inspire confidence. A decided tone in the speech from the Throne will have the effect of calming the excitement, by doubling the confidence in us rather than driving Lombardy to extremes.' At ten minutes past midnight Cavour received the awaited telegram, 'Everything excellent, I approve without reserve.' So the bomb was hurled, but it had been touch and go. Writing the same day (10th) Nigra said, 'In spite of an infinity of obstacles that would have appalled the most determined, I succeeded in making known to you during the night the explicit approbation of the Emperor to the speech from the Throne. I will not tell you now how that was accomplished. It is a history, an *Iliad*, that I will tell you later.'[1]

The effect was tremendous. Delivered firmly and clearly, with all that proud kingliness that marked Victor Emmanuel's public demeanour, it created an indelible impression. The applause was frantic and the exiles from all parts of Italy who crowded the galleries made no attempt to hide their emotion. Cavour tele-

[1] *CCN.*, vol. i. Nos. 186–8, 218–19.

THE EFFORTS OF LORD MALMESBURY 273

graphed to Nigra: 'the speech has been a tremendous success.'[1]

Napoleon's famous words to Hübner and Victor Emmanuel's speech from the Throne combined, opened the sluice gates of European diplomacy. In the torrent of notes and dispatches, projects and counter-projects, that now issued from the Chancelleries, the lead was taken by England, whose Foreign Secretary, Lord Malmesbury, made a great, if unavailing, effort to save Europe from war. Unfortunately he did not understand the position, for he started from premisses which rendered a conclusion of failure inevitable. These premisses were that the Treaties of 1815 should be respected and that no territorial change should be made in Italy. Had he realized Cavour's determination to make Italy a nation, or had he known the terms of the pact of Plombières, he would have understood how impossible it was to win the adherence of either France or Sardinia to such conditions. The position was this. Italy had been bound hand and foot in 1815, and over her had been placed a gaoler, who not only saw to it that the knots kept firm, but occasionally added others of his own. Her efforts to free herself had won a friend who was prepared to remove the gaoler by force, and undo her bonds. Lord Malmesbury, while refusing either to free her or take away her gaoler, was most anxious to make her more comfortable than she was at present, by a slight readjustment of the knots where they galled her most. The rest of Europe was sympathetic but suspicious of the designs of the friend. Lord Malmesbury's diplomacy was vitiated by another fact, although he attached so much importance to the sanctity of the settlement of 1815, he was not prepared to fight to support it, and for the very good reason that he knew the sympathy of his country was with Italy, and would never permit that the armed force of England should be used to perpetuate the tyrannous system of Austria. But this was not the case with Austria, who

[1] See Massari, *Vittorio Emanuele II*, for the scene in the Chamber.

from the first was prepared to use all her strength to retain her hold on Italy.

The reply of Malmesbury to the Emperor's speech was a dispatch to Hudson at Turin saying, 'Be reserved. We shall not support any party that begins the strife, say this and no more.' Austria's reply was to march the Third Army Corps into Italy together with some special troops destined to keep order in Lombardy and the Legations (Jan. 5th). How far the English Foreign Office was from understanding the position is seen from the dispatches to Turin. 'Piedmont's interests will not be considered by France or Austria, her prosperity will disappear, the Italian standpoint is the same now as in 1848: Lombardy does not wish to join Piedmont. Bring these points before Cavour,' and he added, 'A war in Italy might bring about a change of masters, but assuredly will not give them independence without which liberty is hopeless.' When Malmesbury read the *grido di dolore* speech he wrote of the 'terrible responsibility of the head of a Government, unassailed by any foreign Power, and with no point of honour at stake, appearing to invite a European war by addressing himself through his Sovereign to the suffering subjects of other Powers.'[1] To Malmesbury, Italy was still a geographical expression; to Cavour, Italy was a living entity in whose name he spoke. But Malmesbury had hardly got into his stride when Cavour took yet another step forward.

On January 15th Prince Napoleon and his suite arrived at Genoa. Proceeding to Turin he was at once plunged into a combination of business and pleasure. The final revision of the treaties was at once taken in hand. France agreed to take over half the expenses of piercing the Mont Cenis Tunnel, but insisted on the definite cession of Nice as well as Savoy being embodied in the treaty. After the signature, it was dispatched to Paris and by January 29th it was returned duly signed by Napoleon. 'Never have I seen the Emperor in such

[1] F.O. 167, vol. 105.

good humour,' said the official who witnessed the signature, 'he was simply delighted.'[1]

On the 30th, the Prince and the Princess were married in the Royal Chapel and the day after left for Genoa. Their reception was splendid. The populace, once so cold and distrustful, hailed Victor Emmanuel as King of Italy; they cheered for war; then cheered for Italian Independence. 'The first act of the drama closes,' wrote Cavour, 'now we pass on to others still more grave, but which certainly will not be more difficult to carry out. For I can assure you, I have worked harder to bring this about than I have worked for anything else in my life.'

With the signing of the treaty and the marriage of the Prince, the first half of the task Cavour had set himself was accomplished. He now had before him the problem of finding an adequate cause for war, knowing that when that was forthcoming Napoleon would be with him. Though to satisfy his ally he had already put forward a variety of suggestions, he seemed to be relying more on a general policy of provocation than on the discovery of one specific cause. As he put it later, his object was to create a situation which Austria would find unbearable and be driven to attack as the lesser of two evils. In a letter to Villamarina he outlines his line of conduct in these words:

Now that the marriage is a *fait accompli* our thoughts are fixed exclusively on war. On our return we shall demand from Parliament permission to contract a loan of 40 millions, and we shall push on vigorously with our armaments. Our language will always be most moderate and we shall pose as the victims of the threats of Austria. It is essential that the treaty remains secret. Only, now we can say that we have the certainty that, as long as right is on our side, the Emperor will not desert us.[2]

While the alliance of France and Sardinia was being

---

[1] The full text of the treaty is in *CCN.*, vol. i. Appendix.
[2] *CCN.*, vol. i. No. 242.

sealed at Turin, Malmesbury was exploring the Chancelleries of Europe for a road to peace. To Lord Cowley in Paris he wrote that, 'the only security for peace was the strict, even pedantic, observance of the treaties which France had hitherto loyally kept.' But when Cowley interviewed the Prince before leaving for Turin, 'he evinced so little respect for existing treaties and broached a policy of so dangerous a character for Italy' that Cowley spoke to Walewski about it, who replied that the Prince's views were not those of either the Foreign Office or the Emperor. Napoleon himself was enigmatic; as to the great alarm felt 'he was quite unable to divine the reason of it,' but he added, 'I respect existing treaties because they are the only landmarks we have.'[1] Buol at Vienna was at least candid; 'if you wish to preach peace to prevent war,' he said, 'address yourselves with firmness to France and Piedmont. We are not meditating war: we shall not be the aggressors:' 'but,' he added, 'we can never come to an understanding with France, because we do not recognize her as an Italian Power and because she sympathizes and protects the cause of nationalities; we support that of Sovereigns, Governments, and *l'ordre établi.*'[2] The British Minister at Berlin wrote that Prussia reserves complete liberty of action but allows it to be seen that public opinion *may* force Prussia to take part against France. Russia was polite but cold. As to Turin, when Cavour's Minister in London wrote warning him that Malmesbury's attitude was almost threatening, Cavour, remembering the warm support from England promised by Lord Clarendon at Paris, three years before, wrote in reply that he awaited the promised communication with resignation, 'in the meantime,' he said, 'it seems to me that we can say that we trust the *menaces* will have the same value as the *promises*. Whilst we recommend moderation and calmness, Austria accumulates troops. Lombardy is an entrenched camp, and we shall

[1] Cowley to Malmesbury. F.O. 167, vol. 105.
[2] Seymour to Malmesbury, January 20th.

be obliged to take steps for self-defence.'[1] But the activity of Lord Malmesbury, in truth, assisted Cavour's plans. He had feared that when the Prince's marriage was known, Austria would take it as 'morally a declaration of war' and anticipate hostilities by a *coup de main*. But the energy of the British Foreign Secretary's peace propaganda restrained Austria from any such action, and the two divisions Napoleon had made ready at Marseilles, in case Piedmont needed instant succour, remained in camp.[2]

The response of diplomatic Europe to Malmesbury's appeal was a chorus of insistence on the preservation of the treaties of 1815. 'Possible changes in Italy,' said Count Buol, 'was a most dangerous doctrine and subversive of the treaties of 1815.' Even King Leopold of Belgium, who owed his throne purely to the flat defiance of the treaties, wrote to his beloved Niece, 'it was praiseworthy that you said in your speech that treaties must be respected, else indeed we return to the old *Faustrecht* we have been striving to get rid of.'[3] Malmesbury, oblivious to the facts of 1820 and 1848, not to mention the Crimean War, wrote that 'the treaties of 1815 had given us the longest peace on record.' There were just two men in Europe who knew their own mind, Buol and Cavour. Buol, thanks to the warning given by Napoleon to Hübner, was pouring troops into Italy determined to fight for his hold on Italy. Cavour, equally determined, was preparing to fight for Italian freedom and to make Napoleon fight with him.

But the chorus of disapproval that followed his words to the Austrian Ambassador had its effect on Napoleon. Alarmed by the fall on the Bourse and the protests of the commercial classes in France, he hastily published a disclaimer in the *Moniteur*, made a point of being polite to Hübner, and took a step backward. On January 27th Cowley was able to write that 'the general

[1] Cavour to E. D'Azeglio, January 15th.
[2] *CCN.*, vol. i. Nos. 182 and 228.
[3] *Letters of Queen Victoria*, vol. iii.

position was better both in France and Italy, due to the
salutary warning Napoleon has received as to the state of
opinion in Europe, and in no lesser degree to the absence
of Prince Napoleon from Paris.' On February 4th
Napoleon published the pamphlet *Napoléon III et l'Italie*,
outlining his plan of a Confederation of States and his
reasons for it, and another thrill went through Europe;[1]
it was a further step in his education of public opinion.
On the 8th he opened the Corps Législatif: his speech
was anxiously awaited, but nobody got any satisfaction.
It was so carefully phrased that it was impossible to say
what it really meant. 'I did not expect,' wrote Lord
Cowley, 'a document so little adapted to calm the
anxiety which has for the last few weeks pervaded the
public mind. People consider it as leaving matters
exactly as they were.' Walewski, interviewed by Cowley,
endeavoured to explain it, 'but,' he wrote, 'it was clear
to me that he was of the same opinion as myself.' Three
days later, however, he writes to Malmesbury with more
assurance: 'I found Count Walewski this afternoon
more reassured than I have yet found him as to the late
crisis being entirely over. Other information has also
reached me which shows that the Emperor has for the
present at least abandoned all thoughts of war.' Lord
Cowley would have been much interested if he could
have seen the letter Napoleon had written the day before
to Victor Emmanuel. After commenting on the difficulties raised by Prussia's threat of supporting Austria
and by the attitude of England, who through 'jealousy
of France shows herself very badly disposed towards
Italy,' he suggested the following line of action 'to
prepare slowly but seriously for war, that is to say to
make those preparations that demand more time than
money: to arm and strengthen the forts, to accumulate
munitions and provisions, will be of more value than to

---

[1] The pamphlet was written by the Vicomte de la Gueronnière in conjunction with E. Rendu, the friend and correspondent of D'Azeglio. It was
planned by Napoleon and written soon after his return from Plombières.
Later he revised it with great care before publication. See the account
written by Rendu in Chiala, vol. iii. Appendix.

have ready large numbers of men and horses, that cost
much money to keep.' As to policy, to detach Prussia
and England from Austria was the great task. 'There
is no fear of an act of aggression from Austria, she will
do everything possible to escape war.' There was little
comfort for Cavour or his King in this letter. 'I send
you the Emperor's letter,' wrote Victor Emmanuel to
Cavour, 'it is feeble, and I have premonitions of misfortune.'[1] But Cavour understood the difficulty of
Napoleon's position better: 'The conduct of the Emperor appears to me as clever as it is frank, he inspires
me with the greatest confidence,' he wrote to Bixio in
Paris, and Prince Napoleon insisted that 'he was always
the same.' But the moment when diplomatic pressure
compelled Napoleon to reassure Europe by revealing
a sudden disposition towards peace, was always seized
by Cavour to take a step forward, and so on February 9th
he introduced his loan for 50 millions, and in his speech,
which was specially conceived with a view to influencing
English opinion, 'he lavished more praises on the
English than perhaps they deserved,' 'but,' he added,
'it is necessary to make them swallow certain truths
which may not be very palatable.' Malmesbury was
sorely grieved: 'H.M.'s Government must earnestly
implore the Cabinet of Turin to pause in its present
headlong course,' he wrote, and then requested Cavour
to give him a detailed statement of Italian grievances
and no longer talk in generalities. Cavour replied with
an indictment of Austria which was unanswerable.[2] He
now began to give open encouragement to deserters
from Lombardy and young men of all classes, to enroll
in the Piedmontese army; the numbers had reached
5,000 by the end of February. It was a fruitful source
of trouble if Austria demanded their extradition under
the existing treaty, for Cavour meant to refuse. On
February 18th he had written to the Marquis Ridolfi
at Florence asking him to send an envoy to come and

[1] CCN., vol. ii. Nos. 249–50.
[2] CCN., vol. ii. Nos. 268–9; F.O. 167, vol. 105.

see him, 'hitherto I have abstained from giving our
Tuscan friends precise advice,' he said in his letter,
'but now things are changed, it is therefore urgent and
important to take steps to concert together the exact
path to be followed. Tuscany is called upon to play
an important part in coming events.' The next steps
were in preparation; nothing further would be done
until the loan was covered. He must have money.
Then he would 'call out the contingents,' in other words
order a partial mobilization. Austria continued her
preparations for war, every week saw more troops sent
to Italy and increased activity on fortifications at Pavia
and Piacenza. France was doing the same, but less
obtrusively.

But the position of Napoleon was growing very difficult. Even the Prince, ardent advocate of war as he was,
could not fail to see it. Walewski opposed every step
taken by his master and gave all possible encouragement
to the promoters of peace. 'I do not speak of Walewski,'
wrote the Prince to Cavour, 'whose conduct I deplore
and oppose. Your discourse on the loan was very good
and has had a good effect in England, where opinion is
less bad. It is Germany, which rises up as one man to
threaten us.' And then he went on to urge Cavour to
send Nigra back to Paris. So Nigra went back again.
In the same strain the Prince wrote to Victor Emmanuel
advocating 'perseverance and prudence' as the order of
the day. Nigra had an audience with the Emperor on
March 4th. His position, the Emperor said, was more
difficult and dangerous than ever before. There must
be, he said, a temporary suspension in the execution of
their plans, 'a moment of truce to resettle ourselves in
the saddle' were his actual words. During this truce, he
proposed, while continuing to make preparations for
war, to attempt a diplomatic campaign, with a view to
getting public opinion in Europe on their side by insisting on reforms in Italy which Austria would certainly
not either accept or carry out. Whilst Piedmont was
to denounce the extradition treaty with Austria, to

encourage legal and constitutional agitation in Italy, to insist on the demolition of the fortifications at Piacenza and the reforms outlined in Cavour's memorandum; Napoleon, in reply to the question England was continually asking, What do you want done in Italy? was going to outline a plan for a military, political, and economic league, which would completely annul Austria's influence south of the Po. Piedmontese or Federal troops would garrison the places now occupied by the Austrians and wide reforms would be initiated. Finally, war must be postponed until the spring of 1860. 'Of course,' said the Emperor, 'this plan cannot be executed. Nobody would want it, neither the Governments nor the Italian people, and it would not satisfy either France or Piedmont. But I shall have a programme, which I shall try to make England adopt, and with which one can make a species of ultimatum to Europe and Austria.'[1] The very next day in pursuance of his plan Napoleon inserted in the *Moniteur* an article in which he said officially, 'The Emperor has promised the King of Sardinia to defend him against every aggressive act of Austria: *he has promised nothing more and he will keep his word.*'

Now, almost on the same day, Count Buol, interviewing Lord Cowley, sent by Lord Malmesbury on a special mission to Vienna, disclaimed all intention of attacking Piedmont and offered to give this guarantee to Lord Cowley in writing,[2] but at the same time he ordered the 2nd Army Corps to be placed on a war footing and proceed to Lombardy. The significance of these facts was clear. While France took a step towards peace, Austria took one towards war. What was Cavour to do under such circumstances? In the face of this simultaneous advance of his enemy and retreat of his friend to avoid anything of the nature of further provocation would have appeared common prudence. But

---

[1] *CCN.*, vol. ii. No. 282.
[2] Cavour refused to give a similar guarantee except on conditions. See *CCN.*, vol. ii. No. 325.

to leave the country only half prepared, in the face of
the enormous force across the Ticino, was a responsibility that Cavour would not take. He informed
Napoleon that the article in the *Moniteur* forced him
to order partial mobilization, in spite of the appearance of provocation which such an act might have.
Napoleon did not disapprove, and a few days later
30,000 additional men were called to the colours.

On March 6th Cavour in a letter to Paris put down
his policy with his accustomed lucidity.

> I understand the position of the Emperor [he said] and I do
> not blame him. He must sacrifice something to public
> opinion and use pacific language. We do not want to be
> provocative, but in the nature of things we are obliged to
> adopt a firm and decided attitude. It is known already that,
> having enrolled 2,000 Italians of other States in our army,
> we have given Austria a *casus belli* of which she can make use
> in twenty-four hours. Armed, we are masters of the situation
> in Italy; disarmed, we shall be without influence in a fort-
> night, and power passes into the hands of the revolutionaries.
> I make no opposition to a diplomatic campaign, in fact I find
> it most opportune. I do not ask that Austria shall be driven
> to fury with notes and protocols. Let them negotiate, and
> while they do so, *it will be our task to make the situation in-
> supportable.* The Italian emigration continues, in two months
> we shall have 10,000 Lombards, Parmenese, Modenese,
> &c., in our ranks. This fact will be the finest possible
> evidence of the real feelings of Italy and at the same time
> a provocation that Austria will not be able to tolerate.[1]

At this point the policy of Napoleon and Cavour, in
a certain sense, diverge. Napoleon's diplomatic campaign was presently to issue in the idea of a congress,
the purpose of which was not to settle the Italian
question, but to shift the moral responsibility for war
from Paris to Vienna, and create the atmosphere that
would enable Napoleon to open hostilities with public
opinion behind him.[2] But he reckoned without Cavour

---

[1] *CCN.*, vol. ii. No. 290.

[2] *CCN.*, vol. ii. No. 349. Nigra to Cavour: 'The Emperor has charged
me to tell you that he was forced to follow a different road to that of Your
Excellency in order to arrive at the same end.'

if he thought it would take twelve months, for in five weeks the end had been accomplished. Cavour, on the other hand, now concentrates on the task of openly rousing Italy and creating a situation which was an open defiance of Austria.

In the meantime Lord Cowley was at work at Vienna. His instructions were to procure the adhesion of Austria to four points. Security for peace between Austria and Sardinia, evacuation of the Roman States, reform of Italian States, and a substitute for the treaties between Austria and Parma and Modena which obliged Austria to intervene in case of danger. 'These points,' wrote Malmesbury to Loftus, 'form the whole pith of the Italian question and embrace as much as it would be just and politic to ventilate.' To Cowley he wrote that 'if we go farther we shall be at sea.' The outcome of Lord Cowley's mission could hardly be termed satisfactory. Though, according to Malmesbury, Austria 'agreed to all we asked,' such verbal assurances were generally recognized as of little value in face of the fact that she had 150,000 men under arms. Austria, in short, gave the most elaborate assurances of her pacific intentions but would make no concessions. As Napoleon wrote to Cavour, Cowley's mission would come to nothing.

The *revirement* in policy initiated by the article in the *Moniteur* developed before long into the idea of a Congress. It appeared as a Russian proposal, to whom, however, it had been suggested by Napoleon, through Kisseleff, the Russian Ambassador at Paris. The Emperor's idea in this may have been to transfer the diplomatic lead hitherto held by England, who was opposed to his designs, to Russia, who was favourable to them. Cavour received the first notice of the new move on March 17th in a cipher dispatch from Nigra, who added, 'Emperor wishes to consent, thinking Austria will not accept, I have demanded in any case that Piedmont should be represented.' To this Cavour replied: 'Oppose Congress with all your force. Go boldly to Walewski. Exclusion of Sardinia will lead to a crisis.' The next day he telegraphed to the Prince, 'If Piedmont is excluded I should be forced to resign,' receiving the reply, 'to resign would be desertion. Don't think of it. It would lose everything.'[1] Cavour had every reason to distrust the idea of a Congress; since that of Vienna in 1815 nothing had ever come from a Congress that was not adverse to Italian freedom. Even his own herculean efforts in 1856 at Paris had ended in fair words. On the 18th came a long letter from Nigra recounting an interview with the Emperor. The reasons given for his support of a Congress were, the hope of getting something of real value for Italy if it was held, or of winning the support of England and Prussia if it fell through owing to the refusal of Austria to participate in it. Pressed as to his views regarding Piedmont's inclusion, Napoleon replied that the Congress would concern only the five Great Powers, and that if Piedmont was admitted the other States of Italy must be also included. There was not much comfort in this for Cavour. If the Congress divided into two parties, France and Russia on one side against England, Austria, and Prussia, Italy would not get much benefit. The next day Cavour wrote to the Emperor explaining the extreme difficulty in which the proposal placed him. His whole strength, he said, lay in the moral force of his position as the spokesman of Italy. His exclusion would mean the loss of all prestige for himself and his country in the eyes of the rest of Italy, and the collapse of the whole edifice that ten years of diplomacy had built up.[2] Two days later, on March 21st, he received both from Sir James Hudson and the Minister of France formal notice that the Congress would be held, without Sardinia, and, what was worse, a request to disarm. The day following he writes to Nigra,

Make your mind easy. I neither lose my head nor my courage.

[1] Cavour to Prince Napoleon, March 18th, and reply same day. *CCN.*, vol. ii. Nos. 329 and 332.
[2] *CCN.*, vol. ii. No. 336.

The greater the danger the calmer and more decided I shall be. I shall not abandon my post or my King until I have exhausted every means to save Italy from the abyss to the edge of which she is pushed. Repeat, I pray you, to the Emperor that as to disarmament, I reply with a positive refusal. The news arriving from all parts of Italy is excellent. If I was a general instead of a diplomat in fifteen days I should be on horseback with or without France.

Cavour's task, moreover, was not confined to fighting Italy's cause in Paris and London. He had his difficulties at home. The King had bad spells of depression and did not spare Cavour.

> The King [Cavour writes] who up to this had kept calm and hopeful, is now most irritable and discouraged; he said to me to-day with much bitterness that he was scorned and betrayed; that what he had foreseen had happened, that the Emperor having once obtained the hand of his daughter thought no more of keeping his promises; he added that he had yielded to my pressure and advice and that now he must suffer for it. In other circumstances I should not have borne patiently such bitter reproofs. I have put him at the foot of the horrible Calvary on which diplomacy prepares once more to crucify Italy.

The same day came an autograph letter from Napoleon. It was but a repetition of what Nigra had sent. He realized, he said, the difficulties of Piedmont, but his own were even greater; in proposing the Congress Russia had put forward the only means that could once again put him in *le droit commun* without abandoning the cause he wished to serve. Sardinia could not be admitted to the Congress without the rest of Italy. His own conduct appeared clear: 'to show moderation, to gain time, and acquire the adhesion of England and Prussia.' Then he added, 'the difficulty of the moment is to obtain the disbanding of your contingents. England and Prussia insist on it, promising to force Austria also to disband the troops lately sent to Italy.' This letter decided Cavour to go in person to Paris. The idea had already occurred to him. On 22nd he had written to

Nigra: 'I begin to lose patience. I am tempted to go to Paris one of these days and tell the Emperor that I have no intention of allowing myself to be mystified any longer by Walewski.' On the 24th the Prince telegraphed, 'I have proposed you should come to Paris, the idea has been adopted and approved by the Emperor. Come at once without losing an hour. Do not hesitate, it will be a *coup décisif*, give great publicity to your voyage, say that it is to arrange with the Emperor your attitude at the Congress in which you will represent Piedmont. This will have great influence, all may yet turn to your advantage. This step is of the utmost importance, come.'[1] Cavour's reply was, 'I leave to-night.'

In the meantime Malmesbury's efforts elsewhere were not meeting with much success. Russia and Prussia, it was true, agreed to everything, but it was different at Vienna. Austria placed three conditions to accepting the invitation to the Congress: no territorial changes in Italy, the inclusion of the Italian states at the Congress, Sardinia excepted, and the preliminary disarmament of Sardinia. Her grounds for the exclusion of Sardinia were that, in the first place, she was not a great Power and therefore could not be admitted on an equality, and in the second place, the subject of the Congress being the reform of certain Italian states— which did not include Sardinia—she was the one State not required to take part in the Congress. From the standpoint of Austria and England, who still held by the settlement of 1815, these arguments had force, but when seen from the angle of Italy and France they were simply inadmissible, for Sardinia was recognized as the bridgehead through which the attack on the Treaty of Vienna must be made. As to the third condition, disarmament, France refused to ask Sardinia to disarm or to join with England, as Lord Malmesbury suggested, in giving her a five years' guarantee against attack by Austria.[2] Then Russia demanded that if Sardinia was

---

[1] *CCN.*, vol. ii. No. 355.   [2] Malmesbury to Cowley, March 21st.

asked to disarm, Austria should do so too.[1] Austria's next step was to declare that the evacuation of her troops from the Roman States and the internal administration of the others, was not a subject for the Congress to discuss at all, and that the only question for discussion was to find a substitute for the treaties between Austria and Parma and Modena, which was to reduce the Congress to a farce.[2] Finally, Austria insisted on the preliminary disarming of Sardinia and the surrender of all deserters. To these demands of Austria Malmesbury replied that if other Italian States were invited, the exclusion of Sardinia was utterly unjustifiable; that if Austria would withdraw her troops from the frontier the four Powers would summon Sardinia to disarm and station her troops at their usual posts. As to the evacuation of the Roman States, the Powers, he maintained, had a right to interfere because Austria's occupation was becoming permanent, a state of things not contemplated in the original agreement. A confederation of the small states for mutual assistance, he suggested, might replace their agreements with Austria. But Austria held aloof: opinion was hardening in favour of war, and her distrust of France and hatred of Piedmont made the chance of her presence at the Congress sufficiently remote. Such was the state of affairs when Cavour arrived in Paris.

Cavour had a twofold purpose in his visit. The first and most important was to find out whether or not the Emperor was still determined to make war on Austria, provided the sufficient cause was forthcoming, and at the same time to counteract as far as possible the influence of Walewski and the peace party, of which he was the official mouthpiece. The second was to explore the diplomatic situation at first hand and decide on the policy to be pursued. Cavour arrived in Paris early on Saturday, March 26th. After calling on the Prince and King Jerome, he had his first and only audience alone

[1] Malmesbury to Crampton, March 28th.
[2] Malmesbury to Cowley, March 22nd.

with Napoleon. In this interview he sought rather to explore the position than to put forward his own views and those of the King. He did not see Napoleon again until the evening of the next day. In the interval he saw Cowley and Kisseleff and the German Ambassador, Pourtalès. To all of them he adopted a calm and reasonable tone, but was adamant on the refusal to disarm. At his second audience, the Prince and General Niel were present, which imposed upon him a certain reserve. A third meeting was arranged to be held on the Monday afternoon, but the Emperor was seized, perhaps opportunely, with an attack of rheumatism and took to his bed, postponing the audience until 2 o'clock on the Tuesday. Sometime previous to his final meeting with the Emperor he interviewed Walewski. The French Minister told him bluntly that Napoleon was determined to make peace with Austria and not to mix himself further in Italian affairs; whereupon Cavour proceeded to enlighten him as to the responsibility of the Emperor for the present state of things in Italy. This must have convinced Walewski that Cavour had a stronger hand than he thought and that persuasion rather than threats was desirable. Cavour was not one to be ridden over rough-shod. On the Monday (28th) he wrote a long letter to Victor Emmanuel. The Emperor, he said, was more than ever decided on war. His views on the Italian question had not varied, but if anything, were more 'unitarian' than before, 'but,' he added, 'if on fundamentals he is perfectly sound, he is, as to how to execute them, in a condition of perplexity and deplorable uncertainty.' As to the diplomatic situation, the Italian question had been put by the Emperor before France and Europe in the most unhappy manner. The result being that, if war were to be declared immediately, all Germany would rise against France, supported by England, if not with her fleet, at least with her moral influence. As to his admission to the Congress he had peremptorily refused to take part in it except as an equal. To the demand

that Sardinia should disarm he refused to reply, unless
he was admitted to the Congress on an equality, and
Austria reduced her army to the size which it was on
January 1st.[1]

On the afternoon of the following day he had his last
interview with Napoleon, but not as he hoped, alone,
Walewski being present. After this last audience Cavour
wrote a hasty line to La Marmora. He summed up his
impressions under four heads: (i) War inevitable.
(ii) It will be delayed two months at least. (iii) It will
take place on the Rhine as well as the Po. (iv) Piedmont
would have to make colossal efforts. 'The French,
dragged against the grain into war, would never pardon
Italy if the full weight of the campaign fell upon them.'
'Woe to us,' he added, 'if we triumph purely through
the French.' The letter was unfinished, as Cavour had
to hurry away to dine with the Princess Mathilde, and
Nigra added the postscript, 'Count Cavour is not very
satisfied with the Conference held to-day with the
Emperor and Walewski.'[2] The next day he left for
Turin.

Cavour left Paris the evening of March 30th, and
spent the day drawing up a Memorandum or Plan of the
Diplomatic Campaign, to be sent to the Emperor with
a covering letter. The first point was disarmament.
If Italy disarms, he said, the whole nationalist movement
collapses and the Government with it. It is therefore
very important and highly desirable that it is avoided.
If, however, in an extreme case, the Emperor deems it
indispensable, then, if Sardinia is admitted to the
Congress on a footing of perfect equality, with or
without the other States of Italy, it would be possible,
at least in part, to disarm. If this is refused it is impossible to send a single man home.

The suggestion of a collective demand to disarm was
a threat, and France could not permit such to be made
to her ally. The utmost limit to which France could go
was not to oppose such a demand if made by the other

[1] CCN., vol. ii. No. 358.   [2] CCN., vol. ii. No. 360 and note.

Powers. If it is made, he added, Sardinia will reply that she had only armed in self-defence, and therefore Austria, having been the first to arm, must also be the first to disarm. In confidence, he would let the Emperor know, however, that if Austria reduced its army to what it was on January 1st, and dismantled the fortifications of Piacenza, and destroyed the bridgehead at Pavia, then Sardinia will disband the reserves now called up. As to the volunteers, it was an imperious measure of national safety to keep them with the army.

The second point discussed was his admission to the Congress. His right to equality he based on the Protocol to the Treaty of Aix-la-Chapelle in 1818, which stated that, where matters concerned other states besides the Great Powers, they should be summoned under the express reserve of their right to be represented directly or by their plenipotentiaries. Austria, he added, would appear at the Congress both as a Great Power and an Italian Power, and as the other States in Italy were all in dependence on her, she would have no opposition unless Piedmont was represented. Unless admitted as an equal, he would refuse to participate or to accept any responsibility for acts in which his country did not concur. The rest of the memorandum was concerned with the policy to be followed at the Congress, which however did not take place.[1]

With this clear-cut statement Cavour sent a personal letter of a very different tone. It was a strong appeal to the Emperor not to let down his ally. The policy of Walewski, Cavour said, was heading straight for disaster. It would ruin Italy without saving France. His Government would fall, the King abdicate, Italy become the mortal enemy of France in the hands of Mazzini and the revolutionaries. Let the Emperor recall the events of the last year. How at the first appeal the King had responded with complete trust: how, without heeding the dangers to which he exposed his country, he had loyally followed every suggestion of the

[1] *CCN.*, vol. ii. No. 364.

Emperor. Every step taken had been approved by the Emperor. All he asked was not to be placed in a position in which he would be forced to sanction the ruin of his country and the triumph of Austria and the revolution.[1]

Behind this letter lies a depth of personal feeling. Cavour was a realist. He knew that the fate of Italy was in the hands of Napoleon. He could not fight Austria alone and unaided, after giving her six months to prepare for war. If Napoleon, after planning and executing the alliance, after inducing the King to sacrifice his daughter, went back on his word, all Cavour's work for Italy, all the hopes that he had raised, all the regeneration he had accomplished, collapsed. Against him was ranged the whole conservatism of Europe. The old autocratic caste with its dignity and its diplomats, its dread of democracy and fear of revolution. Behind him lay the hopes of a prostrate nation, dragooned by the brutal methods of Austria; ruled by fainéant princelings and corrupt ecclesiastics, exercising their power by virtue of the bayonets of Austria. Alone amongst the rulers of Europe, Napoleon had accepted Cavour's profound belief that force alone could free Italy, that diplomacy was useless to make Austria let go her hold. Would he now, when the test came, fall back on the futile anodynes of protocols and pious resolutions? But it was no easy matter for Napoleon to keep his word. Not only was he faced, like Cavour, with the diplomatic hostility of Europe, Russia excepted, and the possibility of a war on two fronts, but the nation as a whole was not with him. His Ministers, the Senators and Deputies, opposed him just as strongly as they dare. The vested interests of business dreaded war, and all the instincts of a prosperous bourgeoisie— *France en pleine épicerie*—were ranged against him, yet in spite of this Napoleon held firm to his word.

The general impression in diplomatic circles in Paris after Cavour's return was that his visit had been a failure. Walewski declared that Cavour had come to

[1] *CCN.*, vol. ii. No. 361.

Paris with four objectives, his (Walewski's) dismissal, Sardinia's admission to the Congress, or failing this, to induce Napoleon to abandon it, or lastly, to pledge the Emperor to some new conditions through which the same end could be obtained. In none of these had he succeeded. Cowley was equally optimistic. In private conversations it was generally believed that Cavour had established some hold over Napoleon which drove him to war. Malmesbury believed it and Hübner thought it probable. Marliani, the Tuscan envoy in London, told Lord Clarendon that, if the crash came, Cavour would retire to America and publish his correspondence with the Emperor. The fear of assassination was another reason put forward. There is no hint of this in Cavour's correspondence, but the circulation of such rumours deepened the belief in war and discouraged the hopes of peace. Walewski and Cowley were entitled to whatever satisfaction they could get from the thought that Cavour had been defeated and left Paris in anger and disappointment, in which there was no doubt some truth, but the two facts that stood out amid all the uncertainties were Cavour's refusal to disarm and Napoleon's determination to fight. It was this that clogged the machinery of peace. As long as Cavour held firm in his refusal to disarm and France supported him, the Congress could not be held and war grew nearer day by day, for Austrian patience had limits.

But Cavour's journey had not been fruitless. 'The visit of Count Cavour has had good results,' wrote Prince Napoleon to the King, 'the position here without being good, is less bad, opinion is rising against Austria.'[1] Malmesbury wrote that the return of Cavour from Paris 'had unquestionably been followed by active demonstrations in France of an intention to be prepared for all events in Italy.'[2] Hübner noted that since Cavour's visit the French preparations for war had doubled in intensity.[3] The truth was that the position

[1] CCN., vol. ii. No. 367.   [2] Malmesbury, Memoirs of an Ex-Minister.
[3] Hübner, Neuf ans de souvenirs d'un ambassadeur d'Autriche à Paris.

was rapidly passing out of the hands of diplomats into those of the men of war, and for this Austria was mainly responsible. Whatever were the weaknesses of Austrian diplomacy, she had a grasp on facts that prevented all illusion. Her vast preparations were directed more against France than Piedmont. She never deceived herself that France would stand aside and allow her to crush her little Italian neighbour. There were centuries of traditional policy behind French action. After Cavour's return from Paris and the subsequent developments—the increased military activity of France and the intransigent attitude of Cavour on disarmament— Austria's determination was taken. On April 5th the general in command of the second army, Gyulai, was warned that in ten or twelve days he should be prepared to take the offensive against Piedmont. On the same day two further army corps, the 6th and the 9th, were put on a war footing. From now onwards war was regarded as inevitable in the Councils of Vienna.

But this decision, unknown outside the council chamber, did not deflect the energy of diplomacy. The day after Cavour left Paris, Lord Malmesbury suggested at Turin and Vienna that their respective forces should be withdrawn ten miles from the frontier. Cavour accepted, Buol refused. Austria had given her word not to attack Piedmont, replied Hübner, when Walewski made the suggestion, and she would keep it. Austrian guns did not go off by themselves.[1] Malmesbury then approached France as to her willingness to join England, Prussia and Russia in a collective note to Piedmont to disarm. This was the one thing Cavour dreaded. Walewski consulted the Emperor, and instead of the anticipated acceptance that he himself would have freely given, the reply struck a different note. 'France might join,' he said, 'in a collective invitation to be addressed both to Austria and Sardinia to disarm. If Lord Malmesbury drew one up for Sardinia alone, he would show it to the Emperor, but it must be vague and not

[1] Hübner (*Ibid*).

mention either disbanding the contingents or the free
corps. It must only be a recommendation couched in
courteous language.[1] The same day Lord Loftus telegraphed from Vienna that 'Count Buol will insist on the
disarmament of Sardinia, both of her contingents and the
free corps, as a *sine qua non* of her consent to enter the
Congress.' On the same day also we find Lord Malmesbury telegraphing to Odo Russell in Rome his regret
that Rome and Naples will not send representatives
to the Congress. Parma and Modena had already
refused. The prospects of the Congress were growing
very dim.

In rejecting the suggestion that the Austrian troops
should be withdrawn from the frontier, which he
regarded as a threat, Count Buol had dropped some
words to the effect that if it had been a question of
general disarmament it would have been different. The
hint was not lost on Lord Malmesbury, who promptly
adopted the suggestion. At Paris the new idea was
received with cautious favour, for the French army was
still technically on a peace footing, and Napoleon saw
a fresh rebuff for Austria in having to disarm while
the French preparations remained unaltered, and after
some hesitation Walewski accepted it in principle. At
Turin it met with no support, for disarmament of any
kind meant peace, which was the last thing Cavour
desired. To gain time he blocked its progress by laying
down conditions, writing to the Prince that it was
impossible to accept unless Piedmont received a formal
guarantee for the freedom of the right bank of the Po
and the admission of the principle of non-intervention.[2]
On hearing that France had accepted it, he wrote again,
and was at once reassured by the Emperor, who replied
that the new suggestion concerned only the five Great
Powers, Sardinia remaining free. But apart from the
fact that Austria would never accept such an interpretation, which was tantamount to disarming at the dicta-

[1] F.O. 167, vol. 106. Malmesbury to Cowley, April 4th.
[2] *CCN.*, vol. ii. No. 377.

tion of Piedmont, success was vitiated by the simultaneous military measures in Austria.

On the 8th Cavour telegraphed to Paris that he was informed that Austria had called out her whole reserves and that 50,000 fresh troops were under orders for Italy. Napoleon's reply to this was to prepare to call up the men *en congé*, 125,000 troops. But Sardinia was still the stumbling-block. Austria repeated her demand that the reduction of the Sardinian army must precede anything else, but Napoleon refused to coerce her. The exasperation caused by Cavour's obstinacy was extreme. Lord Cowley, in a moment of temper, exclaimed to Hübner, 'You ought to summon the Piedmontese to disarm, cross the frontier, destroy her, and then declare that you are ready to negotiate in Congress when and where we like.' And Hübner replied, 'in my opinion that is what we should do and shall do.' When Napoleon held back from forcing Cavour, England tried her hand at it. On the 14th Sackville-West, in the absence of Hudson—escaped from a hateful task to England— came and demanded disarmament. Cavour played for time, for every hour now was a vital matter. The King was as Pollenzo, when he returned there should be a cabinet meeting. Still assured of French support, Cavour was in reality immovable, and cheerfully wrote to Nigra: 'The demand is for immediate disarmament, accompanied by threats and promises. I shall not let myself be moved by one or other. Say to the Prince and Emperor that there is little generosity, I might even say honesty, in leaving a poor devil exposed alone to the blows of Neptune's trident!' And he held firm.

The sands of Austrian patience were running very low. The attitude of Napoleon convinced her of what she had already feared and suspected, that France was playing for time. Austria could not go into a Congress, of which the first business was to be disarmament, leaving Sardinia armed on her border, while Napoleon completed his preparations, threw up the Congress when all was ready, and declared war. On the 11th

Austria sent to Berlin the Archduke Albert in a last
attempt to win Prussia to a joint attack on France, but
Prussia was not ready and all the English influence was
against it, for next to peace, Malmesbury was bent on
localizing the conflict to Italy. In the meantime Cavour
had replied to England that her position being purely
defensive, the situation *vis-à-vis* to Austria was not
identical with that of this latter Power, but to show his
goodwill he would engage not to call up his remaining
reserves or to move his troops or give the final orders
for mobilization. To further instances from London
he took refuge in his exclusion from the Congress.
Grant him admittance as an equal and he would accept
the same responsibilities as the other members.

On the 13th Hübner wrote in his diary: 'the crisis
we are about to traverse may be summed up in two
words. Will France invite Piedmont officially to disarm? If Napoleon refuses, as he perhaps will, it means
that he wants war. He will have it.' The next day he
was sent for by Walewski, who told him that having to
give advice to the Emperor at this critical moment, he
wished to know the intimate thought of Austria. Hübner
put the case for peace from every aspect. Having
justified Austria's attitude toward Piedmont, after ten
years of defiance and provocation, he outlined the results
for France if she went to war with Austria. If she lost,
the Emperor was doomed, if she won he would have to
face a coalition of Powers, and coalitions were always
victorious. And this was assuming, what was far from
unlikely, that Germany, Russia or England did not
come in against her while the war was still raging.
Walewski passed from Hübner to the Tuileries, where
for three hours he urged peace on the Emperor, and
still failed to convince him. The next day he told
Hübner that the Emperor would ask Piedmont to
disarm, if all the Italian Powers were admitted to the
Congress. 'It is a trap,' wrote Hübner in his diary. It
was Austria who finally cut the knot.

The day after the Archduke Albert had left for

Berlin, Count Buol forwarded to Count Apponyi in London a dispatch in which he used these ominous words:

> The Emperor, our August Master, owes it to his dignity and the security of His Empire, to put an end to a situation so intolerable (i.e. the attitude of Piedmont) by taking the question of Piedmont's disarmament in hand himself, since the good offices of England have failed to do so. With this object we are about to address directly to the Cabinet of Turin a demand to reduce her army to a peace footing and disband the free corps.

This was read to Malmesbury on the 15th, and to it he replied that he had no objection to such action, provided that to such a demand was added Austria's adhesion to the principle of a general disarmament, accepted by France, and that it was indicated that such disarmament was simultaneous. But if it was of the nature of a haughty summons, Piedmont would certainly reject it, and all hope of peace would be lost. From such a tone he therefore begged Austria to refrain. At the same time he telegraphed to West at Turin a summary of this communication, adding that Cavour would be wise to accept it. But the question was, when would it come? [1]

The tension was growing unbearable. Throughout these days Cavour was haunted by the spectre of a joint *démarche* from England and France compelling him to disarm without conditions, followed by the retreat of Austria, and the consequent reaction in Italy. He saw the loyal co-operation of Garibaldi converted in a moment into unbridled rage; he heard the cry of Italy betrayed; he saw the army diverted from war with Austria to the suppression of civil strife; the arrival of Mazzini to fish in troubled waters; the scorn and anger of the Liberals throughout the Peninsula. Could he hold out? Would Austria attack in time? these were the torturing thoughts that pursued him night and day.

---

[1] F.O. 167, Malmesbury to Sackville West, April 16th.

The situation, as it was, was almost beyond his control. Volunteers were pouring into Piedmont. Now, it was Malenchini with 600 Livornese, now, 400 from other districts in Tuscany. Over 12,000 were under arms and the number was increasing almost hourly.

The crisis came to a head on April 18th. The previous day France, Russia, and Prussia had all individually urged on Cavour to accept the principle of disarmament. He had refused. Nothing but a joint demand from France and England would make him yield. All depended on the staunchness of Napoleon. The struggle in the Tuileries redoubled on the 18th, Walewski, Cowley, and Hübner urging the Emperor to yield and join with England, Nigra and Prince Napoleon striving to hold him firm. At last he gave in, and telegraphed to London that, if England would agree to admit Sardinia to the Congress, he would join in a demand for immediate disarmament. On receipt of this Malmesbury delivered his last word. There must be disarmament, *préalable*, effective, and simultaneous, to be carried out by a commission of senior officers, and the Italian States to be admitted on the same footing *as at Laybach in 1821*.[1] Napoleon accepted, and that evening the fatal demand was telegraphed to Turin. The blow had fallen. Late that night Cavour was roused from bed to face the dreaded ultimatum. His agitation was extreme. But he realized that there was no alternative to submission, and replied: 'Since France unites with England to demand from Piedmont disarmament before Congress, the Government of the King, while foreseeing that this measure will have disastrous consequences for Italy, declares that it is disposed to submit.'

On April 19th Cavour was in such a condition of nervous strain that his friends did not like to leave him alone. Two telegrams from the Prince Napoleon somewhat reassured him. His acceptance had created an

---

[1] This ensured Piedmont's presence at the Congress on a footing of equality but not as a great power. Walewski urged upon Cavour to avoid this latter phase, which he said would never be admitted. See Cavour to D'Azeglio on April 20th. Walewski to La Tour d'Auvergne. Matter, vol. iii. p. 181.

excellent effect. Austria was furious. His position at the Congress seems still to have been obscure, but events were soon to render this of no consequence. The next day he was himself again. 'Cavour has slept last night,' wrote the King to Rattazzi, 'he is quite calm. Looks at things optimistically. No longer talks of quitting office and meditates a great speech to the nation next Tuesday, and in the meantime is going to Leri for Saturday and Sunday, happy and content, saying it is necessary to stand fearless at his post.' [1]

Throughout these two days Europe waited in feverish anxiety the final word from Vienna. Would she disarm, accept the Congress, and sit beside Piedmont? On the 21st came the reply:

10.55 a.m. Foreign Office to West.

Tell Cavour that on Tuesday night 19th orders sent from Vienna to Gyulai to summon him to disarm and give an answer in three days. Austria has refused our proposal entirely. I have called a Cabinet meeting for 4 p.m. Lord Derby being at the confirmation of Princess Alice it could not be held before.[2]

MALMESBURY.

The conditions of Plombières were fulfilled, Sardinia was attacked, and the French alliance came into force.

Never, perhaps, has a statesman worked for war with such persistence and grim determination as Cavour. In his passion for the freedom of his country he was ready to see Europe set ablaze, if only out of the ashes he could build a free, united, and independent Italy. And never, perhaps, could a statesman justify with weightier reasons his appeal to the calamitous arbitrament of battle. For ten years the cause of Italian freedom had been pleaded before every court in Europe. Her claims had been put before the Powers in Congress with all the force of which diplomacy was capable. But the principle of the sanctity of treaties, just or unjust, had stultified every effort. The issue was, in truth, one which it was almost beyond the power of diplomacy to solve, for

[1] *CCN.*, vol. ii. No. 402.   [2] F.O. 167, vol. 105.

Austria could not, dare not, admit the principle of nationality upon which Cavour's case rested, without imperilling the entire Imperial structure. Nor could she even alter her system of repression, brutal as it was, without sacrificing her whole method of government. She clung to the treaties of 1815, for upon them her existence rested.

The winning of the French alliance brought the hopes of Italy into the realm of the practical. The skill, the courage, and the determination of Cavour on the one side and the indomitable tenacity of Napoleon on the other, defeated the peace efforts of England, Germany, and even France itself. If Napoleon set the course, Cavour set the pace, and if, disturbed by a head wind, the Emperor tacked, he always came back, though sometimes with much flapping of sails through indifferent seamanship. But the most remarkable evidence of skill in this strange journey, for which Cavour must be given the credit, was that, they not only reached their objective at the exact time set, but they arrived together, when a few lengths difference might have spelt disaster.

On April 23rd Cavour summoned an emergency meeting of the Chamber of Deputies. In a short speech he asked that in the present crisis full powers should be placed in the hands of the King for the defence of the country. He gave a brief history of the negotiations, the final refusal of Austria, and her decision to send an ultimatum, now on its way, to Piedmont. 'Under such circumstances,' he added, 'the steps taken by the Emperor of France are for us both a comfort and a cause for deep gratitude.' Then, cognizant as he was of the support he had received throughout these anxious months from the loyal help and encouragement of Victor Emmanuel, in a voice vibrant with emotion he closed his speech with this brief apostrophe: 'And who can be a better guardian of our liberties? Who more worthy of this proof of the nation's trust? He, whose name, throughout ten years of reign, has been synonymous with loyalty and honour. He, who now, as always, holds high and firm the tricolour of Italy: he, who at this moment prepares himself to fight for liberty and independence!'

The frantic applause that greeted Cavour's words had hardly died down when a hastily written note was brought to him containing the words: 'They are here: I have seen them,' and Cavour hastily left the Chamber to meet the messengers of Austria, remarking as he did so, 'I leave the last sitting of the Piedmontese Parliament; the next will be that of the Kingdom of Italy.' At 5.15 he received with his customary courtesy the Austrian Envoys, and having read Count Buol's ultimatum, fixed the same time three days hence for the delivery of his reply. It was war.

X. THE WAR AND THE PEACE

THE Austrian ultimatum of the 23rd gave Cavour three
clear days before a reply was imperative. They were
not wasted. In response to a telegram, he received word
from Napoleon on the 24th that orders had been given
for the French troops to enter Piedmont by Susa and
Genoa. The next day they were marching through
Savoy.[1] On the 26th he handed his reply to the Austrian
envoys. The day following he expected the invasion
to begin. But Gyulai was both slow and cautious.
Throughout the 27th and 28th he remained motionless.
For this precious gift of time the diplomacy of England
was in some degree responsible. Despite the ultimatum,
Lord Malmesbury, carried forward by the force of his
own momentum, continued to make desperate efforts
for peace. He advised Cavour to word his reply in such
terms as to leave a loophole for negotiations. He
telegraphed to Cowley to offer direct English mediation
between France and Austria, and urged Loftus at
Vienna to take the same line. On the 28th, Cavour,
dreading a successful effort on the part of Lord
Malmesbury, wrote to Villamarina: 'The Austrians
have not moved. Behind this there is some English
intrigue. Publish Buol's letter and my reply.' In
response, came word from Prince Napoleon, 'inaction
of Austria due to offer of mediation by England who
intrigue horribly. Emperor bids me tell you he will
try to reply in a manner that will gain time and give
some days for our troops to arrive *chez vous*, but in a

[1] CCN., vol. ii. No. 412; Chiala, *Lettere*, vol. iii. cxlv.

way Austria cannot accept.'[1] England's offer was accepted by Austria, as between herself and France, but not in regard to Sardinia, and thus the last effort failed.

On the 29th Gyulai crossed the Ticino. Even then a vigorous forward movement, pushed home with superior numbers, would probably have been successful. The small Piedmontese army might have been overwhelmed, Turin occupied, and the French troops caught debouching from the Alps, or by a southern movement the road blocked from Genoa. Cavour dreaded the moral effect of the occupation of Turin. The main Piedmontese railway system, upon which everything depended, was a rough equilateral triangle. One line going north-east from Turin through Vercelli and Novara to the frontier on the Ticino at Buffalora, a second going south-east to Alessandria, with a cross line running from Vercelli through Casale to Alessandria; then continuing south to Genoa. The Piedmontese army lay between Casale and Alessandria with the railway at their back and the river Sesia in front. Gyulai after some hesitation turned north, seized Novara, and advanced along the railway to Turin. He occupied Vercelli, and by May 6th his outposts were on the Dora Baltea, a stream only twenty miles from Turin. The next day they suddenly retired, and the threat to Turin was over.[2] After this ineffective demonstration Gyulai concentrated his forces once more behind the Ticino, and left Napoleon free for a further fortnight to bring his army unmolested in Piedmont.

In the meantime Piedmont went to its battle stations. On the 30th the King had assumed command of the army, choosing as his chief of staff General Della Rocca. La Marmora, vacating the War Office, joined the King in the unsatisfactory post of special military adviser. Cavour, already Minister of Foreign Affairs as well as

[1] *CCN.*, vol. ii. No. 421.
[2] Cavour had ordered the flooding of the district round Vercelli, which greatly impeded the Austrians. The weather was atrocious, raining incessantly. See *CCN.* vol. ii. Nos. 432-3. Thayer, *Cavour*, vol. ii. c. i–ii, for full account of military operations. Maps in Zini.

Minister for the Interior, took over the War Department. It was not a happy arrangement. La Marmora's experience and organizing ability was largely wasted, Cavour overworked, and the King worried by two advisers. The inevitable friction arose. Cavour offered advice that was not taken, La Marmora differed from the King in his opinions, and, ignoring the fact that Cavour had the entire diplomatic situation in his hands, Della Rocca refused to send him either dispatches or even information.

> At Head-quarters [wrote Cavour a few weeks later] it seems orders have been given to tell nobody anything. I have written letters upon letters, multiplied telegraphic dispatches addressed myself to the Emperor, the King, Marshal Vaillant and La Marmora in turn, and heard nothing. In the matter of information I am treated up to now as one treats a clerk one does not trust. It is not only in love that the absent are always wrong.[1]

To Cavour fell the organization of the train service, the dispatch of troops, the provisioning of the armies, and the forwarding of material. From the beginning of May troops poured into Piedmont at the rate of eight to ten thousand a day, and the task of dealing with them taxed the railway service to the utmost. Cavour had a bed installed in the War Office, and snatching what sleep he could, and an hour or two was all he required, he might have been found at all hours of the night clad in a dressing-gown, dictating, dispatching, and issuing orders, first from one Ministry and then from another, for they were all in the same building. It was his war and he fought it with all the strength of his being. On March 12th the Emperor arrived at Genoa. The King and Cavour met him. His reception was magnificent, 'You ought to be content,' Napoleon said to Cavour, 'your plans are being realized.' And Cavour wrote to La Marmora, 'I am very content with the Emperor: he appears to me to be disposed to fulfil his promises,' for Napoleon had pledged himself by publicly announc-

[1] To Prince Napoleon. *CCN.*, vol. ii. No. 461.

ing that he came 'to free Italy from the Alps to the Adriatic.'

The arrival of Napoleon at Genoa set the seal on ten years of diplomacy. That 'terza riscossa'[1] to which Piedmont had calmly looked forward since Novara was a fact at last. In spite of the opposition of Europe, for neither France nor England, nor even Austria, wanted it, war had become a reality. Cavour and Napoleon alone desired it, and the latter would have more than once postponed it, had it not been for the determination and skill of Cavour. But great as such a diplomatic achievement was, it was very fortunate for the allies that when war came, Austria's action put her entirely in the wrong, and prevented the sympathy of England and Prussia taking an active form. Malmesbury declared the neutrality of England as quickly as possible, but he did more than this, for he took immediate steps to keep Germany quiet. In February the Prince of Prussia had written to the Prince Consort asking his opinion as to Prussia's action in certain eventualities, adding, 'Your advice will be decisive for us.' In his reply the Prince Consort used these words: 'In the case of war breaking out I should place the army upon a war footing, and occupy the fortresses, at the same time giving friendly assurances to all the courts.'[2] This line of conduct, which was adopted later, was checked by a dispatch from Malmesbury, sent to all the German Courts on the outbreak of war, in which he said that Her Majesty's Government 'witness with great anxiety the disposition shown by the States of Germany to enter at once into a contest with France. Her Majesty's Government cannot perceive that at the present moment Germany has any grounds for declaring war against that Power,' and he went on to add that England would maintain a strict neutrality and would give 'no assistance to Germany nor contribute, by the interposition of the naval forces of this country, to protect her coast from

[1] 'The third round' is possibly the nearest English equivalent.
[2] Martin, *Life of Prince Consort*, vol. v.

hostile attack.'[1] An even stronger warning had been received from Russia, who wrote offering to guarantee German integrity in return for strict neutrality. In this Gortschakoff was warmly supported by Bismarck, the newly appointed ambassador, so that he was accused by the smaller German States of being more French and Italian than German. When Prussia declared her intention of keeping her complete freedom of action, Russia replied bluntly that, if the confederation declared war against France, and thus placed herself in open contradiction with the treaties by which she existed, Russia would be free to declare war against her.[2] When war came, Prussia issued a circular declaring she would confine herself to protecting Federal territory. This attitude of Russia and England damped the bellicose ardour of the German confederation, and gave the belligerents a clear field for the opening of the struggle.

But no sooner had one cause of anxiety been removed than another took its place. This time it was, what was to happen in Italy when once the Austrians were defeated? The redistribution of Italy, as outlined by Napoleon at Plombières, included, besides the Kingdom of Upper Italy, a Kingdom of Central Italy, of which the nucleus was to be Tuscany enlarged by portions of the States of the Church. But Cavour, though he had raised no objections at the time, was determined, if possible, to thwart this design in the interests of unity, and it was his diplomacy on this question that led to a breach with Napoleon and contributed to Villafranca.

Cavour was anxious, if possible, to keep the resettlement of Italy in the hands of the Italians. He needed Napoleon to drive out the Austrians, but after that he would have gladly applied the principle of non-intervention. His plan was to form an offensive and defensive alliance between Piedmont, Tuscany, and Naples; to induce these two latter States to grant constitutional

---

[1] Text in full in Malmesbury, vol. ii. p. 205. The date is May 2nd, 1859.

[2] Bianchi, *Stor. Doc.*, vol. viii. c. 3. Sauli to Cavour. Gortschakoff to Berlin, March 27th.

Government, and thus prepare the way for the ultimate fusion of Italy in a single constitutional State. In pursuance of this plan Cavour wrote to his Minister at Florence in March 1859, instructing him to urge upon the Grand Duke the desirability of alliance with Piedmont. He would freely stretch the hand of friendship, he said, to all those Italian Governments who would join him in raising the flag of national independence. Piedmont had no intention of interfering with the autonomy of Tuscany, and would refuse to assist any popular rising against the dynasty.[1] But the Tuscan Government would hear of nothing but neutrality. When war became inevitable Cavour renewed his offer. In confidence he let the Grand Duke know that Piedmont was not only supported by France but had the moral support of both Russia and Prussia, while England was ready to acquiesce in the addition of Lombardy and Venetia to Piedmont. He had ready a note asking formally for the alliance of Tuscany the moment war was declared.[2] But nothing moved Leopold from his determination to maintain his neutrality, which, as Cavour pointed out, in a war fought for national independence, was an impossible position. After this refusal the initiative passed from the Grand Duke to his people, and no sooner was war declared than there took place the 'rosewater revolution,' and Leopold departed on the long road to Vienna and exile.[3]

Cavour was equally frank but equally unsuccessful with Naples. The instructions given to the Marquis Gropello, the Piedmontese Minister, were identical with those sent to Boncompagni at Florence, but they failed to shake Ferdinand's determination to remain neutral. Ferdinand was, however, mortally sick, and Cavour turned his attention to his son and successor, Francis, but the Sardinian Minister met with no greater success, and Naples remained sunk in corruption and apathy,

[1] Cavour to Boncompagni, March 14th.
[2] Cavour to Boncompagni, April 12th and 23rd.
[3] Hancock, *Ricasoli and the Risorgimento in Tuscany*, c. vii.

a prey to the first national reaction in favour of liberty.[1] In regard to Modena and Parma, Cavour declared openly that, owing to their alliance with Austria, he considered them as included in the declaration of war.

Napoleon's plan seems to have been to drive out the Austrians first and then to resettle Italy on the lines of the projected Confederation. But Cavour had, through the activities of the National Society, prepared for an immediate demand for union with Piedmont, partly to force Napoleon's hands, partly to leave no opening for Mazzinian intrigues and to avoid all the complications arising from desires for autonomy which had ruined the rising of 1848. His suggested alliance with the Grand Duke and King Ferdinand is not easy to understand, but he may have thought that, if Tuscany and Naples were given constitutions, allied to Piedmont, and the Austrian influence removed, it would prevent a kingdom of Central Italy and enable the question of unity to be deferred until later; at the same time keeping both under the guidance of Piedmont. The withdrawal of the Grand Duke created a new situation. A provisional government was at once formed which promptly offered Victor Emmanuel the Dictatorship of Tuscany. Cavour interviewed Napoleon, and, as a result, the Dictatorship was refused, but Victor Emmanuel accepted the command of the troops and a protectorate for the duration of the war, naming Boncompagni as his plenipotentiary with the title of 'Commissioner Extraordinary of the King for the war of independence.'[2] New Ministers were appointed, including Ridolfi, who was an autonomist, for Foreign Affairs, and Ricasoli as Minister of the Interior, with Boncompagni as President of the Council. Though the country was quiet, Ricasoli was somewhat uneasy. There were no troops to keep order, all the forces being at the moment reorganized by General Ulloa, and undesirable elements were flocking into Tuscany from the Romagna, and

[1] Cavour to Gropello, April 18th. Ferdinand died on May 22nd.
[2] See Hancock, *Ricasoli*. Bianchi, *Stor. Doc.*, vol. viii.

Ricasoli was reduced to governing by proclamation and moral influence, which he did with great success. He was anxious, however, for Cavour to summons the local forces to Piedmont as soon as possible and replace them with Piedmontese troops. The position would probably have righted itself before long, but Vincenzo Salvagnoli, under the impression that the situation was worse than was generally thought, complicated matters by an ill-advised interference. Instead of approaching Cavour with his fears, he interviewed Napoleon. Ten months before at Compiègne he had seen the Emperor and advocated his plan for a Central Kingdom ruled by Prince Napoleon. Whether or not he repeated his suggestion on this occasion is not revealed, but his estimate of the situation persuaded Napoleon to send Prince Napoleon and the 5th Army Corps into Tuscany. Cavour at once endeavoured to stop this arrangement. He hurried to Alessandria and interviewed Napoleon, insisting that the execution of such a plan would arouse the greatest suspicion abroad as to the Emperor's designs. But the Emperor was cold and obstinate. He had, he said, no dynastic ambitions, and he would explain the position satisfactorily to the Powers. It was the opening of the breach between Cavour and Napoleon. The Emperor now saw that, far from being submissive and accepting dictation at his hands, Cavour had designs very different from his own, and intended to do everything possible to carry them to success. The Tuscan policy of Cavour was leading to that of Villafranca.[1]

In preparation for the arrival of Prince Napoleon and his Army Corps, Cavour, on May 20th, wrote a long and important letter to Boncompagni outlining the policy to be followed. The Prince's mission, he explained, had a purely military significance, and in spite of the inevitable rumours his presence had no political importance. The idea that he came as a candidate for the vacant throne was absolutely devoid of foundation. Neither the Prince nor the Emperor had any such

[1] P. Matter, *Cavour*, vol. iii. c. iv.

notion. 'They are both convinced,' he said, 'that to establish their own dynasty in Tuscany would injure both their own and French interests and lead to diplomatic difficulties that would prejudice the issue of the war and the triumph of the Italian cause.' As a practical proposition there were three possible solutions, a return of the House of Lorraine, a republic, or union with Piedmont, and of these, the last was the only desirable one. Boncompagni should, therefore, work for union by preparing the country to demand it when the right moment came. To this end it was desirable that the Palazzo Pitti and the Boboli Gardens should be at once handed over to the public and opened as a Palazzo Nazionale; the administration purged of those attached to the old system; the diplomatic agents of the Grand Duke removed, and Tuscan interests entrusted to Piedmont.[1] The Tuscan question thus became a struggle between the autonomists and the unitarians. The result was not long in doubt. The influence of Piedmont and the determination of Ricasoli soon brought Tuscany over to union, but on one condition, that it was to Italy not to Piedmont that they should be united. The importance of this proviso was seen later. The Prince and his Army Corps did not remain long in Tuscany, and during their stay the Prince fully justified Cavour's estimate of his views. He interfered in no way with politics, confined himself to his military duties, and showed himself a warm supporter of union with Piedmont.

While these political measures were in progress the military situation had rapidly developed. The area that was now to be the scene of operations was a long narrow strip of country lying east and west, in shape not unlike the shell of a modern quick-firer, of which the detonator was Turin and the nosepiece the curving line of her railways, while the line of the Mincio between the fortresses of Peschiera on the north and Mantua on the south provided the base. The southern boundary

[1] *CCN.*, vol. ii. No. 450.

was the course of the river Po, and the northern, the railway line from Turin through Milan to Peschiera. After his withdrawal from the Dora on May 7th, Gyulai made no further move until May 20th, by which date the bulk of the French army was in Piedmont. On that day Marshal Stadion's corps at Stradella was ordered to make a reconnaissance towards Voghera, to test the forces of the enemy on the south edge of the operation area. Stadion advanced along the Po, until at Montebello he met Forey's division. Though outnumbered by three to one, Forey attacked without hesitation. The fighting lasted all day, and in the end Stadion retreated, having lost thirteen hundred men and gained very little information. The prestige of French arms was greatly enhanced when the disparity of the forces was known, and the confidence of the allies in victory increased as the result of their first serious contact with the enemy.

A week after the battle of Montebello the general advance began. The main strength of the Austrians was known to be in the south-east along the course of the Po, while the allied army was still behind the Sesia. Napoleon decided by a bold flank march to transfer the army to the north, cross the Sesia at Vercelli, and advance on Milan, thus turning the enemy's right flank. It was a hazardous measure; it uncovered Alessandria and the road to Turin, and if the enemy penetrated the design, an attack on the allied centre while the army was on the march would spell almost irretrievable disaster. To cover this manœuvre the Piedmontese, who held the left of the line, were ordered to cross the river and occupy the village of Palestro, while the French crossed the river behind them. On the 30th Victor Emmanuel seized the position, and that day and the day following successfully resisted all the Austrian efforts to dislodge him. The failure to recover Palestro decided Gyulai to retire behind the Ticino. Then, following the railway, the allied army marched through Novara to the boundary station at Buffalora, which they found strongly occupied by the enemy. On the 4th of June was fought the battle of Magenta, named after the village near Buffalora, round which the fighting raged.

Magenta was a soldiers' battle in which the fortunes of the day hung on the staunchness of the Imperial Guard, who, through faulty disposition of the reserves, were called on to bear the brunt of the Austrian attack for three hours before they received reinforcements. The arrival of MacMahon's corps decided the day and won their leader a Dukedom. That night Gyulai abandoned Lombardy and withdrew to the Mincio.[1]

Whilst the main armies were thus struggling for victory, Garibaldi and his three thousand Hunters of the Alps were engaged in a little campaign of their own. After three weeks with the regular forces, Garibaldi had been given a roving commission to harass the right flank of the enemy. Crossing the Sesia on May 21st, he was at Varese two days later. Here he found himself opposed by the Austrian General Urban with greatly superior forces. After a successful campaign of nine days Urban suddenly retreated, and on June 5th Garibaldi received news of the victory of Magenta. Grasping the situation at once, he hurried his little force eastwards; passing through Bergamo and Brescia he reached Lake Garda, but on June 20th he received orders to return and guard the Valtelline. The interest aroused by Garibaldi's campaign was perhaps out of proportion to its military value. Its real importance was that it won for him the absolute confidence of his men, enhanced his reputation as a guerilla leader, and maintained the popular belief in his powers, and thus brought him twelve months later to Sicily with the magic of his name undimmed.[2]

The battlefield of Magenta was Napoleon's first real experience of warfare, and it made a deep impression

[1] It was entirely a French battle, Victor Emmanuel being kept all day at Galliate, well out of the fighting.

[2] See Trevelyan, *Garibaldi and the Thousand*, also Thayer, vol. ii.

upon him. It was not merely the horrors of the carnage and the suffering of the wounded that sank into his mind, these might be forgotten; but in those dread hours of waiting, when, without a single battalion to send to their support, he watched the Austrians hammering at his centre, he learnt the real meaning of defeat. A dozen lost battles would still leave Franz Joseph Emperor of Austria, but one might make him an exile and a fugitive. He was one who must conquer and conquer always. Already in Paris a short war was predicted; the *pacifiques*, on the strength of the Empress's words to the *Corps Législatif* at the end of May, were saying that after the first victory the Emperor would make peace with Austria. Already, perhaps, the words he had written to Cavour in the previous November were returning with redoubled force to Napoleon's mind, 'The task we are undertaking is a big thing. Think, without being forced to do it, I am hazarding the future of my country.' [1]

On June 8th Napoleon and Victor Emmanuel made their triumphal entry into Milan amid the frantic rejoicings of the populace. The next day Cavour arrived. He took the opportunity to obtain an interview with the Emperor and tried once more to get his consent to the annexation of Tuscany, but Napoleon refused. On his return to Turin Cavour wrote to Boncompagni that for the present the idea was impracticable, 'such a step would make a bad impression on the Emperor and he would justly complain that the pledges given by the King were not being kept.' 'But,' he added, with his usual fertility in expedients, 'if the Tuscan movement towards union shows itself irresistible, a manifestation, general and spontaneous, conducted in a legal and peaceful manner, ought not, and perhaps could not, be stopped either by the Government of the King or that of Tuscany.' It was becoming a difficult matter for Cavour and the Emperor to work together. Cavour was determined to pick up and pocket the fruits of victory

[1] *CCN.*, vol. i. No. 133.

as fast as they became available, while Napoleon, still engaged in shaking the tree, wished them left where they were until the task was over, and then to share them out.

The thoroughness with which the revolution in the north of Italy had been prepared became apparent immediately after the battle of Magenta. As Cavour had expected, at the first real defeat of the Austrian army, the princelings of the House of Hapsburg fled. On June 10th the Duchess of Parma hastily retired to a place of safety. A few days later, Francis of Modena, after seizing all the money and valuables upon which he could lay his hands, fled to Mantua, where he joined Leopold of Tuscany. Cavour acted at once. To Parma he dispatched Count Pallieri, and to Modena, Farini, as Royal Commissioners, with instructions to organize the Governments, maintain order, and make every possible effort to raise troops for the national cause. The cession of these two Duchies to Piedmont was included in the pact of Plombières, and no opposition was to be expected from Napoleon, but when the revolutionary movement spread to the States of the Church a very much more complex problem arose.

The Papal possessions in Italy were divided into four adjoining areas. There was the Patriarchate of St. Peter, a lozenge-shaped piece of territory stretching up the western coast, from Rome to the Tuscan border. Then came Umbria in the centre of Italy, the chief town of which was Perugia. East and north of Umbria lay the Marches of Ancona and Fermo, stretching along the Adriatic coast from the Tronto river to La Cattolica, of which Ancona and Rimini were the most important towns. Lastly came the Romagna, reaching north to the mouth of the river Po and bounded on the west by the borders of Modena and Tuscany. This area had its centre at Bologna and was sometimes called 'the Legations' from the fact that the chief places Ravenna, Imola, Faenza, and Forli, were ruled by Papal Legates.

It was a significant commentary on the success of the

Pope as a temporal ruler that for many years these territories could only be kept from open rebellion by means of three armies. French troops maintained order in Rome. The Papal troops garrisoned Umbria, and the Austrian army was responsible for the Marches and the Romagna. With the approach of war between France and Austria Cardinal Antonelli became anxious for the safety of the Papal possessions. His chief fear was the withdrawal of the Austrian garrisons, and he lost no time in urging Franz Joseph to maintain them at all costs. The reply was completely reassuring. 'His Imperial Majesty,' wrote Monsignor Franchi from Vienna, 'has given me, personally, the assurance that the Austrian garrisons at Bologna and Ancona will not be withdrawn under any circumstances, not even if the Duchy of Modena is attacked.'[1] The Cardinals' next step was to endeavour to get a similar assurance from France, but Napoleon replied that he could only guarantee public order in those areas that might be occupied by French troops. Antonelli, however, chose to interpret Napoleon's conditional guarantee in his own way (endeavouring thereby to throw the entire responsibility upon the Emperor), writing to the Cardinal Legates that Napoleon 'had pledged himself in the most formal way that no attempt should be made against the person of the Holy Father or against the safety of his temporal power.'[2] Having in this way sought to avoid all responsibility either for order or disorder throughout the Papal territories, Antonelli made an effort to increase his own military resources by offering five times the usual pay to recruits joining the Papal forces. But diplomatic assurances, however formal, had to give way before the logic of facts. After the battle of Magenta the Austrian garrisons were promptly withdrawn. No sooner had the last troops gone than the populations rose, tore down the Papal arms, installed provisional Governments, and with embarrassing unani-

[1] To the Cardinal Legate at Bologna, May 9th.
[2] Circular from Antonelli, May 7th.

mity offered the Dictatorship to Victor Emmanuel and demanded union with Piedmont. The crux of the Italian problem had now to be solved, what was to be done with the Papal States?

On this question Cavour had long ago made up his mind. The abolition of the temporal power was to him the only solution. As a first step the Kingdom of Upper Italy must stretch from the Alps to Ancona, embracing Romagna and the Marches.[1] Ultimately Rome 'surrounded by a garden' was to be the Papal territory. As soon as he received notice of the withdrawal of the Austrian garrisons, Cavour wrote to his Minister at Rome in the following terms: 'if you are sounded as to the action of the Government of the King, you will say that you have no precise instructions, but that you believe the Government intend to preserve public order by the appointment of a Royal Commissioner with a sufficiency of troops under his orders; that it is probable that, if the populations desire to take part in the war, the Government will equip them and embody such forces in her army. If such declarations are not judged satisfactory,' he added, 'you will request your passports and leave the affairs of the Legation in the hands of the French embassy.'[2]

Napoleon, unlike Cavour, was lost in indecision. The presence of French troops in Rome, the necessity for the continued support of the French clericals, the protestations of the Catholic world, and the unceasing lamentations of the Empress, made it almost impossible for Napoleon to acquiesce in the barefaced spoliation of the Pope. But his sympathies were, in reality, with Cavour, if he could have seen his way to sanction his scheme without disastrous results to himself. What he did was to throw the responsibility on Piedmont, keep his own troops out of Papal territory, and endeavour to whittle down Cavour's plan of annexation to a mere

[1] Cavour to Villamarina, November 25th, 1858. 'Sardinia can never be made safe unless it has its head supported upon the Alps and its feet at Ancona.' *CCN*. vol. i. Nos. 149, 151. Chiala, vol. iii. note 2. p. clii.

[2] Cavour to Della Minerva, June 14th.

temporary occupation, to increase the allied military resources, and maintain order. Cavour intended to send Massimo d'Azeglio to Bologna as Commissioner with a body of Piedmontese troops, but, under the storm raised by the idea of occupation, he compromised in so far as to substitute General Mezzacapo with his regiment of Romagnuol volunteers for Piedmontese regulars. Before this took place, however, Cardinal Antonelli took his own steps to deal with the situation. He ordered Colonel Anton Schmidt with his 2,000 Swiss troops, stationed at Spoleto, to advance on Perugia and take severe measures to restore order. Schmidt carried out his orders with thoroughness. He bombarded Perugia, defended by some 600 volunteers, forced an entrance, and then sacked the city with medieval ferocity. Europe was horrified at the brutal methods of the Papal troops, but they were effective, and Umbria remained under the aegis of Rome for another twelve months.

Cavour's path was beset with difficulties. Writing to Prince Napoleon on June 21st he says:

> Your Highness will find perhaps a certain indecision, even perhaps a little weakness, in the direction of affairs. Your Highness is not wrong; but if you were in my place for forty-eight hours you would realize that I am as much to be commiserated as blamed. For the past month I have been inundated with contradictory advice from Paris, from Head-quarters, and from yourself. The whole Romagna cries aloud for the protection and dictatorship of the King, but from Head-quarters I am told—'refuse dictatorship, refuse protection, but accept help for the war.' This means not to send either D'Azeglio or troops. What will happen at Bologna when they hear this? Probably disorder and a violent reaction against the priests.[1]

And again, a little later, he writes:

> Gramont and Walewski are complicating matters hopelessly. Gramont, after giving the most revolutionary instructions to Pepoli—and arriving in the middle of the night to tell me

[1] *CCN.*, vol. ii. No. 466.

what he has done—now fulminates against the movement at Bologna and elsewhere. Calls it sacrilege, profanation! Walewski goes even farther, and threatens me with the thunders of Heaven! I really scarcely know how to reply to so strange an argument.

But Cavour, nevertheless, went his own way. D'Azeglio was sent to Bologna, and officers to train the new levies followed him.

The war was now reaching its final stage. On June 24th, three weeks after Magenta, was fought the last desperate battle of Solferino; the greatest battle, in points of numbers, since Leipzig, in which 260,000 men took part. After the defeat of Magenta, Gyulai was superseded, and the Emperor took command in person, with General Hess as his chief of staff. Determined to make a great effort to recover Lombardy, the Austrians recrossed the Mincio and offered battle on Lombard soil. The plan of the struggle was simple, Napoleon striving to pierce the Austrian centre by the capture of the village of Solferino, whilst the Austrians endeavoured to crush his right wing and roll it back upon the centre. Twelve miles to the north at San Martino, Victor Emmanuel and his Piedmontese flung themselves throughout the day on the Austrian right wing, finally occupying the enemy's position at nightfall. All day long the battle raged, but in spite of the utmost efforts of the Austrians, the French right wing held firm whilst their own centre at last gave way. A terrific thunderstorm broke over the battlefield in the evening, and when it cleared the Austrians were once more in full retreat to the shelter of the Quadrilateral.

The battle of Solferino was to the war in Italy what the fall of Sevastopol had been to the war in the Crimea. It was the victory that determined peace. Napoleon believed in making peace on the crest of the wave. He liked to play the magnanimous victor. There were many reasons for his determination to bring the war to a close. The army was not satisfactory. He may have by now realized his own limitations as a general, he

certainly realized those of his Marshals and his ally.
The conditions were bad. The heat was overpowering.
His casualties and the ravages of malaria had seriously
reduced his fighting strength. The commissariat was
defective and reinforcements were not easy to find, and
the chances of forcing the Quadrilateral were problematical. He was not on the best of terms with his allies
and there is evidence that he was not without jealousy
of Victor Emmanuel. Unpleasant comparisons had
been made between his own conduct and that of the
King, always in the thick of the fighting for sheer love
of it.[1] After Palestro, which was mainly a Piedmontese
victory, Napoleon took care to keep his allies posted in
reserve at Galliate during the battle of Magenta, to the
intense annoyance of Victor Emmanuel, ever impatient
for action. Napoleon was disillusioned, too, over the
response of Italy. From the pictures drawn in the
letters of Cavour and Victor Emmanuel, as to the condition of the country, he might well have expected Italy
to spring to arms after the first victory, but the great
army failed to materialize. In Tuscany, too, the failure
to respond to the appeal for recruits disgusted Prince
Napoleon, who wrote bitterly to Cavour on the subject.
But in Lombardy it was worse, for outside the population of the towns, the reception of the French troops
was so bad that Napoleon said that, in case of a forced
retreat, it would be like passing through a hostile
country. He would have liked to have divided the
Piedmontese army into two, mixed it with the French
army, and let Victor Emmanuel look on from a safe
distance, or, better still, return to Turin.[2] Suspecting
this, the King had recently shown an increasing disposition to regard his army as an independent command.
From the political standpoint the situation in Italy was
equally unsatisfactory. Control of the position was in
the hands of Cavour, not of the Emperor. Though consulted and treated with every respect, it was the Pied-

[1] Malmesbury, *Memoirs of a Minister*, June 3rd.
[2] See Cavour to La Marmora, July 6th.

montese statesman, not Napoleon, to whom every one turned for advice and direction. The insurrection in the Romagna brought him nothing but protests and re-criminations; his influence in Tuscany was negligible; the whole Italian question had assumed a complexion quite alien from what he had anticipated. The deciding factor was the threatening attitude of Germany and the disturbing knowledge that his own army of the Rhine existed chiefly on paper.[1] In such a state of things it was wiser to make peace in the aura of victory than to face a stalemate in the Quadrilateral or be forced to make terms at the dictation of Germany as an alternative to a European war.

The obvious course to be taken in such a position was to call a council of war, take his ally into his full confidence, and discuss the situation in all its bearings.[2] But such a straightforward course was impossible to Napoleon. What he did was to give his ally a hint, and without more ado, set to work to make peace with-out consulting any one. On the eve of Solferino, Napoleon took Victor Emmanuel and his chief of staff aside and read to them a letter from the Empress, depicting the situation in the most gloomy colours. When the Emperor finished the King remained silent. 'He understood as I did,' says Della Rocca, 'that every-thing was over.'[3] That evening Victor Emmanuel sent for Cavour and telegraphed to Prince Eugenio, the Regent, at Turin: 'The Emperor received yesterday a communication from all the Courts, that if he entered Venetia all Europe will be on the side of Austria. The Emperor declares it is impossible to face such a coali-tion and appears disposed to make peace.'[4] Cavour arrived at head-quarters on the 25th, the day after

[1] See Bianchi, *Stor. Doc.*, vol. viii; Thayer, vol. ii. p. 89; Matter, vol. iii. c. iv.

[2] Art. 6 of the treaty read: The High Contracting Parties undertake not to receive any overture or proposition tending to the cessation of hostilities without having previously deliberated in common.

[3] Della Rocca, *Autobiografia di un Veterano*.

[4] *CCN.*, vol. ii. Nos. 471–2; Chiala, vol. iii. Appendix note 2.

Solferino, and that evening had a long conference with the King and La Marmora. When it was over he telegraphed to Turin: 'the difficulties, though serious, are not as great as the dispatch would lead us to believe; Nigra will see the Emperor. According to the result of this interview I shall visit him or not.' On the 27th Cavour saw the Emperor at Cavriana, and the same day returned to the capital.

There is no record of what passed at this interview, but it is evident from Cavour's subsequent letters that Napoleon effectively concealed his intention of making peace *at once*, lulled Cavour's suspicions, and sent him back to Turin satisfied that there was no fear of immediate peace; that Napoleon's main preoccupation was the want of reinforcements; and his chief grievance, the meagre response of Tuscany and Lombardy in the matter of recruits. Immediately on his return Cavour wrote strongly on this matter to Vigliano, the Governor of Milan. But he had already taken a much more drastic step than this, for he had dispatched to Naples the Count di Salmour to endeavour to procure an offensive and defensive treaty with the new King Francis as the one means of obtaining a substantial reinforcement for the Italian forces.[1]

On July 1st Cavour wrote to Prince Napoleon, and without mentioning anything about the danger of immediate peace, expressed his opinion that the important matter at the moment was to frustrate a diplomatic intrigue designed to stop the Emperor's admirable work for Italy by arresting his victorious march upon the Adige, if not upon the Mincio. This Cavour attributed to the joint efforts of Walewski and Cowley, who were trying to get peace by mediation on 'the bases of a new Campoformio.' But, as Cavour saw the political situation, there was nothing to fear as long as England did not pronounce against the Italian programme, and on this point the attitude of the new Liberal Govern-

[1] Bianchi, vol. viii, for instructions to Salmour, but wrongly dated June 25th instead of May 27th. See Trevelyan, p. 129.

ment in England under Lord Palmerston completely reassured him. 'I know in the most positive manner,' he wrote, 'that Lord Palmerston does not share in the least the sentiments and opinions of Lord Cowley, and that he is very inclined to favour the complete emancipation of Italy. I am certain that if the Emperor would interrogate him he would receive the most satisfactory assurances.'[1] On the same day he wrote to La Marmora, again without any apparent disquietude as to peace, discussing at length his plans for increasing the armies. 'The news from London,' he says at the close, 'is good. At Berlin the same undecided and vacillating policy. One day the Regent yields to the war party, the next he gives France the most pacific assurances.' The only bad symptom he noticed was the ill humour of Stackelberg, the Russian Minister, 'but,' he added, 'whether it is due to his liver, or to jealousy or instructions from Gortshakoff, I cannot make out.'[2]

The changed tone of the Russian Minister was probably to be traced to Cavour's intrigues with Hungary and the Principalities. Kossuth was in Piedmont, and had had a long interview with Napoleon, who had given him warm encouragement. Cavour was working for a diversion that would both weaken Austria and compromise Napoleon, but the idea of a revolution in Hungary cooled the support of Russia and the intrigue with Kossuth did more harm than good.[3] In the meantime, unknown either to Cavour or his King, Napoleon was taking steps for an immediate suspension of hostilities. To prevent Germany taking the lead in mediation, the Emperor instructed Persigny, his Ambassador in London, to approach Lord Palmerston to offer mediation. The terms he suggested were: Parma and Lombardy to go to Piedmont; Modena and Venetia independent, under an Austrian Archduke; the Legations to be ruled by a Piedmontese, under the suzerainty of the Pope, and all the States to form a Confederation

[1] CCN., vol. ii. No. 473.   [2] Chiala, vol. iii. No. 673.
[3] Chiala, vol. ii. No. 473.

with the Pope as President. To Palmerston the scheme appeared 'suggested by jealousy of Sardinia and tenderness for the Pope,' and he refused to have anything to do with it.[1] To cover his tracks, Napoleon, while waiting for an answer from London, talked loudly of continuing the war, made preparations for the siege of Peschiera, and urged the King to hasten his reinforcements. But his mind was set on peace. To all his other reasons the slaughter of Solferino had now been added. He had had enough.

Cavour remained suspicious, perhaps, but completely in the dark. On July 6th he wrote to La Marmora a long letter about new regiments, at the close of which he added, 'The Emperor has seen Kossuth. He came to see me yesterday with Pietri and Klapka, and told me word for word what Napoleon had said. The result is that I am convinced that Napoleon expects war with Germany; that he even desires it, if it will not drag England in against him.'[2] A telegram the same day from the Marquis Sauli at St. Petersburg, hinting at Russian mediation, was answered in these words: 'at this moment mediation could only have unfortunate results. It is necessary that Austrian influence disappears completely from Italy if peace is to be lasting.' On this very day (6th) Napoleon sent General Fleury to ask Franz Joseph for an armistice. Two days later Cavour received from La Marmora the following telegram: 'Armistice is being concluded at this moment at Villafranca, where Vaillant and General Martimprey represent France and Della Rocca and Robilant, Piedmont. I find it impossible to discover exactly how and from whom the proposal came.'[3] Unable to do anything that day, Cavour the next morning showed the telegram to Nigra, who said at once, 'This means peace.' 'You think so?' said Cavour, 'then let us go to head-quarters.' That evening, Cavour, Nigra, and Alexander Bixio,

[1] Ashley, vol. ii. p. 158.   [2] Chiala, vol. iii. No. 674.

[3] Ibid. No. 676. See Bolléa, No. 179. La Marmora to Cavour dated July 5th. Word also came from Prince Napoleon, see Comandini, *Il principe Napoleone nel Risorgimento*.

who happened to be in Turin, left Turin for Desenzano, which they reached at dawn on the 10th. As soon as a conveyance could be procured they drove straight to the Villa Melchiorre at Monzambano, which served as the King's head-quarters. A long and stormy interview followed. Cavour, in a desperate state of uncertainty and anxiety, heard from the King the reasons given by Napoleon for the armistice. Furiously angry, his words were as caustic as his criticisms. Then he heard that the two Emperors were to meet the next morning at Villafranca. Powerless to effect the issue, with no certain knowledge even of the purpose of the meeting, but of course expecting peace, Cavour spent all that day and the next in bitter anxiety for the fate of Italy and consumed with anger against Napoleon.[1]

The two Emperors met at Villafranca early the following morning. An hour's conversation sufficed to decide in outline the terms of the treaty. Later in the day Prince Napoleon was dispatched to Verona with the written document, under orders to be back at Valeggio that night by 10 p.m. with the treaty signed. On his return to Valeggio, Napoleon found Victor Emmanuel awaiting him. He explained the terms of peace in as favourable a light as possible, and the King, bitterly dissatisfied, rode back to Monzambano. Avoiding the exasperated Cavour, Victor Emmanuel consulted La Marmora, who later in the day rode over to Valeggio and voiced the King's dissatisfaction to Napoleon. After a long conversation Napoleon suggested the additional phrase 'so far as concerns me' as a saving clause and with this La Marmora returned.[2] At ten o'clock that night, accompanied only by the aide-de-camp on duty, General Solaroli (followed by Nigra in a separate conveyance), Victor Emmanuel once more took the road to Napoleon's head-quarters. The

[1] Mazzini was for once a true prophet when he said, on hearing of the coming war, 'You will be in some remote corner of Lombardy, when the peace that will betray Venice will be made, unknown to you.' Chiala, vol. iii. Introd. 163.

[2] Massari, *Alfonso La Marmora*.

Prince arrived almost at the same time as the King, and the three principals went upstairs to the salon of the Casa Morelli for the signature of the treaty. Victor Emmanuel signed after Napoleon, adding the words, 'en ce qui me concerne.' After Nigra had made a copy of the terms they returned to Monzambano.

The terms of the treaty were as follows:

(1) The Emperors of Austria and France will favour the creation of an Italian Confederation under the honorary Presidency of the Holy Father.

(2) The Emperor of Austria cedes to the Emperor of France all his rights upon Lombardy, except the fortresses of Mantua and Peschiera. The Emperor of France will hand over this territory to the King of Sardinia. Venice will form part of the Confederation remaining in the possession of Austria.

(3) The Grand Duke of Tuscany and the Duke of Modena will return to their States proclaiming a general amnesty.

(4) The two Emperors will ask the Holy Father to introduce into his States indispensable reforms.

(5) A general amnesty.

The fate of Parma and Piacenza was not mentioned, Franz Joseph remarking that, since they were not his possessions, he could not dispose of them. They were destined to be added to Piedmont.

It was after midnight when the two carriages clattered once more through the silent streets of Monzambano and drew up at the Villa Melchiorre, where Cavour, half distraught with impatience and anxiety, awaited the King's return from the fatal meeting. It was a stifling night. The King, on entering the salon, threw off his tunic, unbuttoned his sleeves, lit a cigar, and with his bare arms propped in front of him, seated himself at the table. Cavour sat at his left, Nigra opposite. 'Give the Count the paper, Nigra,' said the King. Nigra handed it across the table. Cavour read it.

At a glance Cavour saw that every condition essential to Italian independence and unity was absent from the terms of peace. Austria, entrenched in the Quadrilateral, with the line of the Mincio and the key-fortresses of Mantua and Peschiera in her possession, was still master of the fate of Italy. Piedmont, reduced to a mere member of a Confederation, lost at once all claim to speak on behalf of Italy. The return of the Duke of Modena and the Grand Duke of Tuscany assured the predominance of Austrian influence throughout the Peninsula. What was the value of pushing back the Piedmontese frontier from the Ticino to the Mincio when the objective of the whole war, independence and unity, was rendered impossible by the restoration of Austrian influence and introduction of the principle of federation? Beside himself at such a betrayal, Cavour's anger blazed forth in a furious denunciation of the treaty. He spared neither Emperor nor King. The King could never ratify such a treaty. It dishonoured the Royal House of Savoy, betrayed Italy, ruined at a blow the whole policy of the Government. Lombardy? What was Lombardy compared to Italian independence? Let the King refuse Lombardy; abdicate; carry on the war alone; anything to show Europe the fatal consequences of such terms and uphold the honour of Italy! Never was Cavour, despite the wildness of such suggestions, so great and true a patriot as at this moment. Angry as he was at Cavour's unmeasured language, the King with admirable self-control did his utmost to calm his outraged Minister and bring him to reason. But nothing stopped Cavour. He at least, he declared, would have no part in such a transaction and offered his resignation. It was at once accepted. But Cavour's action in this hurt the King even more than his angry words, for it looked to him like desertion just when he needed help. 'Ah, for you gentlemen,' said Victor Emmanuel bitterly, 'things always come right, for you settle them by resignation. I am the one who cannot get out of a difficulty so nicely. I cannot offer my resignation. I cannot desert the cause. We work together all right until there comes a difficulty, then I am left alone to face the music. I am the one who is responsible before history and the country.' Then, seeing Cavour about to start again, he cut the interview short, 'You are not in a condition to continue this discussion. Go and get some rest: sleep will bring you sense and calm; to-morrow we will have another talk.'

Accompanied by Nigra, Cavour withdrew to La Marmora's quarters, where a bed had been provided for him. The next day another conference took place at which Prince Napoleon and La Marmora assisted. It was then that the Prince undertook to persuade the Emperor to insist that force should not be used to restore the exiled rulers to their thrones, a clause that did much to save the situation. That night, worn out in mind and body, Cavour returned to Turin. When he arrived at Milan a crowd was waiting at the station to give him an ovation, but on hearing that he was asleep, it dispersed in silence.[1] The day after his arrival Cavour had an interview with Kossuth and Pietri. Once more his anger surged up. 'The terms of this peace,' he thundered, 'shall never be carried out! This treaty shall never be executed! I will take Solaro della Margherita by one hand and Mazzini by the other, if need be. I will turn conspirator. I will become a revolutionary. But this treaty shall never be executed. No, a thousand times No! Never! Never!'

Cavour's words, even when uttered in anger, were never empty phrases. To this thought he returned more than once. Some weeks later, talking over the future with his friends at Geneva, he exclaimed: 'I shall turn my attention to Naples. I shall be accused of being a revolutionary, but above all *il faut marcher et nous marcherons*. Ah well, they will force me to spend the rest of my life as a conspirator!' In the last phase of his work these words had their fulfilment.

Napoleon had never done a wiser or more surprising thing, from his own point of view, than signing the

[1] On the Peace of Villafranca, see the *Frammenti di C. Nigra*; *CCN.*, vol. ii. Appendix II. Extrait du Journal de Voyage de S. A. I. Mgr. le Prince Napoléon. *CCN.*, vol. ii. No. 481. Arrivabene, *Memorie della mia vita*, c. 13. Thayer, for very full account.

Peace of Villafranca. A short and successful war was exactly what he wanted. In little over two months he had transported an army of 200,000 men into Italy, driver the Austrians without a single check out of Lombardy, won two resounding victories, and was back again in Paris almost before Europe had grasped the fact that the war had really begun. He had frustrated all idea of armed mediation, increased the military reputation of France, and enhanced his position in Europe. There was only one flaw—he had broken his word to Italy. Publicly announcing that he came to free Italy from the Alps to the Adriatic, he had stopped in the middle, signed a peace that betrayed his promises and could not be fulfilled, left behind him a sullen and disappointed people, and created for himself a diplomatic imbroglio out of which the determination of Italy and the cleverness of Cavour were destined to achieve results Napoleon neither expected nor desired. Above all, he had failed to settle the Italian question and satisfied no one but himself.

Napoleon, accompanied by Victor Emmanuel, arrived in Turin the day after this interview. His reception, wrote Cavour, was 'cold but *convenable.*' Cavour avoided the State banquet that evening, but afterwards had a short talk with the Emperor. Napoleon justified the peace on military grounds. Assured Cavour that he would plead the cause of Italy at the Congress and confirmed his promise to prevent the forcible return of the exiled Princes. Before he left Turin the Emperor said to Victor Emmanuel, 'your Government will pay me the expenses of the war and we will say no more of Savoy and Nice.'

The new Government took office on the 19th. La Marmora was President, Rattazzi took the Home Office, and the cautious Dabormida returned to the Foreign Office. The same day Cavour left Turin and withdrew to the solitude of Leri. But the short interval of five days was long enough to enable him to give clear and decided marching orders to the Royal Commissioners in the different States. To Farini at Modena he telegraphed, 'arms and money,' to which laconic advice Farini replied: 'note that, if the Duke, relying on conventions about which I know nothing, should make any attempt to return, I shall treat him as an enemy of the King and country. I will be driven out by no one, if it costs me my life.' And Cavour answered, 'The Minister is dead, the friend grasps your hand and applauds the decision you have taken.' To Count Pallieri at Parma he wrote: 'Parma must be annexed to Sardinia. Prepare the oath and act with the utmost energy. I am resigning.' No less clear was the advice given to Bianchi, the Tuscan envoy, sent hot foot to Turin. 'Appoint a Liberal Government prepared to resist equally to diplomatic pressure and armed intervention. Recall Ulloa's troops. If Tuscany holds firm it may save everything.' To D'Azeglio at Bologna his orders were to carry on the Government and rouse the people to their own defence without trusting to Piedmont. The official recall of the Royal Commissioners was soon afterwards sent out. Farini at once resigned, and then, as a simple citizen, was elected Dictator. The others returned. But Parma first and then Bologna placed themselves under Farini, who with Cipriani in the Romagna and Ricasoli at Florence, were the three who rendered the return of the old order an impossibility, except by the use of armed force.

To free the new Cabinet from all embarrassment, Cavour, after a week at Leri, left Piedmont for a visit to his cousins at Geneva. Switzerland was the only place in Europe to which he could go without causing suspicion in diplomatic circles. At first he was moody and difficult, but he quickly recovered his poise and before long was busy with new plans.[1] Cavour's resignation, though given in a moment of anger and regarded as a desertion by the King, was an act of true political wisdom. Only by such a means could he justify his policy before Italy and make a protest against

[1] De la Rive, *Cavour*.

the peace that Europe could understand and appreciate. His own account of the reasons that prompted him appears in a letter to his Minister in London.

> I think you will have understood [he writes] the peremptory reasons that have forced me to resign. I have not been influenced in this by any personal considerations. If I had believed that by remaining in power I should have performed a service to the King and country, I should have sacrificed without hesitation my personal feelings and what little popularity I may have acquired. But my retirement was necessary to attenuate the unhappy consequences of the peace. You know that the policy of the Cabinet has been frankly national; that it had in view, not the enlargement of Piedmont, but the emancipation of Italy; the establishment throughout the Peninsula of a wise liberal system. If the present peace leads to the return of the old régime in Central Italy, it will do more harm than good to the national cause. I could not take the responsibility for it. Moreover, I had no motive to do so, for it was negotiated and settled unknown to me.

But besides being demanded as a justification of his policy in the past, Cavour realized that his resignation was necessary for the future benefit of the country.

> Before a diplomatic tribunal, the cause of Italy, if pleaded by me, would suffer [he went on]. I am the *bête noir* of diplomacy. Walewski detests me for a thousand reasons, and above all, on account of the sarcasms and jokes that Clarendon and I made at his expense during the Congress of Paris. Cowley has nervous spasms when he sees me. I should be a veritable nightmare to the Austrian delegates. These gentlemen would refuse to the individual, what they would, perhaps, concede to the country, provided that our representative was a *persona grata*.[1]

The decision was wise from other points of view. It gave him six months' rest, which he needed very badly. It gave him time to study the new situation and think out a fresh line of policy. His successors would simply mark time, and while they did so the atmosphere would clear and reveal the new landmarks.

---

[1] *La Politique de Cavour*, No. 178. See also Chiala, vol. iii. Nos. 686-9.

Cavour remained in Switzerland until the end of August, then he returned to Piedmont. For the next four months he resided chiefly at Leri. His position was not easy. Though he was anxious not to cause difficulty to the Government, his mere presence brought them embarrassment. The homestead at Leri became the haunt of politicians and ambassadors, unofficial agents came to ask his advice, messengers from Tuscany and the other States found their way to his rice-fields, and if Leri did not become the centre of intrigue against the Government, it was only because of the determination of Cavour not to impede the Cabinet in its difficult task. Cavour watched and waited. He offered his help freely to the Government, and whenever it was asked for, he gave it. But his value as a consultant was not very great. An ordinary performer may consult a master about the fingering of a difficult passage, and even get it right, but that will not ensure that the performance as a whole will be masterly. But the very lack of a positive policy on the part of the Government was at the moment a help.[1] During these six months a new situation was arising and the weakness of the Government threw it into relief, and when the right moment came, the one man capable of dealing with it stepped in and took the helm.

The immediate question was the signature of the Treaty of Peace. For this purpose the plenipotentiaries of France, Austria, and Piedmont met at Zürich in August. But, although the final outcome of their labours was little more than a ratification of the preliminaries of Villafranca, their task was not completed until November 10th. Behind this lay the real problem, what was to be done with the revolted provinces of Italy, Parma, Modena, and Romagna, and above all, Tuscany? Were they to be allowed to join Piedmont, were they to be grouped into a Kingdom of Central Italy, or, were their rulers to be restored? Of these

[1] Treitschke, *Cavour*. 'Good fortune had in those days given Italy an incapable Government.' See Cavour to Dabormida. Chiala, vol. iii. No. 701.

three alternatives the first was the solution desired by England, the second by France, and the third by Austria.

The initial position taken up by Napoleon was defined in his words to the Marquis Pepoli at Turin on July 15th:

> If annexation crossed the Apennines, unity would be made, and I do not wish unity. I want only independence. Unity would bring danger to me in France itself, because of the Roman question, and France would not see with pleasure a great nation armed on her flank which might diminish her preponderance.

But with this veto he coupled the principle of non-intervention, which spoilt Austria's plan of restoring the *status quo* at the point of the bayonet. 'Italy for the Italians' was the motto of England, who lent her full diplomatic support to the principle of annexation. In such a state of things it was clear that Italy herself would largely determine the final decision. It was a great stroke of good fortune that, at this moment, with Cavour out of office and a weak Government at Turin lacking in initiative, Italy found two strong men in Farini and Ricasoli who could neither be intimidated nor cajoled. Their policy was similar but distinct. Both kept strict order and by every means they could devise impressed upon Europe their unalterable determination to annex themselves to Piedmont and thus settle the question of Unity.

Bettino Ricasoli, the Dictator of Tuscany, was a man who, to a somewhat narrow intellect joined an inflexible will. Most of his life had been spent on his estates at Brolio, where he had dedicated himself to the education of his only daughter, the betterment of his estates, and the moral and intellectual improvement of his peasantry. For this latter purpose he instituted a night school conducted by himself. Not content with this, being of a deeply religious nature, he adopted the words of the prayer-book—'that they may know these things the better ye shall call upon them to hear sermons'—and with deep fervour and eloquence preached to his peasants every week on their moral and spiritual responsibilities. When the flight of the Grand Duke and the outbreak of war transferred his activities to Florence, where he became first Minister of the Interior, and then President of the Council, he proceeded to govern Tuscany on the same principles as he had enunciated at Brolio. By means of pamphlets and pro-clamations he 'illuminated' the country districts on the requirements of patriotism and its relation to morality, whilst a carefully controlled Press inoculated the country with his views, and no others. His political purpose was simple and clear. He was determined that Tuscany should be united to Piedmont, but only on condition that the objective was the creation of Italy. The inflexibility of his purpose is seen in the following incident. When La Marmora, seeing no way out of the *impasse*, counselled him to bring back the House of Lorraine on the best terms obtainable, Ricasoli wrote to his brother: 'Tell General La Marmora that I have torn his letter into a thousand pieces.' Such was the temper of the man who more than any one else during these months saved Italy from disruption.[1]

More flexible in mind and less dictatorial in manner, though no less firm in his determination to make Italy, was Carlo Luigi Farini, dictator first of Modena and then of Parma and Romagna as well, which he governed under the inclusive title of Emilia. A doctor by pro-fession, but trained in political life, he revealed at this crisis an energy, initiative, and a capacity to govern, that won the admiration of Italy and demonstrated effectively before Europe the determination of Emilia to unite itself to Piedmont. Farini was anxious that Tuscany and Emilia should act strictly in concert, but to this, beyond a certain point, Ricasoli demurred. He saw clearly that too close a union would create *de facto*

[1] On Ricasoli see Hancock, *op. cit.*; Gotti, *Ricasoli*; Finali, *Contemporanei illustri*, has articles on Ricasoli and Farini; also Martinengo Caesaresco, *Italian Characters*.

that 'Kingdom of Central Italy' which Napoleon had
adumbrated, and that all Napoleon or Europe would
have to do, to establish it *de iure*, would be to dump down
some royalty with the title of King. To Farini, therefore,
he laid down the principle, 'acts identical but distinct.'[1]

As soon as Ricasoli heard that the peace of Villafranca excluded armed intervention, he began to act.
He summoned the Consulta and instructed that body
to make arrangements for the election of an Assembly.
On August 11th the Assembly met in the Palazzo
Vecchio and proceeded to pass the two resolutions
Ricasoli had prepared. The first declared that Tuscany
would never receive back the House of Lorraine whose
conduct had 'rendered its presence absolutely incompatible with the order and happiness of Tuscany.' Four
days later it passed the second, which stated 'the firm
intention of Tuscany to make part of a strong Italian
Kingdom under the constitutional sceptre of Victor
Emmanuel.' The votes on both these resolutions were
unanimous.[2] The Assembly, having done its duty, was
then prorogued. Similar resolutions were passed by
the three States of Emilia, but Ricasoli refused to adopt
Farini's suggestion to wait and present the four simultaneously to Victor Emmanuel. The intention to
present these resolutions caused trepidation in the
Cabinet at Turin. The Treaty of Zürich was not
signed, Napoleon had refused to consider annexation,
they could not be accepted and they could not be
refused, what was to be done? In the end they were
presented and received, the King thanking each deputation in turn, promising to support their wishes before
Europe, but avoided all mention of annexation. The
qualms of conscience displayed by the Cabinet aroused
the sarcasm of D'Azeglio, who wrote that 'Potiphar's
wife had only to deal with one Joseph, but Tuscany
and Emilia had to face six.'

[1] Hancock. Cavour called Ricasoli when he heard this 'a stupid mule', but
Ricasoli was right.
[2] A few voluntarily stayed away not to spoil the unanimity of the vote.

In spite of the hesitation at Turin, both States now set to work to identify their internal organization with that of Piedmont, unifying the currency, weights and measures, customs, postal arrangements, and so forth.[1] They next proposed that the Prince of Carignano should be sent as Regent in the King's name. Once more the Cabinet at Turin, after vainly trying to curb the audacity of the two Dictators, dutifully appealed to the Tuileries, and again Napoleon vetoed the suggestion.[2] But in spite of this, after further negotiations, the principle was at least in part admitted, by the nomination of Boncompagni as the King's deputy's deputy, in which capacity, after Ricasoli had carefully assured his own retention of power, Boncompagni was installed in an inconspicuous Palazzo at Florence. Throughout these months the conduct of Ricasoli was superb. Napoleon's special envoy, the Comte de Reiset, insisted that the union of Tuscany to Piedmont was irrevocably forbidden by the Emperor: the Government at Turin begged him to compromise; his own agents in Paris and elsewhere besought him to make the best of a bad job and call back the House of Lorraine, but the iron Baron contemptuously ignored them. 'Go and tell those gentlemen,' he said to a friend on his way to Paris, 'that I have twelve centuries of existence, I am the last of my line, and I will give the last drop of my blood to maintain the integrity of my political programme,' and he proceeded to add the arms of Savoy on the tricolour flag of Italy, set up the Royal arms on all public places, and to head all public documents with the title *Regnando S.M. Vittorio Emanuele.*

But the good work hitherto achieved by the two Dictators was seriously imperilled early in November by a military intrigue of which Garibaldi was the

---

[1] Farini, in forming the new army of Central Italy, numbered the regiments in continuation of the Piedmontese army numbers.

[2] Cavour when consulted on this advised that the Prince should be nominated by each Assembly without previous arrangement; that he should be named Regent, without saying that he would govern in the name of the King and that the Piedmontese Cabinet should remain extraneous to the whole affair.

leading figure. During these months, the party of
Order was not the only one showing activity. Mazzini,
with the full knowledge of Ricasoli, was concealed in
Florence.[1] La Farina and the National Society were
still alive, and Garibaldi had a post as second-in-
command to General Fanti in the army of Central Italy.
Towards the end of October these elements of the party
of action planned a rising in Umbria. Before the movement came to a head, however, Ricasoli heard of it and
informed Farini that it must be stopped. Difficulties
arose with Fanti, who was not altogether innocent of
connivance. Taking advantage of the confusion, and
believing the King was with him, Garibaldi made preparations for an immediate advance into Umbria. Just
at this moment Cavour happened to come to Turin,
and hearing what was taking place, grasped at once the
serious nature of the position and wrote post haste to
La Marmora: 'the King must act directly and without
hesitation, a delay of twenty-four hours might be fatal.'
The King took the advice and at once summoned
Garibaldi to come to Turin. Garibaldi obeyed, and
after an interview with the one man whose word he
obeyed without question, retired to Genoa on his way
to Caprera to await a more propitious moment for
action. The incident showed how little grip the Cabinet
had on the situation, and the eyes of the nation began to
turn once more to the quick brain and firm hands of
Papà Camillo.

These events revealed the danger of prolonging the
anomalous situation in Central Italy. There were two
lines upon which a solution could be found; either
annexation by Piedmont with the tacit consent of
Europe, or a redistribution of Italy by the mandate
of a European Congress. Everything depended on
Napoleon, who was the central figure of the whole
position. There were two dominant ideas in his mind:
firstly, he desired to obtain Nice and Savoy; and
secondly, he wanted his own solution of the Italian

[1] He was expelled after this incident.

question carried out, but he wanted some one else to shoulder the responsibility for it. The ideal solution would be a Congress that would adopt his suggestions and give him Nice and Savoy for his trouble. The alternative was a private treaty with Piedmont by which permission to annex Central Italy would be paid for by Savoy and Nice, but in this case Napoleon must accept the responsibility and face the consequences.

He began by sounding Piedmont. In October Dabormida went to Paris and had two interviews with Napoleon, at both of which the latter brought up the question of Savoy, leaving Nice in the background. By the treaty of January, he said, Savoy was to be given France, and he would now be glad to accept it, instead of cash, for his expenses. But Dabormida replied that the conditions were that Austria should be completely expelled from Italy, and until that was realized the surrender of Savoy could not be demanded.[1] Having failed with Dabormida, Napoleon then tried Victor Emmanuel. In a long letter the Emperor explained that if a Congress was held and a settlement demanded on the basis of Villafranca, he should keep his word— which meant the return of Tuscany to the Grand Duke and Romagna to the Pope. But he did not state how this was to be accomplished without armed intervention. It was another hint that his consent to annexation was open to sale by private treaty. The King replied that he was as deeply pledged to Italy as the Emperor was to Austria, and that he might be compelled to yield to force, but he would never betray his country. Having failed again, Napoleon next turned to England. When Palmerston urged the annexation of Central Italy to Piedmont, Persigny was instructed to reply that the formation of a strong kingdom on her borders would require a rectification of France's frontier in Savoy. To this Palmerston replied that to filch Savoy from Piedmont was to lower the purpose of the war from generosity to mere self-seeking. Persigny then sug-

[1] Dabormida to La Marmora. Chiala, *Lettere,* vol. ii. Introd. p. 246.

gested that if England herself put forward the idea of giving France Savoy it would heal the wounds of 1815 and be a true act of friendship. To this Palmerston vouchsafed no reply.[1] All his overtures having failed, and the Treaty of Zürich being signed on November 10th, Napoleon allowed the idea of a Congress to go forward and on November 21st the formal invitations were issued.

Napoleon was, in fact, on the horns of a dilemma. He was pledged to Austria by the preliminaries of Villafranca to found a Kingdom of Central Italy. If he kept his word, he would render Piedmont definitely hostile, and he must say good-bye to all hopes of Nice and Savoy. If, on the other hand, he permitted the annexations, he might get the coveted provinces, but at the cost of breaking his word to Austria. In this predicament it was necessary, as Queen Victoria wrote to Lord John Russell, to get some one to pull the chestnuts out of the fire for him, and that some one could only be England. After first sounding Lord Cowley, Napoleon proposed through Walewski, that Lord John should approach Austria and ask her not to insist on the return of the exiled princes and to acquiesce in the union of Central Italy to Piedmont.[2] On December 12th Count Rechberg replied that it was not the intention of Austria to attempt to acquire predominance in Italy or even to mix herself further in Italian affairs. Napoleon's path was now clear. All that remained was to compensate England, wreck the Congress, and enter into negotiations with Piedmont on the basis of Nice and Savoy for the Romagna and the Duchies.

England was at once propitiated by a favourable commercial treaty. The fate of the Congress was settled with equal ease and dispatch. The happy thought had struck Napoleon that the definition of temporal power involved no specified area. In short, that the necessary independence of the Pope would be equally assured, if

[1] Persigny to Walewski, December 2nd and 14th.
[2] Russell to Loftus, December 3rd.

he only possessed 'Rome surrounded by a garden.' In his reply to an address of welcome delivered by the Archbishop of Bordeaux in the previous September, he had given a strong hint of his changing attitude, which he now proceeded to make unmistakably clear in a pamphlet entitled *The Pope and the Congress*, which was issued on December 22nd. In this, the writer, after demonstrating the necessity of the temporal power to preserve the independence of the Pope, proceeded to show that the smaller the area His Holiness had to govern, the better it would be for every one concerned. So that, even if reduced to the city of Rome, or at most to the Patriarchate of St. Peter, his independence would be preserved, and the task of the Holy Father rendered incalculably easier. The parentage and the purpose of the pamphlet was unmistakable.

Amongst those, however, who failed to realize that the proposals of the author were in reality those of Napoleon himself, was the Pope, who, in responding to the felicitations of General Goyon, the Commandant of the French legion at Rome, on January 1st, 1860, after stigmatizing the pamphlet as a 'notable monument of hypocrisy and an ignoble tissue of contradictions,' expressed his belief that the Emperor would condemn the principles contained therein.[1] He was speedily undeceived. A few days later came the famous letter from Napoleon in which he explained 'with sincere regret' that the best solution in his opinion was that the Pope should sacrifice the revolted provinces. 'If the Holy Father,' he added, 'for the peace of Europe, will renounce his claim to these provinces, which for fifty years have caused embarrassment to his Government, and in exchange, demand from the Powers a guarantee for the remainder, I do not doubt the immediate return of order.'[2] Deeply insulted, the Pope at once refused to send a representative to the Congress; whilst Austria,

[1] Text in Zini, vol. iv. No. 254. 'His Holiness added that he had several documents sent to him by the Emperor that were a veritable contradiction of these principles.'

[2] Zini, *Documenti*, No. 254 B.

receiving an equivocal reply to her demand that France would neither propose nor support the opinions put forward in the pamphlet, refused likewise. So the Congress vanished. A circular, dated January 3rd, announced that it was indefinitely postponed. The next day the Emperor dismissed his Foreign Minister, Walewski, whose pro-Austrian proclivities were notorious, and replaced him by his ambassador at Constantinople, Thouvenel, whose sympathies were with Italy. The path was cleared for the new policy.

Cavour saw at a glance the full significance of Napoleon's actions. On January 7th he wrote to de la Rive:

> It is evident to me that, after long hesitations, the Emperor has made up his mind to return frankly to the English alliance for which all his life he has had a decided *penchant*. He has realized that in France the clerical party drag him towards the fatal slope that ruined Charles X; he has sensed a violent reaction against ultra-montanism; and he has broken with Rome. In my opinion the Emperor's decision has been no longer in doubt since the day that he made his famous reply to the Archbishop of Bordeaux, of which the significance, in my eyes, was no less than that of the brochure, *The Pope and the Congress*. After reading that reply I said to myself: 'I forgive the Emperor the peace of Villafranca, he is rendering to Italy a service greater than the victory of Solferino. The English alliance and the rupture with Rome must give a more liberal, or at least a wider and more popular tone to the Emperor's Government. The dismissal of Walewski and the appointment of Thouvenel, an enemy of the priests, confirm this opinion. What will be the result? I cannot say. . . . As to Italy I am convinced that the restorations will not take place, the temporal power of the Pope is destroyed, and that in a very short space of time the principle of unity will triumph from the Alps to Sicily.' [1]

The new situation had arisen. All that was now needed was that the one man capable of using the opportunity effectively should be back in power. Italy had not long to wait.

Towards the end of the year the attitude of Cavour

[1] Chiala, *Lettere*, vol. iii. No. 736.

in regard to the Cabinet completely changed. On his retirement from office he had offered them his loyal support and had kept his word, but the conduct of the Ministry during the last months of the year had completely alienated his goodwill. To some extent this was inevitable. The policy of Cavour, so personal, so secretive, and so intricate, could not possibly be continued by another Cabinet. It was natural that the master craftsman should show irritation at the bungling efforts of his less skilled successors to use the tools his hand had fashioned. Seized once more with the desire to continue his work, with new plans and combinations seething in his mind, Cavour became daily more impatient, and impatience soon led to exasperation. But his growing disgust at the feeble diplomacy of the Cabinet was increased by a more personal source of annoyance. This was due to the sympathy lent by a section of the Cabinet, and notably by Rattazzi, to a malicious and persistent intrigue against his return to power, promoted by the extreme section of the Left. No sooner had Cavour resigned than Brofferio, Sineo, and their following, assisted by the bitter and disappointed Florentine Guerrazzi, who, exiled from Tuscany, was now domiciled at Genoa through the kindness of Cavour, began to plot against him.[1] Through Rattazzi's influence they gained admittance to the palace, and did their best to inflame and poison the mind of the king, already sufficiently irritated by the memories of Monzambano, against his great Minister. Cavour's disgust when he heard this was deep. He may well have remembered that it was just ten years since Victor Emmanuel's father, Charles Albert, had lent himself to precisely the same influences. On that occasion, Gioberti was the victim—and the result was Novara! The plan devised by Brofferio was to split Cavour's majority in the Chamber by uniting as many

---

[1] Guerrazzi at this time confided to Brofferio his three ambitions, to be presented to the King, to be appointed Historiographer Royal, and to be made Governor of Tuscany *vice* Ricasoli. See Ruffini, *L'Opposizione al tempo di Cavour.*

as possible of his supporters in a new organization called the 'Liberi Comizi,' of which the leader was to be Rattazzi, and the mouthpiece, a new journal called the *Stendardo*. To influence public opinion still farther, they bribed certain French journalists, by means of Piedmontese decorations, to depreciate Cavour and exalt Rattazzi in the French Press.[1] To achieve their aim, a name was necessary, and they found little difficulty in inducing Garibaldi, always a child in politics, to lend his support and prestige to the new venture. But the scheme was an utter failure. At the inaugural banquet to which 200 guests were invited less than 40 presented themselves. On the eve of an important meeting of liberal deputies, convened to decide whether or not they would join the 'Liberi Comizi,' a scandalous article in the *Stendardo* against Cavour, written by Brofferio, procured a unanimous vote against having anything to do with the new organization.[2] Garibaldi in disgust resigned the Presidency, and a few days later the 'Liberi Comizi' was disbanded and almost immediately replaced by a new Society to be called *La Nazione Armata*. But the result was the same. La Marmora and Dabormida frowned upon the movement, the public held aloof, and 'The Nation Armed' sank quickly into oblivion, this time to be replaced by what proved a popular appeal. In a manifesto, dated January 4th, 1860, Garibaldi once more issued a call to the nation, concluding with these words, 'with the unanimous consent of all the members I declare the Nazione Armata dissolved, and I invite every Italian who loves his country to assist with subscriptions to procure *Un milione di fucili*. The Million Rifle Fund proved (under Government supervision) as great a success as the attempt to oust Cavour proved a failure.

[1] Charles de la Varenne and Ernesto Resetti both received the Cross of the Order of S. Maurice and S. Lazarus. See extracts from their articles in the French press in Chiala, vol. iii. Introd. p. 286.

[2] Cavour let it be known that if any large section of his party joined he would not go to Paris as representative of Italy at the Congress. Brofferio's article was on the Connubio, it is quoted in the Introduction to Chiala, vol. iii.

One of the malign influences resulting from this
intrigue was the humiliating delay to which Cavour
was subjected in his nomination as plenipotentiary for
Italy at the Congress. For this position no other name
than that of Cavour had ever been considered. After
being informed unofficially that he would be nominated,
the Cabinet kept him waiting three months for the
official announcement, while they deferred once more
to Napoleon as to whether Cavour would be acceptable.
'What credit will I get from a Government,' Cavour
wrote, 'that does not dare to nominate its representative
without obtaining the express permission of a foreign
ruler?' When the offer was finally made to him, he
accepted, 'because,' as he wrote to Farini, 'to refuse
would have proclaimed an antagonism fatal to Italy,'
but with justifiable bitterness he added: 'in accepting,
I have made the greatest sacrifice a political man can
make for his country, not only by bearing in silence the
most cruel slanders, but in accepting a mandate from
a Government that inspires me neither with esteem nor
confidence.'

Cavour's irritation at the subserviency of the Cabinet,
to the Democrats on the one hand and to Napoleon on
the other, was increased by their attitude on a constitutional issue to which he attached great importance.
The Cabinet kept postponing the convocation of Parliament, and, Rattazzi in particular, as Minister of the
Interior, was rushing through a mass of ill-digested
administrative decrees that were causing great annoyance in Lombardy. The reason was obvious. Once
Parliament assembled, with Cavour in opposition, the
Cabinet would not last a week. This conduct was
already causing adverse comment in England, whose
support was vital, and when, after the Congress collapsed, Cavour was invited to undertake a special
mission to Paris and London, a request coming in the
first place from Lord John Russell, he made the immediate assembly of Parliament a condition of acceptance. The Cabinet temporized, and Cavour made up

THE WAR AND THE PEACE

his mind to refuse the mission and return to Leri. Before doing so he went to say good-bye to Sir James Hudson. During his visit General Solaroli came in with some Government papers for Cavour to look at. The question of the mission to London cropped up and Cavour stated his conditions. Solaroli asked him to write them down, but Cavour refused, whereupon Sir James Hudson offered to act as his amanuensis and took down the conditions from Cavour's dictation. The paper, in Hudson's handwriting, was brought to the Cabinet. It was recognized, and La Marmora, roused at the thought of having his policy dictated by the English ambassador, at once resigned. La Marmora's biographer notes that the precipitation with which the General resigned, reveals the 'exquisite delicacy of his feelings,' but his action savours strongly of seizing an excellent excuse to get out of a position he was only too ready to vacate and dragging a somewhat unwilling Cabinet after him, for he had told Cavour on accepting the Presidency that he only held it in preparation for his return.

Cavour's carriage was at the door when the summons to the palace arrived. He went at once. The King was ill in bed. The interview was difficult but satisfactory, and an hour later Cavour left the palace to ring up the curtain for the last act.

XI. ANNEXATION AND CESSION

Policy of Cavour—His Diplomatic Circular—Russell's Four Points—Nice and Savoy—Struggle for Tuscany—The Plebiscite and Annexation—Napoleon demands Nice and Savoy—England's Anger—The Secret Treaty—Its publication—General Election—Tuscany and Emilia—New Parliament—Garibaldi and Nice—Difficulties with France—The Debate on Nice and Savoy.

THE return of Cavour to power was greeted with a chorus of approval. 'You cannot believe,' wrote Farini, 'how much the return of Cavour has raised the spirits throughout Emilia.' From Paris, Vimercati, the King's private channel of information, wrote that the nomination of Cavour had 'met with approval on all sides,' and equal satisfaction was shown in London. Confidence in the future of Italy returned once more, and every one felt that the period of hesitation and inaction was over.[1]

To Cavour himself the line to be followed was clear. 'You know our system,' he wrote to Massimo d'Azeglio the same day that he took office, 'liberal conservatives at home: *italianissimi* to the extreme limits of possibility abroad.' The task that lay immediately in front of him was the annexation of Central Italy to Piedmont and its corollary, the cession of Savoy and Nice to France. On the first of these two questions his resolution was taken. He believed it necessary, and was prepared to take the requisite measures, which included a definite and legal sanction by Parliament as soon as it assembled. If France and England wished it, he was also prepared for a popular vote.[2] Certain of English support, the attitude of Napoleon was the unknown factor.

As to the Emperor of France [he said to Giorgini, sent to him

---

[1] Hudson to Russell, January 21st. 'As soon as it was known that the King had commanded M. de Cavour to form a new Cabinet the city of Milan proposed to celebrate the event by a public illumination; this was prevented by the authorities; but every town, city, and borough on the telegraph line between Piacenza and Rimini did illuminate on the evening of the day of the Count's nomination.' F.O. 167, vol. 115.

[2] Cavour to Em. d'Azeglio, January 24th.

from Florence], after his famous pamphlet he has shut himself in an impenetrable silence, and has made it plain that he does not want any more deputations from Central Italy. I do not expect that he will be in favour of annexation. On the contrary, I believe that he would wish us not to do it, and truly the pledges given at Villafranca make it impossible for him to sanction it. I must assure myself that he will not oppose us too resolutely. It is necessary to study him, to probe his mind, and observe his attitude towards us. What I am resolved to do, whatever happens, is to admit the deputies of Central Italy to Parliament.[1]

As to the cession of Nice and Savoy, however much he regretted it, Cavour believed it to be inevitable. His instinct told him that the surrender of these two provinces was the essential condition upon which the unity of Italy depended. He realized that the fulfilment of his original compact was the necessary sacrifice required to win the consent of France to the annexation of Central Italy.

> The knot of the question [he wrote soon after his return to power] appears to me to be neither the Romagna nor Tuscany, but Savoy. This has been rendered more delicate and difficult by the lack of any accord on the question between France and my predecessors. Walewski told Dabormida that he did not dream of annexing the Alpine valleys and Dabormida took his words as bar-gold. The result was that Rattazzi's instructions to the Governors were strongly anti-separatist, and they have acted accordingly. Though I have received no communication of any kind on this subject, either from Paris or Turin, though Talleyrand has assured me that he had instructions not to speak of Savoy or Nice, I have understood that we have been on the wrong road and I am trying to give our policy a different direction.[2]

But Cavour felt the necessity of going very slowly and cautiously in the matter. In view of the approaching elections he wished to keep this question in the background until the annexations were accomplished, and then the difficulty of parliamentary sanction would be

[1] Bianchi, *Stor. Doc.*, vol. viii. c. 5. See Cavour to Marliani, January 22nd. *CCN.*, vol. iii. No. 507.
[2] Bolléa, No. 201. Chiala, *Lettere*, vol. iii. No. 194.

reduced to a minimum. His immediate task was to let Napoleon know he would be loyal to the promise of Plombières and try and inspire sufficient trust to let him make the annexations first. It was just this want of trust in his loyalty that caused him the greatest difficulty.

Cavour took office on January 20th. His first official act was to dissolve the Chambers, which were still nominally in existence, and decree a general election for the beginning of April, as soon that is, as the electoral lists could be prepared. At the same time he wrote to Farini and Ricasoli to prepare the electoral lists for Emilia and Tuscany, although they were not yet annexed. His plan was that the deputies of these provinces should meet after their election, and having given their sanction to the action of their respective Governments in proclaiming union with Piedmont, come and take their seats in the Chamber at Turin.[1] This simple and direct method had, however, to be modified later by the adoption of the principle of a plebiscite.

In pursuance of his determination to go forward with annexation, Cavour, on January 27th, sent a circular to his diplomatic agents abroad with orders to give it the widest publicity. In this document, after sketching the events of the past six months, he summed up the actual position in these words:

> The prorogation of the Congress, the publication of the brochure,[2] the Emperor's letter to the Pope, and his *rapprochement* with England, these four facts, of which the least important would have been sufficient to precipitate the solution of pending questions, have rendered any longer delay impossible. Fully commented on by the European Press, they have convinced all serious minds that (i) all idea of the restoration of the dispossessed rulers must be given up; it is as impossible now at Bologna and Parma as at Florence and Modena. (ii) The only possible solution lies in the legal admission of annexation, already established in fact both in Emilia and Tuscany. (iii) The Italian populations, having

[1] Chiala, *Lettere*, vol. vi. No. 1680. Cavour to Farini.
[2] *Le Pape et le Congrès.*

waited in vain for Europe to settle their affairs upon the basis of non-intervention and respect for popular opinion, have now the duty of going forward and providing for their own Government.[1]

Two days after the issue of this circular, Cavour was confirmed in his policy by a dispatch from Lord John Russell. On January 15th the British Government had submitted to Napoleon a programme of four points as the basis of a settlement. They included, the admission of the principle of non-intervention by France and Austria, unless invited to intervene by the Five Great Powers; the withdrawal of the French troops from Italy; the recognition of non-interference by the Powers in the internal affairs of Venetia, and a guarantee from Sardinia not to send troops into Central Italy until they had again expressed their desire for union by means of elected assemblies. Sir James Hudson now informed Cavour that these proposals had been favourably received by France. This joyful news Cavour at once forwarded to Bologna and Florence, writing to Ricasoli that 'to-day it may be said that annexation was an accomplished fact and that we have reached the goal of our desires.'

But the path of union was not to be quite so easy. So far, in accordance with what he had written to D'Azeglio in London, 'that for a long time he had thought that the best policy regarding Savoy and Nice was to say nothing about it,' he had carefully kept all reference to the subject in the background, hoping to settle the annexation question before confronting the country with the inevitable sacrifice required by France. But the impatience of Napoleon or his suspicion of Cavour or inability to stem the rising demand for compensation, pushed the question to the front. On January 25th the Emperor permitted the publication of a strong article, on the claims of France to Savoy, to appear in the journal *La Patrie*, followed by a similar article two days later on Nice. The Piedmontese papers

[1] Bianchi, *Stor. Doc.*, vol. iii. c. v.

at once replied and the question immediately engrossed public opinion. Protests and demonstrations against separation from Sardinia followed in both areas, and so strong was the feeling aroused that the Government had to give a flat denial to the rumours of cession, and were promptly accused in the French Press of strangling the free expression of opinions.[1] This controversy not only upset Cavour's plans but produced unexpected results in Paris, and the Emperor published an article in *Le Constitutionnel* designed to calm the excitement. The publicity thus given to the question produced a double result. It aroused the suspicions of Lord Cowley, who asked explanations from Thouvenel, which were so unsatisfactory that the British ambassador quickly divined the truth and wrote to Lord John Russell. His reply to Cowley was to make every effort 'to dissuade the Emperor from a course of conduct that would awake in Europe those very fears and jealousies that Napoleon himself should be the last to wish to see aroused.'[2] The other result was to spur Napoleon to action before Cavour, supported by England, took steps to save the coveted provinces.

A new French Minister, the Baron de Talleyrand, had arrived in Turin during January, but owing to Victor Emmanuel being ill had not as yet presented his credentials. On February 2nd he was received by the King, to whom he handed an autograph letter from the Emperor. This letter contained Napoleon's interpretation of Russell's four points.

> To solve the existing difficulties without going back upon my word [he wrote], four points should be observed. The first is to admit the principle of non-intervention; the second is to obtain a fresh general vote in Central Italy upon their future destiny. The third, to renounce boldly and frankly all idea of encroachment upon neighbouring States; and lastly, to leave the same liberty in Savoy and Nice as in Tuscany, and

[1] Chiala, *Lettere*, vol. iv. Introd. pp. 15 ff.
[2] *Parl. Papers*, 1860.

abide by the wishes of the populations after their free expression of opinion.

He then added that, in the case of the Romagna, a Vice-Royalty under Papal Sovereignty would be necessary until such time as the Pope consented to separation.[1] Cavour, though he was far from accepting all of these proposals, seized the opportunity afforded by this letter to let Napoleon know that he was sound on the question of Nice and Savoy, and Victor Emmanuel replied by return of post: 'I can assure Your Majesty that my Government will not oppose the free manifestation of the wishes of Savoy and Nice.'[2] Cavour here laid down the principle upon which he acted throughout, the principle, that is, of universal suffrage as the deciding factor. This he adopted because it was the basis of Napoleon's right to the throne of France, and by means of it, he intended to acquire Central Italy and find some kind of justification for the surrender of Savoy and Nice.

The next day Sir James Hudson asked for an interview, and in the name of his Government requested to know if it was true that Savoy and Nice were to be surrendered to France. Cavour's reply was of the same diplomatic texture as that of Thouvenel, when asked a similar question by Lord Cowley. Sardinia, said Cavour, had no intention of 'ceding, exchanging, or selling Savoy,' but he then went on to say that 'the question of Savoy was in the hands of the good sense and feelings of the Savoyard people.' In other words, that if the union with France was proclaimed as the result of a plebiscite, Cavour would accept the decision.[3]

When Cavour's reply, revealing the obvious collusion between France and Sardinia, reached Lord John Russell, he was thoroughly indignant, and wrote hotly to Sir James Hudson that 'in the opinion of Her Majesty's Government the King of Sardinia will be-

[1] *CCN.*, vol. iii. No. 512; Bolléa, No. 193; Chiala (vol. iv. Introd.) gives a quite different letter, not reproduced elsewhere, which seems, however, to be later in date, unless two letters followed each other very quickly.

[2] *CCN.*, vol. iii. No. 524, February 3rd.

[3] Chiala, *Lettere*, vol. iv. Introd. p. 31.

smirch the arms of the House of Savoy if he yields to France, the cradle of his ancient and illustrious House.' At this moment, had he chosen to make full use of English support and been prepared to act henceforth without French assistance and to face the possibility of French diplomatic hostility, Cavour might have saved Savoy and Nice. It was a cruel predicament, but one which both Victor Emmanuel and Cavour had foreseen and upon which they had made up their minds. The truth was that the deciding factor in determining the policy of both the King and Cavour was neither France nor England, but Austria. Though Austria had not moved, there was no saying when she might, and in this case England would only protest, while France would act, and it was action alone that would save the situation. Cavour's position was difficult in the extreme. He had to retain the goodwill of France in order to keep the latent hostility of Austria in check, and he needed that of England to overcome the reluctance of Napoleon to see Italy made. Yet whatever action he took must offend one or the other, for the cession of Savoy, while it would placate France, would anger England, and its refusal, which would please England, would alienate Napoleon. The political vision of Cavour was already ranging over Umbria and Naples, and for any successful effort in the south of the Peninsula the tacit consent of France was an absolute necessity. The support of England was valuable, but that of France was vital, and for this reason Cavour prepared for the sacrifice of Savoy and Nice. But upon one thing his mind was made up, that the price paid was nothing less than Tuscany and the Romagna. Both the peace of Villafranca and the Treaty of Zürich had been signed independently of him, and in consequence he felt perfectly free to make his own bargain. In loyalty to his own treaty he would fulfil its terms, but at his own price and for nothing less.

In preparation for the struggle that he saw confronting him, Cavour sent Count Arese to Paris, where his influence with the Emperor might prove of value. At the same time Des Ambrois, who had succeeded Villa-marina on his transfer to Naples, asked to be relieved, and Nigra, as a simple chargé d'affaires, was sent to Paris to take his place. Napoleon's position was almost as difficult as that of Cavour. He had accepted Russell's four points, while still bound by the terms of Villafranca, and the two were incompatible, one of them had to go, and he decided to repudiate Villafranca. Thouvenel was instructed to communicate with Berlin, St. Petersburg, and Vienna on the significance of the British suggestion and to intimate to Austria that Napoleon could no longer be bound by the terms of Villafranca and Zürich. When the replies came to hand it was seen that Russia and Prussia both disliked on principle the right of the people to choose their own sovereigns and reserved their liberty of action. Austria, to whom the new arrangement was explained as the creation of a buffer state, designed to prevent the mutual jealousies of the two countries for predominance in Italy, replied that if a revision was necessary, the original idea of a confederation appeared to her to offer the best solution, but implied that she would not impose a veto or allow the new arrangement to become a *casus belli*.[1] The road to annexation now seemed clear of obstacles, when Napoleon threw everything once more into confusion by a new proposal.

Having thus freed himself from the obligations imposed by the Treaty of Zürich, Napoleon turned his attention to those contained in Russell's four points. Although he had accepted the principle of non-intervention, this did not exclude, in his opinion, an attempt to obtain a solution on lines suggested by himself. He was not only uneasy at the reservations made by Prussia and Russia, dreading above all else a hostile alliance of the Northern Powers, but he could not reconcile himself to the union of Tuscany with Piedmont. 'If union,' he had said, 'crosses the Appenines,

[1] Thouvenel's dispatch and the reply are in *Parl. Correspondence*, 1860, part ii.

Italy is made,' and this he did not wish to see realized. To Monsignor Sacconi, the Papal Nuncio in Paris, Napoleon at this time repeated this opinion. 'I will not allow further annexations to Sardinia,' he said, 'the interests of France, as those of Rome and Naples, require that Central Italy is formed into a strong Kingdom of conservative tendencies, based on the idea of a confederation.'[1] He therefore now proposed the following solution: (i) the definite and immediate annexation to Piedmont of Parma, Piacenza, and Modena; (ii) the creation of a vicariat, embracing the three Papal Legations, to be exercised by Victor Emmanuel under the suzerainty of the Pope; (iii) the erection of Tuscany into a separate Kingdom under a Prince of the House of Savoy; (iv) the cession of Nice and Savoy to France.

Such a scheme was now utterly impracticable. The first clause would not satisfy Piedmont, and the third had already been rejected by Tuscany. As to the suggested vicariat, it had already been put forward and rejected by the Pope. Immediately after Thouvenel's dispatch to Austria on January 31st, realizing the weakened position of Austria as a supporter of Papal policy, Cavour had dispatched the Abbé Stellardi to Rome with an autograph letter from Victor Emmanuel making this very suggestion of a vicariat, which the Pope had refused to consider; moreover, the letter having been passed on to Napoleon, Thouvenel had written strongly to Talleyrand about Cavour's 'intrigues and manœuvres calculated to multiply complications.' A fortnight later he was making the same proposal himself.[2]

Before being put into their final form these proposals were shown confidentially both to Count Arese and Lord Cowley. The former wrote at once to Cavour warning him what to expect, describing it as a kind of ultimatum à l'eau de rose.[3] Two courses were open to

[1] Bianchi, Stor. Doc., vol. viii. p. 389.
[2] Chiala, Lettere, vol. iii. p. 201. Bianchi, Stor. Doc., vol. viii. p. 399, for Letter and Instructions. Thouvenel to Talleyrand, February 24th.
[3] Bonfadini, Vita di F. Arese, February 15th.

Piedmont, Thouvenel said to Arese in their interview, either acceptance of these proposals with the subsequent support and backing of France, or an independent line of action, in which latter case France would at once withdraw her troops from Italy, consult her own interests, and leave Piedmont to face alone what he termed 'the most perilous chances,' which meant, of course, the risk of war with Austria. When they were shown to Lord Cowley he at once objected that they infringed the principle of non-intervention. That being so, he said, he could not hold out much hope of their acceptance by the English Government. He thought, moreover, that the circumstances in which the Emperor felt justified in claiming Nice and Savoy, did not arise if Tuscany was made into a separate Kingdom. Lord Cowley's opinion was fully endorsed by Lord John Russell, who, when informed of the proposed terms, replied at once that, though he could not object to these proposals being made to Sardinia, the British Government could neither approve nor support them, to which Thouvenel in his turn replied that he trusted that Her Majesty's Government would, at least, not put difficulties in the way of Piedmont's possible acceptance, by advising them to persist in annexing Tuscany.[1]

Though Cavour was at the time under the impression that the new plan had the backing of England, for Thouvenel had incorrectly informed Arese that that was the case,[2] he did not hesitate to reject it, and telegraphed at once to Arese that 'rather than concur in forcing Tuscany to accept a solution of which she did not approve, he resigned himself to see the French troops withdrawn and *to run the most perilous chances.*' He followed this up with an urgent letter to General Fanti, his Minister for War. 'It is absolutely indispensable,' he wrote, 'not to lose a minute, to spare neither expense nor effort in preparation for all eventualities. You realize what these words mean: I know the energy of your patriotism: I need say no more.'

[1] *Parl. Corresp.*, 1860, part iii.   [2] Chiala, vol. iii. p. 210. Cavour to Fanti.

Cavour had to deal with this situation from Milan, where with the King and Court he was taking part in a whirl of gaieties in honour of the new union with Piedmont. 'Cavour is never still, he goes everywhere, receives every one, and is the gayest of the gay,' wrote Castelli. But in between dances, so to speak, Cavour dealt with the crisis with indomitable firmness. If Waterloo was to follow, he was prepared to face it. To Ricasoli he telegraphed, 'the moment to take energetic decisions approaches, but not yet arrived; count upon my devotion and, if necessary, even audacity.' Orders followed to Fanti to be ready to mobilize four classes and to prepare to call up the Lombards. He found time to visit Brescia to inspect an armament factory, and wrote complaining of the 'traditional slowness of the artillery so distinguished in other respects.' He returned to Turin before the end of February.

On February 24th Thouvenel's ultimatum was ready. It was dispatched simultaneously to Turin and London with a covering letter of explanation for England. Cavour did not yet know the real opinion of the British Cabinet in regard to the new proposals, but Palmerston had expressed the opinion that he should stand by the four points. Although Cavour was determined to reject the proposals and take his own line whatever it might cost, a joint *démarche* from France and England would be a formidable proposition to flout. It was, therefore, with some uneasiness that he waited to hear whether England associated herself with the French proposals. On the morning of February 28th, Cavour sat writing a letter to Arese on the situation. At two o'clock he had an appointment with the Baron de Talleyrand, who was to read to him Thouvenel's dispatch. 'I will close this letter,' he wrote, 'after the interview is over.' At this point Sir James Hudson was announced. No sooner had his visitor departed than Cavour resumed his letter. 'Sir James Hudson has this moment left my room,' he wrote. 'He came to communicate to me a dispatch from Lord John, who has charged him to declare officially that England disapproves entirely the French proposals, because she finds them subversive of the independence of Italy. I believe Lord Cowley has made an identical communication to the French Government.' In the nick of time Lord John had stolen Thouvenel's thunder.

In due course Talleyrand arrived for his interview. The substance of the dispatch Cavour already knew. It differed only on one point in its final form, and that was for the worse, for the sentences suggesting an Italian Prince for the throne of Tuscany was now omitted. The reasons by which the French Foreign Secretary supported his case were singularly unconvincing, and, further, revealed a genuine failure to understand the real difficulties of the situation. The first reason put forward against annexation was that Piedmont would be incapable of 'assimilating so much new territory', that she would suffer, in fact, from a kind of political indigestion, which, considering the marked ability shown by Piedmont since 1848, was as uncomplimentary as untrue. The next was that the desire of Tuscany to unite to Piedmont was not due to the attraction of Piedmont but to a desire for war with Austria, which was again unhappy, since Tuscany was the least warlike state in Italy. Thirdly, he argued that behind the desire for union was an *arrière-pensée* to recover Venetia and to disturb the possessions of the Holy Father and the King of Naples. Then came the ultimatum. If Piedmont accepted her solution, France would be with her and behind her. If, on the other hand, she took her own line, which Piedmont was fully entitled to do, the Emperor would not at any price consent to take upon himself the responsibility for such a situation, but would take the interests of France as the sole guide of his conduct. The dispatch ended with a 'few words on Savoy and Nice,' to the effect that, 'although by the arrangements developed in this dispatch, the annexation of all the states of Central Italy to Sardinia would not be complete, it is certain that, from the point of view of external relations, it would be equivalent, in reality, to an analogous result,' and therefore Savoy and Nice must go to France.

There was a meanness about this final sentence that must have filled Cavour with disgust. After proposing to deprive Piedmont of Tuscany, and having carefully left a loophole for the installation of a French or Austrian princeling at Florence, and having prepared a veritable bed of thorns for Piedmont in the Romagna, this was to be considered as 'in reality an analogous result' to annexation.

Cavour having listened patiently to the recital of Thouvenel's ultimatum proceeded to give a polite but firm refusal. Even if Piedmont accepted these terms in deference to France, he said, they would be rejected by Tuscany, the Romagna, and the Pope. All he could do was to submit them to Ricasoli and Farini, suggest a vote by universal suffrage, and loyally abide by the decision. He then confronted the French Minister with the dispatch of Lord John Russell, handed to him an hour before by Sir James Hudson, expressing England's opinion that the French proposals were 'subversive of the independence of Italy.' Faced by a position so different from what he had expected, Talleyrand withdrew to telegraph for fresh instructions, and Cavour turned to finish his letter to Count Arese in these words:

Talleyrand has just left me after a conference lasting 2½ hours. I have sent you a *résumé* of my reply by telegraph. To-morrow I will try to write an official dispatch to Nigra. In the meantime I beg you to make it clear that we cannot force Central Italy to accept a solution contrary to the wishes of the people, and that at a moment when every one was convinced that France was ready to give them complete satisfaction. A Cabinet that refused annexation after approval by universal suffrage would not receive ten votes in the Chamber. The Emperor cannot ask us to commit suicide. If we must perish, let us fall with honour at the hands of our enemies. I shall be desolated to be abandoned by the Emperor, but, I repeat it, I believe it to be better to run the risk of being crushed by Austria than to lose all prestige and to be reduced to being able to govern only by bayonets. For nations, as for individuals, there are circumstances when the voice of honour speaks louder than that of prudence.[1]

In response to Talleyrand's telegram, Thouvenel replied, admitting the *revirement* in England's policy, deprecating any appeal to a plebiscite (of which the result was a foregone conclusion in favour of annexation), and advising delay until a fresh plan could be devised. But time was the one thing Cavour was determined not to grant. Realizing that Russell's dispatch had ruined the success of the French proposals, and knowing that Napoleon could not refuse to assent to a verdict based upon the same conditions as those by which he held his throne, Cavour acted at once. Thouvenel's dispatch was immediately forwarded to Modena and Florence, and the vote by universal suffrage no less promptly accepted, and on March 1st the preliminary notices were sent out through Tuscany and Emilia. In vain Talleyrand, urged on by Thouvenel, endeavoured to restrain Cavour's haste; to all his appeals Cavour replied that it was too late, Ricasoli and Farini had gone too far to be stopped.[2]

On March 1st the Emperor was to address the Corps Législatif at the opening of the new session, and Thouvenel's dispatch had been carefully timed so that in case of a favourable reply, a clause could be inserted 'having for its effect to disengage the word of the King *vis-à-vis* to the people of Tuscany and to shift the responsibility for the new arrangement from Sardinia to France.'[3] The reply, however, being a refusal, Napoleon, realizing as he must have done that his plan had failed and Tuscany was lost, put in another of a very different kind, boldly announcing that the terri-

[1] Thouvenel's dispatch and Cavour's reply are in *Correspondence*, 1860, part iii. Cavour's letter to Arese. Chiala, vol. iii. p. 220; *CCN.*, vol. iii. No. 604; and Bonfadini, *Vita di F. Arese*, p. 233, which alone contains the passage referring to Hudson's interview.

[2] 'La scène,' says Cavour's French biographer, Matter, 'est tout à fait jolie.'

[3] *CCN.*, vol. iii. No. 606. Nigra to Cavour.

torial enlargement of Piedmont necessitated, as a measure of safety for France, a demand for 'the French slopes of the mountains,' a euphemism for Nice and Savoy.

Napoleon's words created a sensation throughout Europe and an outburst of indignation and distrust, especially in England and Germany. On receiving by telegraph a summary of the Emperor's speech, Cavour at once took steps to make his position clear in the eyes of Europe. He dispatched an official note to Nigra, in which, after restating Thouvenel's declaration that France had not the least intention of effecting territorial changes contrary to the wishes of the population, or without consulting the great Powers and taking into due consideration the interests of the Swiss, he laid down once again his principle of nationality. The Sardinian Government, he said, would never cede or exchange any part of the national territory, but, at a moment when they demanded that Central Italy should decide upon its own fate, they could not refuse to allow the same freedom to Nice and Savoy *if pronounced in a legal manner and in accordance with the directions laid down by Parliament.*[1] The next day he wrote to the Cavaliere Marliani in London to explain to Lord Palmerston and Lord John Russell that 'in calling the attention of the French Government to the fact that the great Powers were to be consulted, and that the annexation should not be proceeded with until after the vote of the populations and the sanction of Parliament, we have done everything possible in the position in which we are placed, to remove all cause of uneasiness from Europe.'

The storm of indignation raised in England by the Emperor's phrase about Savoy, coupled with the untoward reminder from Cavour of his own conditions, redoubled Napoleon's determination to hasten the cession of the ill-fated provinces. Talleyrand was,

[1] When Cavour's note was published in the *Moniteur*, these words, on which his whole case rested, were deliberately omitted.

therefore, instructed to demand a secret treaty, to be signed at once, ceding Nice and Savoy. Cavour, though somewhat disgusted with Napoleon's indecent haste to get his pound of flesh, acquiesced, and the treaty was drawn up and signed on March 12th. On the same evening came the first notices of the overwhelming success of the voting in Central Italy and the certainty of the union of Tuscany with Piedmont. The next day Lord Palmerston, expressing in the House his genuine satisfaction with the result of this vote, took occasion to pay the following very handsome tribute to Cavour:

> In regard to the Italian statesman, who has so often been censured during this debate—Count Cavour—I limit myself to say that, whatever may be the opinion of those whose political designs, thanks to him, have failed, Italy, present and future, will regard him as one of the greatest patriots that have ever adorned the history of any nation. I know no country that owes so much gratitude to any of its sons, as Italy owes to him. Firm in the knowledge of what he has done for Italy, he may well disregard what foreign critics may say as to his actions.

Now although Cavour regarded the cession of Nice and Savoy as inevitable, and was perfectly ready to assume the responsibility for it, he was determined that it should not be done without a vote of the population and parliamentary acceptance. It was the basic principle of his policy that every step he took towards Italian unity should receive constitutional sanction. Napoleon, on the other hand, was determined to get hold of these provinces at the earliest possible moment. He regarded Cavour's constitutional scruples as finesse, and suspected that he was trying to delay the cession, hoping that Europe, and especially England, would interfere and stop it. He now bethought himself of a decisive method of reaching his objective. The recall of the troops from Lombardy had been imminent for some time. On March 7th Marshal Vaillant had received a telegram to be ready to return homewards in twenty-four hours. The Emperor now proposed to send one-half via Nice and the other via Chambéry, and thus occupy the provinces by military force. When this plan was exposed to Nigra by Thouvenel he was naturally indignant. Such a step, he told the French Minister, was as illegitimate as dishonourable. It would be everywhere condemned by public opinion and regarded either as a hostile act towards Piedmont or as the consequence of a secret treaty which they dare not avow. But, as he foresaw, that if, in his present mood the Emperor was not given satisfaction, the fate of Savoy and Nice would one day be settled by an announcement in the *Moniteur* and a simultaneous military occupation, he proposed to Cavour to convert the secret treaty into a public one, which while safeguarding the vote and parliamentary sanction, would render the passage of French troops legitimate.[1]

In the first rush of anger at Napoleon's want of trust and arbitrary methods, Cavour replied hotly:

> Tell Thouvenel that France can occupy and annex Nice and Savoy, but neither the King nor the Government will ever sign a public treaty without stipulating the manner of votation, nor will they allow the vote to be taken under the menace of French bayonets. We are ready to use all our influence to produce a solution satisfying to France, but we will never consent to methods which are contrary to our institutions or which wound the national honour.[2]

He accepted, however, the idea of a public treaty to be submitted to Parliament, provided it contained a clear definition as to the manner upon which the voting should take place. So Benedetti was sent to Turin with full powers, and the treaty was signed without difficulty on March 24th with Cavour's two stipulations duly included. The final scene has been described by an eyewitness. Cavour, silent and preoccupied, walked up and down the room while the treaty was read. This finished, Cavour with a firm hand signed it, and stood aside for Talleyrand to append his signature. No sooner

---

[1] *CCN.*, vol. iii. No. 696, March 19th.
[2] *CCN.*, vol. iii. No. 699, March 20th.

was that done than Cavour's face cleared, his habitual smile returned, and he remarked: 'Now we are accomplices, Baron!' What lay behind that remark in the far-seeing brain of Cavour, Talleyrand little guessed, the next six months would reveal it.[1]

Cavour was under no delusion as to the gravity of what he had done in ceding two provinces of the Kingdom without the consent of Parliament.

> You know that a treaty entailing a modification of territory [he wrote to Nigra] is only of value if Parliament has given consent to it. So in signing this treaty I commit a highly unconstitutional act, which might have very grave consequences for me. If the Chamber consisted of men like Dabormida and Carutti I should run the risk of being accused of high treason and of finding myself condemned, if not like Strafford to lose my head, at least to some years in a fortress, like Polignac. In spite of this I have not hesitated to advise the King to sign the treaty, for which I assume all the responsibility. But I do not intend to tear up the Statuto and do without Parliament. I believe I can guarantee the adhesion of Parliament, neither the King nor I have any doubt about this, for he risks his crown and I, if not my head, at least my reputation, which is far more dear to me.[2]

On March 25th, the day after the treaty was signed, the general election took place. The fears of Cavour that the agitation in Nice and Savoy would react disastrously on the Government majority were happily not realized, and any adverse influence the excitement may have produced was more than compensated for by the loyal support given to him in the newly acquired provinces. Cavour was returned for eight constituencies, including Turin, Milan, and Florence. The clerical party was almost wiped out, which Cavour regretted, for he wished all interests in the country to be represented.

On April 2nd Parliament was opened by the King in the Palace Madama at Turin. The hall was packed to the doors, and the patriotic phrases of the King's speech were greeted with frantic applause. It was a brilliant assembly. Cavour, smiling and happy, showing

[1] D'Ideville, *Journal d'un Diplomat en Italie.*   [2] Bolléa, No. 234.

little signs of the strain of all that he had been through, stood beside the King. Ricasoli and Farini, now Members of the Order of the Annunciata and cousins of the King, the one Governor of Tuscany, the other Cavour's right-hand man as Minister for Internal Affairs, were both present. D'Azeglio, Cesare Alfieri, who had urged the first reforms on Charles Albert in 1847, Rattazzi, Minghetti, and Lanza, the last three all future Prime Ministers, were noticeable figures. Manzoni, the doyen of Italian literary personalities; Sommeiller, the engineer of the Mont Cenis tunnel; Gualterio, the historian, added distinction to the assembly. Garibaldi, though elected, was not present. Never, perhaps, were so many, whose names have passed into Italian history, gathered together under one roof.

The Royal sitting over, the business of the session commenced. The first trouble was with Garibaldi, who having been born at Nice was raging over its cession to France. His anger at being made 'a foreigner' in Italy was doubled by the thought that his birthplace was to be handed over to Napoleon, whom he hated as 'the man of December' and the extinguisher of the Roman Republic of 1848. Fortunately he had had three months in which to cool the first effervescence of his wrath. As early as January 17th he had sent Colonel Türr to the King to ask if Nice was to be ceded to France, with instructions to 'answer me at once by telegraph Yes or No!' Victor Emmanuel, after he had recovered from the peremptory audacity of the request, replied, 'very well, yes! but tell the General that not only Nice but Savoy as well! And that if I can reconcile myself to lose the cradle of my family and my race, he can do the same.' On April 6th, four days after the session opened, and before the necessary officials and committees had been properly constituted, Garibaldi came down to the Chamber to interrogate the Government on the cession of Nice. Garibaldi was out of his element in the Chamber. He had a hearty contempt for politics and politicians, and, moreover, he was

opposed by a political strategist of the first order. It
was no part of Cavour's policy at this point to have a
stormy debate on the question of Nice, and no sooner
had Garibaldi begun to speak, than Cavour rose and
pointed out that to interrogate the Ministers before
the Chamber was properly constituted, was not only
out of order but unconstitutional, and he should refuse
to answer any questions addressed to him. Cavour was
right, and after an appeal to make this question an
exception had failed, Cavour carried his point and Garibaldi had to postpone his question until the 12th. On
that day he reopened his attack, but once again he was
foiled by Cavour.

Garibaldi's speech, in which the hand of others better
informed than himself was evident, had the virtue of
being short and of being delivered with self-restraint.
After tracing the history of the union with Piedmont,
Garibaldi denounced the treaty as being in contradiction with Article 5 of the Statuto:[1] accused the Government of exercising undue pressure upon the people:
stigmatized the treaty as 'human traffic,' and demanded
that the votation should be suspended until the treaty
had been sanctioned by Parliament. In his reply, Cavour
said that the treaty was not an isolated fact but one in
a series, of which some were already completed, while
others remained for the future to determine. When the
proper occasion arose the Chamber should have the
fullest opportunity for debate, but until the treaty was
presented, he deprecated all discussion. He begged the
Chamber to leave the matter over until then. All he
would say now was that the cession was inevitable and
he did not believe it was unconstitutional. Though
other speakers followed, and an attempt was made to
enlarge the debate, the majority accepted Cavour's suggestion, and passed an order of the day expressing no
blame, but recommending the Government to safeguard
liberty in voting and maintain the constitutional

[1] Art. 5 required the assent of Parliament to any cession of territory.
Cavour had safeguarded this in the treaty.

guarantees. Garibaldi did not get another chance of impeaching the Ministry, for when the Bill was brought in for approval, he was at the crisis of his career on the heights above Palermo. Three days later Victor Emmanuel, accompanied by Cavour and the rest of the Cabinet, left Turin for a visit to Tuscany and Emilia, and the Chambers were adjourned until May 1st.[1]

Cavour at this time was very worried and discouraged. The strength of the opposition in the Chamber, following in the wake of Rattazzi and Garibaldi, proved much stronger than he had anticipated, and gave him much uneasiness. The Government candidate for President had only been elected at the second ballot. 'It is a victory of the same sort as Malplaquet,' Cavour wrote to Nigra; 'it only requires two or three more like it and we shall be lost completely.' Though he had managed to keep the debate upon Nice to the constitutional issue, he confessed that he had found it 'very thorny and difficult to defend.' The debate was in fact neither a victory nor a defeat, but it strengthened his opinion that the passage of the treaty would be no easy matter, and that even a Government defeat was not an impossibility. The position of the Cabinet was still further weakened by the behaviour of France over Savoy and Nice. Once the treaty was signed, Napoleon, in his anxiety to get his new provinces, completely ignored the vote and the parliamentary sanction required by the treaty, and behaved as if they were already French provinces. Over one of the outstanding questions, the delimitation of the new frontier, there were endless difficulties; General Fanti, the Minister for War, repeatedly threatening to resign.

> The conduct of France is provocative and irritating [Cavour writes on April 4th]. In spite of what they say, their presence in Savoy and Nice has taken on all the character of a permanent occupation, they have appointed *commandants de place* from the Staff Officers, just as if it was a matter of French

[1] As some of the Powers instructed their Ministers not to accompany the King, as a protest against the annexation, the Corps Diplomatique was not invited.

territorial divisions. Such a way of behaving makes this unhappy question more complicated and difficult than ever. The retirement of Fanti would ruin me utterly. I shall make every effort to pass the treaty and shall perhaps succeed, but that finished, I shall definitely leave office, my heart full of disgust for the French alliance.

On April 18th and 22nd the voting took place, first in Nice and then in Savoy, and the result was almost unanimous in favour of union with France. This made things easier, for ratification by Parliament after such a majority was inevitable. But the effect on the strength of the Cabinet was keenly felt by Cavour, 'in rushing through the cession of Nice and Savoy,' he writes on April 27th, 'without showing the least regard for the just susceptibilities of the country, the French Government has succeeded in destroying the influence of the Ministry both at home and abroad.'

Now Cavour's position was, in reality, far too strong for defeat to be possible, and he must have known it; his insistence on his weakness thus suggests some ulterior purpose, and it is to be noticed that this is the very argument he used to France as a reason for not stopping Garibaldi and the Thousand, who sailed for Sicily only a fortnight later. The same reason may account for the delay in opening the final debate on the treaty, which did not take place until May 25th, for as long as the treaty was not ratified Cavour had some hold on Napoleon, who knew well enough that his influence would be decisive and this perhaps was in part responsible for the mild nature of the French protests when Garibaldi's departure became known.

The result of the plebiscite, if it made the approval of Parliament a foregone conclusion, did not rob the debate of interest.

When the debate began, the great majority of votes cast in favour of union with France in both Nice and Savoy was unhesitatingly attributed by the opponents of cession to pressure and manipulation, but the evidence was not convincing. There were many powerful reasons contributing to such a result. As Cavour pointed out in his speech, all the material interests of both areas lay in the direction of France rather than Italy. France provided the main market for their produce; France absorbed all their superfluous labour; France found much of the capital invested in the country. 'When, with the introduction of the railways,' said Cavour, 'I saw Paris brought within 12 hours of Chambéry, whereas, to reach Turin 20 or 24 hours was required, from that day, in my opinion, the annexation of Savoy to France was accomplished.' No less convincing were the inducements held out by the French agents. The priests would receive a substantial increase of pay, the Government officials, schoolmasters, and civil servants would have both higher pay and increased pensions. The contadini who migrated into France during the winter would be relieved of the trouble and expense of passports. In language and literature Savoy was French, and Nice was as much French as Italian. Even the army, loyal as it was to the House of Savoy, could appreciate the advantage of serving only seven years with the colours instead of eleven. The attitude of the Government was perhaps a deciding element, for the loyalists found their efforts, if not discouraged, at least treated with an indifference and neglect which revealed the secret intentions of the Cabinet.

The principal opponents of the treaty were Rattazzi, the most influential member of the late Government, and Guerrazzi, who, without the oratorical gifts of Brofferio, had temporarily assumed his mantle as the spokesman of the extreme Left; for thanks chiefly to Cavour, Brofferio had been rejected in both of the constituencies he had contested. The methods and aims of Cavour's two antagonists were entirely different. Rattazzi had no intention of coming to close quarters with Cavour, he knew too well the powers of his redoubtable opponent, and carefully avoiding all irritating personalities, he spoke *on* the treaty, not against it. His first charge was that by this treaty the Government had deserted the great policy of Nationality to which it owed its past success, by ceding Italian soil to a foreign country. His next accusation was that Nice at least could have been saved if the Government had not weakly yielded, and lastly, he blamed the treaty for the absence of any guarantee that the annexation of Tuscany and Emilia would be recognized and supported by France. Guerrazzi, on the other hand, rushed in where Rattazzi feared to tread. His speech was a personal attack on Cavour, bitter, sarcastic, and backed with all the vindictiveness of disappointed ambition. On the political side, in contrast to the robust realism of Cavour, Guerrazzi displayed that pathetic trust in the idealistic goodness of human nature that was so often characteristic of the extreme democratic creed.

> If it had been clearly put before France [he declared] how much blood and treasure Italy had poured out when she followed France from Madrid to Moscow; or, coming to a nearer epoch, if she had been reminded of our work in the Crimea; how Italy, forced to choose between a brother and a friend, had chosen the brother and fought the friend: of the money spent and not refunded: of the dangerin curred in case of disaster, from Austria armed and threatening— I believe, so great is my trust in the generosity of France— that she would have said to us: 'Yes, it is true, rather than accept compensations, we confess ourselves always in debt to you!'

But the pith of the speech was his impeachment of Cavour. In his unbridled egotism he believed that his words would be a 'knife-thrust to his heart.' He had found, he thought, an effective historical parallel to the conduct of Cavour in the incident of Lord Clarendon and the sale of Dunkirk. This is how he put it:

> English history records a fact very similar to that which we discuss to-day. Indeed, to my mind a hundred times less serious. The Earl of Clarendon was a very influential and powerful statesman. He ruled the King with no gentle hand and Parliament with stern severity. This latter, though with an ill grace, supported him. Thinking in his pride that he

could do anything, he suddenly thought of selling Dunkirk to France, putting forward (as usual) arguments of gratitude, of present benefit, and future advantages; in reality to make money for himself. The King let him do it. The bargain settled, he asked approval from the Council of the Crown, which refused it absolutely. He did not ask the consent of Parliament, for, as Macaulay says, he attached no value to it. Accused by Seymour, the House of Commons unanimously decided to impeach him. He tried to resist, but warned by the change in public opinion, saved himself by flight. Condemned to perpetual exile, he died at Rouen, unhinged in mind by his disgrace, and even more, by the consciousness of having too well deserved it.

This little extract from history was packed with innuendoes. The allusion to Clarendon's treatment of the King and Parliament; the suggestion of self-advantage; were all to be found in the current scandal of the day about Cavour.

Cavour's reply to these attacks was a truly masterly performance. The object of his speech was not merely to defend the treaty before the Chamber. He was speaking, he knew, not simply to Italy, but to Europe. His purpose was to explain his policy to Europe, to show its consistency in the past and to reveal its necessary continuance. He meant to drive home the principle of non-intervention, with his face turned to the south. He began his speech with a sentence that at once won for him the sympathy of the Chamber:

If some of the previous speakers [he said] had been able to read the secrets of my heart, if they had been able to appraise how much sorrow it has suffered, perchance, they would have tempered their words; perchance, the honourable Deputy Castelloni-Fantoni would not have launched against me the arrows of his indignant eloquence, and the honorable Guerrazzi would have spared me that full measure of irony, sarcasm, and epigram, with which he has embittered this grave and unhappy discussion.

Then he turned on Guerrazzi:

The honourable member has reminded me of Lord Clarendon; of how he was accused by the Commons, exiled by the

King, condemned to die abroad, and all this for the sale of Dunkirk to France. The honourable member will allow me to add that had Lord Clarendon, in defence of that policy, so much condemned by Parliament, been able to claim that he had freed some millions of English subjects from a foreign yoke, and added some counties to the royal domesne, perhaps Parliament would not have been so severe nor Charles II so ungrateful, to the most faithful of his subjects. But, Gentlemen, since the honourable member wished to give me a lesson in history he should have finished it. He should have reminded me of who those men were that were his adversaries, who accused him, shared the spoils of his fall, and followed him to power. Had he done so he would have told us that the adversaries of Lord Clarendon were that famous group of men, united by no past actions, by no common principles, by no political idea, save the most unbridled egotism. Those men drawn from all parties, professing every variety of principle, in turn Puritans, Presbyterians, Episcopalians, and even perhaps Catholics; men that one day were republicans, the next extreme royalists; demagogues in the Piazza, courtiers in the palace; tribunes of the people in Parliament; favourers of reaction and extreme methods in the Royal Council; those men in short that history has branded with the stigma of the name 'Cabal.' After having thus completed the history lesson of the honourable member, I leave the Chamber and the country to judge what practical lessons may be drawn to fit our case.

It was a severe but deserved exposure, for Guerrazzi and his friends had been a veritable Cabal, conspiring to keep Cavour from power. Republicans by repute, they had sunned themselves gladly in the warmth of the Royal palace, and Cavour's description fitted them like a glove and the Chamber applauded the justice of the denunciation.

Having disposed of Guerrazzi, Cavour plunged into the heart of the question. The policy of the Government had from the outset been based on two principles, in internal affairs, that of Liberty; abroad, that of Nationality. This he illustrated by a survey of national policy from 1850 up to the Treaty of Zürich. Why then, he asked, was the treaty necessary? What was the reason of it? The answer was that it was an integral part of their political system. The cession of Nice and Savoy did not infringe the principle of Nationality, because they were not Italians but French, in language, culture, situation, and interest. It did not infringe the principle of liberty, for, having adopted universal suffrage in regard to Central Italy it could not be refused to Nice and Savoy. Their fate was in their own hands. What then were the recompenses received for the loss they had sustained. The Treaty of Zürich was one, bringing them Lombardy; the Emperor's letter to the Pope was another, for it established the principle of the destruction of the temporal power. On this Cavour spoke strongly, for he was anxious that Europe should realize that the temporal power was doomed, before the time came to destroy it. 'This letter', he declared, 'marks a memorable epoch in the history of Italy; with this letter the Emperor, in my opinion, has acquired a title to the gratitude of the Italians not less than that which he obtained by the battle of Solferino. Because with that letter he put an end to the rule of the priests which is perhaps as harmful to Italy as the predomi- nance of Austria.' Lastly, there was the recompense of Central Italy, which could not have been acquired without the cession of these two provinces. To prove this last assertion he analysed the condition of France. The French support of Italy, absolutely vital as it was, could not be called unanimous. They had against them large and influential sections of the nation. The Legitimists, the Ultramontanes, and above all the com- mercial interests, who condemned Italian unity because it lowered the funds. They had on their side the Emperor and the masses. 'Now, Gentlemen,' he went on, 'if, to the hostility of these various parties was added, I will not say the hostility, but merely the in- difference of the masses, the Emperor, however great his sympathy for us, however much he might be con- vinced of the utility of the Italian alliance, could not translate it into fact, because even his power has certain

limits. Now, gentlemen, I say it with profound conviction, to maintain the mass of the French people
favourable to Italy, the cession of Nice and Savoy was
a necessity. Whether rightly or wrongly I do not wish
to discuss, but they believed and still believe, that these
provinces belong by right to France. It is a false
opinion may be, but that this opinion exists is a fact
that no one who knows France can in good faith deny.'
Then to lend still further weight to this declaration,
Cavour quoted a letter he had received from Alessandro
Bixio: 'Mio caro,' he had written, 'for the love of
heaven, for the love of Italy, sign the Treaty: sign it
if you want the French alliance, because, rightly or
wrongly, if you hesitate, if you refuse, your country,
Italy, will lose all sympathy in France.'

One last point remained to be dealt with, which
Rattazzi had more than once emphasized, the question
as to what guarantee France had offered for the stability
of the new Kingdom in return for the ceded provinces.
In reply Cavour boldly answered that guarantee there
was none. 'Not only,' he continued, 'is there no
guarantee, but we have never asked for one, and I will
go farther and add that, if one had been offered to us,
we should have refused it. To us it is sufficient that
France has solemnly, openly, not to us, but to Europe,
declared that she would respect in Italy the principle of
non-intervention.' He then went on to point out that
such a guarantee as was asked for by Rattazzi would
inevitably entail a species of control, a real tutelage:
'there are certain questions of opinion, certain considerations,' he continued cautiously, 'upon which we
do not see eye to eye with our neighbours across the
Alps, and authoritative advice given to us under the
right of guarantee, might prove very inconvenient and
impede the natural development of events in Italy.'
With Garibaldi at the gates of Palermo there could be
little doubt as to what Cavour was alluding to, and the
Chamber understood and applauded. Finally, reviewing
the policy of the Government as a whole he maintained

that no other system was possible. Two alternatives presented themselves. The one was to give up the bold forward policy hitherto followed and adopt that of economy and internal reform. But to do this in the face of the hostile forces with which they were surrounded would be suicidal. The other possible line of action was to reject the treaty, antagonize France, and assume a position of isolation, which would be equally disastrous. In his opinion the country was too deeply committed to change its course. They must maintain their alliances, and settle all impending questions with the support and approval of their allies. He trusted the Chamber was of his opinion and would vote for the treaty.

Cavour's speech determined the acceptance of the treaty. Though it was characterized by passages of special pleading, especially where he tried to prove that Savoy and Nice were not Italian provinces in the true sense, it was a brilliant effort. The debate continued for some days, but when the division took place 229 votes were cast for acceptance with 35 negatives and 23 abstentions. The debate created little excitement, for the interval of two months since the signing of the treaty had reconciled Piedmont to the inevitable. Besides, the thoughts of Italy were no longer in the north but in the south, where, amid the orange and lemon groves that fringe the Conca d'Oro, the fate of Italy was at that moment being decided in the barricaded streets of Palermo.

XII. CAVOUR AND THE THOUSAND

IN the policy of Cavour Italian independence had always taken precedence of Italian unity. But the two could not remain entirely separated, and at the beginning of 1859, while endeavouring to procure the intervention of France and war with Austria, Cavour had opened negotiations with Florence and Naples. His idea, then, was to secure a union of the three States on the basis of national independence and constitutional government. When war became a reality, the predominance of France induced him to send a special envoy, the Count di Salmour, to Naples, to sound the Government as to an offensive and defensive alliance, the immediate object being to get the help of the Neapolitan army. All these attempts failed. After Villafranca, Cavour having left office, the new Ministry transferred the Marquis Villamarina from Paris to Naples with instructions to promote friendly relations between the two Governments. On his return to power Cavour confirmed this attitude, adding that 'Villamarina must take care not to give the least support to plots against the Government as any revolution in the Two Sicilies would be ruinous to Italy.'[1] These sentiments he repeated later, writing: 'I approve strongly of your prudence and with you I believe that at this moment it is of the greatest importance to stop all revolutionary activity in Italy.'

Towards a policy of friendship with Naples, Cavour was urged by all the Powers. Despite the shocking condition of Southern Italy not one of the Powers was willing to leave Naples to her fate. The dread of revolu-

[1] Chiala, vol. iii, February 11th.

tion and, perhaps, the anticipated intervention of
Russia, whose support of Naples was a maxim of policy,
led them all alike to bolster up the Bourbon throne.
But even Russia saw that only a radical change of heart
could save the young King.

> It is not to the interest of Napoleon [said Gortshakoff to the
> Neapolitan Minister] to extend the revolution to the south
> of Italy. Lord Russell has assured Baron Brunnow that the
> English Cabinet is of the same opinion. Piedmont follows
> the line of a revolutionary, who having obtained power, turns
> conservative. There is no danger for you from outside, if
> you yourselves do not provoke it by an intervention in the
> Papal States. We do not admit the principle of non-inter-
> vention, and still less that of the sovereignty of the people,
> but unless there is a change in your methods, it would require
> a European war to prevent one or the other taking place.[1]

Equally plain speaking was used by the English Minister
at Naples. So hopeless did he consider the condition
of the country that he requested an audience of the
King 'in order,' as he wrote to Lord John Russell, 'that
when the catastrophe arrives I may not have upon my
conscience the reflection that I had not done all in my
power to save an inexperienced Sovereign from impending ruin.'[2] But all efforts were equally useless, and
it was precisely that intervention in the Papal States
against which Russia had uttered a warning that turned
the attitude of Cavour from friendliness to hostility and
precipitated the fall of the Bourbon.

Villamarina had not been long at his new post when
he discovered that the Government, far from responding
to the friendly overtures of Cavour, was engaged in an
intrigue for the recovery of the Romagna and the
restoration of the dispossessed Princes. As early as
January 30th, Villamarina had written to Cavour warning him of what was taking place. The intimation
received from Paris that Napoleon wished to withdraw
the French troops from Rome, as soon as the Papal

[1] Bianchi, *Stor. Doc.* Regina to Carafa, February 2nd.
[2] Elliott, *Diary.*

forces were prepared to undertake their own defence, had stimulated the creation of a Papal army. The French general, Lamoricière, accepted the command, and the Holy Father had issued an appeal to Catholic Europe for recruits. He would not, however, raise his new forces from amongst his own subjects. Cynics might have said that he could not trust them, but the reason given by the Pope was that he could not reconcile it with his conscience to constrain his subjects in large numbers to a celibacy even temporary, though this scrupulous attitude did not apply to the Irish, Belgians, and Austrians, who flocked to the Papal standard.[1] At the close of 1859 the Neapolitan army was concentrated in the Abruzzi, and four new regiments of 'Bavarian,' i.e. Austrian, troops were raised to replace the Swiss recently disbanded.[2] All this was the first-fruits of an intrigue carried on by the Queen Mother, who completely dominated the weak mind of Francis, Cardinal Antonelli, and the Archduchess Sophia at Vienna, backed by Monsignor Ginelli, the Papal Nuncio at Naples, and the Spanish Ambassador, Bermudez di Castro, who talked imposingly of the formation of a great Catholic League.[3]

Cavour replied to Villamarina with great moderation, instructing him to adopt a reserved and prudent attitude, to assure the Neapolitan Foreign Secretary of the sincerity of Piedmont's desire not to see the tranquillity of the Southern Kingdom disturbed, but to be prepared to act with vigour if Naples should attempt to infringe its neutrality by the occupation of Papal territory.[4]

The reason why Cavour was anxious to keep on good terms with Naples is clear. He had no wish for fresh

[1] Cavour to Nigra.

[2] *The Times* correspondent at Naples wrote on January 23rd: 'Here there is in course of formation a body of men amounting to 4,000, hired cut-throats, the scum of Europe.'

[3] Bianchi, *Cavour*, for extracts from correspondence. *Parl. Papers.* Loftus to Russell, December 13th. Corbet to Russell, January 17th, 1860. Villamarina to Cavour, January 30th, in Bianchi, *Stor. Doc.*, vol. viii.

[4] Chiala, vol. iii. p. 233.

complications until the problem of Central Italy was successfully solved. But a deeper reason lay beneath. Cavour's plan was to work from north to south, and between the new Kingdom and Naples lay the Papal States. Trouble with Naples, before the Papal question was settled, would be most undesirable; to attempt to conquer the south by sea was out of the question, and to overrun the Roman territory in order to attack Naples was to bring a hornet's nest about his ears, for Catholic Europe and Napoleon in particular were desperately sensitive where Rome was concerned. By the middle of March Central Italy was safe, and Cavour could turn his attention to the Papal States. His solution of the problem was based upon the withdrawal of the French troops from Rome, to which Napoleon was pledged after his acceptance of Russell's four points. When this took place an insurrection in Umbria was almost inevitable; a situation would at once arise similar to that created in the Romagna on the withdrawal of the Austrian garrisons in the previous May, and then, in the interests of order, Cavour would step in and take over the remaining States of the Church.

These facts were equally clear to Napoleon. His original idea, in his desire to prevent a united Italy, was that unity should not cross the Apennines. Outmanoeuvred by Cavour with the help of England, he now endeavoured to create a fresh barrier on the Roman border. His plan was revealed diplomatically to Cavour by Thouvenel in an interview with Nigra on March 22nd. It was necessary, the French Foreign Secretary said, that Italy should now have a period of quiet to organize the new Kingdom. As long as the French troops were in Rome, order in the Papal States was probably assured. But the recall of these troops was imminent. The Pope demanded it, the Emperor wished it, Europe desired it, and the welfare of Italy required it. Then what would happen? An insurrection would certainly take place at once. How could this be prevented? Some troops must replace the French. The Austrians or the

Spaniards could not be allowed. There remained the Piedmontese and the Neapolitans. The former were excluded by the express desire of the Pope, *ergo* it must be the Neapolitans.[1]

Cavour's reply to this suggestion was characteristically subtle. 'It is a very embarrassing question for me,' he wrote to Nigra. 'At bottom, I would desire this occupation to take place, but I would not wish to recognize its legitimacy.' In other words, he would be glad to see it carried out, provided his sanction was not given, for it would create a situation out of which he could always make trouble; for the presence of Neapolitan troops could always be treated as just as much a foreign occupation as those of France, with this advantage, that he could, with a real chance of success, risk a war with Naples on the question, which he dare not do with France.

This proposal, as put forward by Thouvenel, looked plausible and reasonable enough. He even went so far as to regard it as temporary; statesmen, he said, in the present condition of things could not look more than a year ahead. This plan would lead either to reform in Naples and the States of the Church or to a continuance of present methods, in which latter case insurrection would eventually take place and then the King of Naples would have to concentrate his troops in his own country and Piedmont would take over the Marches. But there was another side to it. It was, in fact, a case of the velvet glove, and what was beneath comes out plainly in a letter written by the French Ambassador at Rome, the Duc de Gramont, to an unnamed Neapolitan diplomat. This is what he wrote:

> It seems to me that your government has overlooked the most important fact, which is the basis of the whole arrangement, namely, that the Emperor would guarantee the Neapolitan troops placed in the Papal States against all aggression on the part of Piedmont. With this guarantee the frontiers of Naples are no longer menaced, since the

Pontifical zone, which the enemy must traverse to reach you, is itself guaranteed from all attack . . . further, it appears to me difficult that the Emperor, after his preventing any attack on Naples by Piedmont through the Papal territory, could approve or tolerate that this Prince should attack Sicily. This arrangement in my opinion increases the security of the Kingdom of Naples more than an addition of thirty thousand troops to the Royal army would do. I do not hesitate to say that your King would be much stronger than ever before. Lastly, there is one circumstance that will not have escaped you; that is, that it will produce this strange result, so little expected, of seeing Piedmont, a rebel to our counsels, isolated by France, and Naples actively associated with our peaceful policy and assisting in our sincere efforts to solve the difficulties of a situation full of dangers.

He then goes on to describe the actual situation, or rather, the alternative to this arrangement, in these words:

you know as well as I do that the revolt of the Marches and Umbria is imminent, that its success is practically certain, and that, in any case, the entry of Piedmont is inevitable, as well as their victorious march to the frontiers of Naples. We shall not be in a position to oppose them, for it is only under the pretext or rather because of our evacuation, that we can impose on the King of Sardinia the obligation of not attacking the Neapolitan army. . . . I ought, in closing this long letter, to remark to you also that there is necessarily a certain correlation between the withdrawal of our troops in Lombardy and that of the Division in the Pontifical States.

Such was the plan as seen by the French Ambassador in Rome. Piedmont, as a punishment for absorbing Tuscany against Napoleon's wishes, exposed on her eastern flank to Austria, with all chance of expansion through the Papal States or Naples blocked by a French guarantee, was to be isolated, and in her place Naples, the worst government in Europe, was to become the protégée of France.[1] Now, if Cavour through his many channels of information learnt the substance of what was contained in this letter, it was more than sufficient to

[1] Bolléa, No. 239, March 20th.

change his attitude towards Naples, and assure his support of any movement that would help to free the oppressed Italians of Umbria before Napoleon's guarantee handed them over to the tender mercies of the Neapolitan soldiery. On March 22nd Cavour heard from Villamarina that Cardinal Antonelli's brother had secretly visited the King at Gaeta to arrange for Neapolitan intervention in the Marches. Cavour replied by telegraph: 'inform Neapolitan Foreign Secretary that if troops enter Papal territory without a previous agreement with us, you are ordered to protest and ask for your passports.' On March 27th we have a second telegram as follows: 'after having received your first dispatch upon the occupation of the Marches by Naples, France has requested us to accede thereto. We have replied that we cannot do so unless the King of Naples recognizes the annexation of the Romagna or we are allowed to garrison Ancona.'[1] These conditions, as Cavour knew well, would never be accepted, and France, when she heard them, offered as an alternative 'a reciprocal guarantee that France will give, simultaneously, to Turin and Naples which would have for its result to stop all conflict between the two nations.' Things had reached this point when King Francis cut short the negotiations by a peremptory refusal. The folly of Francis, who thus threw away the last chance offered him of remaining King of the Two Sicilies, relieved Cavour from a very awkward situation and left the position open once more.

When the danger of a French guarantee of the Papal States and Naples was over, Cavour turned his thoughts to the possibility of insurrection. His first step was to get further information as to political conditions. On March 30th he wrote a long letter to the Marquis Villamarina.

You know [he wrote] that I do not in the least desire to push the question of Naples to a premature solution. On the contrary, I believe that it would be of benefit to us if the actual

[1] Chiala, vol. iii. No. 791.

state of things lasted some years longer. But I know from a good source that even England despairs of maintaining the *status quo*, and it is without doubt in view of a rising in Naples that her fleet is now stationed in those waters. I believe, then, that we shall very shortly be forced to evolve a plan of action that I could have wished to have had more time to mature.

He then went on to ask a series of questions as to the relative strength of political forces in Naples. What support was given to Muratism? Were the republicans strong in Calabria? Was there a possibility of a spontaneous movement such as took place in Tuscany? What was the strength of the French party?[1] While Cavour awaited a reply from his Minister things began to happen.

During the next few days news came through that a rising was imminent in Palermo.[2] Cavour at once quietly sounded his War Minister, General Fanti, as to a suitable officer to be sent to guide it. Fanti suggested General Ribotti, who had been a leader in the Sicilian rising of 1847. On April 2nd the King opened Parliament, and on the 6th came news of the outbreak at the Gancia Convent at Palermo. Garibaldi at that moment was in Turin, come to take his seat as a deputy and interpellate Cavour on the cession of Nice. When the news of the Sicilian insurrection reached Genoa, Nino Bixio and Franceso Crispi at once set off for the capital to persuade Garibaldi to lead an expedition to Sicily; after a long interview Garibaldi finally gave his consent. Immediately this was settled he obtained an audience from the King, told him what was proposed, and boldly asked permission to take with him the Reggio Brigade of regulars commanded by Colonel Sacchi and mainly composed of his old Cacciatori delle Alpi. Victor Emmanuel temporized and consulted Cavour, who vetoed the suggestion, pointing out that

[1] Chiala, vol. iii. No. 793.

[2] Throughout this chapter and the next the stirring events in the south, so vividly portrayed in Dr. Trevelyan's two volumes, *Garibaldi and the Thousand* and *Garibaldi and the Making of Italy*, are seen only from the windows of the Foreign Office in Turin.

it would compromise the Government and promote desertions from the army, and added that, if the expedition materialized, all the regular forces would be needed to deter Austria from active opposition. The King informed Garibaldi of the unwelcome decision and, moreover, induced him to discourage desertions from the regular forces and trust to his volunteers. Furious with Cavour, Garibaldi left the capital for Nice, though the King tried to keep him in Turin. 'I don't believe he will produce much of an effect there,' wrote Cavour. His friends, however, kept him in Genoa and dissuaded him from making trouble in his native town. Amongst those he consulted was Sir James Hudson, who told him that it was better to go to Sicily, where he was wanted, than to Nice where he was not, and that fighting the Bourbon was a more suitable occupation than smashing ballot boxes.[1]

But the expedition of Garibaldi was not the only one in preparation. La Farina, as soon as the outbreak at Palermo was known, determined to provide what assistance he could with the resources of the National Society. He chose as the leader Colonel La Masa, a Sicilian, who, like Ribotti, now sent back to his command, had taken part in the rising of 1847. La Masa applied to Cavour for help, and after some hesitation he consented, and instructed La Farina to provide him with arms and equipment. When he returned to Genoa La Masa found Garibaldi's expedition being organized, but in difficulties, owing to inability to obtain the rifles held by the Million Rifle Fund, which were stored at Milan under Government supervision, and which the Governor, Massimo d'Azeglio, refused to release. After some negotiation, the two expeditions combined, La Masa serving under Garibaldi and La Farina providing the equipment. This amalgamation had a twofold effect. While it diluted the Mazzinian influence and thereby won Cavour's approval, it made it much more

[1] His plan was to raid Nice and destroy the voting papers, then sail for Sicily.

difficult for him to stop it, because to do so would throw La Farina and the moderate Liberal party in the Chamber into opposition, and make it almost impossible to pass the treaty on Nice and Savoy.

Before matters had gone too far to be stopped, Cavour resolved to give King Francis one last warning, and on April 15th Victor Emmanuel addressed a personal letter to his cousin at Naples.

> We have reached a moment [the King wrote] in which Italy may be divided into two strong states, one in the north and the other in the south; which, adopting the same national policy, will uphold the great idea of our age, national independence. But to put this idea into practice it is necessary that Your Majesty abandons the road you have hitherto followed. If you reject my counsel—which, believe me, is the result of my desire for the welfare both of yourself and your dynasty—you will see, perchance, the moment come when I shall be placed in the terrible position of either endangering the most vital interests of my own dynasty or of being the chief instrument in the destruction of yours. The principle of dualism, if firmly established and honestly followed, might at this moment be accepted by the Italian people. If you allow months to pass without heeding my friendly suggestion, Your Majesty will, perhaps, have to experience the bitterness of the terrible words 'too late,' as happened to a member of your family in 1830.

But to these wise and outspoken words no reply was vouchsafed. We cannot suppose that Cavour expected much result from this letter, but at least it justified his attitude before Europe and cleared his own conscience before the blow fell. The same day as this letter was written the King and Cavour left Turin for Florence, leaving behind them at Genoa Garibaldi's expedition in full process of organization.

The credit for the original conception of the expedition of the Thousand must be given to Mazzini. From 1856, when the prestige of Cavour sapped his influence in the north, Mazzini had turned his attention to the Kingdom of the Two Sicilies. The ill-fated expedition of Pisacane in 1857, and the futile rising of Bentivegna in Sicily the following year, had both been his handiwork. Undeterred by these failures, he continued his propaganda, concentrating more especially on Sicily. With his head-quarters in London and an advanced base established at Malta by Nicola Fabrizi, he pushed on his campaign unceasingly. His chief agents were Agostino Bertani, Francesco Crispi, and Rosalino Pilo, who, undaunted by the dangers, visited Sicily, and kept alive the thought of revolution. But Mazzini was not the only one urging the Sicilians and Neapolitans to revolt. La Farina and the National Society had long been an active force in the south, and the cry of 'Unity and Victor Emmanuel' soon proved more popular than the pure republicanism of Mazzini. The advice given by both organizations was similar, only let the Sicilians rise and then aid would come, but in the face of 20,000 Neapolitan regulars, the ill-armed and unorganized Sicilians were apt to say, let the aid come first and then you will see how we will rise!

The return of Cavour to power and the annexation of Central Italy stimulated the efforts towards revolution, but at the same time it increased the difficulties. No organized expedition could start from Genoa without at least the tacit consent of the Government, and anything short of organized assistance was useless; and without its active connivance success on any large scale was impossible. Unfortunately, just at the moment when an understanding between the two principals, Cavour and Garibaldi, would have been most useful, they were personally estranged. Garibaldi's unfortunate association with Brofferio and Guerrazzi in the campaign against Cavour's return to power, and his ill-timed escapade two months before in Emilia, had incensed Cavour as much as the opposition to the Liberi Comizi and the failure of the Nazione Armata, which he attributed to the influence of Cavour, had enraged Garibaldi.

'To bring Cavour and Garibaldi together at the present moment,' wrote Bertani to Panizzi in London, 'would be a difficult thing to do, but nevertheless it would be most useful for the cause. Garibaldi has the King and the nation in his hand; Cavour would supply the intelligence and guidance that fails in the other two. Cavour, with the King and Garibaldi, could free himself in a large measure from the influence of Napoleon . . .'[1] But before even the preliminaries for so desirable a combination could be set on foot, the breach between them became irreparable by the cession of Nice to France. Henceforth Bertani gave up all idea of working with the Government, and bent his energy on carrying out his scheme of national unity with the revolution alone.[2]

But the necessity for some working compromise became evident when the first overtures were made to Garibaldi to take command of such an expedition, for he laid down as his principle of action 'Italy and Victor Emmanuel.' To this Mazzini himself had to bend, and on March 2nd he wrote to his Sicilian supporters, 'it is no longer a question of Monarchy or Republic; it is a question of national unity. If Italy wishes to be a Monarchy under the House of Savoy, well and good. If later, it wishes to proclaim the King and Cavour as Liberators or anything else, let it do so. That which all now desire is that Italy shall be made.' This attitude made possible the final solution, which was that the expedition of Garibaldi won the sympathy and support of all the active forces of the nation from the King and Cavour to Mazzini himself.

The expedition of Garibaldi came as no surprise to Cavour; he had expected it and foreseen it; for when the national determination for unity and independence, which had first turned eastward, was blocked by Napoleon at Villafranca, Cavour realized that it must now turn south.[3] As soon then as Cavour knew, after Garibaldi's

[1] January 19th, 1860.   [2] See Chiala, vol. iii. Introd. p. xciii.
[3] Bolléa, No. 306. Cavour to Nigra: What has happened was easy to foresee and I can say I had foreseen it. The expedition of Garibaldi is the consequence of the cession of Nice as the violence of the unitarian movement is the result of Villafranca.

interview with Victor Emmanuel, that he had consented
to lead an expedition to Sicily, he had to choose between
two possible lines of action. His own plan had been
to secure the Papal States before attempting any action
farther south. The reason was obvious: Naples could
neither be attacked nor governed with the States of the
Church intervening. Negotiations for the evacuation of
the French troops from Rome had been proceeding for
some time. Their withdrawal was to begin in July.[1]
From the situation that must arise when the protecting
troops had gone, Cavour hoped to achieve his object
of annexation. But this process was slow and uncertain, for very little pressure would be required to make
Napoleon stop evacuation and Italy must remain quiet
until it was completed. But it had the great advantage
of keeping the control of the national movement in
Cavour's own hands and of thus giving Europe the
assurance that the development of Italian unity would
proceed on the correct lines hitherto followed. The
alternative to this was to support Garibaldi, and in so
doing, to sacrifice his own solution, and against all the
principles upon which his policy had been hitherto
based, acquiesce in an unorthodox revolutionary movement with Mazzini at the back of it and Garibaldi in
the front.[2]

Cavour could have stopped Garibaldi had the expedition remained purely Mazzinian, but when it coalesced
with La Farina and the National Society, it became
almost impossible at any lesser price than resignation.
Now Cavour could not resign; he was pledged to pass
the treaty with France and procure the cession of Nice
and Savoy, which was not only the payment promised
for Tuscany, but the condition necessary for the future
connivance of France in the completion of unity. For
some time Cavour had been very uneasy about the
stability of his Government. The support given to

[1] Cavour to Ricasoli, June 3rd. Cowley to Russell, May 18th.

[2] It is at this point that we realize the full meaning of Cavour's words after
Villafranca. 'Ah well, they will force me to be a conspirator for the rest
of my life . . .' and a conspirator he became. See de la Rive, *Cavour*.

Rattazzi's candidature for the Presidency of the Chamber, and the opposition manifested to the cession of Nice, evoked by Garibaldi's interpellation in the Chamber, together with Fanti's repeated threat of resignation over the delimitation of the new frontier, had convinced Cavour that unless some action was taken that would rally the country round him, the successful passage of the treaty was very problematical. Nothing was so well calculated to bring support and popularity to the Government as to let Garibaldi go. It would please the King, turn the attention of the country from Nice and Savoy to Sicily, and, if successful, achieve in a few months the work of years of diplomatic action. The danger, apart from the diplomatic storm that Cavour would have to face, lay in the fact that Cavour could not control the movement. Garibaldi would certainly not follow his advice, and although Cavour trusted his loyalty to the King, the extent of the Mazzinian influence upon him was difficult to gauge. On the other hand, Cavour's lack of influence would prevent his premature recall if demanded by foreign pressure.

Weighing the two sides of the question Cavour decided to adopt towards Garibaldi the policy he asked Europe to adopt towards Italy—that of non-intervention. He would not stop and he would not encourage him. He would leave the onus of responsibility upon Garibaldi while he prepared himself for either contingency. If Garibaldi did not go, Cavour would return to his own policy of working from north to south; if he went, Cavour would leave the Papal States until later, and exploit and support the new effort for all it was worth. In spite of appearances, this was neither a policy of weakness nor of indecision, but an example of Cavour's method of opportunism, of adapting himself instantly to a new phase of the situation and being ready to use whichever of two or more lines of action promised the greatest success.

But Cavour was under no illusion as to the hazardous nature of the enterprise. If Garibaldi met the fate of

Murat or Pisacane, or if his ships were sunk by the Neapolitan cruisers, an outburst of national wrath might drive him to declare war on Naples with all European opinion against him. More than once he discouraged the attempt by pointing out the dangers. But beyond this expression of personal opinion he never made the least attempt to stop it.

> The expedition of Garibaldi is a very serious matter [he wrote to Ricasoli after his departure] all the same I believe that we could not nor ought not to have stopped him. Whether it prove a blessing or a disaster it was in any case inevitable. Now we are once more on the high seas in the midst of storms and dangers. But what can we do? As long as Italy is not made one cannot think of reposing in the calm of the past years.[1]

The first step, once his decision was taken, was to conceal all suspicion of Government complicity. From the first he kept Nigra in the dark as to his support of the expedition and gave him to understand that he was opposed to it. He harped perpetually on the theme that the conduct and methods of France over the cession of Nice and Savoy was steadily weakening his position in the country, and eventually gave this as his reason for inability to stop Garibaldi.[2] To divert French uneasiness he threw suspicion of complicity upon England. Lord Palmerston, he told the French Government, was working resolutely to procure the freedom of Sicily and Egypt, and when this was achieved he intended to ensure its continuance by extending English protection over both. This started a persistent rumour that Piedmont would surrender Sicily to England in exchange for acquiring Naples. Cavour, of course, denied this flatly, and there was not the least truth in it, but the idea of English complicity served to divert French indignation from Piedmont to England and made France hesitate to be too dictatorial when the news of Garibaldi's departure reached France.[3]

[1] Chiala, vol. iii. No. 809.   [2] Bolléa, No. 267, Cavour to Nigra.
[3] CCN., vol. iii. Nos. 743. 826. 840.

On his arrival at Florence with the King, Cavour found Villamarina's reply to his questionnaire awaiting him. As to the general situation in the south he was assured that it was certainly not the French that would command the greatest support. The masses were entirely against France. At no price would they put up with the dominance of Napoleon. As to support given to the cause of Murat there was some amongst the bourgeoisie, but none in the army. There was no chance of any movement similar to that which had taken place in Tuscany. 'At Naples,' wrote Villamarina, 'the King has without doubt the army with him, I repeat what I wrote before, the Government is strong, very strong, when it is a question of repressing the populace. No insurrection could break out here as in Sicily that might lead to the fall of the Monarchy.' As to Sicily, it was unanimous in favour of annexation to Piedmont. Republicanism was dead even in Calabria. In regard to the probable attitude of the foreign Powers, Russia would protest, but probably bow to the inevitable, and England would accept the free expression of the popular will.[1]

This dispatch must have relieved Cavour. It dissipated his fears of Murat and republican support, and reassured him as to the annexationist tendencies of Sicily. But it did more than that, for it revealed that, rotten as the political edifice was, the pressure that was required to overturn it must come from outside; Naples, in short, was waiting for just such a shock as Garibaldi was admirably equipped to give.

Cavour did not stay long in Florence, he found the warmth of his reception embarrassing: 'The Florentines are very kind to me,' he wrote to Nigra in Paris, 'I cannot go out without provoking unexpected demonstrations, of which, perchance, there is some jealousy in certain quarters.' After visiting Pisa, he left for Spezia from Leghorn in the cruiser *Marie Adelaide*. Realizing the importance of the navy at this crisis, Cavour had

[1] Chiala, vol. iv. Introd. p. cxxxv.

detached the Ministry of Marine from that of War and taken charge of it himself. Already while at Florence he had dispatched two frigates, the *Authion* and the *Governolo*, to Sicilian waters for observation, and some days later he concentrated the rest of the available ships at Cagliari in Sardinia. A central position in telegraphic communication with Turin, and almost equidistant from Genoa, Naples, and Sicily.

After breaking his journey at Spezia, where he examined the new naval base in course of construction, Cavour arrived at Genoa on April 22nd. That evening he had an interview with the Vice-Governor. As, a few days later, La Farina was informed by this official that certain 'cases of books,' in reality, rifles, had arrived and were at his disposal, the instructions given to him by Cavour are sufficiently obvious. The following morning Cavour was visited by Sirtori, one of Garibaldi's most trusted lieutenants, with the knowledge of Bertani but unknown to Garibaldi. He laid before Cavour the pro-posed plan of action; his reply was that, as to any expedi-tion to the Marches, the Government would oppose it 'by every means in their power,' but in regard to Sicily, he said, 'Well and good: begin from the south and come up north. When it is a question of undertakings of that kind, however bold they may be, Count Cavour will be second to none.' That evening Cavour returned to Turin.

The impression left on Cavour's mind by his visit to Genoa was far from satisfactory. He returned to Turin very uncertain as to Garibaldi's power of resis-tance to Mazzinian influences, and more than uneasy as to the prospects of success if the expedition started. For the first time in his political career he had sanc-tioned a movement which had Mazzini behind it, and over which, in consequence, he had not complete control. Writing to Farini after his return, he says, 'In Genoa I found the minds very restless through the intrigues of Garibaldi, around whom the Mazzinians are gathering and beginning to raise their heads. To increase the restlessness, the attitude of the more advanced party (not Mazzinian) contributes, for they are openly raising the flag of opposition, taking the questions of Nice and Sicily for their base of operations. Nevertheless I do not anticipate serious trouble there.' But whatever happened, all suspicion that the Government was implicated had to be allayed, and in a letter to Nigra in Paris after describing the situation in similar terms, he added, 'they want to force the Government to help the Sicilians. They are collecting arms and money. I suspect the King of imprudently favouring these projects. I have given orders to watch and, if possible, stop these desperate efforts.'[1] These last words, no doubt, refer to the mission of Colonel Frappolli whom Cavour sent the next day to Genoa to dissuade Garibaldi (almost as uncertain of success as Cavour) by pointing out the results of failure. After this Nigra was not likely to strengthen French suspicions of Cavour's complicity. As to the political attitude of Garibaldi Cavour was reassured by La Farina, 'I have been to Genoa,' he wrote to Cavour on the 24th, 'Garibaldi wished to see me and we had a long conversation as to what is to be done in regard to Sicily; he is desirous of working with me; there is no collusion between him and the Mazzinians, rather pronounced disaccord. The same attitude is taken by Medici, Bixio, Besana, and Sirtori.'[2] But Garibaldi's expedition was by now daily passing out of the hands of any one party and becoming a national affair. No sooner was the rising in Sicily known than committees of help sprang up all over the country. Subscriptions poured in; municipalities voted substantial sums of money and young men in thousands applied to fight under Garibaldi.[3] While the union of La Farina and the National Society, with the original committee presided over by Bertani, widened the basis of the whole movement.

During these weeks Cavour was overwhelmed with

[1] Golléa, No. 261.　　[2] La Farina, *Epistolario*.
[3] See Trevelyan, *Garibaldi and the Thousand*.

work. He had not only a vast amount of administrative work, co-ordinating the old and new provinces, but he had to attend regularly in the Chamber, where the new deputies, unaccustomed to the rules and procedure of Constitutional Government, had to be taught and guided. In addition, he was fighting a difficult rear-guard action with France over the new frontier between Piedmont and Nice and Savoy. In accordance with his policy he had during these weeks adopted an attitude of *laissez faire* towards the expedition organizing at Genoa. During the last ten days of April the prepara-tions were conducted with an openness that scorned concealment. Train loads of enthusiastic volunteers were crowding into Genoa, provided for largely by the Committee of Help, nine-tenths of whose funds were supplied by the Vice-Governor, coming direct from the King.[1] Their destination was an open secret, and we find the French Consul at Leghorn writing to the Quai d'Orsay on the 25th: 'with the connivance of the Government an expedition is preparing at Genoa and Leghorn simultaneously.' At the height of the excite-ment the Baron de Talleyrand paid a visit to Genoa in person. With his own eyes he saw what was going on and promptly dispatched an energetic protest to Cavour.[2]

But it chanced that just at this moment the prospects of the expedition received a sharp setback. Bad news came from Sicily. A telegram from Fabrizi depicted the situation there as almost hopeless, and Garibaldi, with tears in his eyes, declared that it would be 'madness to go.' The expedition seemed abandoned. Cavour at once used this information to reassure diplomacy, but on the night of the 29th he heard that preparations for departure were again in full swing. Crispi had produced reassuring telegrams and hope revived once more. Cavour, when this information reached him, found his position awkward, and, thinking discretion the better part of valour, decided to leave Turin until Garibaldi

[1] Nazari-Michele, *Cavour e Garibaldi*, p. 70.
[2] D'Ideville, *Memoires d'un Diplomat.*

had sailed. He had anticipated some such situation as this, for some days before he had written to Nigra: 'the King leaves for Bologna on Wednesday, he will stay there three or four days. I shall, perhaps, be obliged to join him there.' It was just as well to be out of Turin during the final stages of Garibaldi's departure, which, moreover, raised important questions that would have to be settled. So, on the first of May, taking with him General Fanti, the Minister for War, Cavour left for Bologna to join the King. On the same day Victor Emmanuel accompanied only by Farini drove across the Apennines from Florence.[1] They arrived within an hour of each other, and either that day or the next a meeting took place to settle the questions arising out of Garibaldi's departure.

In the one account we have of this meeting at Bologna the writer maintains that Cavour wished to stop the expedition and to arrest Garibaldi, and declared that if no one else would do it he would do it himself, but that finally he gave in to the pressure of the King.[2] Not only is this unsupported, but the whole political position is against its probability. If Cavour had intended to stop Garibaldi he would have done it a month before. He did not stop him because to do so would have prevented the passage of the treaty over Nice and Savoy. The arrest of Garibaldi at the last minute, or even the display of force that would be necessary to stop him, added to the irritation already existing against the treaty, would have certainly provoked an opposition that would have forced the Government to resign. The new Cabinet would have had to refuse the cession of Nice, if not of Savoy as well, and then France would assuredly have marched in troops and occupied both provinces by force and the position of the country and the Government would have been humiliating. Everything was, in fact, in favour of letting Garibaldi go. It

[1] Chiala, vol. iv. Introd.; Nazari-Michele, p. 82; Matteuzzi, *L. C. Farini*; all agree on the presence of Fanti and Farini at the meeting at Bologna. The former arriving with Cavour, the latter with the King.

[2] D'Haussonville in the *Revue des Deux Mondes*, September 15th, 1862.

would divert attention from Nice, gratify the King, and most important of all, give the Government the full support of the country. The political position was not bad. England would certainly not interfere. France would protest officially, but Napoleon was disgusted with Naples, and the brusque refusal of Francis to accept a French guarantee for his kingdom was too fresh to be forgotten, and Savoy and Nice were not yet quite safe. With England and France as accomplices Austria would not move. As to Prussia and Russia they would be very angry, especially the latter, but could do little. Looked at broadly, the question at issue was whether the diplomatic storm that would follow the departure of Garibaldi would be more dangerous to the country than the internal trouble that would result from stopping him, and Cavour chose what he believed to be the lesser of the two evils.

What took place at the meeting is fairly clear from Cavour's subsequent letters. It was decided not to interfere with the expedition provided that no attack was made on the Papal States.[1] It was further decided to lend the help of the Government as long as this could be done without compromising it in the eyes of Europe. As to the consequences, it was expected that Naples would send an ultimatum which might mean war at once, and the Piedmont brigade of infantry was held ready at Genoa prepared for immediate embarkation. The next day Cavour as Minister of Marine ordered Admiral Persano to leave Leghorn and proceed to Cagliari, but without using his engines.[2] With the navy in a central position and 150,000 men under arms[3] Cavour was prepared for all eventualities. He remained at Bologna some days longer, looking at pictures and waiting for news of Garibaldi's departure. On May 5th

[1] This decision was conveyed to Bertani from Farini by means of the deputy Finali. See *Nuova Antologia*, April 1909.

[2] This phrase has been much discussed but the meaning is clear. There was no hurry as the expedition had not yet started. Persano was to save coal in case a declaration of war made it necessary for the fleet to put to sea at once.　　　　　[3] La Farina, *Epistolario*.

he returned to Turin in time to hear by telegraph the details of the final stages of the embarkation.

The historic embarkation of the Thousand took place at Quarto a few miles from Genoa in the early hours of May 6th. The smoke of the two vessels, the *Piemonte* and the *Lombardo*, had hardly disappeared below the horizon when the diplomatic protests commenced. The Baron de Talleyrand, who had kindly kept Cavour informed of all that had been going on at Genoa during the preceding weeks, was amongst the first to voice the official indignation of Europe. Cavour replied that Garibaldi had grossly, brutally deceived him, that he had given his word not to take part in the expedition, 'but as it has turned out otherwise,' he added, 'I must confess that his absence diminishes considerably the difficulties existing at this moment. He was the centre of the discontented throughout the country; as long as he was here I was like a sick man, now I am myself again.'[1] Talleyrand reported Cavour's attitude in a note to Thouvenel, but he had to admit that it was the general opinion of diplomacy at Turin that it would have been 'a dangerous experiment for M. de Cavour to enter on a serious struggle to stop the embarkation of the volunteers, for whatever the result the Government would certainly have had to resign after so unpopular an act.' Russia was profoundly indignant. Gortschakoff declared that 'had the situation of Russia been different' he would have interfered by force in spite of the principle of non-intervention. Prussia lamented the distance and the absence of ships in Sicilian waters, but lent her moral support to Naples, whose Minister at Berlin telegraphed that 'this help would be ruined in a moment if time was allowed to a thousand bandits, the scum of the earth, to raise the fatal flag of the theory of universal suffrage,' adding, as an afterthought, 'but the Minister of this court at Turin is an imbecile.'[2] The language of Naples, and

---

[1] Talleyrand to Thouvenel 9th May.
[2] See Bianchi, *Cavour*, for extracts from diplomatic correspondence.

no one had been better informed of what was preparing, was a shriek of indignation, but the ultimatum that Cavour naturally expected did not materialize, and her conduct justified Cavour's stigma that 'the behaviour of the King of Naples is so ignoble that he has no claim to continue on the throne.' To these protests Cavour replied as best he could. If Austrian, Belgian, Irish and French subjects were allowed by their Governments to flock to Rome and form a Papal army, he replied, whose purpose was to attack Piedmontese territory, he could not stop the Sicilians of the north from helping their brothers in the south. To England and the Emperor he was more candid. He wrote to Nigra:

> I have not stopped Garibaldi from carrying out his project because it would have required force to have done so. Now the Government is not in a position to face the immense unpopularity which an attempt to stop Garibaldi would have aroused against it. Having need of the support of all shades of opinion in the Liberal party, to defeat the intrigues of the opposition and get the treaty passed, I could not take the strong measures that were necessary if the help destined for Sicily was to be stopped. But I have omitted nothing to dissuade Garibaldi from carrying out his mad attempt.[1]

To D'Azeglio in London he scarcely troubled to offer any explanation, the interests of England and Sardinia in regard to Sicily were identical, he said, to deliver the island from subjection and give to it a real and lasting independence. He had not encouraged Garibaldi to undertake this expedition which he considered rash, but he had respected the highly honourable motives that inspired him, and did not believe it was right to stop him by force. Finally, he added that, owing to the pressure of Russia, he had been obliged to insert in the Official Gazette an article denying the rumours of the complicity of the Government.[2]

But while with one hand Cavour sought to reassure Europe and reconcile diplomacy to the flagrant breach of international law at which he had connived, with the

[1] Bolléa, No. 267.   [2] Politique de Cavour, No. 182.

other he was actively helping Garibaldi. When Cavour
let the expedition sail he knew that it could only be
justified by success. If it failed, the reaction in the
country would probably throw him from power or force
him to declare war on Naples. So from the first he did
his best to assist, but in such a way that the Government
would not be compromised. Having given Garibaldi
twenty-four hours' start Cavour telegraphed to Nigra:
'after having promised to give up the expedition,
Garibaldi, on receiving false news from Sicily, left
yesterday at 3 a.m. We have immediately telegraphed
to Sassari and Cagliari to stop him executing his project.' The order received the same day (7th) by Admiral
Persano from the Governor of Cagliari was to arrest
the expedition if it stopped at any port in Sardinia but
to leave it alone if it was met with on the high seas.[1]
Garibaldi, however, had gone down the Tuscan coast,
stopped at Talamone, where he had landed sixty men
under Zambianchi to raise an insurrection in the Papal
States,[2] and bluffed the commander of the Fort at
Ortebello into furnishing him with munitions. He
arrived there on the 7th, and left for Sicily on the
morning of the 9th, arriving at Marsala two days later.

On the 10th Persano, finding his orders ambiguous,
sent word to Cavour that if the expedition was really
to be stopped would he telegraph 'Cagliari,' if not, the
word 'Malta.' On the 11th, the day Garibaldi landed
at Marsala, Persano received a telegram, 'the Cabinet
has decided for "Cagliari",' but the Admiral taking this
to mean that Cavour in person did not agree with the
Cabinet, replied, 'I understand,' and did nothing.[3]
From this exchange of telegrams it is clear that Cavour's
orders were not only ambiguous, but either by design
or by accident were always too late to achieve their
apparent object. Cavour, however, being anxious that

[1] Persano, *Diario Privato.*

[2] Nazari-Michele gives Garibaldi's orders to Zambianchi signing himself,
'G. Garibaldi, General of the Roman Government, elected by universal
suffrage and with extraordinary powers.'

[3] Persano, *Diario Privato.*

it should appear that he had done his best to stop Garibaldi, and he was certainly very annoyed over the incursion into the Papal States, wrote to Nigra on the 12th and said:

> As the news from Palermo announced that the state of siege had ceased and that the insurrection was on the point of collapsing, I believed that Garibaldi whether he wished to or not would have to keep quiet. I should never have thought that he would be mad enough to land in Umbria, where La Moricière and Goyon have much superior forces to those he has been able to collect. That would suffice, at need, to stop my being accused of connivance with him; for one would not suppose me, I hope, fool enough to desire an insurrection in Umbria at the present moment. As I telegraphed, I had already given orders to Admiral Persano to stop the expedition if found in Sardinian waters. Yesterday, immediately I received notice that a number of Garibaldians had disembarked at Talamone, I gave orders to stop the ships wherever they were found, except in Sicilian waters, for the King of Naples has no need for us to act as police for him. Will you explain all this to Thouvenel.[1]

The next day Cavour received word of Garibaldi's safe arrival at Marsala. Writing to Baron Ricasoli a day or two later he expresses his opinion and outlines his future policy in these words:

> Garibaldi has disembarked in Sicily. Now what will happen? One cannot foresee. Will England help him? It is possible. Will France oppose him? I don't think so. And we? To help him openly we cannot, to stop individual assistance we cannot either. We have then decided not to permit new expeditions from Genoa or Leghorn, but not to stop the forwarding of arms and munitions, if carried out with prudence. I cannot hide from myself the inconveniences of so badly defined a line of action, but I cannot think of another that would not be far more difficult and dangerous.

But once Garibaldi was safe in Sicily Cavour had very little to say in the matter of helping him, beyond permitting it, for the country took the matter up with a thoroughness and determination that rendered pre-

[1] Bolléa, No. 267.

ventive Government action impossible. A week after his letter to Ricasoli *The Times* correspondent described the condition of things in these words:

nothing is done here except in the fullest daylight; another expedition is planned; it will prepare and set out under the very nose of Count Cavour who might as soon dream of forcing back the Po from Adria to Monte Viso as think of interfering with the preparation or the execution of the scheme. I can positively assure you, and do not mind doing it for the hundredth time, that men of all classes, of all ages, of all parties, have only one business, have only one object and subject—how to help Garibaldi. To live in Turin or Genoa in Milan or Florence, and not to be Garibaldi-mad is impossible.

XIII. THE CONQUEST OF THE SOUTH

Garibaldi's Arrival—Help from Cavour—Protests of Diplomacy—England and France—Capture of Palermo—Problem of Annexation—La Farina—Naples and France—Cavour and Naples—Projects of Garibaldi—Cavour's Plan to forestall Garibaldi at Naples—Napoleon and the patrol of the Straits—England refuses to join France—Garibaldi crosses the Straits—The March on Naples—Failure of Cavour's Plot—The Royal Army enters Umbria—Fears of Revolution—Castelfidardo—The Volturno—Victor Emmanuel and Garibaldi—Demand for Cavour's dismissal—Parliament Assembles—Bill for Annexation—Cavour's Speech—Austria, Prussia, and Russia at Warsaw—Fear of Attack from Austria—Meeting of Garibaldi and the King—Lord Russell's Dispatch —the South won for Italy.

THE safe arrival of Garibaldi at Marsala brought Cavour face to face with a new situation. Though the chances of his success looked sufficiently remote, such was the magic of Garibaldi's name and so precarious was the hold of Naples over Sicily that almost anything was within the bounds of possibility. Cavour's first care was to lend what support and guidance he could, without compromising the Government, to the movement for providing Garibaldi with reinforcements. There were three organizations assisting the expedition: La Farina and the National Society, the Million Rifle Fund, and the Committee presided over by Bertani. To facilitate matters Cavour purchased the rifles and equipment guarded by the impeccable D'Azeglio at Milan 'to arm the national guard' and passed them on to La Farina, but at the same time he put his foot down on the plan devised by Garibaldi and Bertani for dispatching the volunteers, organized by Cosenz and Medici, to the Papal States to attack Naples from the north. 'If France regards an expedition to Sicily with tolerance,' he wrote, 'she is inflexible upon not allowing an attack on the State of the Church,' and in due course the reinforcements were sent to Sicily.

While these arrangements were being carried out *sub rosa*, Cavour was busily engaged with the diplomatic imbroglio created by the expedition. He was surprised at the mild nature of the protests from France. On the

first receipt of the news, Garibaldi had been stigmatized
in the Press as a filibuster and a pirate, but the treaty
on Savoy and Nice was not yet passed, and Napoleon
had no desire to exasperate Italian opinion before the
discussion, so on a hint from the right quarter Garibaldi
rapidly became no more than a patriot *un peu imprudent,
un peu ardent.*[1] Reassured as to France, Cavour turned
his attention elsewhere. His chief anxiety, as usual, was
Austria. Vienna, as Berlin and St. Petersburg, was
furious, and collective action either directly against
Piedmont or indirectly by support of Naples was by no
means an impossibility. Fortunately for Cavour any
power that interfered in Italy would have to reckon
with France, and Napoleon had his own reasons for
preventing anything in the nature of a coalition of the
Northern Powers, and all immediate danger speedily
evaporated under French diplomatic disapproval.

Cavour did not expect much help from France in the
task before him. Napoleon was by no means reconciled
to Italian unity, but Cavour believed that the Emperor
was too deeply involved in the work already accomplished to allow his handiwork to be ruined or even
imperilled by Austria. To counteract the passive
attitude of France Cavour looked to England. 'I would
wish England to do for the south of Italy what France
has done for the north,' he wrote. A strong Italian
power as a counterpoise to the influence of France in
the Mediterranean, would, he knew, be welcomed by
England, but it was a delicate task to work both powers
together, for they were already deeply suspicious of
each other's aims in Italy.

England feared that France would demand Genoa
as the price of acquiescence in the conquest of the
south, and France suspected England of a desire to
obtain Sicily. On May 22nd Sir James Hudson was
instructed to ask Cavour to declare that (i) Sardinia
would not commit any aggressive act against Austria or
the Kingdom of the Two Sicilies, and (ii) to promise

[1] *CCN.*, vol. iii. No. 826. Nigra to Cavour.

that Sardinia would not make to France any territorial concession beyond those established by the Treaty of Turin on March 24th. To these demands Cavour adhered, but guarded himself as to his relations with Naples, by stating that he could not guarantee to stop by force the manifestations of sympathy arising throughout Italy for the people of the Neapolitan Kingdom. Lord John Russell was not altogether satisfied and showed it, so that Cavour wrote to d'Azeglio that the 'platonic sympathy' of England was insufficient, implying that the alternative was further dependence on France.[1]

The primary object of Napoleon at this stage was to obtain from England the recognition of the principle of 'dualisme,' the division, that is, of Italy into a Northern and a Southern Kingdom, and thus save Naples from extinction and at the same time prevent the creation of Italian unity. The recognition of this principle would, moreover, checkmate any desire of England to obtain Sicily if she was thinking of so doing. But the true crux of the situation was the existence of the Papal States as an independent kingdom; until a solution to this problem was found Italy could not be made. For this reason it is doubtful if any one at this moment believed in unity as a practical proposition. Neither Napoleon nor Hudson accepted it,[2] and as late as June 30th Lord John Russell wrote that after all 'it would be better for every one if Italy was divided into two groups on good terms with each other, and united by a common interest, rather than pursue the ideal of unity, perhaps impossible to realize, and of which the immediate result would infallibly be a new war with Austria.[3]

Cavour had hardly had time to reply to the indignant protests of diplomacy at the departure of Garibaldi, when news arrived (May 31st) of the capture of Palermo. Following his successful landing at Marsala on the 11th,

[1] *Parl. Papers*, 1860, part vii. Cavour to E. d'Azeglio. *Politique*, No. 182.
[2] Hudson to Russell, May 8th.   [3] Persigny to Thouvenel.

Garibaldi had marched boldly inland, and after routing
Landi at Calatafimi on the 15th, had made his initial
attack on Palermo on the 27th. After three days of
desperate street fighting, Lanza, the Neapolitan commander, had asked for an armistice. This was later
extended to June 7th, between which date and the 19th,
Lanza's garrison of 20,000 men was shipped to the
mainland. The surrender of Palermo decided the
question of unity. It convinced Cavour that no other
solution was possible, as it likewise convinced Hudson
and Sir Henry Elliott, the British Minister at Naples,
who now began jointly the task of converting Lord
John Russell.[1] Cavour's first thought was for the
immediate annexation of Sicily. This alone would cut
short the intrigues of France for a Bourbon Prince and
prevent all fear of a movement for independence. It
was in line with his policy during the war of 1859, which
so estranged Napoleon, of gathering the fruits of victory
at the earliest possible minute. Against it was the fact
that, once Sicily was annexed, Cavour could no longer
claim that he had no influence over Garibaldi and would
become responsible for his actions, and if the Powers
vetoed his passage to the mainland, Cavour would have
to stop it, and besides the danger of a serious breach
with Garibaldi in consequence, the conquest of Naples
and prospective unity would be indefinitely postponed.
But Garibaldi had no intention of complying with any
such proposal. It would deprive him of the Dictatorship, take away his freedom of action, and make him
responsible to the Government of Turin. Much as
Cavour wanted annexation, nevertheless, he would not
attempt it without the consent of Garibaldi, but to try
and gain his end he sent La Farina to Palermo in the
first days of June.

Cavour's choice of an agent was unfortunate. La
Farina was not only the personal enemy of Crispi, who
was acting as Garibaldi's Secretary of State, but he

[1] On the conversion of Hudson and Russell to the idea of Italian unity, see
the extracts from the Russell Papers in Trevelyan, *Garibaldi and the Making
of Italy*, Appendix A.

was hated by all the Mazzinian element for his intimacy with Cavour. In carrying out his difficult mission he showed little tact. Almost his first act was to plaster the walls of Palermo with demands for annexation, a method of propaganda scarcely calculated to propitiate Garibaldi. He took small notice of Cavour's advice not to be in a hurry, but to let the men around the Dictator prove their incapacity before urging his own case. His letters to Cavour painted the misgovernment of the island in the blackest colours, and although Cavour was not altogether deceived by them, he failed to realize, perhaps, how much the conduct of La Farina prejudiced Garibaldi against any thought of immediate annexation. The Dictator put up with La Farina's unwelcome activities for a month, then his patience gave out, and he was arrested and sent back to Genoa.

There was no fighting in Sicily during the month of June. Garibaldi was occupied with the evacuation of the Neapolitan troops from Palermo and the organization of a new army—thanks to reinforcements arriving from Turin—with which he intended to cross the Straits and conquer Naples. Diplomacy, however, was feverishly active, the lead being taken by Naples, who hoped to stem the tide of disaster through the good offices of France. Napoleon on his side was lavish with good advice as to reforms and concessions. 'We shall second him in regard to the continent,' wrote Cavour, 'since the macaroni is not cooked: but as for the oranges already on the table we are well decided to eat them.'[1]

On receipt of the news of the armistice at Palermo, the King convened a meeting of the Foreign Ministers accredited to the Court of Naples, and tried to obtain from them a guarantee for the maintenance of the dynasty and the immunity of the kingdom from attack. But the ambassadors refused to commit their Governments, and the Marquis d'Azeglio telegraphed from

[1] For the explanation of Cavour's unusual phrase see the amusing letter of Nigra to Cavour, Appendix D.

London that Lord John Russell had replied that he would take care to sanction nothing of the kind. Cavour in his turn sent word to Villamarina that he protested in advance against all interference of foreign Powers in Italian affairs, basing this on the principle of non-intervention proclaimed by France and England. This checked Francis's second move which was a direct appeal to Austria for help, which, however, was not forthcoming. All that remained was now an appeal to France, and on June 7th De Martino, the Neapolitan Envoy at the Court of Rome, was dispatched to Paris to endeavour to win over the Emperor.

Nothing, however, could be got from Napoleon but a repetition of the suggestions put forward by Thouvenel in a note to Cavour, namely, autonomy for Sicily under a Bourbon Prince, a Constitution of Naples and Palermo, and an alliance with Sardinia.[1] Of these it was the last upon which the Emperor laid most stress and which caused equal repugnance and embarrassment to both the proposed allies. Alliance was hateful to King Francis and impossible to Cavour. But Talleyrand was instructed to urge it, and in this he was warmly supported by Russia and Prussia. Cavour had no intention of accepting these terms, but he was anxious to show himself reasonable and not slam the door in the face of diplomacy, so he replied that he had no objections to make—provided that they were freely accepted by the people of Sicily. A condition which he well knew was equivalent to rejection.[2] Francis, in the meanwhile, forced by circumstances to stomach the bitter humiliation of the terms proposed by France, issued a Sovereign Edict, which, after proclaiming a general amnesty, a constitution, the adoption of the Italian flag, and a Bourbon Prince and a constitution for Sicily, announced with unhappy assurance that 'an accord will be estab-

[1] *CCN.*, vol. iii. No. 814, dated May 9th. The same letter in Bolléa bears the date June 9th. This latter is the right date as can be seen by the letter dated June 5th in *CCN.*, vol. iv. No. 884. See also for a full account of De Martino's mission, Bianchi, *Stor. Doc.*, vol. viii.

[2] *CCN.*, vol. iv. No. 896.

lished with S.M. the King of Sardinia for the common interest of the two crowns in Italy.'

Even though he had been personally willing to promote this 'marriage of the carp and the pike' Cavour could not have carried it through. The King, the country, and, above all, Garibaldi, would not hear of it. In Parliament, the debate on the loan for 150 millions gave occasion for a very decided expression of opinion. 'We hear,' exclaimed Guerrazzi, 'with as much amazement as disgust, that Naples holds out to us its hand, still smoking with the blood of Sicily: reject it: with Naples it would be no alliance but a punishment, a corpse bound to a living body,' and other speakers, if less dramatic, were equally decided against it. The Press was unanimous in opposition. In an article in *l'Opinione*, the leading Ministerial paper, the fundamental paradox of the proposed alliance was ruthlessly exposed:

> The promised concessions have for their objective to keep Naples in subjection and regain the mastery over Sicily. How can Piedmont consent to an alliance whose supreme end is to turn our arms against Sicily? Can we deny to Palermo the principles we have supported, defended, and caused to triumph, at Modena, Parma, Florence, Bologna, and Ferrara? If the Government of Naples, in its present conditions, believes for one instant that Piedmont will enter into an alliance, it has fallen into an illusion that will quickly be dissipated. Our Government has nothing to gain and everything to lose by such an alliance. It would impose upon us obligations that would cost us dear and would offer no recompense either for our own interests or those of Italy.[1]

With this feeling in the country Cavour had only one course to pursue, but he was sorely embarrassed to know how to refuse the alliance and satisfy diplomacy.

After his unsuccessful mission to Paris, De Martino returned to Naples to become Foreign Minister in the new Constitutional Cabinet. He at once opened negotia-

---

[1] Chiala, *Lettere*, vol. iv. Introd.

tions with Villamarina, who asked for instructions from
Cavour and received the following reply. He was to
be very reserved, but to let it be known that Piedmont
would abstain from creating difficulties, and, if the new
Cabinet adopted a truly national policy, would support
it. As to an alliance, it was necessary that Naples should
break with Austria, endeavour to make the Papacy
accept a national programme, and renounce all idea of
recovering Sicily by force. A policy which would admit
civil war was incompatible with that of Turin. The
real significance of these terms is summed up in a letter
of Cavour to Nigra: 'if Naples accepts our conditions
she is lost, for the sacrifice of Sicily will take away the
only support which might have enabled the Government
to overcome the difficulties in the country. If they are not
accepted, we shall wash our hands of the whole business
and leave the King to his fate.'[1]

June passed into July and nothing was settled, in
fact the problem became still more intricate. Prince
Napoleon was writing urging Cavour to a policy of
audacity, to drop finesse, lay the whole position before
the Emperor, and go straight for national unity.[2]
Ricasoli in Florence was even more peremptory. He
not only demanded immediate annexation of Sicily, but
was talking of leading the levies being openly raised in
Tuscany in an incursion into the Papal States and there
joining hands with the malcontents. Ricasoli had to
be called to Turin and made to see reason. But no
sooner was he back in Florence than his four-page
letters on the weakness and hesitation of the Government at Turin recommenced. At last Cavour lost
patience and wrote to Prince Eugenio in Florence that
'if the Baron Ricasoli has another policy to propose to
the King, let him propose it, and if His Majesty agrees,
I am ready to yield the reins of Government to him.
But if he has not the courage and energy necessary to
put in practice the commonplaces with which he regales
me every morning, let him allow those who are carrying

an extraordinary heavy burden on their shoulders to do it in their own way.'[1]

The problem over which Cavour was pondering day and night had its centre in Garibaldi. His fabulous success on the one hand, and the cruelty, cowardice, and ineptitude of the King of Naples on the other, had given an irresistible impetus to the national demand for unity. The concessions of the King had made no difference, for no one believed his word, and besides, Garibaldi would have nothing to do with him. The only thing to be done was to let him fall—*en sauvant les apparences*. That accomplished, the alternative was annexation or revolution. Cavour did not fear revolution, for he thoroughly trusted Garibaldi's loyalty to the King, in spite of the fact that his *entourage* was Mazzinian. But the trouble lay in this, that Garibaldi, intoxicated by success, no longer restricted his view to Naples, but spoke openly of going on at once to Rome and after that to Venice; finally, of presenting Victor Emmanuel on the steps of the Quirinal with a united Italy. If this had been mere boasting little notice need have been taken of it, but the danger lay in the possibility of at least some measure of success. If Garibaldi conquered Naples as easily as he had done Sicily, if the army of King Francis revolted or refused to fight, what was there to stop him passing on from Naples to Rome? The likelihood of this becoming a reality was brought daily nearer by the disintegration that was taking place throughout the Neapolitan Kingdom. For this to happen meant war with France, national humiliation, and the collapse of Italian unity. The problem was how was Garibaldi to be stopped?[2]

Cavour saw three possibilities. The immediate annexation of Sicily would lessen the prestige of Garibaldi, remove the halo of the Dictatorship, and make him amenable to reason. But Cavour, in spite of the impatience of Ricasoli and the advice of Nigra, would not attempt this without Garibaldi's consent.

[1] Bolléa, Nos. 312. 324.   [2] *CCN.*, vol. iv. No. 940.

If I was to enter upon a struggle with Garibaldi [he wrote] it is probable that I should have the majority of the old diplomats on my side, but public opinion would be against me, and it would be right, for Garibaldi has rendered to Italy the greatest service that a man can render. He has given the Italians confidence in themselves; he has proved to Europe that the Italians know how to fight and die upon the battlefield to reconquer their country! this service all the world recognizes.

The second possibility was the one finally adopted, the march of the Piedmontese army through the Papal States, but this was not yet more than an outline. The third was to promote a revolution in Naples before Garibaldi arrived there, to procure the flight of Francis and the installation of a provisional Government, so that on Garibaldi's arrival the reins of power would be already in Piedmontese hands.

The morality of this last proposal cannot be defended. By men like Massimo d'Azeglio and Sir Henry Elliott it was condemned unreservedly. But nevertheless it has to be remembered that Cavour was pledged to England not to make open war on Naples, which in any case he was anxious to avoid; that he was only promoting a line of action which any other people less demoralized and corrupted than the Neapolitans would have carried out of their own accord, as the Tuscans and Modenese had done, and as the papal subjects would also have done but for the French garrison. But even if such a revolution took place, the march through the Papal States was bound to be the last act of the drama. Unity could only be sealed by an imposing display of the principle of monarchy. The King, not Garibaldi, must dominate the final scene, and law and order not revolution must be the prevailing note of it, and unity without the Papal States was impossible.

Garibaldi proved obdurate on the question of annexation, he would not lay down his Dictatorship until what he believed to be his mission was accomplished. Instead he asked for Agostino Depretis to be sent to

Sicily to take over the civil administration, and Cavour, though he thought the choice was bad,[1] acquiesced, and Depretis was installed as Pro-Dictator. The question of annexation now took second place and Cavour concentrated on the insurrection at Naples. His chief instruments were Villamarina and Admiral Persano.[2] The former was to try and get influential adherents to the cause of unity in the court circles, whilst the latter was to try and seduce the fleet. Three important conquests were made. The King's uncle, the Count of Syracuse, Liborio Romano, the Minister of the Interior, and General Nunziante. One small war vessel, the *Veloce*, came over, but no more. In spite of all efforts the Neapolitans would not move.

The diplomatic crisis as to the fate of the south took place towards the end of July. On the 4th, following the advice of Prince Napoleon, Cavour had written fully to Nigra and outlined the policy that in view of the situation he thought must be carried out. The Bourbon must go, and a provisional Government be installed at Naples before the arrival of Garibaldi. Umbria and the Marches must be annexed, but Rome remain intact, unless the Pope left it of his own accord. He did not expect, he said, that Napoleon would approve such a programme. The necessity of keeping on good terms with Russia and Prussia might require a public disavowal of it, but if the Emperor would give his tacit consent, Cavour would guarantee order and a stable government in the new kingdom. This letter was read to the Emperor by Dr. Conneau, and on July 13th Nigra was summoned to St. Cloud.

After declaring the Prince's programme 'absurd' and finding fault with the want of cleverness in Cavour's handling of the situation, Napoleon's real opinion came out.

I do not love the Bourbons of Naples [he continued], they

---

[1] He would have preferred Lorenzo Valerio as a stronger man.

[2] The young Marquis Visconti Venosta was a very active agent in Naples at this time.

have never listened to me. The Pope for his part has lost
my sympathies if he ever had them. But it is not necessary
that every one should believe that we are working to overthrow
the thrones of Naples and Rome. I am not opposed in
principle to Italian unity, but I believe the task is beyond
your powers. I do not think that the King of Naples can keep
his throne for long, but it is necessary to let him fall under the
weight of public opinion in his own country. It is neither
Piedmont nor France that should dethrone the King of
Naples, but his own Parliament and people. It is necessary
to be able to wait. It is a question of putting him in the wrong
and posing conditions that will be impossible for him to accept.

On receiving this summary of the Emperor's reply from
Nigra, Cavour wrote cheerfully to the King, 'after
having lectured us as one lectures a son who contracts
debts, the Emperor has finished by showing himself
disposed to pay them. In short, he accepts our programme, provided we are strong and clever enough to
execute it. He suggests the *forme* and in that he is
very right.[1]

But the way was not yet cleared for the execution of
Cavour's programme. In the middle of July two
Neapolitan diplomats, MM. Manna and Winspeare,
arrived at Turin to negotiate for the alliance. Cavour
received them, put them off and tried to gain time.
Conversations had, in fact, been proceeding for some
time between France and England as to a possible
settlement of the situation in Sicily. Thouvenel had
suggested a truce for three or six months. Lord John
Russell suggested in reply that Garibaldi should hold
Palermo and Catania, and the Neapolitans Messina and
Syracuse, and that the Sicilians should be invited to
form a Government in the middle. It was not very
hopeful, but as everything depended on Garibaldi,
Cavour was approached to give his consent and use his
influence to restrain the Dictator. Cavour replied that
the Government had no influence over Garibaldi, that
they had sent him a representative, La Farina, who had

[1] *CCN.*, vol. iv. Nos. 966 and 973.

been arrested and sent back to Genoa. So the plan dropped through. Then the French Minister at Naples, Brenier, and the French Admiral, de Tinan, realizing that the position in Naples was growing steadily worse, and that Garibaldi's arrival on the mainland would mean the collapse of the Bourbon régime, urged Thouvenel to approach England with the suggestion that the Straits should be patrolled by a joint French and English squadron and Garibaldi forcibly prevented from landing. Thouvenel acquiesced and instructed Persigny to approach Lord John Russell. A favourable result seemed in prospect when Cavour learnt what was taking place. On the suggestion of Hudson he sent word to Sir James Lacaita, a personal friend of the Russell family, to try and see Lord John and prevent England from accepting. The move was successful, and at a Cabinet meeting held on July the 25th it was decided to reject Thouvenel's proposal.[1]

While this was taking place in London, Talleyrand informed Cavour of the proposal for a six months' truce. Cavour replied that the idea was excellent if one knew what Garibaldi would do, and if Sicily could produce a Ricasoli to keep the Sicilians in order. 'The idea is good,' he said, 'but inapplicable.' Almost at the same time came news of Garibaldi's victory at Milazzo and the surrender of Messina, and the probability of Garibaldi consenting to sit still for six months vanished.

> Please convey my warm and sincere thanks to General Garibaldi [Cavour wrote to Persano] after so splendid a victory I do not see how he can be stopped from crossing to the Continent. It would have been better that the Neapolitans should have completed or at least begun the work of regeneration; but since they do not wish or are not able to move, Garibaldi must do it. The work cannot stop half-done. The national flag raised in Sicily must be unrolled on the mainland and stretch along the coast until it floats over the Queen of the Sea.

[1] *Parl. Corresp.* For the details of Lacaita's mission see Trevelyan, *Garibaldi and the Making of Italy*, pp. 105 ff.

But Cavour could not refuse some satisfaction to the pressure of diplomacy, and he agreed to ask the King to use his influence to restrain the Dictator from crossing the Straits, and in a letter dated July 23rd Victor Emmanuel wrote as follows:

Dear General,

You know that when you departed for Sicily your expedition had not my approval. I have now decided, in the grave conditions that exist at this moment, to offer you a suggestion, knowing the sincerity of your feelings in my regard.

To put an end to the war between Italians and Italians I counsel you to renounce the idea of crossing the mainland with your brave army, provided that the King of Naples pledges himself to evacuate the island and leave the Sicilians free to decide their own future. In the event of the King of Naples not wishing to accept this condition I reserve my full liberty of action.

General, think over my advice and you will see that it is useful to Italy, towards which you can increase your debt by showing to Europe that, as you know how to conquer, so you know how to make the best use of your victories.

V. E.

But, alas, for the honesty even of a Re Galantuomo in the face of necessity, together with this impeccable epistle, Count Litta Modignani was the bearer of another which ran thus:

Now after having written as King, V. E. suggests to you that you reply in these terms which I know are your own. Say that the general is full of reverence and devotion for the King, that you would wish to be able to follow my advice, but that your duties towards Italy will not allow you to refuse help to the Neapolitans when these call to you to free them from a government which no good and loyal Italian can trust, so not to be able to adhere to the wishes of the King desiring to keep your full liberty of action.[1]

When Garibaldi read this second letter, he laughed, and then sat down and wrote his reply, which differed

[1] The original of this famous letter has never been forthcoming and its authenticity has been in consequence impugned. See Curatulo, *Garibaldi Vittorio-Emanuele, Cavour, nei fasti della patria*.

only from that suggested by the King in the terms in which it was expressed.

Whilst this little comedy was being enacted, Cavour at last received the good news for which he had long hoped. The English Cabinet having dispatched to Thouvenel a note in which it not only refused to join with France in blockading the Sicilian coast, but added that, if France did so alone, England would protest against her action, Napoleon gave in, and wrote to Persigny that he only desired that 'Italy should be pacified, *no matter how*, but without foreign intervention.' Cavour asked for nothing more.

For three months Cavour had kept the ring for Garibaldi in the face of an angry and scandalized diplomacy. He had made such good use of the friendship of France, thanks in no small measure to the cession of Nice and Savoy, that all efforts at interference on the part of Russia and Austrian had been nullified by the action of Napoleon; and then, when he proposed to interfere himself, Cavour had used England to prevent it. For all this he had neither recognition or gratitude from Garibaldi. But Cavour was thinking not of himself but of Italy, and the rancour and hatred of Italy's idol did not disturb him. He appreciated Garibaldi at his just value. 'He has a generous character and the instincts of a poet,' he wrote to Nigra, 'but at the same time he has a primitive nature on which certain impressions trace an indelible imprint. The cession of Nice has wounded him deeply; in a sense he regards it as a personal injury, with the result that he desires, I verily believe, to overthrow the Government as much as to drive out the Austrians.' He divined Garibaldi's course of action accurately. 'He will not proclaim the republic at Naples,' Cavour wrote on the first of August, 'but he will not permit annexation and he will keep the Dictatorship.' But while Cavour knew that Garibaldi, personally, could be trusted to be loyal, he realized that the political side of the campaign would be in the hands of men much more dangerous for the future of Italy. 'If his government acts at Naples as it did at Palermo,' he wrote, 'in a week there will be neither army, navy, or finances.'

All these reasons weighed with Cavour in his deter- mination to stop Garibaldi before he went too far, but the dominant motive was the revolutionary atmosphere that was implicit in the whole undertaking. It was true that he himself was an accomplice; he had allowed Garibaldi to be supplied with men and munitions; he had recently guaranteed a loan of two millions to his government in Sicily, and now, as far as diplomacy could achieve it, he had assured Garibaldi's passage to the mainland. But here his active support ended. What he dreaded now was less his failure than his success. Henceforth, until Garibaldi was once more safe at Caprera, Cavour's policy was directed to one end, to secure the prestige of the Crown.

Now the only way to achieve this object and put Garibaldi and his redshirts in their true relation to the Kingdom of Northern Italy, was to dominate them at the critical moment with an imposing display of the regular forces of the Crown with the King at their head. This could only be done by marching south through the Papal States and risking war with Austria, but Cavour made up his mind to do it. On the first of August he wrote to Nigra his reasons for this momen- tous decision and a statement of the risks it involved.

If Garibaldi crosses to the Continent and conquers the King- dom of Naples and its capital as he has done Sicily and Palermo, he becomes entire master of the situation. The King will lose almost all his prestige; he becomes in the eyes of the majority of Italians no more than the friend of Garibaldi. He will probably preserve his crown, but this crown will shine only with such reflected light as an heroic adventurer will judge well to throw upon it.[1] Disposing of the resources

[1] This is by no means as great an exaggeration as might appear. An English journalist, G. S. Lang, a keen supporter of Garibaldi, in an interview with Lord J. Russell gave his opinion that 'the crown of Naples will be given to Victor Emmanuel not by the voice of the people but by the will of Gari- baldi.' If this reflects truly the opinions of Garibaldi's supporters, Cavour's fears were justified. See Curatulo, *op. cit.*, p. 268.

of a kingdom of nine millions, surrounded by an irresistible popular prestige, we cannot struggle with him. He will be stronger than we are. Then what are we to do? There is only one thing to be done. Associate ourselves with him frankly and go together to make war on Austria. The King cannot accept the crown of Italy at the hands of Garibaldi; it would sit too uneasy on his head. To restore the prestige of the throne, the King must mount his charger and in the centre of the famous quadrilateral the adventures of Sicily will be effaced. Palermo and Milazzo will be forgotten in the taking of Verona and Venice.[1]

But Cavour held his hand for a moment before taking this desperate resolution. The arrival at Turin of a certain Baron Nisco decided him to make one last effort to dethrone Francis by an insurrection before Garibaldi arrived. Ricasoli was summoned to Turin, and together with Farini they devised the *modus operandi*. Baron Nisco was to be conveyed to Naples in a warship, carrying a consignment of arms and a detachment of Bersaglieri to be put at the disposal of Liborio Romano and General Nunziante. Under cover of protecting the Countess of Syracuse, by birth a Piedmontese, Persano was to take his flagship to Naples prepared to assist and supervise the conspiracy. If a successful insurrection broke out, Liborio Romano was to assume the leadership of the movement at the head of a provisional government, and at once to invoke the protection of Piedmont. The King would accept it and dispatch a division of regular troops to control the situation and prevent Garibaldi's march on Rome. Having set this plan in motion and dispatched the 'Centurione' with arms and men to Naples, Cavour turned his attention to stopping a movement against the Papal States which had its source nearer home.

Garibaldi's original plan for the conquest of Naples had envisaged a simultaneous attack from both north and south. Bertani, with Mazzini behind him, had never given up this design. While La Farina and the National

[1] *CCN.*, No. 1022.

Society, assisted by the Government, had been hitherto responsible for the reinforcements sent to Garibaldi, Bertani had retained his volunteers for the projected invasion of the Papal States. He had now 6,000 men equipped and ready in Genoa and over 2,000 more under Nicotera in Tuscany. But he reckoned without Cavour, who, having decided to send the regular army from the north, was in no mood to see his plans forestalled by the irruption of Bertani's volunteers, whatever their chances of success, which were doubtful enough. Farini was sent to Genoa to tell Bertani that his men must go to Sicily, and Ricasoli was sent back to Tuscany with orders to disband the troops under Nicotera. Farini arranged that Bertani's troops should depart for the Golfo degli Aranci in Sardinia, and then go on to Sicily. The mistake was made of letting Bertani go with them. He left them in the Gulf, and hastened on alone to meet Garibaldi, whom he hoped to persuade to lead his troops to their original destination in the Papal States. Garibaldi set off the same day for Sardinia with Bertani, only to find half the troops already on their way to Sicily escorted under compulsion by Piedmontese warships. Cavour had been too quick for them. Bertani was wild with rage, but Garibaldi was more philosophic, and needing men for his own purpose took the rest with him back to Sicily. Nicotera's men met the same fate. After a bitter quarrel with Ricasoli over disbanding his men, the Iron Baron compromised, and they were all dispatched to Garibaldi in Sicily. Having safely disposed of the active elements, Cavour now stopped all organized recruiting in Piedmont and cleared the road for the employment of the regular forces.

By the middle of August Cavour realized that the crisis was upon him. Three possible solutions of the situation were apparent. Either Francis would fall through the success of an internal revolution or through the work of Garibaldi, in either of which cases Cavour would go boldly forward, or, Garibaldi would be defeated, the insurrection would fail, and Cavour would resign, and his place be taken by a cabinet 'more conservative in tone and more amenable to the advice of diplomacy.'[1] The political position was intricate and uncertain. Austria, trusting to Russian support made possible by the Czar's irritation over Naples, was assuming a threatening attitude. Prussia, though she had not pledged herself to help Austria if attacked only by Italy, had recognized that Venetia was necessary to Austria and had undertaken never to recognize the union of the Kingdom of Naples with Piedmont.[2] Russia tended to shift her support from France to Austria, whilst England openly supported Garibaldi. As to the Emperor, Cavour found him 'enigmatic and irritable from the failure of his astute and undecided policy.' But Cavour felt pretty certain of at least the passive support of France. The feeling in England against Napoleon was very strong, and the Emperor had no desire to drive his neighbour to exasperation by thwarting the success of Garibaldi. Though the Emperor, when pressed by Prince Napoleon to say whether he would aid Piedmont if Austria attacked her again, had refused to give a definite reply, merely remarking that, 'sometimes it is well to have no *parti pris*,' nevertheless, when Thouvenel read to him yet another note of threats and remonstrance against Piedmont, he put his pen through it, saying to his Minister that Piedmont knew very well that France would never take action against her, even if she disregarded French advice; that it was therefore useless to write notes: too many had been written already, and besides, it was not advisable to oppose a policy the application of which might become necessary by oneself later.[3]

Cavour had not long to wait for a solution of the situation. On the night of August 18th, Garibaldi

[1] Chiala, vol. iii. p. 332. Cavour to Cassinis, August 16th.

[2] This was the result of the meeting of Franz Joseph and the Prince of Prussia at Teplitz in July.

[3] Bolléa, No. 332.

successfully crossed the Straits and landed at Melito in Calabria. On the 21st he captured Reggio, and three days later started on his amazing journey to Naples, miles in front of his troops, accompanied only by a few of his staff and an assortment of English civilians who could afford to pay for conveyances. The collapse of all effective resistance and the rapidity of his advance created consternation in official circles at Naples. Before Garibaldi had reached Monteleone, dreading above all else a repetition of the bombardment suffered by Palermo, the Neapolitan Government sent to Cavour through Villamarina a proposal that Naples should be neutralized and considered as an open town. Cavour seized on the suggestion as a last hope of getting hold of Naples before Garibaldi, and in forwarding the letter to Victor Emmanuel, after remarking that to ask a general to consent to the neutralization of the enemy's base of operations appeared to him ridiculous, suggested a reply of the following tenour: 'you cannot undertake to make such an absurd demand to Garibaldi. If the King and the diplomatic body desire to save Naples from the disaster of war, it is necessary for the King to leave the city and consent to the formation of a provisional government, giving us permission to garrison the forts.'[1] Cavour's purpose was not only to dethrone the King, but to be able to dispose of the army and navy. If his proposal had been accepted, it was his intention to send as large a proportion as possible of the Neapolitan troops to strengthen the Piedmontese forces in Lombardy, while the King came south through the Papal States. Believing that the success of Garibaldi would demoralize the fighting forces of Naples, he wanted to be in a position to send them north while they were still intact and under discipline. This would not only avoid the possibility of a collision between the garrison and the residents and remove the

---

[1] In the original draft after the words 'leave the city' the King added in pencil 'and if he cannot defeat them in the field and if he has no pluck in him', a characteristic touch.

dangers of a bombardment, but would enable Cavour
to present a formidable opposition to Austria.

But all attempts at a revolution without Garibaldi
failed. Cavour's agents were badly chosen. Villamarina
was hopeless as a conspirator and Persano was not the
man to take responsibility in a crisis. Baron Nisco
proved useless, and neither General Nunziante nor
Liborio Romano had any real influence. But the
decisive factor was the unexpected loyalty of the army.
The officers were unreliable enough, but the rank and
file remained firm to their oath. Though the country,
from the Royal Family downwards, was seething with
treachery and disloyalty, no one had the courage to
head the movement or come into the open with a
demand for the King's abdication. As to the people,
their profound distrust of their rulers and their dread
of a bombardment kept them silent and motionless.
Not a finger would they raise to drive out the hated
Bourbon, not one effort would they make to win their
own freedom. There was just one solution—the coming
of Garibaldi. So Naples waited, silent and expectant,
secure that the predestined deliverer 'will come in
thunder from the stars and save her.'

In the meantime Garibaldi, oblivious to all the
diplomatic entanglements he was creating for Cavour,
was pursuing his victorious march towards the capital
as fast as transport would permit. On August 30th he
was at Soveria where Ghio and 10,000 men surrendered.
The next day found him at Cosenza, sacred to the
memory of the two brothers, Attilio and Emilio Ban-
diera, who in 1844 had attempted to raise the flag of
liberty and had been shot by the Austrians a few miles
outside the city, in whose cathedral their bodies were
interred. After leaving Cosenza, Garibaldi found the
road blocked by the demoralized troops of Caldarelli
retreating on Naples, he therefore made for the coast
and sailed round to Sapri, where the ill-fated *Pisacane*
had landed three years before. Here he found Colonel
Türr with 1,500 men brought up by sea, and putting

THE ARRIVAL AT NAPLES 421

himself at their head struck inland, and rejoined the
trunk road at Il Fortino. A few miles farther on he
overtook Caldarelli's force which, like that of Ghio,
surrendered without trouble. Any expectation that the
King would attempt to defend his capital, by opposing
Garibaldi south of Naples, vanished on September 5th
when—thanks in part to bogus telegrams sent from
Eboli by 'Garibaldi's Englishman' Peard—the formidable garrison of Salerno was ordered to retire northwards. Garibaldi entered the day following. That
evening news arrived that the same day Francis and
his Queen had left Naples by sea for Gaeta and that the
capital anxiously awaited the coming of Garibaldi. On
September 7th he took the train for Naples from the
terminus two miles outside Salerno, and accompanied
by a frenzied cheering crowd, that reduced the speed of
the train to a walking pace, made his triumphant entry
into the capital, and

> The air broke into a mist with bells
> And the old walls rocked with the crowd and cries.

News of the unhindered progress of Garibaldi had
rapidly convinced Cavour that all idea of a revolution
at Naples without him must be abandoned, and on
August 31st, when the Dictator was at Cosenza, he
wrote to Persano that 'what would have been most
opportune a fortnight ago, would now be fatal: that
the Government accepts the arrival of General Garibaldi as inevitable, only it trusts that all honest men,
aided by himself and Villamarina, will unite to persuade
him not to repeat the errors committed in Sicily, and
to call to power persons devoted to the cause of liberty,
order, and unity.' To try and improve their personal
relations Cavour sent an old friend of Garibaldi's,
Captain Laugier, to explain the policy he intended to
adopt, and a personal letter in which he expressed the
hope that the mission of Laugier would re-establish
'that complete confidence which existed two years ago
between us, when I prepared the war in which no one

believed and which many feared.' This effort was but half successful. Garibaldi began well. He appointed a cabinet of moderate men and handed over the fleet to Persano. But before long the real power fell into the hands of Bertani and Crispi, and the arrival of Mazzini and Cattaneo made the anti-Cavourian influence once more predominant.

The two methods of achieving national unity championed respectively by Garibaldi and Cavour came face to face once the Dictator was in possession of Naples. In refusing to allow the annexation of Sicily, Garibaldi laid down his point of view in these words, 'annexation, or to put it more exactly, the proclamation of United Italy and its King Victor Emmanuel, must not be announced until the Italian people, fighting from the extremity of Sicily, has arrived victorious at Rome the capital of the Kingdom. Annexation means detaching one part from its revolutionary solidarity with the rest. The revolution is our redeemer: annexation is the negation of it.'[1] So far as Garibaldi ignored the authority of the Government, his action was truly revolutionary, it was saved by his loyalty to the King. Cavour's view was different, 'there is no revolution,' he wrote, 'when all the people consent in the form of government, when the government is the reflection of public opinion, having legal means to urge it or restrain it in accordance with the popular will . . . if, therefore, those popular forces, improperly called the revolution, constitute one of the greatest assets of the Government in the work of national redemption, they only preserve their efficiency and utility as long as it is the government that moderates and directs them.'[2] This, then, was the question which had to be decided, whether the final decision was to be given by the constituted authority or not.

The arrival of Garibaldi at Naples forced Cavour to act. The compelling reason was simply that north and south must be joined, for unity could not become a

[1] Garibaldi to Depretis.   [2] Cavour to Cesarini.

reality with the Papal States intervening. Nor could this task be left to Garibaldi, for he would embroil himself with the French garrison and ride roughshod over the susceptibilities of the Catholic world. This reason was perhaps too crude to put forward officially, so Cavour made use of another in dealing with diplomacy. This was the fear of revolution, which throughout his political career Cavour had used as one of his principal weapons for winning the support of the Powers. He had systematically represented his Government as the one barrier between Europe and this nameless catastrophe, of which Mazzini was the personification, and now, with that arch-conspirator at Naples, his appeal had real force behind it. Yet Cavour must have known, in spite of Garibaldi's flamboyant talk about winning Rome, Venice, and even Nice and Savoy, that the hero had his Achilles' heel, namely, his unswerving loyalty and obedience to Victor Emmanuel, and that, in the last instance, there was no danger of civil war with the consent of Garibaldi or even of a republic.

What Cavour did fear was delay. The moment had come to dominate the triumph of popular force in the interests of order and the prestige of the monarchy. If Garibaldi was wounded, or his army seriously checked or defeated, there was no saying what might not happen. Delay might mean an attack by Austria in the north or the union of the Papal army with that of Naples, with the consent and assistance of Austria. Given time, Russia, Prussia, and Austria might come to a working agreement that might ruin Italian unity. In any case delay was a danger and Cavour was resolved to act at once. The moment was not unpropitious. The week before Garibaldi's arrival, Napoleon visited his new province of Savoy, accompanied by the Empress. It was an opportunity not to be missed, for although his mind had been prepared by Nigra for Piedmontese intervention in the Papal States, the Emperor had not expressed his approval. Cavour now dispatched Farini and General Cialdini to Chambéry to explain the situation and the steps it was proposed to take. The interview took place on August 28th and was entirely satisfactory, and the next day, after the return of his emissaries, Cavour wrote to Nigra: 'The Emperor has been perfect. Farini, following Conneau's advice, explained to him in detail the plan we have adopted. The Emperor approved everything. Diplomacy he said would make a great fuss—he would find himself in a difficult position, but he would put forward the idea of a Congress. We touch the supreme moment. With God's help Italy will be made before three months are passed.' As to an Austrian ultimatum or invasion Cavour saw reasons to doubt it. Writing to La Marmora to keep what forces he had in readiness for instant action, he added, 'I believe an aggressive movement on the part of Austria unlikely. In the actual internal conditions of the country the slightest reverse would be very dangerous for her. It might mean the total ruin of the Empire. But it is all the same possible.'

The same day as Garibaldi reached Naples Cavour wrote a peremptory dispatch to Cardinal Antonelli, demanding the immediate disbanding of the foreign troops, and on his refusal the Piedmontese army crossed the frontier (Sept. 11th).

But if Cavour, trusting in Garibaldi's loyalty to the King, did not in reality fear any revolution, he was under no illusion as to the intensity of the hostility that the Dictator bore to himself. The wound inflicted by the cession of Nice was kept open and envenomed by Bertani and Mazzini, whose plans Cavour had thwarted and whose policy he had systematically defeated. The immense prestige of Garibaldi, his headstrong character, and the extremist opinions held by the men around him, had become a real danger to the peaceful solution of the problem confronting the country. If Garibaldi deliberately ignored the decisions of the Cabinet at Turin, the King might find himself so placed as to have to choose between the two, and opposition between the King and his Government at such a moment would be as calamitous as a breach with Garibaldi. Prepared to make any sacrifice for his country's welfare, Cavour, as early as the first half of July, had considered the desirability of offering his resignation as a means of putting the Government on good terms with Garibaldi, but had put it aside as impracticable.[1] At that time Nigra had written suggesting that Parliament should be summoned and the country made to choose between Garibaldi and himself. Cavour had replied that if by so doing he might save his prestige, he would lose Italy, adding that 'he would rather lose his reputation but see Italy made.' But now the crisis had come; in spite of all his efforts Garibaldi had refused to listen to the advice offered, so to prevent the charge being brought against him that he had clung to power to the detriment of the country, and to remove the one obstacle to co-operation between Garibaldi and the Cabinet, he offered his resignation to the King together with that of Farini. In doing so he explained that a dispatch received from Persano left no doubt as to the hostility of Garibaldi towards his colleague and himself; that the choice of another Cabinet would make it easier to avoid the probable conflict with the Dictator over Southern Italy; that the change could be made now without loss to the dignity or authority of the Crown, but that if the existing breach became public, the Cabinet could not resign without injury to the Constitution, because that would mean that the policy of the King had been dictated by a subject.[2] The King refused absolutely to accept either resignation, announced that he would deal with Garibaldi himself, and would carry out his purpose even if it meant using force. Cavour, having done all that was possible, withdrew his resignation.

[1] *CCN.*, vol. iv. No. 961. To Nigra. 'If a change of Government would establish harmony between Garibaldi and Turin one ought, perhaps, to do so. But who to put in our place? At the moment I believe Rattazzi impossible. Besides he is too reasonable to accept Garibaldi's programme. This latter puts faith in Depretis. But Depretis would not be tolerated either by the country or by Europe.'

[2] See the full text in the Memoria given by Luzio in *Garibaldi, Cavour, Verdi*, p. 291. The date is September 9th.

Two days later (Sept. 11th) Garibaldi wrote two letters to the King. The first was a request to send the Marquis Giorgio Pallavicino to Naples as Pro-Dictator, the second was a demand for the dismissal of Cavour: 'I have been silent up to now,' he wrote, 'as to the infamous opposition suffered by me at the hands of Cavour, Farini, &c., but to-day when we approach the crisis of the great Italian drama, I must implore from your Majesty, for the good of the holy cause I serve, the dismissal of those individuals.'[1]

The King sent this letter to Cavour who forwarded it to Nigra, remarking, 'I believe all commentary useless. Show it to M. Thouvenel, but without giving him a copy, and ask him if after this there was any other line to take except that we have been obliged to adopt. The King has at once replied to Garibaldi in a tone calm and categorical.'

Having assured himself of the support of the King, Cavour now decided to summon Parliament, demand a vote of confidence in the Government, and ask for powers to annex the newly acquired provinces. The step was a bold one, for the breach with Garibaldi could not be concealed from Parliament, and Garibaldi's immense prestige would find great support in the Chamber. But Cavour believed in constitutional methods and trusted to the good sense of Parliament to see the necessity for supporting his action.

In the meantime the royal army was rapidly carrying out its task. Fanti divided his forces into two corps, one under Della Rocca, whose task was to overrun Umbria; while the other, under Cialdini, had Ancona for its objective. The rapidity with which invasion followed the ultimatum disconcerted La Moricière, who was given no time to call in the troops occupying the towns of Umbria. He decided to try and reach Ancona with his main body, but Cialdini was too quick. Divining his intention, by forced marches he intercepted La Moricière at Castelfidardo and scattered the

Papal forces beyond recovery. The news of Cialdini's victory came as an immense relief to Cavour. Determined to make the most of the victory as an offset to the triumphs of Garibaldi, he celebrated the occasion with all possible pomp.

> The military triumph is great [he wrote to Cialdini] but the political victory is greater. You have solved the problem which was the *raison d'être* of the expedition in the most satisfactory manner. It was not merely a question of winning, but of winning quickly. Now the political horizon has cleared; the dangers that threatened us on all sides have either disappeared or are reduced to such a point as to be easily overcome.

Della Rocca's corps, having freed Perugia and the rest of Umbria, now turned east and joined Cialdini before Ancona. Orders had been sent to Persano to leave Naples and bring the fleet round to Ancona to assist in the siege, which lasted until September 29th when the town surrendered.

While these events were taking place Cavour was carefully watching the development of Garibaldi's policy at Naples. On the 12th, the day after the royal army crossed the Papal frontier, the King wrote a personal letter to Garibaldi. After congratulating him on his great work 'for the common cause,' and having informed him of the entrance of the northern army into Papal territory, he continued, 'This move, added to what you have done, has much alarmed the Powers, and we may be attacked by Austria; it is therefore necessary that military action in Italy shall be under one command, and that no expedition or attack shall be made without my order. The bearer of this will tell you my proposals verbally. You will please inform him how many of the old Neapolitan troops I can dispose of for Northern Italy and how much material can be sent with them.' Garibaldi's reply is not known, but he had certainly nothing to offer in the way of troops and supplies, and his own position was difficult enough. At the moment he was engaged in concentrating his army as it arrived in detachments from the south, most of his troops having marched from Calabria. The southern half of the Neapolitan army had been disarmed and disbanded, but the northern half, encouraged by the presence of the King and his brave consort, was concentrated round Capua on the line of the Volturno and outnumbered Garibaldi's forces by two to one. But if Garibaldi's military dispositions were sound, his political arrangements were, in Cavour's phrase, 'deplorable.' He first refused the request of his Pro-Dictator, Depretis, to permit the annexation of Sicily;[1] then he refused to accept his resignation, which he came to Naples to offer, and sent him back to Sicily with full powers, making only one exception, that annexation should in future not be mentioned until 'our programme has been realized at Rome and I have obtained the certainty of the fulfilment of the following two conditions: (i) that the King recognizes by Royal Decree the rank of the officers of the southern army as they are at the time of the proclamation of the Italian Kingdom; (ii) that S.M. promises me, with his royal word, to continue the Italian Movement until the whole natural frontier of Italy is reached, and promises me to march with the army to the frontier, in fulfilment of our desire and that of the entire nation.'[2] A little later, when Depretis renewed his request to resign, Garibaldi accepted it, and departing suddenly for Palermo installed a republican, Mordini, in his place, seizing the occasion to harangue the Palermitans on his determination to proclaim Victor Emmanuel King of Italy on the steps of the Quirinal. 'Alas,' wrote Cavour to Villamarina, 'the honeymoon with Garibaldi has been of short duration. His choice of ministers has been good, but his address to the Palermitans is a political programme with which we cannot associate ourselves. The proposal to attack the French, announced to Europe, obliges us to separate our cause from his.'[3]

[1] This request he received at Il Fortino, and only for Bertani's inopportune protest he would have probably granted it. See Trevelyan.
[2] Bolléa, No. 352, September 14th.   [3] Bolléa, No. 355, September 17th.

Not content with thus advertising his march on Rome, Garibaldi dispatched the Marquis Pallavicino, his newly appointed Pro-Dictator at Naples, back to Turin with a letter to the King again demanding the dismissal of Cavour. The King was furious, and not only sent a peremptory refusal, but decided at once to depart for Ancona and take command of the army in person and thus deal with Garibaldi himself. In writing to Prince Eugenio, who was hastily summoned as Regent to Turin, Cavour added, 'it is this insolent ultimatum brought by this imbecile Pallavicino that has decided the King.'[1] Cavour was still haunted by the fear of a march on Rome by Garibaldi before the Royal Army could get between him and his objective, and he feared, too, the possibility of a clash between the red-shirts and the regulars. He dreaded an Aspromonte as much as he did a Mentana. But events were soon to simplify the situation. Ancona fell on the 29th, and the same day Victor Emmanuel left Turin to join the army before the captured fortress. On October 1st Garibaldi was attacked by the full strength of the Neapolitan army. Victory rested with Garibaldi, but it paralysed his advance on Rome and kept him on the defensive until the Royal Army joined him from the north. The battle of the Volturno removed Cavour's anxiety. 'Garibaldi is no longer to be feared,' he wrote to the King, 'he has lost all moral force and his material force is much weakened. Not only can he no longer oppose Your Majesty, but it is almost impossible for him to resist an advance of the troops of the King of Naples. Villamarina has sent me a courier telling me of his condition and Medici also makes it clear in his letter. Both beg Your Majesty to hasten your advance on Naples, if you do not want to find that city fallen again into the power of the Bourbon.'[2]

On October 2nd the Parliament met at Turin and

[1] *CCN.*, vol. iv. Nos. 1138 and 1147; Bianchi, *Politique*, No. 195.

[2] *CCN.*, vol. iv. No. 1154. At the same time Cavour hurried what troops he could find to Naples by sea and this created an excellent impression both on the populace and on Garibaldi.

Cavour laid the issue before the country in a single-clause Bill stating that,

> The Government of the King is empowered to accept and confirm by Royal Decree the annexation to the State of those Provinces of Central and Southern Italy, in which is freely manifested by direct universal vote the desire of the people to make an integral part of one Constitutional Monarchy.

In introducing it Cavour laid down the reasons for the Bill. The danger of prolonging the present state of things; the need to return as soon as possible from revolutionary to constitutional methods, lest Europe should be given reason to believe that, in Italy, revolution was not the means but the end. He then stressed the necessity for a vote of confidence in the Government to strengthen the hands of the Cabinet, especially as 'one voice justly dear to the people has made plain to the Crown and the country its distrust of us.' The debate began on October 5th, and on the 11th Cavour wound it up with a great closing speech.

He began by congratulating the Chamber that 'with one splendid exception' the Chamber was unanimous on the immediate annexation of the Central and Southern Provinces. Then he proceeded to deal with the principal criticisms put forward in the debate. The first was the contrast in method between the immediate annexation of the south and the long delay over that of Emilia and Tuscany; which Cavour effectively disposed of by a rapid summary of the political conditions after Villafranca, which had made immediate annexation impossible. Then he came to a more difficult criticism; the Ministry, it had been said, wished to make the Chamber the judge, not of itself but of Garibaldi, and from the expressions used it might have been thought that the illustrious general was a prisoner at the bar of the House. Such, said Cavour, was not the intention of the Government. Far from slighting General Garibaldi, in thus asking for a vote of confidence in the Government, the Cabinet believed that they had rendered him the greatest homage which could be paid to a citizen. A profound difference of opinion had arisen between the General and the Government. The Government had not provoked it and they had done their best to avoid it. As long as they could do so they had concealed this dissension from the public, but when it became known, they considered the fact of sufficient gravity to invite Parliament to say if this dissension did not modify the vote of confidence in the policy of the Government given some months ago. Such action appeared to him to be a compliment rather than an injury to General Garibaldi. Not to have appealed to Parliament would have given a handle to their political opponents to take action against them.

The last criticism with which Cavour dealt was the suggestion of the Left that the Government in the circumstances should have resigned. To this Cavour replied that he agreed with this suggestion, and that the Cabinet, after considering the position while the dissension was still unknown to the' public, had offered their resignation, but the King had refused to accept it. He did not fail to add, however, that once the quarrel was known to the public resignation was impossible, for, if the Crown on the demand of a private citizen, however illustrious or well-deserving of his country, had changed its advisers, it would have given the constitutional system a grave, almost a mortal, blow.

> In short, gentlemen [he added], in coming to you and frankly asking for a vote of the Chamber, not upon the conduct of General Garibaldi but upon our policy, we shall obtain this result that, if your vote is against us and a ministerial crisis follows, it will be in accordance with sound Constitutional practice and will confirm rather than contradict the principles I have enunciated. If, on the other hand, your vote is favourable to us, we trust that it will exercise a very great influence on the generous mind of General Garibaldi.[1]

It is impossible not to admire the fairmindedness of Cavour. Not a word of censure or condemnation of Garibaldi escaped him. While freely admitting the

[1] Discorsi, vol. xi. p. 237.

conflict of opinion which had arisen between the Dictator and the Government, he put the issue before the Chamber without the least bias. He refrained from pleading his own case or attempting to prejudice that of Garibaldi. He put himself in the hands of the Chamber, as the constitutional mouthpiece of the nation, and left them to decide. But Cavour could not confine himself to the question of annexation. It was necessary before closing to deal with the problems that lay beyond, and let Italy and Europe know what was the attitude of the Government towards Rome and Venice.

> It is a serious thing [he went on] for a responsible Minister to give his opinion on the big questions of the future; nevertheless, I recognize that a Statesman, to be worthy of the name, ought to have certain fixed points, or, so to speak, a polar star, to guide him on his path, reserving to himself the choice of means and the right of changing them if necessary, but always keeping his eye fixed upon the point at which he aims. For the last twelve years the polar star of King Victor Emmanuel has been national independence; what will be his polar star in regard to Rome? Our polar star, gentlemen, I declare it openly, is to make the Eternal City, upon which twenty-five centuries have heaped every kind of glory, the splendid capital of the Italian Kingdom.

To achieve this end he relied on moral, rather than physical, force, basing his belief upon the ever-growing conviction in European thought that liberty is highly favourable to the development of true religious feeling.

> When this great principle will be generally accepted [he added] the great majority of earnest Catholics will accept the truth that the Holy Father will exercise greater influence, and at the same time be more truly independent in his sublime office, when guarded by the love of twenty-two millions of Italians than when defended by twenty-five thousand bayonets.

Lastly came Venice. To break with Austria now was impossible. Their army was not ready and Europe was against them. It was necessary to change public opinion. To do this they must prove two things to Europe: first, that they knew how to make themselves a strong and well-ordered nation; and secondly, that it was impossible to reconcile the Venetians to any kind of Austrian rule. Venice must belong to Italy, for in the moral order there is an analogous law to that of the physical world; attraction is in proportion to the mass: the stronger and more compact Italy becomes so much the more powerful and irresistible becomes the attraction that she exercises over Venice. When this is recognized by France, England, and Germany, Venice will join her Mother Country.' When Cavour brought his speech, amid tumultuous applause, to a conclusion, the voting was at once demanded. The Bill before the House and the vote of confidence were passed without a dissentient voice, preceded by an order of the day couched in the following terms,

> The Chamber of Deputies, whilst applauding the splendid valour of the sea and land forces and the generous patriotism of the volunteers, attests the national admiration and gratitude to the heroic General Garibaldi, who, succouring with magnanimous ardour the people of Sicily and Naples, has, in the name of Victor Emmanuel, won for the Italians so great a portion of Italy.

Assured the country was behind him, Cavour wrote hastily to Farini who was with the King: 'The result of the debate has been splendid. The opposition utterly discomfited. We are masters of the terrain. It is necessary to make use of it. To act and act quickly. Beg the King not to allow the troops to waste time anywhere. They must be at Naples before the Conference at Warsaw hatches any scheme to our detriment.'

The mention of Warsaw reveals the central point of European policy at the moment. No sooner had Cavour sent the army on its fateful journey south than the diplomatic storm had burst upon him. France had been the first to protest, by the immediate withdrawal of her Minister from Turin. Cavour was surprised at so precipitate an action after the Emperor's attitude to Farini at Chambéry, but he understood.

I see clearly [he wrote to Nigra] that France ought not to have the appearance of being our accomplice. To those who have not carefully weighed the difficulties of our position our plan must appear as a *coup de tête*. What seems to me probable is that, while making no part of the secret thought of the Emperor, Thouvenel has felt it necessary to separate, with some emphasis, the policy of France from that which circumstances impose upon us.

The real inconvenience was the withdrawal of Nigra from Paris and in consequence the absence of direct communication with the Emperor. Russia followed the example of France and withdrew her Minister. But the critical point was Austria. Since the beginning of August, Austria had been quietly increasing her army in Lombardy in a manner that half convinced Cavour that she meant to fight. Uncertain as to how far French support would be forthcoming, Cavour began to prepare for all eventualities. But the same uncertainty as to France's action held Austria back. A conference was arranged between Russia, Prussia, and Austria to meet at Warsaw on October 20th, and upon this everything depended.

But, unknown to Cavour until later, both England and France were working for a peaceful solution to Italian unity. Lord John Russell had accompanied the Queen to Coblentz in September and had obtained a promise from the Prince Regent that, if France did not assume an aggressive attitude, Prussia would not encourage Austria. Though Prussia protested, her Minister was left at Turin, and when he read to Cavour the note of the Prussian Foreign Secretary, Cavour replied, 'I console myself with the thought that on this occasion I have given an example that before long Prussia will probably be very glad to imitate.' Russia assured Napoleon that 'conciliation not coalition' was the purpose of the Warsaw Conference, and France, having given a formal promise not to support Piedmont in an *offensive* war against Austria, a peaceful outcome became assured.

While these negotiations were proceeding, Cavour, deprived of Nigra, turned to Prince Napoleon for information. The Prince proved an alarmist, being certain Austria would attack, though, out of respect for France, not Lombardy but the Duchies. The Emperor had replied to his fears by saying that Austria 'would not dare,' but the Prince remained unconvinced. Cavour left nothing to chance, and every available man and gun was pressed into service. The National Guard was armed and mobilized, and arrangements hurried on for transports to convey troops northwards from Naples the instant war was certain. Never, perhaps, throughout his political career had Cavour so anxious a month as October 1860, for the fate of Italy hung in the balance and he was unable to affect the issue. The meeting of Victor Emmanuel and Garibaldi on the one side and that of the rulers of Prussia, Russia, and Austria on the other, must decide the destiny of Italy while Cavour at Turin was powerless to influence either of them.

Cavour had now little fear of civil war, but he was desperately anxious that the Garibaldian epic should close on a note of friendship and generosity on both sides, worthy of the spirit of the whole great adventure. Above all he wanted it to end quickly so as to present Europe with a *fait accompli*. But Victor Emmanuel was in no very good humour with Garibaldi, whose dictatorial methods he resented. General Fanti, a hard bitten old regular, very jealous of the traditions of the army, had no love for either the volunteers or their general, and proposed to solve the question of their future by sending them all home with a gratuity. But Cavour knew well that such services as they had rendered to Italy were not to be paid for by cash, and he tried to get Fanti sent back to Turin, to deal with the situation in the north, and leave the task of settling with the Garibaldians in the more sympathetic hands of Cialdini. He kept writing to the King and Farini in this strain, declaring that he would go and bury himself at Leri rather than be a party to an ungenerous treatment of the volunteers. He wanted a mixed commission to decide their future. To incorporate the best elements in the regular army; to form a special corps of Cacciatori delle Alpi with their own officers and grades of seniority, and disband the indifferent elements with a gratuity. But now, as before, when he was safely out of range and surrounded by his soldiers, the King took little notice of Cavour's advice. Had it been taken there would afterwards have been less heartburning in the ranks of the volunteers.

In the meanwhile the political problem in the south was solving itself on the lines Cavour desired. Bertani, the most dangerous of Garibaldi's advisers, had retired and returned to Genoa. His place was taken by Crispi. Between Crispi and Pallivicino, the Pro-Dictator, a struggle ensued as to whether the vote for union should be entrusted to a constituent assembly (a return to the views of 1848) or to a plebiscite as Cavour desired. Pallavicino, backed by public opinion, triumphed; Crispi resigned, and on October 21st the plebiscite, held simultaneously in Naples and Sicily, voted for union by an overwhelming majority. A similar vote in Umbria and the Marches followed a few days later. On the same day Cavour wrote to La Marmora: 'The Emperor, interrogated directly upon the intentions of the Austrians, has informed me that Count Rechberg had assured the Minister of France that Austria did not think of aggression. He added that he was convinced that under no circumstances would Lombardy be attacked. Lord John has expressed the same conviction, adding that Prussia had pledged herself to him to preach moderation at Warsaw. The fear of an immediate attack thus seems to be dissipated.' Cavour's satisfaction with this good news was destined to be short-lived, for the very next day he telegraphs to Admiral Persano, 'a telegram announces that the Emperor of Austria is about to make large concessions to Hungary and has named the Archduke Albert Commander of the Army of Italy with General Benedek as chief of staff. This is very threatening and it is necessary to be prepared for anything.' Austria was determined to be ready if her colleagues at the Conference gave her support. Once more Cavour threw himself into preparations for war. With feverish anxiety he urged on his preparations. 'I am calling the levy under arms,' he writes to Fanti. 'We are ready for anything. Come what may, if we have to fall we will do it bravely, and in saving the good name of Italy we shall assure her future.' On the 29th he got word of the results of the Conference; they were good but not convincing. 'Austria has not presented an ultimatum and declares her intention of remaining on the defensive, at least for the present. London confirms this,' he wrote to La Marmora. The moment was critical; it was England who came to the rescue, for on the 27th Lord John Russell had written his famous dispatch in which he boldly declared that 'Her Majesty's Government can see no sufficient ground for the severe censure with which Austria, France, Prussia, and Russia have visited the acts of the King of Sardinia. Her Majesty's Government will turn their eyes rather to the gratifying spectacle of a people building up the edifice of their liberties and consolidating the work of their independence.' When Cavour looked up from reading this dispatch, wrote Hudson, there were tears in his eyes. 'Behind your dispatch,' he added, 'he saw the Italy of his dreams, the Italy of his hopes, the Italy of his policy.'

The outspoken words of Lord John Russell, coming at the moment when diplomatic Europe was waiting for a lead, cleared the air, and with a bad grace the continental Powers watched in silence the final stages of the Garibaldian drama. On October 26th, while Cavour was still firm in the belief that Austria meant war, Garibaldi met Victor Emmanuel at Teano. On November 2nd Capua fell before the royal army, and on the 8th Victor Emmanuel, with Garibaldi by his side, made his state entry into Naples. At dawn two days later, while the city was still asleep, Garibaldi embarked on the *Washington* with 1,500 lire borrowed from a friend and a bag of seedcorn, and left Naples for his rocky home at Caprera.

On the 7th of January this year Cavour, after studying the European situation, had written to a friend, 'as to Italy, I am convinced that the dispossessed Princes will never return, that the temporal power of the Pope is destroyed, and in a short space of time the principle of unity will triumph from the Alps to Sicily.' Eleven months later all that remained of Central and Southern Italy, outside the dominions of Victor Emmanuel, was the Patriarchate of S. Peter and the fortress of Gaeta, where for another two months the last of the Bourbons defied, with the help of the French fleet, the efforts of the royal army.

XIV. ROME AND DEATH

Condition of Italy—Naples—Venice and Rome—Diomede Pantaleoni—
Negotiations with Rome—A Free Church in a Free State—The
Negotiations Fail—The first Italian Parliament—Cavour on Rome—
Garibaldi and Cavour—Scene in Parliament—Negotiations with
Napoleon for Evacuation of Troops from Rome—The Conditions—
Cavour Accepts—Treaty drawn up—Cavour's sudden Illness—His
Death.

THE retirement of Garibaldi to Caprera and the return
of Mazzini to England left Cavour in possession of the
field. Without a moment's pause he turned to the task
of making unity a reality. The Royal Commissioners
for Umbria and the Marches, the Marquis Pepoli, a
cousin of Napoleon's, and Lorenzo Valerio, the Governor of Como, had left with the army and at once taken
over the administration of Central Italy. Farini now
resigned his post as Minister of the Interior to become
Royal Commissioner for Naples, while the Marquis
Montezemolo, accompanied by two experts, La Farina
and Cordova, both Sicilians, was sent to Palermo.

Italy had been made with such amazing rapidity that
there had been no time as yet to make any serious
attempt at administrative or legal unification. The
Lombards were still living under Austrian law, and the
British Consul-General at Milan, reporting on the condition of that province at the close of the year, remarked
that the uncertainty was such as to make accurate
information impossible, a condition of things which
would probably continue until the fate of Venetia was
decided.[1] Central Italy proved the area quickest to
adapt itself to the new régime, for such was the relief
at the removal of Papal methods of Government that
little difficulty was experienced in introducing the
Piedmontese system. The conditions in the south were
appalling. The administration was a mass of corruption; the people, steeped in ignorance and superstition,
were devoid of the very elements of political knowledge.

[1] *Parl. Papers*, 1860, part vii.

The hasty reforms of Garibaldi had made matters worse, and Sir Henry Elliott reported that 'a large proportion of the persons who occupied places of trust and importance were, no doubt, corrupt or incompetent, but they have been removed without discrimination and replaced without care; and, if I am to believe the accounts of those who were no friends of the late state of things, malversation, corruption, and oppression are greater at the present moment than they have been at any previous period.'[1] Mazzinians, Bourbonists, Republicans, and Monarchists all had their own following, and whatever reforms and regulations were introduced, bitter opposition from one quarter or another was assured beforehand. Sporadic brigandage was already making its appearance, and all these difficulties were intensified by the continued resistance of King Francis, shut up in the fortress of Gaeta. Behind all these troubles lay the questions of Venice and Rome, without a solution of which Italy could never be peaceful or satisfied.

Cavour's panacea for all these evils lay in the immediate assembly of the national Parliament. 'The salvation of Italy lies in Parliament,' he wrote, 'if it provides us with an honest majority opposed to the sects, I fear nothing. But if the majority is sectarian in character and too small numerically, I could not foresee what calamities might not overtake us.'[2] Cavour's opinion was not that of every one. Many thought he was going too quickly. 'Napoleon,' wrote Vimercati from Paris, 'persists in believing that it is a mistake on the part of the Count to unify Italy through Parliament; that it is only possible by a strong, almost absolute power in the hands of Cavour, who ought to go to Southern Italy to provide for all their urgent material needs which alone in the present circumstances can win over the Neapolitans.'[3] But Cavour remained

[1] Elliott to Russell, October 15th.
[2] Chiala, vol. iv. Cavour to La Farina, December.
[3] Castelli, Carteggio, p. 348.

staunch to his constitutional ideal, and to similar suggestions made by his friend the Comtesse de Circourt he replied in a noble passage:

> For my part I have no trust in Dictators, especially civilian Dictators. I believe that one can do with Parliament many things that would be impossible to absolute power. Thirteen years' experience has convinced me that an honest and energetic Government, that has nothing to fear from parliamentary disclosures, and will not allow itself to be intimidated by the violence of parties, has everything to gain by parliamentary struggles—I never feel so weak as when the Chambers are closed. Besides, I cannot betray my origin or deny the principles of my whole life. I am the son of liberty and to her I owe all that I am. If it is necessary to veil her statue it is not for me to do it.[1]

Many who approved of the principle urged that January 1861 was too soon; that it did not give the country time to provide the machinery or choose suitable candidates. But Cavour was adamant: 'to delay calling Parliament together,' he wrote, 'cannot be allowed. We are lost if the elections are postponed until March. They must be carried through now. Even January is late, but to delay them further would be the greatest mistake.' Cavour was thinking of the effect on Europe. He knew the value of a solemn national sanction given by a freely elected chamber upon England and the Emperor, and irregularities due to haste could easily be rectified later. So the writs for the first Italian National Parliament were issued for January 1861.

The immediate problem, however, was Naples. No sooner had Francis shut himself up in Gaeta than Napoleon, to save him from that humiliation of surrender, which he himself was destined to pass through ten years later, ordered his fleet to prevent an attack on the fortress by sea, by blocking the roadstead. Cavour protested; Victor Emmanuel first wrote, and then sent Count Vimercati to Paris to negotiate. England, urged by Cavour, protested as well. After

[1] Nigra, *Le Comte de Cavour et La Comtesse de Circourt.*

two months of exasperating vacillation Napoleon withdrew the fleet in the middle of January and left the
unhappy Francis to his fate. Three weeks later the
fortress surrendered and the King and Queen retired
by sea to make more trouble in Rome. But the fall of
Gaeta proved of small value. The task of pacifying
Naples was to take years not months, and the brigandage
organized from Rome, with Neapolitan gold and Papal
benedictions, was to tax the resources of the new
kingdom almost to breaking point.

Farini found Naples a very different problem from
Emilia. There the people were with him and he had
only to swim with the stream. Here the currents were
against him and he found himself in a whirlpool.
Instead of acting on his own initiative he named a
Consulta, and the result was indecision and delay.
Already discouraged, the sudden death of his newly
married son-in-law broke down his morale, and he
resigned his post. In December Cavour sent Prince
Eugenio di Carignano, with Nigra as his chief of staff,
to replace Farini, but this combination was little more
successful than its predecessor.

The condition of Naples was a ceaseless anxiety to
Cavour, but he put a brave face on his troubles. The
presence of Victor Emmanuel, who was still in the
southern province, did not make matters easier. He
became the centre of intrigues which complicated the
work of restoring order. More than once Cavour
thought of going to Naples in person, but the 'memories
of Monzambano' and the impossibility of finding a
successor at the Foreign Office kept him in Turin.[1]

I am too far away and not sufficiently informed to give you
advice as to what should be done [he wrote to the new Minister
of Public Works at Naples]. It appears that things are going
badly enough at Naples. I am grieved at it, but I am not
surprised nor discouraged. Nations are not regenerated in
a week. I have faith in the future. Italy must be made and

[1] Cavour to La Marmora, November 15th. Bolléa. Cavour to Cassinis,
December 14th.

shall be made. We shall try to overcome the difficulties by reasonable means, but if that does not suffice we shall use extreme methods. . . . I do not fear Bourbonists or Mazzinians. They will protest, make demonstrations, even perhaps rebel; I am ready to fight them either in Parliament or on the piazza.[1]

Cavour could do no more. Having given Naples the best men he could find he perforce must leave them to do their best. But the strain put upon him was desperate. Every one turned to him for everything, and work as he might there were limits even to his colossal strength.

There was need for a very clear head and a very firm hand at this moment. All over Italy national feeling, over-excited by success, was clamouring for the completion of national unity by the acquisition of Rome and Venice. 'Half the youth of this place,' wrote the British Consul at Milan, 'is running wild after military adventure and leaving trades, professions, and employments.' Garibaldi was always a danger centre and the King himself needed little encouragement to seek further adventures. But Cavour kept his head. He had made up his mind that for the present Venice must be left alone and that Rome was a question for diplomacy not force. 'As to Venice,' he wrote to General La Marmora, 'we have need of two years at least to put our fighting forces in order. It would be folly to declare war before then. If we keep the peace an attack from Austria is not probable, therefore, I believe we are in for a spell of quiet.' To the King at Naples he wrote with even more decision.

Above everything we must be prepared for struggles in the constituencies, in Parliament, and, perhaps later, on the piazza. But conflict is the life of free countries; it is this that keeps them healthy. The Government in consequence is not alarmed at the prospect of it. We shall be as immovable as Your Majesty was in '58 on the question of the clergy. Your Majesty may be certain that the Garibaldini will be kept quiet either *per amore o per forza*. To provoke Austria at the present

---

[1] Chiala, vol. iv. Cavour to Devincenzi.

moment would be an act of madness. We shall not do it and
we shall not allow it to be done, until the great day when
Your Majesty will give the signal for the final struggle that
will render your name more glorious than that of Napoleon.

But if Cavour felt it necessary to wait for Venice, the
question of Rome he held to be urgent. He had already
told the country that Rome must be the capital. It
was the historical and geographical centre of the kingdom, and the only city whose claims, Turin, Florence,
and Milan, would not dare to contest. But there was
another aspect of the Roman question which to Cavour
was of even greater importance than that of the future
capital; this was the opportunity afforded by the present
situation to put the relations of the Church and State
upon a new and more satisfactory basis. The relations
between the civil and ecclesiastical governments had
in the past been regulated by a series of Concordats.
The Leopoldine Laws in Tuscany, the Tannuccian in
Naples, and those dating from Joseph II in the Austrian
provinces, governed their several relationships with the
Church. A revision of the entire situation was, of
course, now inevitable, and Cavour hoped to carry
through an amicable arrangement based on the principle
of 'a free Church in a free State.' To induce the Papacy
to surrender the meagre remnant of the temporal power
in return for a national guarantee of security, an assured
income, and a full measure of spiritual independence.

All his political life Cavour had held that the only
solution of the religious question was the abolition of
the temporal power. 'Statesmen may be able to hasten
it or retard it,' he wrote, 'but they cannot stop it. The
progress of ideas, the development of civilization must
of necessity lead to it at no distant date. In the next
century it will be an accomplished fact accepted by all
parties.' But he did not want to employ force. The
withdrawal of the French garrison and the subsequent
occupation of Rome by Italian troops, following trouble
between the Pope and the people, might solve the civil
question of the capital but not the religious question.

He was convinced that nothing was to be obtained from the Papal Government without conceding a large measure of spiritual liberty, but he made the mistake of believing that to gain this the Church would give up the loaves and fishes of material power. All arrangements founded on purely temporal interests would be impossible, because the Pope could not yield a yard of territory without destroying the principle of 'inalienability' which was his one moral force. The liberty Cavour proposed to give would, he knew, meet with deep and widespread opposition, so profound was the national distrust of clerical influence. But Cavour's faith in liberty strengthened him to face it. 'I do not fear liberty in any of its applications,' he said.[1]

Living at Rome at this time was a certain well-known medical practitioner named Diomede Pantaleoni. A staunch liberal, twice expelled from the Papal States for his opinions, a friend of Massimo d'Azeglio, he had by long study become an expert on the Roman Question. In October he wrote to Cavour offering his services as an intermediary. Cavour accepted, and throughout the autumn Pantaleoni worked unceasingly to find a basis for negotiations. In this he was aided by an influential Canonist, Father Passaglia, a personal friend of Pio Nono. At the end of November his two unofficial negotiators drew up and forwarded to Cavour an outline of conditions necessary 'to assure the spiritual independence of the Holy Father and the exercise of his spiritual authority over the Catholic world' to which was added a second set suggested as 'A basis of agreement between the Papacy and the Kingdom of Italy in regard to the settlement of ecclesiastical affairs.'[2]

The rapid and unexpected success which attended these first overtures disquieted Cavour, for experience had taught him to distrust rapidity when dealing with the Papal Court. In returning the proposals with his comments and reservations, he therefore emphasized

[1] Chiala, vol. iv. Cavour to Pantaleoni; Cavour to Vimercati, January 4th.
[2] Full text in Chiala, vol. iv. pp. 102 ff.

the need for great caution and secrecy. 'I do not think,' he wrote, 'that the time has come to open negotiations seriously. At this stage an official proposal would run great risk of being rejected without examination, and that would compromise and retard our final object of an accord with the Holy See.' But in spite of Cavour's warning matters went forward far quicker than he anticipated. Pantaleoni was in touch with Cardinal Santucci who was the leader of the party most definitely opposed to the policy of Cardinal Antonelli.

At the end of January Cavour received a letter from Pantaleoni which revealed how far things had gone:

> Cardinal Santucci [wrote Pantaleoni], in spite of my expressed desire, has esteemed it his duty to tell everything to the Pope, who asked him what was the nature of this suggested agreement. Cardinal Santucci spoke to him of the inevitable loss of the temporal power; the proposals were received in an amicable spirit. The Pope showed himself resigned to everything. Antonelli was sent for. At first he offered opposition, but afterwards appeared to resign himself and requested that His Holiness would release Cardinal Santucci and himself from their oath in order to negotiate.[1]

Close behind the arrival of this letter at Turin came Father Passaglia in person. After long conferences with Cavour and Minghetti he returned to Rome bringing with him definite proposals. Owing to the absence of the King at Milan his credentials were delayed and followed him to Rome a week later by the hand of an 'honest Rosminian' Father Molinari. It is in these proposals and instructions that we see most clearly the meaning of Cavour's phrase, 'a free church in a free state.' In return for the surrender of the temporal power the following offer was made:

The Pope should retain all the dignity and inviolability of kingship; the right to nominate representatives at foreign Courts and free communication with the same. The Cardinals should rank as Princes with all the prerogatives of that position. The Pope should retain

---

[1] Chiala, vol. iv. p. 149.

the full right of legislation in all spiritual matters;
freedom of communication with the faithful and for the
convening of synods and councils. Liberty of preaching,
printing, association, and religious teaching, so long as
this did not disturb public order. In all temporal
matters the clergy would be treated as ordinary citizens.
The financial clauses contained provision for handing
over to the Papacy securities sufficient to maintain an
adequate civil list and the support of the Sacred College.
A sum to maintain the clergy, chapters, and cathedrals
would be a fixed charge on the national budget. Finally,
the Crown surrendered its rights in the appointment
of bishops and other dignitaries and abrogated all Laws
and Concordats, Customs and Privileges, at variance
with the principle of the freedom and independence of
Church and State. If accepted, these terms were to be
submitted to Parliament and embodied as an integral
part of the fundamental law of the kingdom.[1]

In the instructions which accompanied these proposals Cavour warned his negotiators that the policy of
Rome would probably be to regard these proposals as
a suggested modification of existing concordats, but
this was to be resisted. 'We do not treat,' said Cavour,
'of simply composing certain differences between
Church and State, but of changing the basis of these
relations, and of substituting for the troubles existing for
the last three or four centuries, an harmonious system
of reciprocal independence and mutual liberty.' But
Cavour was too keenly aware of the astuteness of Papal
diplomacy not to safeguard himself against negotiating
on a false basis, and therefore, in addition to his instructions, he sent definite credentials which were only
to be presented to Antonelli when his agents were convinced that proceedings were to open on the basis of
the surrender of the temporal power.

Napoleon, who was kept informed of what was going
on, was sympathetic, but did not expect Cavour would
have much success. Cavour could do nothing further

[1] Bianchi, *Stor. Doc.*, vol. viii. pp. 420 ff.

but wait for the issue of the negotiations. He was not too hopeful. 'Do we deceive ourselves or not,' he wrote after Passaglia's departure from Turin, 'on Antonelli lies the heavy burden of a reply. In any case it is much that one of the most learned and virtuous theologians of the Church, a professor of Canonical science at Rome, a collaborator with the Pope on the Dogma of the Immaculate Conception, has accepted and approved our proposals.'[1]

The success or failure of the negotiations, as Cavour well knew, lay more with Antonelli than with the Pope. As early as the previous December Cavour had opened secret negotiations with the all-powerful cardinal but nothing was concluded.[2] So long as the remotest chance of a reaction in favour of the temporal power was a possibility Antonelli would not negotiate. France had not yet recognized the new Kingdom of Italy, and as long as the French troops remained in Rome the temporal power was safe. Antonelli's strong suit was Naples. If the south was not quickly pacified it might be possible to revive the federal solution after which Napoleon still hankered. Cavour's sheet anchor was Napoleon; with very few exceptions France was against him. The ardent Catholicism of Rome's new guests, the King and Queen of Naples, strengthened Antonelli's hand and he decided to crush all hope of a peaceful solution. In this he was aided by the extreme irritation of the Pope. While Cavour proposed peace, his two commissioners, Valerio in the Marches and Pepoli in Umbria, both promulgated laws closing certain categories of convents, and now a more drastic law regulating ecclesiastical affairs, known as the Mancini Law, was issued by the Government at Naples. In addition, the

[1] On these negotiations, see Pantaleoni, *l'Idea Italiana nella soppressione del potere temporale dei Papi*; Bianchi, *Stor. Doc.*, vol. viii; V. Benoit, 'Le formule de Cavour', in *Revue des Deux Mondes*, July 15th, 1905; Chiala, *Lettere*, vol. iv.

[2] Cavour's agents in these obscure negotiations were a Vercellese named Bozino, the Cavalieri Isaia Secretary to Card. d'Andrea and an official in the Dateria named Aguglia, in close touch with Card. Antonelli. See the Letters in Chiala and the account given by Bianchi.

debate in the French Chamber of Deputies and the speech of Prince Jerome in favour of Italian unity added to the Papal anger. Antonelli's task was not difficult. All that was necessary was to delay the presentation of Cavour's instructions and credentials until he could assert his influence over the Pope. When Father Molinari arrived at Ancona with the documents, he found precise instructions awaiting him from the General of his Order to avoid Rome and proceed direct to Naples. While Cavour's credentials were thus travelling about Italy, Antonelli acted. The Pope responded quickly to the advice of his Secretary of State, and Pantaleoni suddenly received orders to leave the Papal States in twenty-four hours. Cavour had failed, for the resort to force which he sought to avoid was the only argument to which Rome would yield.[1]

While Cavour was thus engaged on his unsuccessful attempt to reconcile Church and State the first Italian Parliament met at Turin. The elections which took place on January 27th returned a solid majority for the Government. A special building had to be erected to accommodate the Chamber of Deputies, now increased to more than double their original number. The session opened on February 18th amid a scene of great enthusiasm. Conspicuous amongst the members in the diplomatic gallery was the Prussian Minister, St. Simon, accompanied by General von Bonin, both newly decorated with the green ribbon of the Order of St. Maurice.[2] Cavour had been quick to see the rising star of Prussia. In January he had sent General La Marmora to Berlin to compliment the new King on his accession to power. In return General von Bonin and a special mission were now in Turin. The address from the throne was brief and tactful, punctuated with vigorous applause, the allusion to the new King of Prussia being warmly acclaimed. When the royal session was over, Cavour introduced without delay a Bill proclaiming Victor

[1] Chiala, vol. iv. Pantaleoni to Cavour, March 10th, p. 187.
[2] de Bunsen, *In Three Legations*.

Emmanuel King of Italy. When this was accepted and passed, Cavour surprised the Chamber by announcing that the Government, feeling that the King should have a free hand in selecting the first Cabinet destined to preside over the new kingdom, had resigned. In submitting the resignation of the Cabinet to the King Cavour suggested that it would be opportune to consult the opinion of the more eminent men at present in Turin such as Ricasoli, Farini, Rattazzi, and Poerio. Victor Emmanuel not only took this advice but offered the Premiership to Ricasoli. He was quickly persuaded, however, that Cavour was indispensable, and with some reluctance sent for him once more.[1]

Cavour reconstructed the Cabinet. Francesco de Sanctis, a Neapolitan, was made Minister of Public Instruction. The portfolio of Public Works was bestowed upon Peruzzi a Florentine, and a Sicilian, Giuseppe Natoli, became Minister of Agriculture and Commerce. As soon as the new Cabinet was in working order Cavour decided to open up once again the question of Rome. It was necessary, to forestall untoward incidents, that the Government should give the country a lead on this vexed question. On March 22nd, apparently before receiving news of Pantaleoni's expulsion from the Papal States, he wrote to him saying that, in his opinion, an admission in Parliament that the State was prepared to grant large concessions in spiritual matters could do no harm and would facilitate the negotiations; that if Rome persisted in its refusal to negotiate, a knowledge of the conciliatory offer of the Government would win over public opinion; 'a frank and loyal explanation of the line the Government intends to take,' he said, 'will, I believe, be far preferable to a not very dignified silence.' So on March 25th, and again two days later, Cavour made two speeches in support of a carefully worded order of the day proclaiming the necessity of the union of Rome with Italy.

As long as this question was one for the future [he said] it

[1] Chiala, vol. iv. Cavour to the King, p. 195. See Thayer, vol. ii. p. 453.

was desirable not to bring it into the open; but now that it was being discussed all over Europe it would be weakness on the part of the Government not to say distinctly what attitude it took upon the question. Rome must be the capital of Italy, because without Rome Italy could not be constituted, and until this was accomplished there must be dissensions and difficulties between the different parts of the Peninsula. But they must only go to Rome on two conditions, in concert with France, and, without subjecting the Church to the dominance of the State in spiritual matters. The first of these conditions was in reality dependent on the solution of the second, for, if Italy could show that the independence of the spiritual authority of the Church was not impaired by the presence of the civil power in Rome, an accord with France would be easily established.

Unfortunately [he continued] many Catholics sincerely believed that if Rome was joined to Italy the Holy Father would become merely the Grand Almoner or Chaplain-General of the King. If this happened it would be fatal, not only to Italy but to Catholicism, for no greater disaster could take place than the union of the civil and spiritual powers in the hands of one authority. It meant either that a sacerdotal caste would usurp the civil power or that this latter would become a power of the nature of a Caliph or Sultan.

Cavour's next point was that the temporal power did not assure papal independence. Since 1789, he said, the basis of civil government was no longer divine right but consent, and since 1814 the history of the Papal States was one long protest against the methods of its government. The temporal power had only been kept in existence by foreign soldiery, and when a sovereign has to beg troops and money from other Governments it is evident that such power is proof not of independence but of dependence. Cavour next emphasized the fact that owing to the double nature of the authority residing in the Pope, reform of the Papal States from within was impossible, because as Pope he could not sanction reforms which as a temporal sovereign he might think desirable. He could not, as Pope, sanction civil marriage. Religious scruples prevented him enlisting troops amongst his own subjects.

The only solution was to separate the two powers and thus give the Pope that real spiritual independence it was impossible to give him as long as he was also a temporal ruler. Then, after outlining the offer already embodied in the proposals forwarded to Pantaleoni, he closed his speech with these words:

> Thus will it be given to this generation, after having called back a nation to life, to prepare an act greater and more sublime still, an act whose influence is incalculable; to have reconciled the Papacy with the Civil Power; to have signed peace between Church and State; between the spirit of religion and the great principles of liberty. I trust it may be given to us to do these two great things which will of a surety win for this generation the blessing and gratitude of the generations to come.[1]

In the meantime Cavour had heard of the expulsion of Pantaleoni from the Papal States. He was not unduly depressed. He did not accept it as final, trusting in the changeable character of the Pope and the influence of public opinion. But as it became clear that any further direct negotiations had small chance of success, he fell back on his alternate line of action. He would have preferred an amicable arrangement with the Papacy, followed by the withdrawal of the French garrison; this having failed, he now reversed his plan and sought a withdrawal of the garrison as a means of bringing about the arrangement with the Pope. Vimercati in Paris was now urged to make evacuation his principal objective.

At the end of March Cavour's preoccupation with Rome was interrupted by renewed political activity on the part of Garibaldi. His withdrawal to Caprera, which had thrilled Europe by its dramatic simplicity and self-abnegation, had not, in reality, been free from an admixture of wounded vanity. All the King had offered him, wealth, rank, or position, he had refused, and the one thing he had asked for, the dictatorship of the south for a year, was just what neither Victor Emmanuel or Cavour would grant, and a feeling of anger and resent-

[1] Discorsi, vol. xi. p. 314.

ment had in consequence marked his return to Caprera. He had genuine cause for bitterness. The King had been inconsiderate and tactless, and the reception accorded to Garibaldi and his army by Fanti and other highly placed officers had caused much bitterness and heartburning in the ranks of the southern army. Cavour had been afraid of this, and had done his best to prevent it. He had begged the King to be generous; he had tried to get Fanti sent back to Turin and have the command transferred to the more *simpatico* Cialdini, but when Victor Emmanuel was at the head of his army Cavour had little influence over him. The result was doubly unfortunate, for not only did it give Garibaldi a genuine grievance but it increased his anger against Cavour, at whose door he laid the entire blame.

Garibaldi at Caprera soon became a centre of disaffection. Cavour's old enemies of the Left, Rattazzi, Brofferio, and their following, quickly got in touch with the Hero, seeking to use him as before for their own political ends. Deputations from the south full of grievances, malcontents of all kinds, found their way to his island and incensed him against the Government. But the last straw was the alleged injustice of the treatment meted out to his old soldiers and officers. Garibaldi wanted his army kept intact. This was impossible, and a commission was appointed to demobilize it, incorporating the best elements in the regular army.[1] The methods of the commission caused a stream of complaints and Garibaldi determined to go to Turin and protest.

Cavour in a quiet way had kept an eye upon Garibaldi all along. He had hit upon the ingenious plan of putting a warship at his disposal in order to follow his movements. On the last day of March he received word from the commander that Garibaldi had requested to be conveyed to Genoa and that he was sailing that same day.[2] 'Garibaldi has arrived at the moment when we

[1] For Cavour's reasons, see *CCN.*, vol. iv. No. 1171 to Bixio.
[2] Chiala, vol. iv. Del Sarto to Admiral Serra; Serra to Cavour.

least expected him,' Cavour wrote a few days later, 'what is the real motive of this return to the political scene? He gives as a pretext that he has come to make a protest on behalf of his officers, and to tell the truth, it is not devoid of foundation, for Fanti has been desperately slow in settling the fate of the Garibaldians.' No sooner had he arrived than Garibaldi began to make trouble. With an utter lack of political sense he irritated every one by his comments on the Government. To a deputation of Milanese workmen he remarked that 'Italy, in spite of the sad effects of a policy unworthy of the country, in spite of this crowd of lackeys who support this policy, must be made,' adding that the King was surrounded 'by a poisoned atmosphere but that he hoped to put him on the right road. . . .' So insulting were his remarks that Ricasoli, next to Cavour the most authoritative voice in the Chamber, was roused to address the House on the reputed words of Garibaldi. The words attributed to General Garibaldi, he said, had wounded the feelings of every Deputy, offended the Majesty of Parliament and the inviolability of the King. The Liberator of Italy was the King, and under him all were equal. If some had had greater opportunities than others they should thank God for the privilege. At the most they had but done their duty. It was impossible, he concluded, to believe that Garibaldi had used the words imputed to him.

Ricasoli's words made a great impression on the Chamber and especially on Cavour. 'I know now,' he said afterwards, 'what true eloquence is. If I die to-morrow there stands my successor.' Garibaldi was not in the Chamber when Ricasoli spoke and he delayed his reply for a week. The Bill before the House was Fanti's Army Bill, which provided for the absorption of a large proportion of Garibaldi's soldiers in the royal army. Every one realized that a storm was brewing. The King sent for Garibaldi and tried to pacify him; Ricasoli interviewed him, and some arrangement was made as to what he would say; Rattazzi, it was said, provided him with notes for a speech. Cavour on his side talked over the matter with his trusted counsellor Michelangelo Castelli.[1]

Cavour was a born fighter. A political struggle with Garibaldi would have rejoiced him, but it could have had but one issue, for Cavour was on his own ground, he had a large majority at his back, and had he sought a personal victory over his opponent the result was assured beforehand. Once before he had been in a somewhat similar position. At the famous sitting of April 8th, at the Congress of Paris, Cavour might have won just such a personal triumph over Count Buol, but he refrained. For Italy's sake he put his own feelings on one side and spoke with restraint and moderation. He did the same now. In spite of his exasperation at Garibaldi's unjust accusations, in spite of the strength of the case that he could have brought against his opponent, he realized that a bitter feud throughout Italy might be the consequence; so on April 9th he went down to the Chamber determined on peace not war.

Garibaldi was not present when the sitting opened, but soon afterwards an outburst of cheering outside the Chamber announced the approach of the popular hero. Avoiding the main entrance, Garibaldi entered by a side door supported by two friends, for he was very lame from rheumatism, and made a dramatic appearance behind the topmost seats on the left, clad in his red shirt and grey poncho. Another ovation greeted him, all the deputies rising to welcome him. Ricasoli spoke and Fanti replied, then in a tense atmosphere of expectancy the President called on Garibaldi. He commenced by reading his speech, but, unable to see it, after a few halting sentences he flung aside his notes and began to speak *ex tempore*. Anger quickly got the upper hand of discretion and his speech became a personal attack on Cavour. He accused him of having done his best to compromise the expedition to Sicily, of having accepted national unity only at the

[1] Matter, *Cavour*, vol. iii; Thayer, vol. ii; Castelli, *Ricordi*.

last minute after having all along opposed it, and of having treated the conquerors of the south with contumely and injustice. At these false and bitter words angry murmurs rose on all sides, but Garibaldi went on unheeding: 'Never can I grasp the hand of the man who has made me a foreigner in Italy,' he declared; and then, turning to the question of the southern army, 'I ought above all,' he said, 'to relate their glorious feats. The prodigies they achieved were only stopped when the cold and treacherous hand of this very ministry sought to foment a fratricidal war.'

At these last words a storm of anger swept through the Chamber. The Left cheering, the rest shouting in protest at the insult to the Chamber and the Government. Up to this Cavour had held himself in, but at these last words he leapt from his seat as if stung, shouting and protesting at the infamy of such a statement. In a moment pandemonium was let loose. The deputies left their seats and crowded down the gangways to the floor of the Chamber shouting and gesticulating. The sitting was suspended until order could be restored. When the sitting was resumed Garibaldi finished his speech, but without a word of explanation or apology. Nino Bixio followed and made a noble plea for concord. Then Cavour spoke. By a tremendous effort of self-control, after what he had been through, Cavour spoke with perfect calmness. 'I could not have believed it possible,' wrote one who watched the whole scene, 'after seeing him so roused to anger, that Cavour could have got sufficiently calm in so short a time to answer as he did. He must have wonderful power of self-command.'[1]

'The Chamber will permit me,' Cavour began, 'to give an explanation to General Garibaldi; not that I flatter myself that I can restore that concord for which General Bixio so nobly pleaded; I know that a fact exists that creates an abyss between General Garibaldi

[1] de Bunsen, *op. cit.* Mme de Bunsen was an eyewitness of the whole scene. See Thayer for a very full account.

and myself. . . . I believe that I fulfilled a grievous duty, the most grievous of my whole life, when I counselled the King and proposed to Parliament the cession of Nice and Savoy to France. From what I myself have suffered I can understand what General Garibaldi has felt, and if he cannot pardon me for this act I cannot reproach him for it.' Then he turned to the question of the volunteers, claiming, as he had every right to claim, that the charge that he was hostile to them was false, for they were his own creation. He, not Garibaldi, had called them into existence in 1859, had provided for their training and equipment in the teeth of opposition from his own military staff and that of France. He raised, supported, and refused to disband them, defying Europe in the process, because he wished to prove that not only the Piedmontese, but all Italians, knew how to fight and die for Italy, and he was proud to think that in that faith he was not mistaken, 'after having done that,' he added, 'after having taken upon myself so grave a responsibility as the creation of the volunteers, without the permission of Parliament, with opposition at home and abroad, who can say that I am hostile to them?' But Cavour had no intention of pursuing the advantage this explanation gave him or of using his great powers to put Garibaldi in the wrong as he might so easily have done. When the applause that greeted this explanation died down, he added simply, 'deeply as I feel the injustice of certain charges made against me, I accept without hesitation the appeal made to me by General Bixio. As far as I am concerned the first part of this sitting is buried and forgotten.'[1] A storm of cheering relieved the tension of the Chamber at these generous words, and Cavour passed quietly on to a discussion of the Bill before the Chamber as if nothing had happened.

The sitting of April 9th was after all but an episode in Cavour's life, in his own words in reference to it a *fatalità*, but it had results few expected. Walking

---

[1] Per me la prima parte di questa seduta è come non avvenuta.

back with him, after it was over, Lanza noted Cavour's obvious distress. The tremendous effort to control that choleric, volcanic nature had had its effect. Garibaldi had struck a shrewder blow than he knew: Cavour was never the same again. Not long afterwards when Count Salmour, one of his oldest friends, told him that he did not look well, Cavour sadly admitted that he had never been right since that *maledetta* struggle with Garibaldi.

But Cavour had no time to dwell upon the past or consider his own health, and no sooner was this painful scene over than he was once more immersed in the problems of the hour. Chief amongst them was Rome. Day and night the problem was with him. The question was now before Europe, and public opinion must be formed in favour of Italy before it would be safe to enter the Eternal City. The withdrawal of the French garrison was henceforth his principal objective. When that took place the end would be near. Count Vimercati in Paris was already placing this judiciously before the Emperor, but Cavour's best helper was, as so often before, Prince Napoleon. Already in his speech to the Senate at the opening of the Corps Législatif on the 1st of March he had boldly championed Italian unity and the need for the withdrawal of the French garrison, and Cavour in writing to thank him declared that he had rendered a very great service to Italy. 'If half that the Prince said,' wrote Prosper Mérimée to Panizzi, 'was authorized by the Emperor, we are about to quit Rome and the Papacy is routed.'

Cavour now put the whole position before the Prince *in extenso*—The two main difficulties with which he had to contend were the presence of the French garrison and the refusal of the Emperor to recognize the new kingdom. The retirement of Francis II to Rome and the attitude of General Goyon, the French Commandant, who treated him as the legitimate King of the Two Sicilies, had put fresh heart into the Papal Court and strengthened their belief in the possibility of re-establishing the old kingdom and recovering the lost

Papal provinces. Rome and the Patriarchate had now become the centre of organized brigandage, dignified by the name of a Holy War, which was rendering the pacification of the south more and more difficult. The reaction against this state of things in the new kingdom was disastrous. It encouraged the party of direct action which sought to put Garibaldi at the head of a fresh expedition; it kept alive the hopes of the partisans of Murat in the south, and prevented Italy settling down to the great work of reconstruction.

The Prince replied to Cavour's letter on April 13th: without being able, he said, to say anything official, he could, he thought, indicate the general ideas of the Emperor. Napoleon was genuinely anxious to evacuate the city and escape from the false position in which he found himself, but only on condition that the principle of non-intervention, upon which his policy regarding the Papacy was based, should be observed. If Cavour would guarantee not only to respect the independence of Papal territory himself, after the garrison was withdrawn, but would undertake to defend it against attack by Garibaldi or any one else; if he would likewise acquiesce in the formation of a Papal garrison, drawn either from the Pope's own subjects or from abroad, limited to a maximum of 10,000 men, then he believed the Emperor would at once withdraw his troops and recognize the Kingdom of Italy. 'You will obtain no more than this from the Emperor,' he added.[1]

At first Cavour doubted his ability to control such a situation. Could he keep Garibaldi and the party of action in the leash? But Cavour never shrank from responsibility, and trusting to his influence and the good sense of Italy he decided that these terms must be accepted. He at once submitted them to the King who agreed. Then, to strengthen his position in the Chamber, he called Ricasoli and Minghetti into consultation. They were not enthusiastic, but after some hesitation and not without 'very obvious repugnance,'

[1] Bolléa, No. 515.

agreed to support him. In his reply to the Prince he summed up the bases of the proposed agreement under five heads. (1) That the treaty or agreement should be concluded directly between France and Italy without the intervention of Rome. (2) That France having secured the Pope from all attack should withdraw her troops in a specified time, a month at the farthest. (3) That Italy pledged herself not to attack Papal territory and to oppose by force an attack by any one else. (4) That Italy would not take umbrage at the formation of a Papal army, and undertook to negotiate with Rome in regard to the debts of the Papal territory now forming part of the Italian Kingdom. (5) The recognition of Italy by France was to follow the signature of the agreement.[1]

Negotiations on these bases were at once initiated. There were many obstacles and difficulties, but at last, on May 10th, Vimercati was able to write privately to his friend Castelli, 'we have come to a settlement, and on the 20th of next month the recognition of Italy by France will be an accomplished fact and the withdrawal of the Roman garrison will have already commenced. Nothing must transpire before the 10th of June when the Chambers close and the Senators and Deputies will have gone home.' Rome the Capital seemed drawing very near. The new arrangement caused changes in Italy. Nigra was wanted to take up the post of ambassador at Paris. So Nigra and Prince Eugenio were recalled from Naples and Count Ponza di San Martino took their place. It was necessary, too, to come to an understanding with Garibaldi. After the scene in the Chamber the King had effected a partial reconciliation.

My interview with Garibaldi [Cavour wrote to Vimercati] was courteous without being affectionate. Nevertheless, I explained to him the line of conduct the Government intended to take towards Austria and France, making it clear that there could be no compromise in the matter. He declared that he accepted our programme and was ready to promise

[1] *CCN.*, vol. iv. No. 1294, also in Bolléa and Chiala, vol. vi.

not to obstruct it. I do not think we have finished with Garibaldi, but I believe that for some time he will remain quiet.

Absorbed as he was in this question of Rome it was only one of a number of tasks with all of which Cavour was occupied. He was preparing an elaborate scheme for the amalgamation and reorganization of the northern and southern fleets and the creation of an Italian navy. He was supervising and assisting Minghetti[1] in the difficult problem of a unified internal administration, in which the dangers of a centralized system, like that of the French departments, had to be balanced against the fear of separation involved in a 'regional' solution. 'After working up to midnight at the Navy Bill,' we find him writing to Minghetti, 'I have given four hours to your laws, as you can realize by the notes you will find appended to the enclosed.' In the Chamber he had to explain and defend an intricate Bill on the extension of the tariff to the new provinces. But light was beginning to dawn. In another month the treaty with France would be signed and the garrison would be withdrawn. There would be an anxious time, but before long Rome would belong to Italy. Then Naples would be pacified, and brigandage, which had its base and source of supplies in the Papal States, be rooted out. Venice must wait, but Cavour's thoughts were already turning to Prussia.

Cavour was utterly overworked but nothing stopped him, and to the world he seemed as energetic and resilient as ever. On May 27th he came down to the Chamber and spoke on the tariff reforms proposed for Tuscany. It was a splendid speech, enlivened by characteristic touches of humour and revealing a masterly grasp of the whole economic position. On the 28th and again the next day he spoke on a question of military rewards and pensions. The question was thorny, but Cavour treated it with a breadth of view and a sense of justice that won the warm support of the

[1] Minghetti had succeeded Farini as Minister for the Interior.

Chamber. Pleading for a real spirit of conciliation, for national gratitude towards all who had helped to win the freedom and independence of Italy, regardless of differences in their political ideals, he ended his speech with these words:

> This thought of concord is expressed in the order of the day; it means that all who have fought, even under a Republican banner previous to 1859, have all deserved well of Italy; with this sentiment we associate ourselves, and in so doing, fulfil, I believe, the greatest act of conciliation that in the actual circumstances it is possible for us to perform.

They were Cavour's last words to Parliament. A week later he was dead.

It was Carnival time in Turin. Never had the city been more gay or the Festival of the Statuto kept with more brilliance. Turin was crowded with strangers, Tuscans and Milanese and Neapolitans, happy and proud in the first flush of their nationality. Horse-races, reviews, concerts, and balls, above all the great Charity Bazaar, the Fiera di Beneficenza—held in the Royal Gardens and organized by the wealth and beauty of Turin—kept the city in a round of festivities. Suddenly into these scenes of gaiety came report after report with heartbreaking rapidity—Cavour was ill— he was seriously ill—Cavour was dying. A pall of consternation fell upon the city. The festivities closed. Day and night a crowd of his beloved Turinese stood or knelt before Cavour's palazzo. Never again would those worthy bourgeois see the familiar figure of Papà Camillo with the bright smile and the cheerful nod walking briskly beneath the arcades of the Via di Po. For a month now Cavour had not slept. He had passed the nights reading or dozing on a couch. At all hours his faithful majordomo, old Martin Tosco, had heard him pacing, pacing, up and down his room. The night after his last speech he had a sudden attack. The symptoms were not new, but from the first there was no hope. The doctors were useless. The distress of his friends was tragic. D'Ideville, the Secretary of the French Legation, wandering disconsolate into the Whist Club, found Sir James Hudson with his head between his hands and tears coursing down his cheeks with the latest bulletin before him. The angel of the house inside the Palazzo was his devoted niece, the Countess Alfieri. Cavour himself soon realized the end had come. He sent for Farini, for Castelli, and other intimate friends. He had a last interview with his King, and when the time came summoned his faithful parish priest, Fra Giacomo, who, braving the thunder of the Vatican, for Cavour was excommunicated, administered the last rites of the Church.

On the 6th of June the end came: 'Italy is made, all is safe,' he murmured, and with these last words Italy's great statesman passed away.

APPENDIX A

In the Proclamation of Moncalieri, the full text of which will be found in Massari, *La Vita e il regno di Vittorio Emanuele*, D'Azeglio put these words into the mouth of the King:

I have signed an honourable and not ruinous treaty with Austria, as the welfare of the country demanded. National honour and the sanctity of my oath both required that it should be faithfully executed without cavil or duplicity. My Ministers requested the assent of the Chamber, which attached a condition that made their assent inacceptable, because it destroyed the reciprocal independence of the three powers and thus violated the statute of the Kingdom.

I have sworn in that statute to maintain liberty and justice for all. I have promised to safeguard the nation from the tyranny of parties whatever may be the name, the aim, or the position of the men that compose them. These promises I am fulfilling by dissolving a Chamber become impossible, and by immediately convoking another. But, if the country, if the Electors, deny me their co-operation, not upon me will fall the responsibility of the future; and, in the disorder that may arise, they must lay the blame not upon me but upon themselves.

If on this occasion I feel it my duty to utter severe words, I trust that the good sense of the public and its feeling of justice will recognize that they are inspired by that profound love of my people and of their welfare that spring from my determination to maintain their liberty and defend them alike from domestic and foreign foes.

Never, hitherto, has the House of Savoy appealed in vain to the loyalty, the good sense, and the love of its people. I have the right to trust in them now, and to rest assured that together we shall be able to save the country and its statuto from the dangers that threaten them.

VICTOR EMANUELE.

20 Nov. 1849.

APPENDIX B

ALTHOUGH a devout Catholic, the Church refused the Sacrament to Santarosa on his death-bed unless he made a categorical repudiation of his responsibility for the Law on the Foro Ecclesiastico which he had supported. Santarosa refused, and died without the last rites of the Church. A grave scandal in Turin resulted. The Government, fearing a popular outbreak against the priests, sent General La Marmora to interview the archbishop, and it was only when he intimated that the archbishop would be held responsible for any disturbance that he permitted Christian burial. It was in view of this event that when the Law on the Convents was before the country, Cavour sent for his friend and almoner, Fra Giacomo, who promised that he should receive the last rites of the Church, no matter what took place, a promise he faithfully fulfilled before Cavour's death. See Cavour's letters in Chiala, vol. i. pp. 134–7.

APPENDIX C

COUNT OLDOFREDI, one of Cavour's secretaries at the Conference, in a letter dated March 14th to the Marchesa di Collegno, gives a diverting account of this incident.

They were discussing the free navigation of the Danube, according to the privileges sanctioned by the never sufficiently praised treaties of 1815. Buol, as if by accident, proposed to slip in the words: *sauf les droits acquis*. Il Mandarino (Cavour) was on his own ground; for an hour and a half he amused himself by playing the innocent as to the meaning of 'free navigation.' What did the treaty of 1815 say about it? Buol replies with a long historical-diplomatic dissertation. Il Mandarino answers, *C'est très beau tout cela, mais je ne comprends rien*. What did the phrase *les droits acquis* signify to His Excellency the Plenipotentiary of Franz Josef? And Buol responded with a second dissertation upon Bavaria and other places more or less unknown. At last, always with the air of a small boy asking his teacher what is the capital of France, he asks Buol, 'Voyons, M. le Comte, if a Turkish Company wished to send their steamers up to Vienna, would you consent to it?'
Bang! the bomb was thrown, and Buol, wriggling in his chair,

exclaims, 'No, no, Monsieur.' 'Good,' replied Il Mandarino—
'liberty of navigation, then, according to the treaties of 1815,
means privileged liberty for Austria only, to the exclusion of the
Turks, English, French, Sardinians, in fact all the Congress?'

The scene was comic. Lord Clarendon was delighted; he
added some caustic phrases and asked Buol to explain himself.
The latter having no notion how to get out of it declared that
he would ask for further information from Vienna. Il Mandarino
was and is the lion of the Conference, he is the most eminent
man here.

APPENDIX D

THE following extract is from a letter from Nigra to Cavour,
dated June 17th, 1860. It needs no comment.

The sojourn at Fontainebleau for the second series of guests
has proved a most amusing time. The absence of the Emperor
had increased the usual vivacity of the Empress. We have
scoured the forest, which is truly magnificent, on foot, on
horseback, and in carriages. We have rowed on the small lake,
we have had a tilting match, we have danced, had plays at the
theatre, and charades. Amongst these last there has been one
that has been much applauded and which V. E. will be interested
in hearing about. They wanted to play a charade on Garibaldi,
but as the word did not lend itself easily, it was altered to
Gargantua divided into *gare*, *gant*, and *tua*. The first syllable
was presented as the opening of a new railway station. Most
suitably, we had the Minister of Public Works amongst the
guests, who made a speech; young ladies presented bouquets;
M. le Maire was present, also Mme la Maire, the latter being
represented by M. Thouvenel dressed *en femme*. The whistling
of the locomotive and the locomotive itself—nothing was
wanting. To present the second syllable the Empress threw
a glove in the midst of the lists. Immediately various cavaliers
à cheval upon chairs, with *boucliers impossibles* and billiard cues
for lances, played a very amusing kind of tournament. I am
pleased to tell you that M. Thouvenel was one of the knights.
The last syllable was represented as some sort of mythological
personage. Finally, we had to represent the whole—Gargantua
himself! Here the Empress had a brilliant idea. Putting

spectacles on one of the guests she said, 'You will be M. de Cavour who is the Gargantua of modern times.' They then came and asked my permission, which I gave at once. A table was then laid before Your Excellency and they brought you first *stracchino* (Lombard cheese), then Parmesan, followed by Mortadella di Bologna (Bologna sausage); V. E. accepted everything, found them delicious and ate them all with relish. Then they brought you *l'aleatico* (the white grapes of Central Italy), next came Sicilian oranges, which you ate amid the applause and acclamation of the assembly. Finally, they offered you *Macaroni*; but you replied, 'that is enough for to-day, keep that for to-morrow!' As V. E. can imagine, the charade was much enjoyed and there has been much laughter over it at the Palace.

BIBLIOGRAPHY

THE following list contains the more important sources for the study of Cavour's political life. It may be supplemented by consulting Lemmi's volume, *Il Risorgimento*, in the Guide Bibliografiche series published by the Fondazione Leonardo per la cultura Italiana. For earlier publications and articles in periodicals Buzziconi's *Bibliografia di Cavour* (Roux Frassate, Torino, 1898) will be found useful.

Unpublished English sources.

Public Record Office. F.O. Papers. Sardinia, Tuscany, &c., 1848–61.
Russell Papers.
Clarendon Papers.

Speeches.

Discorsi Parlamentari del Conte Camillo di Cavour. 11 vols.
Opera Parlamentari del Conte di Cavour. 2 vols. Livorno, 1862 (selection).
Il Conte di Cavour in Parlamento, Artom e Blanc. A selection with a reminiscent introduction by Cavour's secretary, I. Artom.

Letters.

BERT, A. Nouvelles Lettres Inédites de Cavour. Written to his friend and banker, Émile de la Rue, and concerned mainly with public and private finance. Valuable for the earlier years 1848–52.
BOLLÉA, C. Una 'Silloge' di lettere del Risorgimento. An important collection taken from the archives of Turin, 1839–73. Fratelli Bocca. Turin, 1919.
BIANCHI, N. La politique de Cavour. To E. d'Azeglio, Minister in London, 1851–61.
CARTEGGIO CAVOUR-NIGRA.
   Vol. i. Plombières.
   Vol. ii. La Campagna diplomatica e militare del 1859.
   Vol. iii. La cessione di Nizza e Savoia e la annessione dell' Italia Centrale.
   Vol. iv. La Liberazione del Mezzogiorno. Zanichelli, Bologna. The most recent and important contribution for the study of Cavour's policy.
CHIALA, L. Lettere edite ed inedite di Camillo Cavour. 6 vols. with full introductions.

MAYOR, E. Nuove Lettere Inedite del Conte di Cavour. Contains many letters to Sardinian Diplomats abroad, especially to the Marchese Villamarina in Paris.

NIGRA, C. Le Comte de Cavour et La Comtesse de Circourt. A small collection of interesting private letters.

VISCONTI, E. Cavour Agricoltore. Letters to his factor at Leri on farm and business matters. Barbèra. Firenza, 1913.

Contemporary letters bearing on Cavour.

D'AZEGLIO, C. Souvenirs Historiques. Letters to E. d'Azeglio, Sardinian Minister in London, from his mother. Charming and valuable, 1835–61.

D'AZEGLIO, E. Carteggi e Documenti Diplomatici Inediti, 1831–54, per cura di A. Colombo.

D'AZEGLIO, M. Correspondance Politique de Massimo d'Azeglio, par E. Rendu.

Lettere Inedite a cura di N. Bianchi.

La Politica di M. d'Azeglio. N. Bianchi, 1848–59.

CASTELLI, M. Carteggio Politico, 1849–64. One of Cavour's most intimate friends.

MAINERI. Lettere di V. Gioberti e G. Pallavicino.

Lettere di D. Manin e G. Pallavicino.

LA FARINA. Epistolario. 2 vols.

MINGHETTI, M. Miei Ricordi. 3 vols.

Diaries and Memoirs.

BUNSEN, M. DE. In three Legations.

DELLA ROCCA. Autobiografia di un Veterano. 2 vols.

D'IDEVILLE, H. Journal d'un diplomate en Italie, 1859–62. 2 vols.

CASTELLI, M. Ricordi.

COLLEGNO, M. Provana di: Diario Politico, 1852–6.

ELLIOTT, SIR H. Diary: reprinted in Some revolutions and other Diplomatic Experiences. Murray, 1922.

HÜBNER, COMTE DE. Neuf ans de Souvenirs d'un Ambassadeur d'Autriche à Paris, 1851–9. 2 vols.

LANZA. La vita e i tempi de G. Lanza. 2 vols.

MALMESBURY, EARL OF. Memoirs of an ex-Minister. 2 vols.

PERSANO, C. DI. Diario privato-politico-militare, 1860.

RUSSELL, LORD JOHN. Later Correspondence of. 2 vols.

VISCONTI-VENOSTA, E. Memoirs of Youth.

Biographies.

CESARESCO, E. M. Cavour. English and Italian.

MATTER, P. Cavour et l'Unité Italienne. 3 vols. Alcan, 1927. Full and accurate, the most recent biography.

MASSARI, G. Il Conte di Cavour: Ricordi Biografici.

MAZADE, C. Le Comte de Cavour.

ORSI, P. Cavour. English and Italian.

470 BIBLIOGRAPHY

PALÉOLOGUE, M. Cavour. English and French.
RIVE, DE LA. Le Comte de Cavour. Italian Translation. An
intimate study of the man.
THAYER, W. R. The Life and Times of Cavour. 2 vols. Houghton
Mifflin, 1912. The standard life of Cavour.
TREITSCHKE, H. Cavour. Italian translation. A brilliant political
essay.
ZANICHELLI. Cavour.

General Histories.

BOLTON KING. The History of Italian Unity. 2 vols.
BERSEZIO. Il Regno di Vittorio Emanuele II. 8 vols.
CESARESCO. The Liberation of Italy.
MASSARI. La Vita e il Regno di Vittorio Emanuele II di Savoia.
MASI, E. Il Risorgimento Italiano. 2 vols.
RINAUDO. Il Risorgimento Italiano. 2 vols., illustrated.
TIVARONI. Storia Critica del Risorgimento Italiano. 7 vols.
ZINI. Storia d'Italia. 4 vols. Valuable for documents.

Miscellaneous.

ALBERTI. Per la Storia dell' Alleanza e della campagna di Crimea.
Biblioteca di Storia Italiana Recente. Vol. IV.
BIANCHI, N. Storia Documentata della Diplomazia Europea in
Italia. 8 vols.
BONFADINI. Vita di Francesco Arese.
BROFFERIO, A. Storia del Parlamento Subalpino. 6 vols.
CHIALA, L. Une Page d'Histoire du Gouvernement Représentatif
en Piémont. A valuable study of Parliamentary history from
1848–52.
CURÀTULO, G. E. Garibaldi, Vittorio Emanuele, Cavour nei fasti
della Patria.
CAMOZZINI, F. Cavour Economista.
COMANDINI, A. Il Principe Napoleone nel Risorgimento Italiano.
GONNI. Cavour Ministro della Marina.
HANCOCK, W. R. Ricasoli and the Risorgimento in Tuscany.
La Questione Romana negli anni 1860–1. Commissione Reale
Editrice. 2 vols.
LUZIO, A. Studi e Bozzetti. 2 vols.
Garibaldi, Cavour, Verdi.
MAZZIOTTI. Napoleone III e l'Italia.
NAZARI-MICHELE. Cavour e Garibaldi nel 1860.
PANTALEONI, D. L'Idea Italiana nella soppressione del Potere
Temporale dei Papi.
Parliamentary Papers for the Period.
TRÉSAL, J. L'Annexion de la Savoie à la France.
TREVELYAN, G. M. Garibaldi and the Thousand.
Garibaldi and the making of Italy.

INDEX

474 INDEX

Foreign Minister, 98; on the Sequestration Decree, 111; opposes Cavour's offer of troops, 126, 127, 128, 130; refuses payment of troops, 137; his case for Piedmont, 139; his obstinacy, 141–143; resigns office, 144; mission to Czar, 226; becomes Foreign Secretary on Cavour's resignation, 328; mission to Paris, 337.

D'Auvare, Admiral, 63, 65, 69, 70, 71.

D'Auvergne, Prince de la Tour, French Minister at Turin, 245.

D'Azeglio, Marchesa Costanza, 244.

D'Azeglio, Marquis Emanuele, letters to, 130, 199 ff.

D'Azeglio, Marquis Massimo, becomes Premier, 31; life and character, 34; dissolves Chamber, 40; Proclamation of Moncalieri, 40; returns to power, 41; his policy, 41; Bill on the Foro, 47; on Cavour, 56–57; contrast with C., 81; Press Law, 86; on Rattazzi, 90; offers resignation, 90; resigns, 97; his work as Premier, 99; letter to the King, 180; refuses to go to Paris, 194; refuses rifles to Garibaldi, 382.

D'Azeglio, Marquis Roberto, 75.

De Martino, Neapolitan envoy to Paris, 405; becomes Foreign Minister, 406.

De Tinan, French Admiral, suggests patrolling the Straits, 412.

Deforesta, Giovanni, Minister of Justice: his Press Law, 86.

Della Rocca, General, A.D.C. to King, his mission to Paris, 247; Chief of Staff, 303, 320; overruns Umbria, 426.

Depretis, Agostino, Pro-Dictator of Sicily, 409, 425 n.; resignation refused by Garibaldi, 428; letter to, 428; resignation accepted, 428.

Desambrois, Senator, refuses Premiership, 179; amendment to Convent Bill, 182; Minister in Paris, resigns, 352.

Drouyn de Lhuys, French Foreign Secretary, 131, 139.

Durando, General, speech on Crimean Alliance, 145; Minister for War, fails to form a government, 179 ff.

Elliott, Sir Henry, British Minister to Naples, 375; favours unity, 403; condemns Cavour's insurrection policy, 409.

Emilia, 333.

Fabbre, 26.

Fabrizi, Nicola, 384, 392.

Fanti, General, in command of Central Italian army, 336; Minister of War, 354; threatens resignation, 365; meets King at Bologna, 393, 426; attitude to Garibaldi, 435.

Farini, L. C., editor of *Il Risorgimento*, 80; Minister of Education, 90; works for Rattazzi, 90; view on Dissolution, 119; Royal Commissioner for Modena, 314; Dictator of Emilia, 329; work in Emilia, 333; presents resolutions for union, 334; Minister of the Interior, 363; accompanies King to Florence and Bologna, 393; interviews Napoleon at Chambéry, 423; offers resignation, 425; Governor of Naples, 439; resigns, 442.

Ferdinand IV, King of Naples, refuses to send representative to the Congress, 294; refuses alliance with Piedmont, 307.

Ferrara, Francesco, 119.

Fleury, General, 323.

Forey, General, 311.

Foro Ecclesiastico, Bill for abolition of, 48 ff.

Francis II, King of Naples, refuses alliance with Piedmont, 321; Gortschakoff on his policy, 375; Sir Henry Elliott on his policy, 375; refuses to replace French in Papal States, 380; the King's letter to, 383; meeting of Foreign Ministers, 404; his Sovereign Edict, 405; leaves Naples, 421; the battle of the Volturno, 429; besieged in Gaeta, 441; retires to Rome, 442.

Franz Josef, Emperor of Austria, his flight to Olmütz, 15; the Decree of Dec. 1849, 107; visits Milan, 233; reassures Rome, 315; takes command of army, 318; meets Napoleon at Villafranca, 324; the Conference at Warsaw, 434.

Frappolli, Colonel, 391.

Gaeta, Pius IX escapes to, 26; Leopold of Tuscany escapes to, 26; siege and capitulation of, 441–442.

478

INDEX

Russell, Lord John, on the Piedmontese Alliance, 134, 136, 139; his four points, 348, 349, 350, 354–356, 359, 402, 403, 411, 412, 437.
Russell, Lord Odo, 269.

Sacconi, Mons., 353.
Salasco, Armistice of, 7.
Salmour, Count di, 243, 321.
Salvagnoli, Vincenzo, 258, 264, 309.
San Martino, Count Ponza di, Minister of the Interior, 94, 98; Governor of Naples, 460.
Sanctis, Francesco di, 450,
Santarosa, Count Pietro, death of, 58 and Appendix B.
Santucci, Cardinal, 446.
Sauli, Marquis, Minister to Tuscany, 187; Minister to Russia, 323.
Schmidt, General Anton, 317.
Scialoja, Antonio, 115.
Siccardi, Count, 47, 48, 68.
Sirtori, Giuseppe, 390.
Solferino, Battle of, 318.
Stadion, General, 311.
Strassoldo, Count, 106.
Syracuse, Count of, 410.

Talamone, 397.
Talleyrand, Baron Charles, 349; interview with Cavour, 356; visit to Genoa, 392; his note to Thouvenel, 395.
Tchernaia, Battle of, 190.
Thouvenel, Edward, French Foreign Minister, his appointment, 340, 352, 354, 355, 356; interview with Nigra, 377, 378, 379; suggests six months' truce in Sicily, 411; withdraws minister from Turin, 433–434.
Toffetti, Count, 124 and n.

Urban, General, 312.

Valerio, Lorenzo, 17, 37; Royal Commissioner for Marches, 439; Ecclesiastical Decrees of, 448.
Victor Emanuel II, King, ascends the throne, 31; appoints D'Azeglio Premier, 34; Proclamation of Moncalieri, 40; on Cavour, 59; dislike of Connubio, 92; welcomes Crimean Alliance, 123; interviews French Minister, 131, 138, 141; reviews troops, 150; Embassy to Rome, 159; death of mother, wife, and brother, 163 ff.; character, 165; Calabiana offer, 175; public

feeling against, 179; D'Azeglio's letter to, 181; recalls Cavour, 181; decorates Cavour, 221; anger with Austria, 234; the letter to Della Rocca, 248, 263; the speech from the Throne, 270 ff.; marriage of Princess Clotilde, 275; disgust with Napoleon, 285; letter to Rattazzi, 299; Cavour on, 300; in command of army, 303; Palestro, 311; enters Milan, 313; San Martino, 318, 319; interviews Cavour, 324; Villafranca, 324; signs peace, 325; with Cavour at Monzambano, 325; returns to Turin, 328; Napoleon's letter, 337; summons Cavour, 344; letter to the Pope, 353; opens Parliament, 362; the message from Garibaldi, 363; opens Parliament, 381; refuses a brigade to Garibaldi, 381; letter to King Francis, 383; leaves for Florence, 383; aids Garibaldi, 392; meeting at Bologna, 393; letter to Garibaldi, 413; refuses Cavour's resignation, 425; refuses Garibaldi's demand for dismissal of Cavour, 426; letter to Garibaldi, 427; decides to take command of army, 429; leaves for Ancona, 429; meets Garibaldi, 437; enters Naples, 437; sends Vimercati to Paris, 441; Cavour's letter to, 443; interviews Garibaldi, 454; accepts terms for evacuation of Rome, 459; last visit to Cavour, 463.
Villamarina, Marquis Salvatore, Piedmontese Minister to France, sent for as possible Foreign Minister, 180; accompanies Cavour to Congress, 196; transferred to Naples, 374; warning to Cavour, 375; Cavour to, 380; his reply, 389; agent for insurrection at Naples, 410.
Vimercati, Count, sent to Paris, 441; negotiates for evacuation of troops from Rome, 452.

Walewski, Count, French Foreign Minister, presides over Congress, 197, 203, 206, 212, 245, 267, 288, 291, 293; dismissed, 340.
Warsaw, Conference of, 433–434.
West, Sackville, 294.
Winspeare, Francis, 411.

Zambianchi, Colonel, 397.
Zürich, Treaty of, 331, 338.